# OUR SMITH FAMILY

## Descendants of
## JASPER SMITH
### of Maidenhead, New Jersey, New York and Pennsylvania and Beyond

*Compiled by*
*Mary Smith Jackson*

HERITAGE BOOKS
2025

# HERITAGE BOOKS

*AN IMPRINT OF HERITAGE BOOKS, INC.*

## Books, CDs, and more—Worldwide

For our listing of thousands of titles see our website
at
www.HeritageBooks.com

Published 2025 by
HERITAGE BOOKS, INC.
Publishing Division
5810 Ruatan Street
Berwyn Heights, MD 20740

Heritage Books by Mary S. Jackson:

*Marriages and Deaths from Tompkins County, New York Newspapers*

*Marriage and Death Notices from Schuyler County, New York Newspapers*
Mary Smith Jackson and Edward F. Jackson

Our Smith Family: Descendants of Jasper Smith of Maidenhead, New Jersey, New York
and Pennsylvania and Beyond

International Standard Book Number
Paperbound: 978-0-7884-5307-6

# Introduction

Jasper Smith of Maidenhead, NJ was the son of John Smith of Bedford, NY and many of Jasper's descendants are contained in this book. The earlier records are taken from the NJ Genealogies 'Smith families of Bedford, NY and Maidenhead, NJ'. Later records were researched by various members of the Smith families in census records, County records, wills, cemetery records, bibles and personal family records.

Some members of this family moved into central NY State about 1800. From there many of them migrated to Pennsylvania, Michigan and further west. Of course, some of them were very difficult to find and some were never found. We have tried very hard to include as many of the descendants as possible.

This book will not be published or made available to the public. Only a few copies are being printed for family use. One of the reasons we decided not to publish is because not all the sources we have used have been verified to our satisfaction. We would not want to publish something that has the possibility of being incorrect.

We do hope that the members of the family that receive a copy will enjoy it.

# OUR SMITH FAMILY

## First Generation

1-    SMITH John was born ca 1650 and died in 1684 in Bedford, Brooklyn, NY. His mother was named Anna Cathryn and he married Susannah (unknown maiden name). She later married Captain Ralph HUNT who also moved to Maidenhead, NJ. In John's will dated December 7, 1683 and proved October 8, 1684 he mentions his wife and left the property to his sons (unnamed). When the property was sold in 1696 the deed was signed by Thomas and Jasper and each of them named an eldest son John.

        i- SMITH Thomas born ca 1675
2-     ii- SMITH Jasper born ca 1678

## Second generation

2-    SMITH Jasper (*John*) was born 1678 in Bedford, Brooklyn, NY son of John SMITH and Susannah. He removed to Maidenhead, NJ about 1699 and died March, 1770 in Lawrenceville, NJ. His will proved April 11, 1770 devises to eldest son John the plantation on which he now dwells, to grandson Waters Smith the plantation on where his father, my second son Jasper Smith dwelled when he died, to third son Thomas the plantation where he lives, to fourth son Samuel 20 shillings, to grandson John Smith fourth son of of my son Samuel 100 acres from the plantation where I live, said grandson to maintain his mother Elizabeth, his father's wife, to grandson Jasper, second son of my son John, 2 acres of meadow, to my youngest son Joshua the rest of the plantation where I live, he to pay my son Ralph, his brother 100 lira and the moveable estate to my sons Samuel, Ralph and Joshua. His wife not named, predeceased
Children:
3-        i- SMITH John born 1700 in Lawrenceville, NJ
4-       ii- SMITH Jasper Jr. born 1701 in Lawrenceville, NJ
5-      iii- SMITH Thomas born 1703 in Larenceville, NJ
6-       iv- SMITH Samuel born 1705 in Lawrenceville, NJ
7-        v- SMITH Ralph born 1707 in Lawrenceville, NJ
8-       vi- SMITH Joshua Sr. born ca 1714 in Lawrenceville, NY

2

## Third Generation

3-    SMITH John (*Jasper, John*) was born 1700 in Maidenhead, NJ son of Jasper SMITH and died there intestate November 1799. He married Isabel TINDALL born ca 1722 in Ewing, NJ daughter of Joseph TINDALL Sr. and Mercy HART.
Children born in Maidenhead, NJ:
9-        i- SMITH John born 1735
10-      ii- SMITH Jasper born 1740
11-      iii- SMITH Joshua born 1745
12-      iv- SMITH Elizabeth born by 1750

4-    SMITH Jasper Jr. (*Jasper, John*) was born 1701 in Lawrenceville, NJ second son of Jasper SMITH and died September 19, 1754 in Lawrenceville, NJ. He married ca 1725 Keziah SMITH who was born 1702 in Jamaica, Long Island daughter of Thomas and Rachel SMITH and died November 2, 1799 in Lawrenceville, NJ, both are buried in Upper Burying ground.
Children born in Lawrenceville:
13-      i- SMITH Waters Sr. born 1732
14-      ii- SMITH Jasper III born 1737
15-      iii- SMITH Catherine born 1738
16-      iv- SMITH Israel Sr. born 1738
          v- SMITH Benjamin born ca 1740

5-    SMITH Thomas (*Jasper, John*) was born 1703 in Lawrenceville, NJ third son of Jasper SMITH and died after 1769. He married Hannah HUNT who was born March 21, 1708/09 in Newtown, Queens Co. NY daughter of Edward HUNT and Hannah HAZARD and died August 17, 1759 in Lawrenceville, NJ, buried in Upper Burying Ground.
Children born in Maidenhead, NJ:
          i- SMITH Nathaniel born August 18, 1735
          ii- SMITH Elizabeth born April 20, 1738
17-      iii- SMITH James born July 3, 1740 in Morristown, NJ
18-      iv- SMITH Abigail born March 21, 1742/43
          v- SMITH Christian born May 4, 1747
          vi- SMITH Sarah born October 6, 1749
19-      vii- SMITH Elijah born August 13, 1755

6-    SMITH Samuel (*Jasper, John*) was born 1705 in Lawrenceville, NJ son of Jasper SMITH and died after 1760. He married Elizabeth (unknown maiden name).
Child:
20-      i- SMITH John born ca 1730

7-    SMITH Ralph (*Jasper, John*) was born July 1707 in Maidenhead, NJ son of Jasper SMITH and died July 1784 in Hanover, NJ. He married Rachel ANDERSON born in Trenton, NJ daughter of Enoch ANDERSON and Catherine OPDYKE and died September 1805 in Hanover, NJ. Ralph's will was proven July 15, 1784 and names wife Rachel and children:

21-    i- SMITH William born 1740 and died December 1774 in Morris Co. NJ
22-    ii- SMITH Jasper born ca 1741
       iii- SMITH Catherine born ca 1736 and married Jonathan CHEEVER who was born 1744 and died October 14, 1794. Unknown children.
23-    iv- SMITH Ralph born ca 1745
       v- SMITH Sarah married ____ LEWIS


8-    SMITH Joshua (*Jasper, John*) youngest son of Jasper SMITH was baptised June 22, 1714 in Maidenhead, NJ and died 1784 in Oxford, NJ. He married Keziah PELTON who was christened October 9, 1729 in Huntington, NY daughter of Benjamin and Keziah PELTON and died October 9, 1834.
Children born in NJ:
24-    i- SMITH Mary born ca 1743 in Maidenhead, NJ (see #11)
25-    ii- SMITH Christian born ca 1745
26-    iii- SMITH Joshua born ca 1750
27-    iv- SMITH Platt Pelton born ca 1755
28-    v- SMITH Jasper born November 15, 1758 in Maidenhead, NJ
29-    vi- SMITH Obadiah born September 29, 1764 in Maidenhead, NJ
30-    vii- SMITH Annanias born June 21, 1767 in Maidenhead, NJ
       viii- SMITH Benjamin
       ix- SMITH Keziah


Fourth Generation


9-    SMITH John (*John, Jasper, John*) was born 1735-40 in Maidenhead, NJ eldest son of John SMITH and Isabel TINDALL and died September 1812 in Lawrenceville, NJ. He married Catherine J. (unknown maiden name) who was born 1744 and died February 2, 1834 age abt 90 years. His will proved October 9, 1812 devises one third to wife Catherine and two thirds divided among children, except son Jasper to have two shares. They are buried in Presbyterian Churchyard in Lawrenceville.
Children born in Maidenhead, NJ:
       1- SMITH Jasper born ca 1782
31-    ii- SMITH Sarah born 1784
       iii- SMITH Mary born 178__ (see Benjamin SMITH #45)

10-    SMITH Jasper (*John, Jasper, John*) was born 1740 in Maidenhead, NJ son of John Smith and Isabel TINDALL and died April 10, 1820 in Lawrenceville, NJ. He married Jemima

LANNING born 1744 in Ewingville, NJ daughter of Daniel LANNING and died August 28, 1836 in her 93rd year, both buried in Upper Burying Gound.
Children born in Maidenhead, NJ:

      i- SMITH Jasper died 1832
32-    ii- SMITH Daniel born 1750
33-    iii- SMITH Asher
      iv- SMITH Enoch born 1763 and died February 9, 1817 in Sunbury, Pa. Spouse and children unknown
34-    v- SMITH Hannah born ca 1768
35-    vi- SMITH Sarah born 1770
36-    vii- SMITH Elizabeth born 1771
37-    viii- SMITH Prudence born 1778

11-    SMITH Joshua (*John, Jasper, John*) was born 1745 in Maidenhead, NJ son of John SMITH and Isabel TINDALL and died November 1785 in Maidenhead. He married his first cousin Mary SMITH born 1752 daughter of Joshua SMITH and Keziah PELTON and died October 9, 1834 in her 83rd year. (see #24) They are buried in the Upper Burying Ground.
Children born in Maidenhead, NJ:
38-    i- SMITH Sarah born August 11, 1778
39-    ii- SMITH William born 1779
40-    iii- SMITH Matilda born March 2, 1783
41-    iv- SMITH Keziah born October 7, 1784
42-    v- SMITH George W. born 1789

12-    SMITH Elizabeth (*John, Jasper, John*) was born 1750 in Maidenhead, NJ daughter of John SMITH and Isabel TINDALL. She married Ralph LANNING who was born 1723 son of Robert LANNING and Martha HART and died December 1800 in Hopewell, NJ. Ralph married (1) Mary HART daughter of Amos. He left a will proved January 31, 1801 naming wife Elizabeth and children. He was a second Lieutenant in Capt. Hunt's Co. of Hunterdon Co. militia.
Children by Ralph's first marriage:
      i- LANNING Amos born ca 1763
      ii- LANNING Daniel
      iii- LANNING Noah
      iv- LANNING Ralph
      v- LANNING Elizabeth born October 29, 1765, married William CORNELL born March 30, 1759 son of Edward CORNELL and Sarah BURTT
      vi- LANNING Mercy who married ____ REED
One child by second marriage:
      vii- LANNING Elizabeth
43-    viii- LANNING Jasper born July 10, 1790 in Lawrenceville, NJ

13-    SMITH Waters Sr. (*Jasper Jr., Jasper, John*) was born 1732 in Lawrenceville, NJ eldest son of Jasper SMITH Jr. and Keziah SMITH and died August 17, 1820 without issue.

He married (1) January 17, 1770 Jane **VAN CLEVE** daughter of John **VAN CLEVE** and Sarah Couwenhoven **CONOVER** and she died March 23, 1809. He married (2) Lammetje **BERGEN** born April 9, 1758 daughter of George **BERGEN** and Marie **PROBASCO** and widow of Garrett **COVENHOVEN** and she died after August 30, 1817. No issue

14- **SMITH** Jasper III *(Jasper Jr., Jasper, John)* was born 1738 in Lawrenceville, NJ son of Jasper **SMITH** and Keziah **SMITH** and died October 5, 1813 without issue. He married (1) October 1765 Eleanor **RYERSON** widow of Berent **GOUVENEUR** who was born April 11, 1741 daughter of Martin **RYERSON** and Catherine **COXE** and died November 22, 1766. He married (2) December 9, 1767 Theodosia **REID** who was born November 24, 1738 daughter of Col. John **REID** and Mary C. **SANDS** and died May 2, 1810. He married (3) January 3, 1811 Ann **PECK** who was born 1772 and died October 5, 1839. Unknown children. He left a will proved September 7, 1820 naming nephews. He is buried in the Upper Burying Ground in Lawrenceville.

15- **SMITH** Catherine *(Jasper Jr., Jasper, John)* was born ca 1738 in Lawrenceville, NJ daughter of Jasper **SMITH** Jr. and Keziah **SMITH** and died after 1817. She married Thomas **STEVENS** who was born 1735 in Maidenhead, NJ.
Children:
     i- **STEVENS** John born 1757 in Maidenhead, NJ and died August 13, 1843 in Lawrenceville, NJ, buried Upper Burying Ground
44-     ii- **STEVENS** Thomas Jr. born 1761 in Maidenhead, NJ
     iii- **STEVENS** Israel born 1763 in Maidenhead, NJ and died October 16, 1848 in Lawrenceville, NJ. He married Ruth **ROZELL** who died February 23, 1851 age 81 yrs. daughter of John **ROZELL** and Anna **VAN CLEVE**

16- **SMITH** Israel *(Jasper Jr., Jasper, John)* was born 1738 in Lawrenceville, NJ son of Jasper **SMITH** Jr. and Keziah **SMITH** and died there July 1, 1818. He married Johanna **HILL** who was born ca 1745 daughter of Samuel and Christian **HILL** and died August 16, 1819 in Lawrenceville.
Children:
45-     i- **SMITH** Benjamin born 1774, married Mary **SMITH** (see #41)
46-     ii- **SMITH** Waters born 1779
47-     iii- **SMITH** Israel born 1782
48-     iv- **SMITH** Elizabeth born September 22, 1791

17-     **SMITH** James *(Thomas, Jasper, John)* was born July 3, 1740 in Maidenhead, NJ son of Thomas **SMITH** and Hannah **HUNT** and died there December 1810. His will proved January 16, 1811 names wife Charity and children. He married (1) Mehitabel (unknown maiden name) born 1751 and died September 27, 1778 age 27 years. He married (2) June 27, 1779 Charity **PITNEY** who was born ca 1738 and died February 15, 1819 aged 81 years.
Children by first wife:
49-     i- **SMITH** Hannah born February 8, 1772 (see #44)
50-     ii- **SMITH** Sarah born October 12, 1773 (see #33)

51-     iii- SMITH Mehitable born August 13, 1775
        iv- SMITH Thomas born May 30, 1777 and died June 26, 1785

18-     SMITH Abigail (*Thomas, Jasper, John*) was born March 21, 1743 in Maidenhead, NJ daughter of Thomas SMITH and Hannah HUNT and died May 24, 1812. She married Joseph TINDALL Jr. who was born 1736 in Ewing, NJ son of Joseph TINDALL and Mary HART and died in Ewing June 13, 1812.
Children born in Ewing:
        i- TINDALL Hannah born ca 1765
53-     ii- TINDALL Joseph born ca 1764
54-     iii- TINDALL Elizabeth born ca 1766
        iv- TINDALL William born ca 1767, married in Middlesex Co. NJ April 27, 1797 Christina COUWENHOVEN (or CONOVER) born ca 1776 daughter of John COUWENHOVEN and Rachel TINDALL. nfi
        v- TINDALL Ralph born ca 1768, married Mary LANE born ca 1770 daughter of Adam LANE. nfi
        vi- TINDALL Nathaniel born ca 1769, married Marcia JONES born ca 1773 daughter of John JONES.
55-     vii- TINDALL Thomas born ca 1770

19-     SMITH Elijah (*Thomas, Jasper, John*) was born August 13, 1755 in Hunterdon Co. NJ son of Thomas SMITH and Hannah HUNT and died March 11, 1835 in Jacksonville, Ill. He married November 15, 1780 Elizabeth LAUGHLIN who was born May 10, 1757 in Black Fort, Va. daughter of James LAUGHLIN and Mary Jane DUNKIN and died ca 1828. She married (2) Burton Caleb LITTON and had 2 children.
Children:
56-     i- SMITH Nathaniel born November 15, 1781 in Va.
57-     ii- SMITH Virginia Jane born January 28, 1783 in Va.
58-     iii- SMITH Thomas Hunt born August 20, 1786 in Va.
        iv- SMITH Elizabeth born December 22, 1788 in Va. and died December 15, 1879. She married (1) ____ SHOEMAKER and (2) John G. BROWN
        v- SMITH Elijah born May 23, 1791 married Anna TEAL
        vi- SMITH Burton L. born October 2, 1793 married Tabitha Duncan MC FERRIN born ca 1797 in Tn. daughter of William MC FERRIN and Jane Duncan LAUGHTON and died July 13, 1829
        vii- SMITH Christianna born February 22, 1797 married Elias ELDER
59-     viii- SMITH Cynthia Ann born July 6, 1803

20-     SMITH John (*Samuel, Jasper, John*) was born ca 1730 in Maidenhead, NJ son of Samuel and Elizabeth SMITH. He married Anne HOUGHTON born 1732 in Hopewell, NJ daughter of Thomas HOUGHTON and Mary MERSHON.
Children born in Amwell Twp. NJ:
60-     i- SMITH Absolom born ca 1755
        ii- SMITH John born January 4, 1762, married Rebecca GRIFFIN born ca 1776 in

Amwell, NJ
   iii- **SMITH** Sarah born November 19, 1764
   iv- **SMITH** Mary born August 5, 1767
   v- **SMITH** Amos born January 7, 1769 and died 1830
   vi- **SMITH** Andrew born December 10, 1772

21-   **SMITH** William (*Ralph, Jasper, John*) was born ca 1740 son of Ralph **SMITH** and Rachel **ANDERSON** and died in Morris Co. NJ December 1774. He married Elizabeth **SMITH** born ca 1745 daughter of John **SMITH** and Hannah **WATERS**.
   i- **SMITH** William Ames born 1775

22-   **SMITH** Jasper (*Ralph, Jasper, John*) was born ca 1741 in NJ son of Ralph **SMITH** and Rachel **ANDERSON**. His spouse unknown
Children:
   i- **SMITH** Ralph born ca 1765
   ii- **SMITH** William Melville born ca 1767

23-   **SMITH** Ralph (*Ralph, Jasper, John*) was born ca 1745 in Lawrenceville, NJ son of Ralph **SMITH** and Rachel **ANDERSON** and died July 1784 in Hanover Twp. NJ. He married Elizabeth **SMITH** born ca 1745 daughter of John and Hannah **SMITH**. One child:
   i- **SMITH** Charles born ca 1768 in NJ

24-   **SMITH** Christian (*Joshua, Jasper, John*) was born 1745-52 daughter of Joshua **SMITH** and Keziah **PELTON**. She married John **BILES** born ca 1735 in NJ son of John **BILES** and Elizabeth **FREEZE** who died by 1812. He married (2) Sarah (unknown maiden name) and had 4 known children, Abraham, John, Samuel and Sara D.
One known child by first marriage:
61-   i- **BILES** George born November 1771

25-   **SMITH** Joshua (*Joshua, Jasper, John*) was born ca 1750-60 in Plainfield, NJ and came to Hector, Schuyler Co. NY about 1800. His wife was Sarah (unknown maiden name). Joshua died 1829/1830 probably in Hector, NY (possibly buried in Eddy cemetery with his son William, no stones remaining) His wife Sarah moved to Sullivan Twp. Tioga Co. Pa. where she died March 28, 1849. According to her gravestone, she was born November 18, 1771. She was listed as living in Sullivan Twp. Tioga Co. Pa. when she sold her 59 acres on lot #45 in Hector, NY on February 23, 1838.
Joshua's children have been accounted for. The following are his known children:
62-   i- **SMITH** William H. born ca 1794
63-   ii- **SMITH** Joshua Jr. born 1797
64-   iii- **SMITH** Charles born December 27, 1799
65-   iv- **SMITH** Anna born January 11, 1801
66-   v- **SMITH** Daniel T. born 1810/15
67-   vi- **SMITH** Jasper born May 19, 1805
68-   vii- **SMITH** George F. born June 1, 1814

8

viii- **SMITH** daughter born 1810-1815
69-    ix- **SMITH** Obadiah born November 14, 1815

26-    **SMITH** Platt Pelton (*Joshua, Jasper, John*) was born ca 1755 in Maidenhead, NJ son of Joshua **SMITH** and Keziah **PELTON** and died after 1830 in Tompkins Co. NY, buried Jacksonville, NY. He married Johannah (Hannah) **SCHOONOVER** born ca 1760 daughter of Benjamin and Margaret **SCHOONOVER**.
Children born in Smithfield, Pa.
70-    i- **SMITH** Benjamin born 1780-82
71-    ii- **SMITH** Joshua November 1783 in Smithfield, Pa.
       iii- **SMITH** Peggy born November 15, 1785 (see (#86)
72-    iv- **SMITH** Mary born August 4, 1788
73-    v- **SMITH** Johannah born May 12, 1789
74-    vi- **SMITH** Keziah born 1790
       vii- **SMITH** Elijah born January 16, 1791
76-    viii- **SMITH** Robert P. born 1797
77-    ix- **SMITH** Alvah born 1802
78-    x- **SMITH** Lavina born 1806

27-    **SMITH** Jasper (*Joshua, Jasper, John*) was born November 15, 1758 in Maidenhead, NJ son of Joshua **SMITH** and Keziah **PELTON** and died May 6, 1838 in Hector, NY, buried in Reynoldsville cemetery. He married Jerusha **WIND** (**WING** or **WINE**) born Delaware Co. NY. She married (2) Enoch **PIXLEY** who was born 1765 son of Elijah **PIXLEY** and Charity **REYNOLDS** and died in Poland, Chautauqua Co. NY
Children born in Hector, NY:
       i- **SMITH** William born March 26, 1824 and died September 1, 1828 in Hector, NY, buried Reynoldsville cemetery
79-    ii- **SMITH** Lafayette born February 24 1825
       iii- **SMITH** Keziah born August 24, 1829. She married Enoch **LODER** and moved West. (not found in 1880 census)
       iv- **SMITH** Jesse W. born December 24, 1832 and died December 30, 1917, unmarried. He named nieces and nephews in his will.
80-    v- **SMITH** Charlotte born February 4, 1837

28-    **SMITH** Obadiah (*Joshua, Jasper, John*) was born November 9, 1765 in Maidenhead, NJ son of Joshua **SMITH** and Keziah **PELTON** and died October 15, 1827 in Covert, NY, buried Grove cemetery. He married Elizabeth **TOWN** who was born April 5, 1773 daughter of Benjamin and Abigail **TOWN** and died May 17, 1826 in Tompkins Co. NY
Children:
       i- **SMITH** Nancy born August 14, 1793 and died September 2, 1865, buried Grove cemetery
       ii- **SMITH** Benjamin born April 2, 1796 and died October 3, 1817
81-    iii- **SMITH** Obadiah born October 7, 1798
82-    iv- **SMITH** Annanias (twin) born July 15, 1801

v- **SMITH** Berentha (twin) born July 15, 1801 and died November 22, 1869, buried Grove cemetery

    vi- **SMITH** Amandy born November 9, 1803 and died January 29, 1853

83-    vii- **SMITH** Robert T. January 25, 1806

84-    viii- **SMITH** Clement H. born May 20, 1808 and died March 27, 1887

85-    ix- **SMITH** John T. born August 16, 1810

    x- **SMITH** Richard born April 17, 1813 and died January 8, 1845

    xi- **SMITH** Elizabeth born September 17, 1818 and died April 17, 1845, second wife of Abraham M. **CREQUE**. They had a daughter Ann Elizabeth born March 28, 1845 and died September 17, 1850. They are buried in Grove cemetery.

29-    **SMITH** Annanias (*Joshua, Jasper, John*) was born June 21, 1767 in Maidenhead, NJ son of Joshua **SMITH** and Keziah **PELTON** and died February 21, 1855 in Tompkins Co. NY. He married Mary **HARTSOUGH** who was born August 31, 1768 daughter of Zachariah and Sylvia **HARTSOUGH** and died November 29, 1840 age 72 yrs 2 months and 29 days. They are buried in Quaker Settlement cemetery in Ulysses, NY

Children:

86-    i- **SMITH** Joshua born 1784-1790 died October 26, 1839

87-    ii- **SMITH** Peter H. born ca 1786

88-    iii- **SMITH** Nancy born 1795

89-    iv- **SMITH** Elizabeth born 1799

90-    v- **SMITH** Benjamin born 1791-1800 and died 1852

91-    vi- **SMITH** Sally born 1801-1810

    vii- **SMITH** Bartemus born 1801-1810. He married Marilla J. **RUMSEY** who was born ca 1806 daughter of Isaac and Jane **RUMSEY** and died September 16, 1853 age 47 years, buried in the Rumsey family cemetery in Enfield, NY.

30-    **SMITH** Benjamin (*Joshua, Jasper, John*) was born ca 1767 in Maidenhead, NJ son of Joshua **SMITH** and Keziah **PELTON**. He is listed in Hector, NY in the 1820 census with 1 male and 1 female. nfi

## Fifth Generation

31-    **SMITH** Sarah (*John, John, Jasper, John*) was born 1784 in Maidenhead, NJ daughter of John and Catherine J. **SMITH** and died April 1859 in Maidenhead. She married (1) Chrienyonce **VAN CLEVE** who was born ca 1782 in Lawrenceville, NJ son of John **VAN CLEVE** and Elizabeth **MOORE** and died before 1805. She married (2) March 7, 1805 Nathan **FISH** who was born December 10, 1779 son of Benjamin **FISH** and Abigail **HOWELL** and died July 7, 1865.

Child by first marriage:

92-    i- VAN CLEVE Chrienyonce Jr.
Children by second marriage:
       i- FISH Mary born ca 1805
       ii- FISH Elizabeth born ca 1806
93-    iii- FISH Eliza born October 11, 1811?


32-    SMITH Daniel (*Jasper, John, Jasper, John*) was born 1750 in Maidenhead, NJ son of
Jasper SMITH and Jemima LANNING and died April 6, 1810 in Milton, Northumberland Co.
Pa. He married (1) November 28, 1773 Joanna GARDINER who was born January 21, 1753
and died April 15, 1785. He married (2) September 29, 1788 in Morristown, NJ Sarah
PIERSON born 1763 in Morristown, NJ daughter of John PIERSON and Ruth HOWELL
Children by first marriage born in Morristown, NJ:
       i- SMITH David born October 17, 1744 and died before 1780
94-    ii- SMITH Joseph Gardiner born September 17, 1776
       iii- SMITH Daniel born August 31, 1778 and died before 1794
       iv- SMITH David born February 19, 1780
       v- SMITH William born February 2, 1783
Children by second marriage born in Morristown, NJ:
       i- SMITH Joanna born July 3, 1789
       ii- SMITH Grace married October 20, 1813 in Hopewell, NJ Daniel SCUDDER son
of Elias SCUDDER and Sarah SMITH (see #97)
       iii- SMITH Daniel born 1794


33-    SMITH Asher (*Jasper, John, Jasper, John*) was born in NJ son of Jasper SMITH and
Jemima LANNING. He married Sarah SMITH born October 19, 1773 daughter of James and
Mehetable SMITH. (see #17)
One child:
95-    i- SMITH Mehetable born 1795


34-    SMITH Hannah (*Jasper, John, Jasper, John*) was born in Maidenhead, NJ daughter of
Jasper SMITH and Jemima LANNING and died in November 1803. She married Daniel
CLARK who was born ca 1731 son of Daniel CLARK and Elizabeth LOTT and died in 1803.
Children:
       i- CLARK Charles born ca 1781, married Elizabeth LYON born ca 1785 in Danbury,
Pa.
96-    ii- CLARK Mary born ca 1783, married Joshua ANDERSON
       iii- CLARK Elizabeth married (1) Henry RUNYAN (2) ___ KINGMAN
       iv- CLARK Jemima born ca 1784, married Thomas COMBS
       v- CLARK William born ca 1786, married Sarah GRAHAM born ca 1790 in
Philadelphia, Pa.
       vi- CLARK Smith born ca 1788
       vii- CLARK Enoch born ca 1790, married Mercy GREEN born ca 1797 in Easton, Pa.
daughter of Benjamin GREEN and Elizabeth TRAIL

35-    SMITH Sarah (*Jasper, John, Jasper, John*) was born 1770 in Maidenhead, NJ daughter of Jasper SMITH and Jemima LANNING and died January 30, 1853 in Ewing, NJ. She married Elias SCUDDER born 1767 son of Daniel SCUDDER and Mary SNOWDEN. He died January 20, 1853 in Ewing, both are buried in the Presbyterian Churchyard in Ewing. Children born in Trenton, NJ:
97-     i- SCUDDER Daniel (see Grace SMITH #32)
98-     ii- SCUDDER Jasper Smith born October 17, 1797
99-     iii- SCUDDER John born August 17, 1796
100-    iv- SCUDDER Abner Smith born May 8, 1800

36-    SMITH Elizabeth (*Jasper, John, Jasper, John*) was born 1771 in Maidenhead, NJ daughter of Jasper SMITH and Jemima LANNING and died June 28, 1837 in Ewing, NJ, buried Presbyterian Churchyard. She married Richard HILL who was born ca 1759 in Amwell, NJ son of Jonathan HILL amd Sarah SMITH (or Samuel and Christianna) and died December 1826 in Ewing, NJ
Children:
        i- HILL Jonathan born ca 1791 went to New Orleans and never heard from
        ii- HILL John born ca 1793
        iii- HILL Jasper Smith born ca 1796 and died February 3, 1847 in Trenton, NJ age 51, unmarried
        iv- HILL Samuel born 1798 and died July 14, 1825
101-    v- HILL Enoch born ca 1798     moved to Mt. Pleasant, Iowa
102-    vi- HILL Sarah Ann born ca 1800
        vii- HILL Daniel born ca 1802
        viii- HILL Elias born ca 1804. He married Elizabeth ANDERSON born 1807 in NJ.
103-    ix- HILL James ca 1805
        x- HILL Theodore Wallace born ca 1814 and died September 4, 1884 in Ewing, buried Presbyterian Churchyard. He married Caroline GILKYSON who was born 1810 in Bucks Co. Pa. daughter of Elias G. GILKYSON and died November 18, 1911.

37-    SMITH Prudence (*Jasper, John, Jasper, John*) was born 1778 in Maidenhead, NJ daughter of Jasper SMITH and Jemima LANNING and died June 6, 1867 in Lawrenceville, NJ, buried Presbyterian Churchyard. She married (1) William MERSHON who was born March 1, 1769 and died April 1814. She married (2) Joseph PATTERSON born March 6, 1780 and died July 1, 1838, buried Presbyterian Churchyard.
Child by first marriage:
104-    i- MERSHON Samuel Davies born December 5, 1804
Child by second marriage:
105-    i- PATTERSON Mary born May 18, 1817

38-    SMITH Sarah (*Joshua, John, Jasper, John*) was born August 11, 1778 in Pennington, NJ daughter of Joshua and Mary SMITH and died July 26, 1824 in Pennington. She married Ephraim PHILLIPS who was born June 14, 1770 in Lawrenceville, NJ son of William PHILLIPS and Ruth TITUS and died March 5, 1834 in Lawrenceville.

Children born Lawrenceville, NJ:
106-    i- **PHILLIPS** George born September 11, 1803
107-   ii- **PHILLIPS** Mary born September 10, 1805

39-     **SMITH** William (*Joshua, John, Jasper, John*) was born 1779 in Lawrenceville, NJ son of Joshua and Mary **SMITH** and died April 20, 1855 in Lawrenceville. He married Elizabeth **REYNOLDS** who was born ca 1824 in Mercer Co. NJ and died 1859 in Lawrenceville.
Children born in Lawrenceville:
108-    i- **SMITH** Charles born May 16, 1845
109-   ii- **SMITH** David born ca 1847
110-  iii- **SMITH** Amanda born ca 1848

40-     **SMITH** Matilda (*Joshua, John, Jasper, John*) was born March 2, 1783 in Maidenhead, NJ daughter of Joshua and Mary **SMITH** and died August 15, 1832 in Pennington, NJ, buried in Presbyterian Churchyard in Pennington. She married November 3, 1799 Enoch **KETCHAM** who was born July 4, 1774 son of Levi and Elizabeth **KETCHAM** and died March 5, 1850, buried in Presbyterian Churchyard.
Children:
      i- **KETCHAM** Joshua born September 14, 1800 and died January 27, 1860
     ii- **KETCHAM** Sarah born May 29, 1804 and died June 12, 1832
   iii- **KETCHAM** Meriah born June 6, 1809 and died February 10, 1832
   iv- **KETCHAM** Matilda born January 12, 1813 and died January 17, 1888
    v- **KETCHAM** William Smith born October 27, 1814 and died September 25, 1896
   vi- **KETCHAM** Louisa born September 19, 1816 and died July 29, 1900. She was living in Pennington, NJ in 1880 with niece Mary M. **HAGAMAN** age 25, nephews Joseph **HAGAMAN** age 26, George W. age 4 and Clarence age 2 yrs.
111-  vii- **KETCHAM** Enoch Jr. born October 30, 1818
  viii- **KETCHAM** Elizabeth born April 5, 1822 and died March 8, 1832
   ix- **KETCHAM** George born August 9, 1824
112-    x- **KETCHAM** Henrietta born December 29, 1827

41-     **SMITH** Keziah (*Joshua, John, Jasper, John*) was born October 7, 1784 in Lawrence, NJ daughter of Joshua and Mary **SMITH** and died January 19, 1866 in Pennington, NJ. She married May 26, 1804 Daniel **COOK** born July 16, 1780 in Hopewell, NJ son of Samuel **COOK** and Prudence **LANNING** and died July 20, 1837 in Pennington.
Children born in NJ:
113-    i- **COOK** Prudence born 1813
114-   ii- **COOK** Aaron H. born ca 1814
115-  iii- **COOK** Samuel B. born ca 1815
116-  iv- **COOK** Absalom Price born ca 1816
    v- **COOK** Elizabeth born ca 1817
117-  vi- **COOK** William born ca 1818
118-  vii- **COOK** George Rea born March 6, 1819
119-  viii- **COOK** Mary born ca 1820

13

120-     ix- **COOK** Jesse Moore born ca 1822
121-     x- **COOK** Lewis D. born ca 1824
          xi- **COOK** Amanda born ca 1825
122-     xii- **COOK** Edmund Burroughs born March 19, 1831

42-     **SMITH** George W. (*Joshua, John, Jasper, John*) was born 1780 in Lawrenceville, NJ son of Joshua and Mary **SMITH** and died July 10, 1848 in Philadelphia, Pa., buried First Baptist Churchyard cemetery. He married (1) Elizabeth (unknown maiden name) born ca 1785 and he married (2) December 26, 1826 in Philadelphia Sarah Ann **GARDNER**.
Children by first marriage:
          i- **SMITH** William born ca 1805, married December 14, 1826 in Philadelphia, Pa. Sarah Ann **GARDNER** and had son William
          ii- **SMITH** George W. Jr. born ca 1806
          iii- **SMITH** Henry H. born ca 1807

43-     **LANNING** Jasper (*Elizabeth, John, Jasper, John*) was born July 10, 1790 in Maidenhead, NJ son of Ralph **LANNING** and Elizabeth **SMITH** and died August 9, 1865 in Enfield, NY. He married Margaret **VAN KIRK** who was born ca 1793 in NJ and died May 9, 1876 in Enfield, NY. They are buried in Rolfe cemetery in Enfield.
Children:
123-     i- **LANNING** Charles W. born ca 1812
124-     ii- **LANNING** William born 1815
•125-    iii- **LANNING** Caroline born 1817
126-     iii- **LANNING** Joseph born ca 1828
127-     iv- **LANNING** Horace born ca 1830
          v- **LANNING** Monroe born ca 1832 (not found in 1880 census)
128-     vi- **LANNING** Harrison H. born ca 1838

44-     **STEVENS** Thomas Jr. (*Catherine, Jasper Jr., Jasper, John*) was born 1761 in Maidenhead, NJ son of Thomas **STEVENS** and Catherine **SMITH** and died May 24, 1824 in Lawrenceville, NJ, buried Upper Burying Ground. He married (1) Cornelia **VAN CLEVE** who died June 2, 1794 age 23. He married (2) Hannah **SMITH** daughter of James and Mehitabel **SMITH** (see #17).
Children by first marriage:
129-     i- **STEVENS** Elizabeth born ca 1789
130-     ii- **STEVENS** Catherine born ca 1794

45-     **SMITH** Benjamin (*Israel, Jasper Jr., Jasper, John*) was born 1774 in Lawrenceville, NJ son of Israel **SMITH** and Johannah **HILL** and died December 18, 1825 in Lawrenceville. He married in 1802 Mary **SMITH** daughter of John and Catherine J. (see #9). His will was proven January 10, 1826 and names his children.
Children born in Lawrenceville, NJ:
131-     i- **SMITH** Samuel H. born 1802
132-     ii- **SMITH** Theodosia born ca 1804

      iii- **SMITH** Jasper Brown born ca 1806 and died 1843 in Mercer Co. NJ

      iv- **SMITH** Elizabeth born ca 1808

      v- **SMITH** Jane born ca 1809

      vi- **SMITH** Lamatta Ann born ca 1811

46-     **SMITH** Waters (*Israel, Jasper Jr., Jasper, John*) was born 1779 in Lawrenceville, NJ son of Israel **SMITH** and Johannah **HILL** and died November 2, 1865 in Lawrenceville. He married July 25, 1805 Bathsheba **ROZELL** who was born 1786 in Maidenhead, NJ daughter of John **ROZELL** and Anna **VAN CLEVE** and died August 26, 1865. They are buried in Lawrenceville.

Children:

      i- **SMITH** Jane

      ii- **SMITH** John R.

47-     **SMITH** Israel Jr. (*Israel, Jasper Jr., Jasper, John*) was born 1782 in Lawrenceville, NJ son of Israel **SMITH** and Johannah **HILL** and died August 16, 1840 in Troy, Miami Co. Ohio. He married February 15, 1809 in Kingwood, NJ Maria **RUNYAN** who was born 1872 in Kingwood daughter of Hugh **RUNYAN** and Sara **HILL** and died September 21, 1840 in Troy, Ohio.

Children:

133-     i- **SMITH** Benjamin Clark born April 21, 1811

      ii- **SMITH** Lammata Bergen born 1816 and died December 4, 1834

      iii- **SMITH** Waters born June 2, 1821

      iv- **SMITH** Israel Stevens Christened June 12, 1830 in the Presbyterian Church in Lawrenceville, NJ

48-     **SMITH** Elizabeth (*Israel, Jasper Jr., Jasper, John*) was born 1791 in Lawrenceville, NJ daughter of Israel **SMITH** and Johannah **HILL** and died August 4, 1817. She married March 2, 1814 Samuel **BREARLEY** who was born January 17, 1792 in Lawrenceville son of George **BREARLEY** and Ann **GILLINGHAM** and died May 27, 1848 in Trenton, NJ. They are buried in the Presbyterian Churchyard. Samuel married (2) December 16, 1818 Sarah **SMITH** born ca 1798 and (3) October 13, 1830 Mary Ann **SMITH**

Children by first marriage:

      i- **BREARLEY** Elizabeth (Eliza) born December 11, 1814 married Thomas R. **ENGLISH** born ca 1820 nfi

      ii- **BREARLEY** Jane born 1816 in Trenton and died there September 21, 1817, buried Presbyterian Churchyard

Children by second marriage:

      iii- **BREARLEY** Theodosia born 1819 in Trenton, NJ and died September 3, 1820

134-     iv- **BREARLEY** William Armstrong born ca 1821

      v- **BREARLEY** Amanda H. born 1825 and died July 13, 1825

49-     **SMITH** Hannah (*James, Thomas, Jasper, John*) was born February 8, 1772 in Maidenhead, NJ daughter of James and Mehitable **SMITH** and died July 6, 1861. She married

Thomas **STEVENS** who was born 1761 in Maidenhead, NJ son of Thomas **STEVENS** and Catherine **SMITH** and died there May 24, 1824. His first wife was Cornelia **VAN CLEVE** who was born 1771 daughter of Benjamin **VAN CLEVE** and Mary **WRIGHT** and died May 24, 1794. They had two children.

50- **SMITH** Sarah (*James, Thomas, Jasper, John*) was born October 12, 1773 in Maidenhead, NJ daughter of James and Mehitable **SMITH**. She married Asher **SMITH** (see #33)

51- **SMITH** Mehetable (*James, Thomas, Jasper, John*) was born August 13, 1775 in Maidenhead, NJ daughter of James and Mehitable **SMITH**. She married February 27 1808 John **PHARIS**. nfi

52- **TINDALL** Hannah (*Abigail, Thomas, Jasper, John*) was born ca 1762 in Ewing, NJ daughter of Joseph **TINDALL** and Abigail **SMITH**. She married Benjamin **GREEN** born ca 1762.
One child:
　　　　i- **GREEN** George born ca 1788. He married ____ **TEMPLE**

53- **TINDALL** Joseph (*Abigail, Thomas, Jasper, John*) was born ca 1764 in Ewing, NJ son of Joseph **TINDALL** and Abigail **SMITH**. He married Phebe **HENDRICKSON** who was born March 26, 1774 in Ewing, NJ and died after 1793.
One known child:
135-　　i- **TINDALL** Mercy born August 17, 1793 in Ewing, NJ

54- **TINDALL** Elizabeth (*Abigail, Thomas, Jasper, John*) was born ca 1766 in Ewing, NJ daughter of Joseph **TINDALL** and Abigail **SMITH**. She married (1) Benjamin **GREEN** born ca 1762 widower of her sister Hannah (see #52). He died before 1796 and she married (2) August 18, 1796 Jacob **HENDRICKSON** born ca 1768 son of Benjamin **HENDRICKSON** and Mercy **JONES**.
Children by first marriage:
　　　　i- **GREEN** Hannah born ca 1780 married John **HULL**
136-　　ii- **GREEN** Thomas born ca 1781
137-　　iii- **GREEN** Noah born ca 1788
138-　　iv- **GREEN** Benjamin IV born ca 1789
Child by second marriage:
　　　　i- **HENDRICKSON** Letetia born ca 1793

55- **TINDALL** Thomas (*Abigail, Thomas, Jasper, John*) was born October 27, 1785 in Ewing, NJ son of Joseph **TINDALL** and Abigail **SMITH** and died September 10, 1831 in Tecumseh, Mi. He married May 26, 1808 Elizabeth **HOWELL** who was born July 23, 1791 daughter of Noah **HOWELL** and died December 2, 1831 in Tecumseh, Mi. They are buried in Brookside cemetery.
Children born in NJ:

i- **TINDALL** Noah Howell born January 4, 1810
139-    ii- **TINDALL** Jesse born 1812
iii- **TINDALL** Elizabeth born February 3, 1814 and died April 17, 1814
iv- **TINDALL** Benjamin born April 16, 1815
v- **TINDALL** Henry born August 14, 1817 and died September 30, 1817
140-    vi- **TINDALL** Enoch born July 13, 1819 and died January 3, 1897 in Tecumseh, Mi.
vii- **TINDALL** George Phillips born April 29, 1822 and died September 8, 1894
viii- **TINDALL** James White born February 21, 1826 and died June 4, 1849 in Platte River, Col.
ix- **TINDALL** Joseph born March 9, 1830 and died June 24, 1837 in Tecumseh, Mi.
x- **TINDALL** Sarah E. born November 13, 1831 in Tecumseh, Mi. and died September 2, 1867 in Ft. Larned, Ks., buried Brookside cemetery in Tecumseh.

56-    **SMITH** Nathaniel (*Elijah, Thomas, Jasper, John*) was born November 15, 1781 in Va. son of Elijah **SMITH** and Elizabeth **LAUGHLIN** and died February 27, 1862 in Whitley Co. Ky. He married Charlotta **WHITE** who was born July 2, 1785 in NC and died February 7, 1872. They are buried in Steeley cemetery.
One child:
i- **SMITH** John Speed born ca 1808 in Knox Co. Ky. He married June 24, 1832 Cecelia **WEBB** born ca 1815.

57-    **SMITH** Virginia Jane (*Elijah, Thomas, Jasper, John*) was born January 28, 1783 in Va. daughter of Elijah **SMITH** and Elizabeth **LAUGHLIN** and died by 1849. She married August 19, 1802 in Knox Co. Ky. Burton C. **LITTON** born April 2, 1780 in Russell Co. Va. son of Solomon S. **LITTON** and Martha **DUNKIN**. He married (2) May 7, 1849 in Whitley Co. Ky. Jane **COX**
Children:
i- **LITTON** John Speed born 1803
ii- **LITTON** Thomas Jefferson
iii- **LITTON** Thomas Wesley

58-    **SMITH** Thomas Hunt (*Elijah, Thomas, Jasper, John*) was born August 20, 1786 in Abington, Va. son of Elijah **SMITH** and Elizabeth **LAUGHLIN** and died July 17, 1856 in Pontotoc Co. Ms. He married 1806 in Tn. Mary **TABOR** born ca 1785 in Rutherford Co. Va.
Children:
141-    i- **SMITH** James Laughlin born ca 1808 in Tn.
142-    ii- **SMITH** Burton Lytton born 1810 in Tn.
143-    iii- **SMITH** Susannah T. born 1813 in Tn.
144-    iv- **SMITH** William Preston born January 1822 in Russelville, Franklin Co. Ala.

59-    **SMITH** Cynthia Ann (*Elijah, Thomas, Jasper, John*) was born July 6, 1803 in Va. daughter of Elijah **SMITH** and Elizabeth **LAUGHLIN**. She married May 23 1822 in Rutherford, Tn. Joseph **KNOX** born 1799 in NC son of Thomas **KNOX** and Mary **ARMSTRONG** and died in Cannon, Tn.

Children:

    i- **KNOX** James B. born 1824 in Rutherford, Tn., married January 3, 1850 Salina Jane **COX** born 1830

    ii- **KNOX** Thomas born 1826 in Rutherford, Tn.

145-    iii- **KNOX** Elijah Smith born 1828 in Cannon, Tn.

146-    iv- **KNOX** Joseph A. born 1834 in Cannon, Tn.

    v- **KNOX** William A. born 1836 in Cannon, Tn.

    vi- **KNOX** John G. born 1843 in Cannon, Tn.

    vii- **KNOX** Emeline S. born 1845 in Cannon, Tn.

60-    **SMITH** Absolom (*John, Samuel, Jasper, John*) was born November 20, 1757 in Amwell Twp. NJ son of John **SMITH** and Mary **HOUGHTON** and died December 28, 1834 in Williamsburg Twp. Clermont Co. Ohio. He married Susannah (unknown maiden name) born 1757 in Amwell Twp.

Children born in Pa.:

    i- **SMITH** George born 1785, He married June 18, 1812 in Clermont Co. Ohio Margaret **TROUT** born 1789 daughter of John **TROUT**

    ii- **SMITH** Andrew born July 7, 1789 and died March 27, 1868. He married June 18, 1812 married Elizabeth **ANDERSON** (or **LEONARD**)

    iii- **SMITH** Joab born ca 1791

    iv- **SMITH** Jacob born ca 1792, He married March 23, 1815 in Clermont Co. Ohio Hollender **MARLATT** born ca 1794

    v- **SMITH** Margaret born 1795, married February 18, 1816 John **LEONARD** born ca 1791 in Clermont Co. Ohio.

147-    vi- **SMITH** Ann born 1800

    vii- **SMITH** Abraham born 1802 and died January 2, 1880

    viii- **SMITH** Rebecca born 1806, married Michael **SHEARER** born ca 1802.

148-    ix- **SMITH** John born July 21, 1809

61-    **BILES** George (*Christian, Joshua, Jasper, John*) was born 1771 in NJ son of John **BILES** and Christian **SMITH** and died May 1841. He married Mary (unknown maiden name) June 22, 1772 and died May 8, 1842. They are buried in the Moravian cemetery in Hope, NJ. Children born in Hope, NJ.

149-    i- **BILES** Elizabeth ca 1798

150-    ii- **BILES** William born ca 1800 and died before 1841 (possibly the father of Sarah Ann **BILES** born ca 1837 and was living with Phillip and Elizabeth **SCHOONOVER** in 1850)

    iii- **BILES** Mary married William **ARCH** nfi

151-    iv- **BILES** Anna born November 22, 1803

152-    v- **BILES** Jane born 1810

153-    vi- **BILES** Electa

    vii- **BILES** Rachel

154-    viii- **BILES** (possibly) Annanias who married in Hope, NJ July 10, 1841 Sarah **ATTEN**

62-    **SMITH** William H. (*Joshua, Joshua, Jasper, John*) was born ca 1794 in New Jersey.

He married Catherine **LEONARD** who was born 1800 in Schoharie Co. MY, believed to be the daughter of Abraham **LEONARD** altho she was not mentioned in his will dated 1830. It was Abraham Leonard who sold property to William Smith on December 24, 1816, for the sum of $550.00, 15 acres which was part of lot #48 in the town of Hector. An unusual part of this deed states that William "is not on any account to make sale of the premises afore mentioned without the consent of the party of the first part".(Abraham Leonard) Catherine is buried in the Johnson Cemetery in Howard, NY

William died in August/September 1820 leaving a will which was probated in Tompkins Co. NY October 1820. Copied from his will:

I, William H. Smith, of Hector, Tompkins Co. and State of New York, sensible of the uncertainty of life and being weak and debilitated of body but of sound mind and judgement, do make and publish this my last will and testament.

First, I give and bequeath my soul to Almighty God who gave it me and my body to be decently interred on my own farm in Hector in a rise of ground East of my dwelling house. (This became Eddy cemetery) Second, my will is that all my personal property shall within two months after my decease, be sold at public auction or vendue by my Executors or the survivor of them on such time as they may think most conducive to the benefit of my estate, and with the proceeds thereof, pay my debts and with the residue apply to such means as they may, said Executors, may think most beneficial to said estate.

Third, my will is that all my real estate situate on lot # 48 in Hector aforesaid shall be kept by my said executors or the survivor of them until my children (vis Sally, Abraham and John) shall have all arrived to the age of twenty-one which will be on the second day of February in the year eighteen hundred and forty one; at which time my will is, that said estate shall be equally divided among them. Fourth, my will is, that of the portion of my said estate aforesaid, that my beloved wife Catherine may be entitled to, she may have, hold and enjoy the same during the time she may remain my widow or until her decease, at which time the reversion or remainder, to be applied by my executors equally in manner and time afore mentioned for the benefit of my children. I make ordain and appoint my beloved and truly friend William Wiggins and my dear and affectionate brother Joshua Smith Jr., both of Hector aforesaid executors of this my last will and testament, and the survivors of them etc. dated the seventh day of August 1820. This will was probated on October 21, 1820.

Children born in Hector, NY:

155-     i- SMITH Sally born ca 1817
156-     ii- SMITH Abram L. born May 2, 1818
157-     iii- SMITH John L. born February 2, 1820

By 1824 Catherine had married Ambrose **DUNHAM** who was born 1794 in New Brunswick, NJ son of Thomas **DUNHAM** and Anna **CORRELL** and died in Howard, NY 1868. His first wife was Prudence **KIRKPATRICK** born 1795 and died 1818. She is buried in Ovid, NY. They had one daughter, Mary born 1813 who married Benjamin C. **ERWAY** of Hector, NY. In 1824 Ambrose and Catherine removed to the Town of Howard in Steuben Co. NY. They had four children:

i- **DUNHAM** Elizabeth born ca 1828 who married Daniel **PLANK**. No children
ii- **DUNHAM** Richard born ca 1831 who married Sarah **AUSTIN**
iii- **DUNHAM** Ira born can 1833
iv- **DUNHAM** Laura born October 16, 1843 and died March 27, 1923, buried Hope cemetery in Hornell. She married Aaron M. **ARWINE** born ca 1850 and had son Bert born ca 1876 in Hornellsville, NY

63-     **SMITH** Joshua Jr. (*Joshua, Joshua, Jasper, John*) was born ca 1796/7 in New Jersey. He came to Tompkins, Co. NY about 1800 with his father. He married (1) Lydia **CLARK** and moved to Sullivan Twp. Pa. Lydia died ca 1840 and he married (2) about 1842 Diadema **ROBLYER** and married (3) Charity (____) **CLARY**. He committed suicide April 1859 in Sullivan Twp. Tioga Co. Pa. According to his will, Charity signed off as adm. and was called Charity **BOSARD** so she apparently remarried. In 1870 census she is living with her daughter

Olive as Charity Bosard.
Children:
158-      i- SMITH Dennis T. born April 26, 1823 in Hector, NY
159-      ii- SMITH Philetus P. born January 13, 1825 in Sullivan Twp.
160-      iii- SMITH Ephraim C. born January 1826/27 in Sullivan Twp.
         iv- SMITH Burinthea born ca 1825/29 and died before 1840, scalded to death
         v- SMITH Joshua burned to death in coal fire as infant
161-      vi- SMITH Olive Rebecca born April 11, 1835
162-      vii- SMITH Diantha born ca 1836
163-      viii- SMITH Lydia born ca 1845/46 by his second marriage

64-      SMITH Charles (*Joshua, Joshua, Jasper, John*) was born December 27, 1799 in New
Jersey son of Joshua and Sarah SMITH and died September 20, 1885 aged 86 yrs. in Sullivan
Twp. Pa. He married September 10, 1822 Elizabeth THOMAS who was born March 3, 1805
in NJ and died December 1, 1874 in Sullivan Twp. Pa. They are buried in Ames Hill cemetery.
Children:
164-      i- SMITH David Thomas born November 18, 1824
165-      ii- SMITH Isaac born June 1827
         iii- SMITH Jackson died before 1885
         iv- SMITH Charles born March 2, 1831 in Hector, NY and died June 12, 1850 in
Sullivan Twp. Pa., buried Ames Hill cemetery
166-      v- SMITH George born December 29, 1832 in Jackson, NY
167-      vi- SMITH Mary
         vii- SMITH Jonathan
         viii- SMITH William
         ix- SMITH Jason born July 8, 1858 and died August 1, 1858, buried Ames Hill
cemetery
         x- SMITH James R. born October 10, 1845 and died September 29, 1849, buried
Ames Hill cemetery

65-      SMITH Anna (*Joshua, Joshua, Jasper, John*) was born January 11, 1800 in Hector, NY
daughter of Joshua and Sarah SMITH and died February 14, 1879 in Sullivan Twp. Pa. She
married Isaac RICHMOND who was born January 11, 1807 and died May 14, 1877 in Sullivan
Twp. They are buried in Ames Hill cemetery.
Children born Tioga Co. Pa.:
168-      i- RICHMOND Lois ca 1823
169-      ii- RICHMOND Annanias born August 25, 1824 in Hector, NY
170-      iii- RICHMOND Albert born March 9, 1827 in Hector, NY
171-      iv- RICHMOND Melissa born ca 1829 in Pa.
172-      v- RICHMOND Obadiah H. born May 19, 1832/33 in Sullivan Twp. Pa.
173-      vi- RICHMOND Matilda born ca 1834/35 in Sullivan Twp. Pa.
174-      vii- RICHMOND Elizabeth born ca 1836 in Sullivan Twp. Pa.
175-      viii- RICHMOND Malinda born January 14, 1840 in Sullivan, Twp.
176-      ix- RICHMOND Lyman born February 13, 1844 in Sullivan Twp.

66- **SMITH** Daniel T. (*possible son of Joshua, Joshua, Jasper, John*) was born 1810-1815 in Hector, NY son of Joshua and Sarah **SMITH** and died February 20, 1877. He married Sally **HALL** who was born ca 1821 daughter of Richard **HALL** and Susannah **KINDRED** and died May 19, 1875. She is buried in Reynoldsville cemetery.
Children born in Hector, NY:
177-     i- **SMITH** Matilda born 1818
178-     ii- **SMITH** Mary Elizabeth born 1826
179-     iii- **SMITH** Susan M. born 1832
         iv- **SMITH** Richard H. born ca 1840
180-     v- **SMITH** Nelson born January 14, 1839
         vi- **SMITH** Henry born 1845
         v- **SMITH** Charles D. born 1849. He was a minister. He died 1924 and is buried in Tyrone cemetery in Tyrone, NY

67- **SMITH** Jasper (*Joshua, Joshua, Jasper, John*) was born May 19, 1805 in Hector, NY son of Joshua and Sarah **SMITH** and died October 9, 1884 in Sullivan Twp. Pa. He married (1) Elizabeth **HALL** born 1807 and died 1875 and married (2) Caroline (unknown maiden name) born 1822 and died 1884.
Children:
181-     i- **SMITH** Alexander C. born December 13, 1826 in Hector, NY
182-     ii- **SMITH** Lufannie born July 1, 1829
183-     iii- **SMITH** Huldah born December 16, 1833
184-     iv- **SMITH** Arad T. III born August 2, 1839
         v- **SMITH** David (idiot in 1850 census, died before 1884)
         vi- **SMITH** William Harrison born 1841
185-     vii- **SMITH** Lyman R. born June 1843

68- **SMITH** George F. (*Joshua, Joshua, Jasper, John*) was born June 1, 1814 in Hector, NY son of Joshua and Sarah **SMITH** and died March 8, 1896 in Roseville, Rutland Twp. Pa. and is buried in Watson cemetery in Sullivan Twp. (stone reads death date 1895) He left a will naming wife Millie (Amelia), children and grandchildren. He married (1) March 2, 1836 Keturrah Rebecca **HODGES** who was born March 2, 1818 in NY State daughter of Nehemiah **HODGES** and died December 6, 1868 in Sullivan Twp., buried in Hodges cemetery. He married (2) after 1868 Amelia **WILSON** daughter of Samuel and Betsey **WILSON** who was born 1837 and died 1902, buried Watson cemetery.
Children by first marriage born in Sullivan Twp.:
186-     i- **SMITH** Mary Jane born May 8, 1838 married George **SQUIRES**
187-     ii- **SMITH** Sally Ann born April 16, 1841 died before 1896
188-     iii- **SMITH** Nehemiah born June 27, 1844
189-     iv- **SMITH** George Manley born July 23, 1846 died before 1896
         v- **SMITH** Emma Keturrah born May 22, 1848 (see #187)
190-     vi- **SMITH** Charles Wesley born November 18, 1849
191-     vii- **SMITH** Frances Augusta born August 3, 1855 died before 1896
Children by second marriage:

192-    i- SMITH Anna R. born January 27, 1876 in Gray Valley, Pa.
193-    ii- SMITH George F. Jr. born ca 1876
194-    iii- SMITH Effie Sarah born November 20, 1877

69-    SMITH Obadiah (*Joshua, Joshua, Jasper, John*) was born November 14, 1815 in Hector, NY son of Joshua and Sarah SMITH and died June 7, 1905 in Sullivan Twp. Pa. He married ca 1844 Nancy Ann WELCH who was born January 25/27, 1817 in Pa. and died July 18, 1898 in Sullivan Twp. Tioga Co. Pa. They are buried in Gray Valley cemetery. He married (2) at age 83 years at his home in Sylvania, Pa. June 29, 1899 Mrs. Kate CANADY age 55 years of Troy, Pa.
Children born in Sullivan Twp. Pa.:
195-    i- SMITH Ellen Jane born ca 1845
196-    ii- SMITH Cornelius born ca 1847 and died 1931
        iii- SMITH Martha born ca 1847 and died 1929
        iv- SMITH Cora
        v- SMITH Emeline (Elinor) born ca 1851
197-    vi- SMITH Albert Obadiah born December 1853
        vii- SMITH Charlotte
        viii- SMITH Glen

70-    SMITH Benjamin (*Platt, Joshua, Jasper, John*) was born ca 1781 in NJ son of Platt Pelton SMITH and Johannah SCHOONOVER and died July 24, 1849 in Tompkins Co. NY. He married Sarah MUNDY who was born 1787 daughter of Beniah MUNDY and Catherine SCHOONOVER and died August 23, 1861, no issue. She married (2) D. Alonzo FOSTER.

71-    SMITH Joshua (*Platt, Joshua, Jasper, John*) born November 1783 in Smithfield, Pa. son of Platt SMITH and Johannah SCHOONOVER and died March 22, 1850. He married Elizabeth VAN AUKEN who was born May 9, 1781 daughter of Casperus VAN AUKEN and Johannah VAN DERMARK and died May 24, 1851, buried in Quaker Settlement cemetery.
Children:
198-    i- SMITH Benjamin Schoonover born September 15, 1804
199-    ii- SMITH Hannah born 1806
200-    iii- SMITH Casparus Van Aukin born July 21, 1807
        iv- SMITH John Anderson born November 14, 1809
201-    v- SMITH Elijah born February 11, 1811
202-    vi- SMITH George Washington born April 17. 1814
203-    vii- SMITH Mary Ann born 1820
        viii- SMITH Polly Ann born March 5, 1825/6
204-    ix- SMITH Horace David born March 19, 1827

72-    SMITH Mary (*Platt, Joshua, Jasper, John*) was born August 4, 1787 daughter of Platt SMITH and Johannah SCHOONOVER and died June 7, 1855 age 67 years 11 months 6 days. She married (1) December 29, 1805 George VAN HORN who died 1813. His wife Mary was apppointed administrator of his estate. She married (2) Simeon VAN HORN who was born 1795 son of Simon VAN HORN and Sarah DUNNUM or DUNHAM and died October 12, 1883. They are buried in Mc Intyre Settlement cemetery in Hector. Simeon married (2) Mary A. MOORE who was born in Ohio daughter of Daniel T. and Hannah MOORE and died February 25, 1907.

Children by first marriage (George):
205-    i- VAN HORN Margaret born November 19, 1807
        ii- VAN HORN Cornelius
206-    iii- VAN HORN Beniah
207-    iv- VAN HORN Hannah born 1815
Children by second marriage (Simeon):
208-    v- VAN HORN Matilda born 1818 and died 1850-60
209-    vi- VAN HORN Oliver born October 5, 1821
210-    vii- VAN HORN Angeline Adelia born 1827
211-    viii- VAN HORN Ann Eliza born 1829
        ix- VAN HORN Orsemus born 1829 and died 1858


73-    SMITH Johannah (*Platt, Joshua, Jasper, John*) was born May 12, 1789/90 daughter of Platt SMITH and Johannah SCHOONOVER and died March 30, 1849, buried Jacksonville cemetery. She married Nathaniel RICHARDS who was born September 17, 1788 in Wyoming Co. Pa. son of (?) RICHARDS and Rachel DAVENPORT and died August 6, 1846.
Children:
212-    i- RICHARDS Platt born September 1809
213-    ii- RICHARDS Benjamin born September 20, 1810
214-    iii- RICHARDS Alvah born 1811
215-    iv- RICHARDS Hannah born 1812 and died 1879
216-    vi- RICHARDS Robert born June 13, 1814
217-    vii- RICHARDS Albert born 1816
        viii- RICHARDS Rachel Emeline born September 14, 1818, married Benjamin S. WOODWARD (see #220)
218-    ix- RICHARDS Louisa M. or Mary Louisa born 1822
219-    x- RICHARDS William born 1824


74-    SMITH Keziah (*Platt, Joshua, Jasper, John*) was born 1790 in Smithfild, Pa. daughter of Platt SMITH and Johannah SCHOONOVER and died December 16, 1863 in Tompkins Co. NY, buried Grove cemetery in Trumansburg, NY. She married Samuel WOODWARD.
Children born in Covert, NY:
220-    i- WOODWARD Benjamin S. born April 22, 1819
        ii- WOODWARD Buell born March 3, 1822 and died September 5, 1865, married Catherine (unknown maiden name) born 1827


75-    SMITH Elijah (*Platt, Joshua, Jasper, John*) was born March 1811 son of Platt SMITH and Johannah SCHOONOVER and died February 20, 1865 in Marion, Iowa. He married October 21, 1817 Jerusha SOUTHWICK who was born 1797 and died after 1880.
Children born Walnut Twp. Ind.:

i- SMITH John born 1828, listed in 1880 census living in Apol, Iowa age 52 with wife Mary age 51, daughter Emma age 8 yrs and Mother Jerusha age 83 yrs.

ii- SMITH Calvin born 1831 and died bef 1878

iii- SMITH Melissa born 1834 and died aft 1878

iv- SMITH Nancy M. born 1836 and died bef 1878

76- SMITH Robert P. (*Platt, Joshua, Jasper, John*) was born ca 1797 in NJ son of Platt Pelton SMITH and Johannah SCHOONOVER and died November 17, 1869 in Ulysses, NY. He married Elizabeth MILLER who was born ca 1801 in NY daughter of Ziba MILLER and Sally SMITH and died June 7, 1867.

Children:

i- SMITH Sarah M. born 1822 and died May 22, 1842 age 19 years 11 months and 23 days, buried Quaker Settlement cemetery in Ulysses, NY

ii- SMITH Irvin J. born March 18, 1825 and died July 7, 1844

iii- SMITH Adeline L. born born 1828 (see (#209)

iv- SMITH Calista Matilda born 1829 (see #209)

221- v- SMITH Harriet born July 22, 1833

vi- SMITH Julius born 1841 and died May 26, 1842 age 10 months 21 days, buried Quaker Settlement cemetery in Ulysses, NY

vii- SMITH daughter born 1843 and died June 20. 1843

77- SMITH Alvah (*Platt, Joshua, Jasper, John*) was born 1802 son of Platt SMITH and Johannah SCHOONOVER and died November 22, 1871, buried Trumbull's Corners cemetery in Newfield, NY. He married December 22, 1822 Sarah DICKERSON who was born November 8, 1804 daughter of Lewis DICKERSON and Mary COLLINS and died (np date September 1837). He married (2) Lydia Ann (unknown maiden name) born ca 1824 and died 1857-60.

One child by second marriage:

i- SMITH Sarah Ann born 1842 and died before 1872. She married Robert PHILLIPS. nfi

78- SMITH Lavina (*Platt, Joshua, Jasper, John*) was born 1806 daughter of Platt SMITH and Johannah SCHOONOVER and died December 9, 1846. She married David VAN AUKEN who was born 1803 and died June 9, 1864. He married (2) Elizabeth Jane MESSLER who died February 22, 1855 age 24 years 11 months. They are buried in Grove cemetery.

One child:

222- i- VAN AUKEN Horace J. born ca 1830

Children by second marriage born in Covert, NY:

i- VAN AUKEN Catherine A. born January 31, 1848

ii- VAN AUKEN (twin) infant born February 1, 1851

iii- VAN AUKEN Calvin J. (twin) born February 1, 1851 and died September 16, 1919, buried Grove cemetery. He married Anna WIGHTMAN of Ovid Ctr. NY

79- SMITH Lafayette (*Jasper, Joshua, Jasper, John*) was born February 24, 1825 son of

Jasper **SMITH** and Jerusha **WIND** and died November 24, 1904 in Hector, NY. He married Lovina **BORDEN** who was born September 25, 1830 in Steuben Co. NY daughter of Horace and Minerva **BORDEN** and died April 5, 1901 in Perry City, NY. They are buried in Jones cemetery town of Hector. They were living in Tioga Co. Pa. in 1850 and then moved back to Hector, NY before 1860.

Children:

      i- **SMITH** Horace born 1851 and died by 1865

      ii- **SMITH** Jane born December 1857

223-    iii- **SMITH** Alice Amelia born May 1861

224-    iv- **SMITH** Mary F. born 1869


80-    **SMITH** Charlotte (*Jasper, Joshua, Jasper, John*) was born February 4, 1837 in Hector, NY daughter of Jasper **SMITH** and Jerusha **WIND** and died before 1917. She married Abraham **BROWER** born 1814/34 (possibly the Abram Brower buried in Grove cemetery who died November 30, 1913.

Children:

      i- **BROWER** Mary born 1856

      ii- **BROWER** William born 1859 and died July 29, 1948, buried in Grove cemetery.


81-    **SMITH** Obadiah Jr. (*Obadiah, Joshua, Jasper, John*) was born October 7, 1798 in NJ son of Obadiah **SMITH** and Elizabeth **TOWN** and died February 8, 1881 probably in Hector, NY, buried Grove cemetery. He married February 9, 1817 Ann **CULVER** who was born June 14, 1798 and died January 28, 1890.

Children:

225-    i- **SMITH** Elizabeth born April 5, 1818

      ii- **SMITH** Herman C. born February 20, 1820

      iii- **SMITH** Mary Ann born April 5, 1822

      iv- **SMITH** William H. born August 26, 1824

      v- **SMITH** Caroline M. born April 16, 1828 in Tompkins Co. NY and died May 28, 1887. She married ____ **TALMADGE** who died before 1850 census (possibly Hanford **TALMADGE** born ca 1819 in Ct. son of Henry and Hannah **TALMADGE** and died April 1850 in Enfield, NY)

226-    vi- **SMITH** Berentha born October 10, 1830

      vii- **SMITH** Martha Jane born May 27, 1833

227-    viii- **SMITH** Gideon Osborne born January 17, 1836

228-    ix- **SMITH** Harris Irvin born September 24, 1838


82-    **SMITH** Annanias (*Obadiah, Joshua, Jasper, John*) was born July 15, 1801 son of Obadiah **SMITH** and Elizabeth **TOWN** and died December 30, 1871 in Lansing, NY. He married Anna **DRAKE** who was born May 8, 1809 daughter of John **DRAKE** and died May 8, 1858. They are buried in the Lansingburg cemetery.

Children:

229-    i- **SMITH** Francis Drake born January 8, 1828

      ii- **SMITH** John D. C. born 1830

iii- **SMITH** Laura Ann born 1832

iv- **SMITH** Rufus H. born August 1835, listed in 1880 census living in Lansing, NY with sister Salina, died after 1900

v- **SMITH** Salina born April 1844 and died after 1900 unmarried

vi- **SMITH** Reuben M. born April 6, 1853 and died December 1, 1917 in Lansing, NY, married Emma L. (unknown maiden name)

83-    **SMITH** Robert T. (*Obadiah, Joshua, Jasper, John*) was born January 25, 1806 in Covert, NY son of Obadiah **SMITH** and Elizabeth **TOWN** and died November 17, 1881. He married Hannah **NORTON** who was born December 30, 1811 daughter of Smith and Abigail **NORTON** and died January 13, 1880.

Children:

230-      i- **SMITH** Melissa born September 1831

231-      ii- **SMITH** Jehiel born September 15, 1834

232-      iii- **SMITH** Abigail N. born September 5, 1836

84-    **SMITH** Clement H. (*Obadiah, Joshua, Jasper, John*) was born May 20, 1808 in Covert, NY son of Obadiah **SMITH** and Elizabeth **TOWN** and died March 27, 1887. He is buried in Hayt's cemetery in Ithaca, name on Brotherton monument. He married Lucy **SAVAGE** born May 1, 1808 in Mass. daughter of Elisha and Elizabeth **SAVAGE** and died January 25, 1884 age 74 years 3 months and 25 days. They are buried in Hayt's cemetery in Ithaca, NY.

Children born in Tompkins Co. NY:

233-      i- **SMITH** William C. born November 20, 1831

          ii- **SMITH** Mary born 1834

234-      iii- **SMITH** Elizabeth born 1836

235-      iv- **SMITH** Alonzo born April 17, 1840

236-      v- **SMITH** Julia M. born 1843

237-      vi- **SMITH** Laura A. born 1844

238-      vii- **SMITH** Frances born July 20, 1848

85-    **SMITH** John T. (*Obadiah, Joshua, Jasper. John*) was born August 16, 1810 in Covert, NY son of Obadiah **SMITH** and Elizabeth **TOWN** and died March 11, 1865. He married (1) Emeline **COLE** who was born November 13, 1814 daughter of David **COLE** and Rachel **TOWNSEND** and died February 22, 1848. He married (2) Margaret **GILMORE** who was born July 15, 1821 daughter of John **GILMORE** and Rachel **QUIGLEY** and died September 2, 1905. They are all buried in Grove cemtery.

Children by first marriage:

          i- **SMITH** David Cole born October 1837 and died December 9, 1838, buried in Sebring cemetery

239-      ii- **SMITH** Gilbert Cole born July 27, 1839

240-      iii- **SMITH** Delos H. born December 1841 in Covert, NY

          iv- **SMITH** Francis Asbury born May 1843

241-      v- **SMITH** Athena born March 13, 1845

          vi- **SMITH** Wilbur Fish born March 20, 1847 and died 1904, buried Walnut Hill

cemetery in Kingman Co. Ks. He married Evis W. (unknown maiden name) born ca 1854
Children by second marriage:
242-    vii- SMITH Emeline born June 3, 1849
        viii- SMITH Diademma Robbins born October 23, 1851
        ix- SMITH John Wilbur born August 1, 1855
243-    x- SMITH Herman Towne born August 8, 1864


86-    SMITH Joshua (*Annanias, Joshua, Jasper, John*) was born 1784-1790 son of Annanias
SMITH and Mary HARTSOUGH and died October 25, 1839. He married his first cousin once
removed Peggy SMITH born March 27, 1784 in Smithfield, Pa. daughter of Platt SMITH and
Johannah SCHOONOVER and died 1840-43 (see #26)
Children:
244-    i- SMITH Mary Jane died before May 21, 1864
245-    ii- SMITH Priscilla born 1811
246-    iii- SMITH Lovina born July 9, 1813
247-    iv- SMITH Lewis Hartsough born October 9, 1816 in Ulysses,
248-    v- SMITH Daniel Tompkins born 1821
        vi- SMITH Sally Betsey Ann born January 7, 1826


87-    SMITH Peter (*Annanias, Joshua, Jasper, John*) was born ca 1786 in NJ son of Annanias
SMITH and Mary HARTSOUGH and died May 25, 1849?. He married Elizabeth MOORE
who was born 1794 daughter of John MOORE and Esther HOLMES and died August 18, 1863.
They are buried in Forest Lawn cemetery in Buffalo, NY.
Children:
249-    i- SMITH George Washington born ca 1814
250-    ii- SMITH Christina G. born 1816
251-    iii- SMITH William Henry born 1826


88-    SMITH Nancy (Ann) (*Annanias, Joshua, Jasper, John*) was born 1795 in NJ daughter
of Annanias SMITH and Mary HARTSOUGH and died 1864 in Tompkins Co. NY. She
married Elias LANNING born 1794 in NJ and died 1882. They are buried in Hayt's cemetery
in Ithaca
Children:
        i- LANNING Ann born 1817 and died December 18, 1869 in Ithaca, NY
        ii- LANNING Martha Maria born 1823
252-    iii- LANNING Gideon W. born 1827


89-    SMITH Elizabeth (*Annanias, Joshua, Jasper, John*) was born 1799 in NJ daughter of
Annanias SMITH and Mary HARTSOUGH and died June 6, 1872. She married Ezra
GANOUNG who was born 1799 son of Joseph and Amelia GANOUNG and died June 6, 1866.
They are buried in Hayt's cemetery in Ithaca.
One child:
253-    i- GANOUNG Lovisa born 1826

90-    SMITH Benjamin (*Annanias, Joshua, Jasper, John*) was born 1791-1800 in NJ son of Annanias SMITH and Mary HARTSOUGH and died 1852 in Tompkins Co. NY. He married Charlotte GIBB who was born 1797 daughter of James GIBB and Jennet ANDERSON and died January 25, 1872, buried Oak Grove cemetery in Hillsdale, Mi.

Children:
254-    i- SMITH William H. born 1822 and died October 14, 1908
        ii- SMITH Annanias born 1826
        iii- SMITH Eliza A. born 1829
        iv- SMITH Charlotte born 1831
255-    v- SMITH John H. born 1837 and died August 20, 1899
256-    vi- SMITH James Tuttle born 1840 and died April 2, 1902 in New Rockford, ND, buried Oak Grove cemetery in Hillsdale, Mi.

91-    SMITH Sally (*Annanias, Joshua, Jasper, John*) was born 1805 in Enfield, NY daughter of Annanias SMITH and Mary HARTSOUGH and died 1890 in Enfield, buried Summerton cemetery. She married John SUMMERTON who was born 1803 son of Thomas and Marilla SUMMERTON.

Children:
        i- SUMMERTON daughter born 1820
        ii- SUMMERTON daughter born ca 1825
257-    iii- SUMMERTON Thomas born February 18, 1829
        iv- SUMMERTON Francis born 1832 and died 1913. His wife Sophronia was born 1834 and died 1906, buried Summerton cemetery
258-    v- SUMMERTON Alonzo born 1835
        vi- SUMMERTON infant son died March 9, 1838
259-    vii- SUMMERTON Nancy born 1839


Sixth Generation


92-    VAN CLEVE Chreinyonce Jr. (*Sarah, John, John, Jasper, John*) was born ca 1807 in Lawrenceville, NJ son of Chreinyonce VAN CLEVE and Sarah SMITH. He married ____ VAN BRIGHT born ca 1813 in New Brunswick.

Children:
        i- VAN CLEVE Cornelius born ca 1829
        ii- VAN CLEVE Ely born ca 1830
        iii- VAN CLEVE Rachel born ca 1831
        iv- VAN CLEVE Jane born ca 1832, married Samuel KETCHAM born ca 1828
        v- VAN CLEVE Anne born ca 1833, married Liverton MATHEWS born ca 1830


93-    FISH Eliza (*Sarah, John, John, Jasper, John*) was born ca 1807 in Lawrenceville,

NJ daughter of Nathan **FISH** and Sarah **SMITH** and died October 23, 1889. She married Abram **SKIRM** who was born February 22, 1807 in Hamilton Twp. NJ son of Joseph **SKIRM** and Elizabeth **ANDERSON**.
Children:

    i- **SKIRM** Asa F. born ca 1825, married Margaret **COOK** born ca 1825 daughter of William Smith **COOK** and Sarah **SCUDDER**. (see #93) Unknown children.

    ii- **SKIRM** Margaret born ca 1826, married James G. **VAN CLEVE** born ca 1824 son of John Moore **VAN CLEVE** and Martha Anthony **GREEN**. Unknown children

    iii- **SKIRM** Elizabeth born June 8, 1831, married Benjamin **VAN CLEVE** born ca 1825 in NJ son of John Moore **VAN CLEVE** and Martha Anthony **GREEN**.

260-    iv- **SKIRM** Charles Henry born July 29, 1832

    v- **SKIRM** Emily Maria (twin) born April 30, 1836

261-    vi- **SKIRM** Ferdinand (twin) born October 30, 1836


94-    **SMITH** Joseph Gardiner (*Daniel, Jasper, John, Jasper, John*) was born September 17, 1776 in Morristown, NJ son of Daniel **SMITH** and Joanna **GARDINER**. He married (1) April 3, 1803 in Morris Co. NJ Mary **CASTERLINE** who was christened September 22, 1797 in Hanover, NJ daughter of Jacob **CASTERLINE** and Eunice **SQUIRE** and died April 15, 1785 in Morristown, NJ.
Children of 1st marriage born in NJ:

262-    i- **SMITH** James Henry born March 16, 1805

    ii- **SMITH** Susannah born March 1807

    iii- **SMITH** son born September 1809 and died infancy

    iv- **SMITH** Lydia born June 1812


95-    **SMITH** Mehitabel (*Asher, Jasper, John, Jasper, John*) was born 1795 in Lawrenceville, NJ daughter of Asher **SMITH** and Sarah **SMITH** and died February 25, 1855, buried in Lawrenceville. She married James **BREARLEY** son of George **BREARLEY** and Ann **GILLINGHAM**. He died May 25, 1872.
Children:

263-    i- **BREARLEY** Caroline born ca 1820

    ii- **BREARLEY** Elizabeth born ca 1821

264-    iii- **BREARLEY** Charles born ca 1826

    iv- **BREARLEY** Sarah born ca 1823

265-    v- **BREARLEY** George born ca 1824


96-    **CLARK** Mary (*Hannah, Jasper, John, Jasper, John*) was born in NJ daughter of Daniel **CLARK** and Hannah **SMITH**. She married Joshua **ANDERSON** born ca 1790 in Scotland.
One child born NJ:

266-    i- **ANDERSON** Catherine born June 8, 1813


97-    **SCUDDER** Daniel (*Sarah, Jasper, John, Jasper, John*) was born ca 1794 in Trenton, NJ son of Elias **SCUDDER** and Sarah **SMITH** and died January 1829. He married October

20, 1813 Grace **SMITH** (see #32) daughter of Daniel **SMITH** and Sarah **PIERSON**.
  i- **SCUDDER** Mary married Thomas **HEPBURN** in Northumberland Co. Pa. nfi

98- **SCUDDER** Jasper Smith (*Sarah, Jasper, John, Jasper, John*) was born October 17, 1797 in NJ son of Elias **SCUDDER** and Sarah **SMITH** and died October 20, 1877 in Trenton, NJ. He married Mary Stillwell **REEDER** who was born May 20, 1797 in NJ daughter of Amos **REEDER** and died December 16, 1882.
Children:
  i- **SCUDDER** Daniel died young
267-  ii- **SCUDDER** Edward Wallace born August 11, 1822
  iii- **SCUDDER** Christina born October 26, 1823

99- **SCUDDER** John (*Sarah, Jasper, John, Jasper, John*) was born August 17, 1796 in NJ son of Elias **SCUDDER** and Sarah **SMITH** and died May 2, 1840. He married Nancy **GREEN** who was born 1807 daughter of James B. **GREEN** and died 1882.
Children:
  i- **SCUDDER** Alfred born June 1827 and died August 1827
  ii- **SCUDDER** Sarah Smith born August 10, 1828 (see Jesse Moore **COOK** #120)
  iii- **SCUDDER** Alexander March 8, 1831 and died September 1831
  iv- **SCUDDER** Catherine G. born September 4, 1832
  v- **SCUDDER** John born June 6, 1835 and died July 14, 1889
  vi- **SCUDDER** William born February 7, 1838 and died November 8, 1863

100- **SCUDDER** Abner Smith (*Sarah, Jasper, John, Jasper, John*) was born May 8, 1800 son of Elias **SCUDDER** and Sarah **SMITH** and died November 10, 1878. He married Hannah **REEDER** born August 30, 1804 and died May 22, 1869. They are buried in the Presbyterian Churchyard cemetery in Ewing, NJ
Children born in NJ:
  i- **SCUDDER** Edwin born July 22, 1831 and died July 30, 1831
  ii- **SCUDDER** Jasper Smith born 1828 and died 1914. He married Mary **HART** born 1839 and died 1904

101- **HILL** Enoch (*Elizabeth, Jasper, John, Jasper, John*) was born ca 1801 in Flemington, NJ son of Richard **HILL** and Elizabeth **SMITH**. He married January 30, 1827 Delia Ann **STILLWELL** who was born August 20, 1801 in NY daughter of William **STILLWELL** and Hannah **SEABROOK** and died January 2, 1886.
Children:
  i- **HILL** William Richard born May 9, 1828
  ii- **HILL** Jasper Smith born August 10, 1831
  iii- **HILL** Cordelia born June 6, 1834

102- **HILL** Sarah (*Elizabeth, Jasper, John, Jasper, John*) was born ca 1802 in Flemington, NJ daughter of Richard **HILL** and Elizabeth **SMITH**. She married Morgan **SCUDDER** who was born October 31, 1797 in Ewing, NJ son of John **SCUDDER** and

30

Mary **KEEN** and died May 10, 1868. He married (1) Ellen **SMITH** (2) Sarah **HILL** (3) Sarah L. **COOLEY** and (4) Phebe **LIVERTON**. He had 3 children by third marriage.

103-   **HILL** James (*Elizabeth, Jasper, John Jasper, John*) was born ca 1805 in Flemington, NJ son of Richard **Hill** and Elizabeth **SMITH** and died in Mt. Pleasant, Iowa. He married Mary **ASHMORE** who was born ca 1806 in NJ and died in Mt. Pleasant, Iowa. One known child:
   i- **HILL** Elizabeth born ca 1827

104-   **MERSHON** Samuel Davies (*Prudence, Jasper, John, Jasper, John*) was born December 5, 1804 in Maidenhead, NJ son of William **MERSHON** and Prudence **SMITH** and died December 12, 1888 in Lawrenceville, NJ. He married December 13, 1825 in NJ Mary Stocton **SHREVE** who was born August 5, 1808 in NJ daughter of Caleb **SHREVE** and Frances **HUNT** and died January 18, 1892 in Lawrenceville, NJ. Children born in Lawrenceville, NJ:
   i- **MERSHON** William born December 10, 1806 and died 1907
268-   ii- **MERSHON** Frances Shreve born March 31, 1828
   iii- **MERSHON** Joseph Patterson born February 26, 1830, probably died before 1850
269-   iv- **MERSHON** Louisa born March 17, 1832
   v- **MERSHON** Jasper born May 27, 1834
   vi- **MERSHON** son born ca 1836 nfi
   vii- **MERSHON** Caleb Shreve born Mary 25, 1838
   viii- **MERSHON** Mary born 1843 and died 1844 in Lawrenceville
   ix- **MERSHON** Joseph born June 8, 1850

105-   **PATTERSON** Mary (*Prudence, Jasper, John, Jasper, John*) was born May 18, 1817 in NJ daughter of Joseph **PATTERSON** and Prudence **SMITH** and died January 3, 1893. She married May 25, 1836 Allison Ely **PERRINE** who was born October 23, 1805 in Millstone, NJ son of John **PERRINE** and Sarah Ely **ALLISON** and died February 6, 1881. They are buried in the Presbyterian cemetery in Lawrenceville, NY. Unknown children

106-   **PHILLIPS** George (*Sarah, Joshua, John, Jasper, John*) was born September 11, 1803 in Lawrenceville, NJ son of Ephraim **PHILLIPS** and Sarah **SMITH** and died July 7, 1869 in Lawrenceville. He married September 21, 1825 Abigail **KETCHAM** who was born ca 1806 in Pennington, NJ daughter of Levi **KETCHAM**. Children born in Lawrenceville:
   i- **PHILLIPS** Sarah Elizabeth ca 1827
270-   ii- **PHILLIPS** William Wilson Latta born ca 1830
271-   iii- **PHILLIPS** Ephraim born ca 1839
   iv- **PHILLIPS** George Eugene born ca 1840
   v- **PHILLIPS** Frances E. born ca 1841

107-   **PHILLIPS** Mary (*Sarah, Joshua, John, Jasper, John*) was born September 10, 1805

31

in Lawrenceville, NY daughter of Ephraim PHILLIPS and Sarah SMITH and died after 1887 in Newton, Pa. She married February 26, 1836 David FEASTER who was born February 26, 1808 in Northampton, Pa. and died January 10, 1873.
Children probably born in Northampton, Pa.:
      i- FEASTER Mary E. born ca 1836
      ii- FEASTER Aaron born ca 1837
      iii- FEASTER Theodore born ca 1838
272-   iv- FEASTER Ephraim P. born November 5, 1841
      v- FEASTER John born ca 1842

108-   SMITH Charles (*William, Joshua, John, Jasper, John*) was born May 16, 1845 in Lawrenceville, NJ son of William SMITH and Elizabeth REYNOLDS. He married February 5, 1868 Martha Hughes SMITH born May 24, 1847 (not related)
Children:
273-   I- SMITH Edgar born ca 1868
274-   ii- SMITH Charles H. born ca 1870
      iii- SMITH Lambert H. born ca 1871, married Fannie WITHERS born ca 1871 daughter of James B. WITHERS and Jane E. HUNT.
      iv- SMITH Emma born ca 1872 (see #279)

109-   SMITH David (*William, Joshua, John, Jasper, John*) was born ca 1847 in Lawrenceville, NJ son of William SMITH and Elizabeth REYNOLDS. He married Emma STUART born ca 1850.
Children:
      i- SMITH Frederick born ca 1873
      ii- SMITH Walter born ca 1874

110-   SMITH Amanda (*William, Joshua, John, Jasper, John*) was born ca 1848 in Lawrenceville, NJ daughter of William SMITH and Elizabeth REYNOLDS. She married James WOODS born ca 1843 in Hamilton Square, NJ. son of Edwin WOODS and Mary LOVELESS
Children born in Trenton, NJ
275-   i- WOODS Harry A. born ca 1870
      ii- WOODS Anna May born ca 1871
276-   iii- WOODS Barton H. born ca 1872

111-   KETCHAM Enoch Jr. (*Matilda, Joshua, John, Jasper, John*) was born October 30, 1818 in NJ son of Enoch KETCHAM and Matilda SMITH and died December 26, 1896. In 1880 census he was living in NYC with wife Eliza born 1826 in NJ and daughter Lizzie age 15

112-   KETCHAM Henrietta (*Matilda, Joshua, John, Jasper, John*) was born December 29, 1827 in NJ daughter of Enoch KETCHAM and Matilda SMITH and died July 13, 1867. She married Phineas POTTER born March 4, 1822/32. Listed in the 1880 census in

Millston, NJ with wife Henrietta and children Edwin age 25 and Julia E. age 20
Children:
   i- POTTER Louisa K. born ca 1849
   ii- POTTER Edwin born ca 1855
   iii- POTTER Julia E. born ca 1860

113-   COOK Prudence (*Keziah, Joshua, John, Jasper, John*) was born 1805 in NJ
daughter of Daniel COOK and Keziah SMITH. She married March 5, 1832 Abner B.
TOMLINSON who was born October 30, 1801 in Ewing, NJ son of Joseph TOMLINSON
and Jane BUCKMAN and died in 1863, buried Riverside cemetery in Trenton, NJ.
Children born in NJ:
   i- TOMLINSON Eliza born ca 1832
   ii- TOMLINSON Mary born ca 1834, probably died before 1835
   iii- TOMLINSON Elizabeth W. born ca 1834
   iv- TOMLINSON Mary born ca 1835/45

114-   COOK Aaron H. (*Keziah, Joshua, John, Jasper, John*) was born ca 1804 in NJ son
of Daniel COOK and Keziah SMITH. He married (1) Mary READING born ca 1800 and
he married (2) Elizabeth FONNER born ca 1802.
Children by first marriage:
277-   i- COOK Caroline born ca 1822
   ii- COOK Mary Jane born ca 1823
   iii- COOK George R. born ca 1824
Children by second marriage:
   i- COOK Rosalia born ca 1825
   ii- COOK Salinada born ca 1826

115-   COOK Samuel B. (*Keziah, Joshua, John, Jasper, John*) was born ca 1815 in NJ son
of Daniel COOK amd Keziah SMITH. He married Elizabeth DEAN born ca 1818 in
Ewing, NJ daughter of Stephen and Mary DEAN.
Children born in NJ:
   i- COOK Priscilla born ca 1839, married John STEPHENS born ca 1835 in
Phillipsburg, NJ
   ii- COOK Emily born ca 1840, married Grenville B. LITTLE born ca 1835 in
Freehold, NJ
   iii- COOK Adeline born ca 1841
   iv- COOK Lewis D. born ca 1842
   v- COOK Mary K. born ca 1843
   vi- COOK Edward born ca 1844
   vii- COOK Milcelet born ca 1845
   viii- COOK Edwin born ca 1847

116-   COOK Absolom Price (*Keziah, Joshua, John, Jasper, John*) was born ca 1816 in NJ
son of Daniel COOK and Keziah SMITH. He married Margaret WYNKOOP born ca

1820.
Children born in NJ:
      i- COOK Sarah Elizabeth born ca 1841
      ii- COOK William born ca 1842
      iii- COOK Carolina Wynkoop born ca 1843 in Pennington, NJ

117-    COOK William Smith (*Keziah, Joshua, John, Jasper, John*) was born ca 1818 in NJ son of Daniel COOK and Keziah SMITH. He married Sarah SCUDDER who was born ca 1794 daughter of Richard SCUDDER and Jemima BURROWS.
Children:
      i- COOK Charles Scudder born ca 1815
      ii- COOK Frances born ca 1817
      iii- COOK Alfred D. born ca 1818
      iv- COOK Robert H. born ca 1819
      v- COOK Ella born ca 1820
      vi- COOK Margaret born ca 1825 (see #93)

118-    COOK George Rea (*Keziah, Joshua, John, Jasper, John*) was born March 6, 1819 in Hunterdon, NJ son of Daniel COOK and Keziah SMITH. He married December 22, 1842 in Hunterdon Rebecca Elizabeth BLACKWELL who was born February 11, 1822 in NJ and died March 3, 1903. They were living in W. Windsor in 1880.
Children:
278-    i- COOK Amanda born January 2, 1844
279-    ii- COOK Thomas B. born May 18, 1847
280-    iii- COOK Daniel Livingston born ca 1849
281-    iv- COOK Hiram Augustus born ca 1850/59

119-    COOK Mary (*Keziah, Joshua, John, Jasper, John*) was born ca 1820 in NJ daughter of Daniel COOK and Keziah SMITH. She married as his fourth wife Alexander B. GREEN who was born ca 1810 in NJ son of James B. GREEN and Catherine ANTHONY. He had three children by his first wife Mary Ann CHAMBERS daughter of John

120-    COOK Jesse Moore (*Keziah, Joshua, John, Jasper, John*) was born ca 1822 in Hopewell, NJ son of Daniel COOK and Keziah SMITH and died September 17, 1896. He married (1) December 28, 1848 Sarah Smith SCUDDER who was born August 10, 1828 daughter of John SCUDDER and Nancy GREEN and died February 3, 1858 in Philadelphia, Pa. (see #99) He married (2) January 4, 1860 her sister Catherine G. SCUDDER born September 4, 1832 and died August 20, 1889. They were living in Fairmont, Md. in 1880 with the two daughters and mother-in-law Nancy Green.
One child by first marriage:
      i- COOK Catherine born ca 1855
Child by second marriage:
      i- COOK May born ca 1862

121-  COOK Lewis D. (*Keziah, Joshua, John, Jasper, John*) was born 1826 in NJ son of Daniel COOK and Keziah SMITH and died 1891. He married Ellen Palmer SKILLMAN born January 1828 and died 1902. They are buried in Mountain Ave. cemetery in Bound Brook, NJ.
Children:
282-  i- COOK Emma born February 11, 1853
ii- COOK Ella born ca 1859
iii- COOK Lewis Jr. born ca 1864
iv- COOK Laura born January 1866
v- COOK Fred born ca 1868
vi- COOK Jessie M. born January 21, 1870 in Bound Brook
vii- COOK unknown
viii- COOK unknown

122-  COOK Edmund Burroughs (*Keziah, Joshua, John, Jasper, John*) was born March 19, 1831 in Hopewell, NJ son of Daniel COOK and Keziah SMITH and died in Trenton, NJ. He married Sarah D. HOWELL born ca 1836 in Somerset, NJ daughter of Joseph HOWELL and Sarah TITSWORTH and died in Trenton, NJ.
Children born in NJ:
283-  i- COOK Charles Howell born ca 1857
284-  ii- COOK George R. born ca 1858 in Hopewell, NJ, died 1907
285-  iii- COOK Edmund Dunham born ca 1859
iv- COOK Minnie born ca 1860
v- COOK Mary born ca 1861, died Trenton, NJ, married J. Russell BEEKMAN

123-  LANNING Charles W. (*Jasper Lanning, Elizabeth, John, Jasper, John*) was born 1812 son of Jasper LANNING and Margaret VAN KIRK and died in Enfield, NY March 1, 1877. He married September 27, 1832 Orrinda THOMAS of Trumansburg, NY who was born December 12, 1813 daughter of Elias THOMAS and Jane FORRESTER and died May 20, 1888 in Enfield, NY. They are buried in the Rolfe cemetery. Unknown children.

124-  LANNING William (*Jasper Lanning, Elizabeth, John, Jasper, John*) was born 1815 son of Jasper LANNING and Margaret VAN KIRK and died 1895 in Enfield, NY. He married Rebecca H. TABER who was born 1820 and died 1904 in Enfield. They are buried in Rolfe cemetery.
Children:
286-  i- LANNING Jasper P. born 1842
ii- LANNING John born 1843 and died 1911. His wife Katherine S. was born 1854 and died 1928, buried Grove cemetery. Possibly the John Lanning listed in 1880 census in Ithaca, NY born 1844, wife Cassie born 1854 and 2 daughters Winnafred born 1869 and Neva born 1879
iii- LANNING Sarah E. born 1845 and died March 22, 1870, buried Rolfe cemetery. She married William LAMPMAN, buried Rolfe cemetery no dates

125- **LANNING** Caroline (*Jasper Lanning, Elizabeth, John, Jasper, John*) was born 1818 in Enfield, NY daughter of Jasper **LANNING** and Margaret **VAN KIRK** and died 1894. She married Ezra **TUCKER** who was born 1817 and died 1898. They are buried in Rolfe cemetery.
Children:
287-     i- **TUCKER** William W. born 1841
         ii- **TUCKER** Albert born 1842 and died 1864. His wife Lavina was born 1841 and died 1906. They are buried in Mechlinburg cemetery.
         iii- **TUCKER** George Smith born 1845
         iv- **TUCKER** Amos D. born 1846 and died March 2, 1865 in Battle of Petersburg. He was with Co. C. 179th Reg. NY Inf. His wife Martha E. died July 21, 1877 age 28 years. They are buried in Grove cemetery.
         v- **TUCKER** Sarah Ann born 1848
288-     vi- **TUCKER** Mary Jane born 1839/49
         vii- **TUCKER** Ezra Jr. born 1851 and died June 24, 1855
         viii- **TUCKER** Charles A. born 1853 and died May 25, 1855, they are buried in Rolfe cemetery
         ix- **TUCKER** Fred born 1856
Note: 1850 census for Enfield, NY lists William **LANNING** age 71 as father-in-law. This is probably in error.

126-     **LANNING** Joseph I. (*Jasper Lanning, Elizabeth, John, Jasper, John*) was born January 30, 1828 in Tompkins Co. NY son of Jasper **LANNING** and Margaret **VAN KIRK** and died June 6, 1901 in Enfield, NY. He married Marilla (unknown maiden name, possibly **KIRBY**) born April 28, 1829. They are buried in Rolfe cemetery.
One known child:
         i- **LANNING** Arthur born November 18, 1865 and died August 16, 1901. His wife Jennie was born December 1, 1863 and died August 6, 1904. They are buried in Rolfe cemetery.

127-     **LANNING** Horace (*Jasper Lanning, Elizabeth, John, Jasper, John*) was born November 17, 1829 son of Jasper **LANNING** and Margaret **VAN KIRK** and died November 7, 1904. His wife Ursala (unknown maiden name) was born April 28, 1837 and died January 12, 1913. They are buried in Rolfe cemetery.
Children:
         i- **LANNING** Ida born ca 1863
         ii- **LANNING** Charles born ca 1865
         iii- **LANNING** Cora born ca 1875

128-     **LANNING** Harrison (*Jasper Lanning, Elizabeth, John, Jasper, John*) was born 1836 in Tompkins Co. NY son of Jasper **LANNING** and Margaret **VAN KIRK** and died 1913. He married June 15, 1861 in Enfield, NY Olive **SMITH** who was born 1842 daughter of Christopher **SMITH** and died 1923. They are buried in Grove cemetery.
Children:

i- LANNING Lettie born ca 1867
ii- LANNING Glennie born ca 1873

129- STEVENS Elizabeth (*Thomas Stevens Jr., Catherine, Jasper Jr., Jasper, John*) was born ca 1789 in Maidenhead, NJ daughter of Thomas STEVENS and Cornelia VAN CLEVE. She married May 14, 1818 Benjamin Mershon PHILLIPS who was born November 17, 1790 in Lawrenceville, NJ son of John PHILLIPS and Hulda MERSHON. Children born in Princeton, NJ:
   i- PHILLIPS Catherine Mathilda born February 3, 1819, married George BODINE born ca 1815
   ii- PHILLIPS Mary born April 2, 1819
   iii- PHILLIPS Mary Hanna born July 29, 1823 married (1) James TITUS born ca 1820 and (2) October 27, 1868 William WEST born ca 1819
   iv- PHILLIPS William Henry born February 19, 1825, married November 26, 1879 Hannah TINDALL born ca 1830
   v- PHILLIPS Elizabeth Stevens born April 23, 1826
   vi- PHILLIPS Margaret Ann born January 23, 1828
   vii- PHILLIPS Abigail Rozell born December 22, 1829 married (1) William WEST born ca 1825 and (2) December 25, 1868 Richard COOK born ca 1824
   viii- PHILLIPS Randall H. born May 26, 1833
   ix- PHILLIPS John Stevens born July 29, 1835
289-    x- PHILLIPS Robert Phares born November 17, 1837

130- STEVENS Catherine (*Thomas Stevens Jr., Catherine, Jasper, Jr. Jasper, John*) was born ca 1794 in Maidenhead, NJ daughter of Thomas STEVENS Jr. and Cornelia VAN CLEVE. She married James Armstrong PHILLIPS who was born 1795 in Princeton, NJ son of John PHILLIPS and Huldah MERSHON and died January 1871 in Lawrenceville, NJ
Children born in Lawrenceville, NJ:
   i- PHILLIPS Ann (twin) born September 21, 1826
   ii- PHILLIPS Ellen (twin) born September 21, 1826
   iii- PHILLIPS Jane Stevens born October 29, 1827 (see #265)
290-   iv- PHILLIPS Ellen born February 18, 1829
   v- PHILLIPS Elizabeth Frances born December 21, 1831
   vi- PHILLIPS Louisa Frances born October 23, 1834
   vii- PHILLIPS Cornelia Ann born March 22, 1836
   viii- PHILLIPS James Woodhull born April 30, 1839, married Susan MORTIMER born ca 1835
   ix- PHILLIPS Sarah Smith born August 1, 1841

131- SMITH Samuel H. (*Benjamin, Israel, Jasper, Jasper, John*) was born 1802 in Lawrenceville, NJ son of Benjamin and Mary SMITH and died November 26, 1865 in Lawrenceville. He married (1) February 10, 1837 Johannah SMITH born June 20, 1813 and died December 20, 1841. He married (2) Joanna (unknown maiden name) born October

2, 1817 and died October 5, 1887 in Lawrenceville. They are buried in Upper Burying ground in Lawrenceville.
Children by second marriage born in Lawrenceville, NJ:
    i- SMITH Theodosia E. born 1845 and died October 5, 1872
    ii- SMITH Benjamin H. born September 13, 1847 and died September 13, 1847
    iii- SMITH John E. born October 31, 1850 and died same day
    iv- SMITH Mary J. A. born September 14, 1852 and died October 9, 1853
    v- SMITH Wesley F. born September 14, 1854 and died same day
    vi- SMITH Walter S. born 1853 and died June 21, 1871

132-    SMITH Theodosia (*Benjamin, Israel, Jasper, Jasper, John*) was born ca 1804 in Lawrenceville, NJ daughter of Benjamin and Mary SMITH. She married October 8, 1829 George W. JOHNSON born ca 1800.
Note: Theodosia Johnson is listed in the 1880 census in Le Roy, Mi. born 1803 with son Franklin H. born 1833, his wife Sally A. born 1838, child Nettie born 1859 and brother Crowell born 1842.

133-    SMITH Benjamin C. (*Israel Jr., Israel, Jasper, Jasper, John*) was born April 21, 1811 in Lawrenceville, NJ son of Israel SMITH Jr. and Maria RUNYAN and died June 3, 1888 in Philadelphia, Pa. He married June 16, 1834 Sarah SUTTON who was born October 16, 1816 daughter of Oswin SUTTON and Sarah ALLEN and died October 4, 1892 in Philadelphia.
Children born in Phildalphia:
    i- SMITH Benjamin born March 17, 1835 and died May 24, 1835
    ii- SMITH Osborn S. born December 29, 1837
    iii- SMITH Sarah Virginia born July 16, 1850 and died May 25, 1915
291-     iv- SMITH Peter Teneyck born November 9, 1843
    v- SMITH William Henry born September 17, 1845 and died December 13, 1862 at battle of Fredericksburg.
292-     vi- SMITH Ella Maria born October 14, 1847
    vii- SMITH Mary Adda born October 1, 1854

134-    BREARLEY William Armstrong (*Elizabeth, Israel, Jasper, Jasper, John*) was born October 8, 1821 in Trenton, NJ son of Samuel BREARLEY and Elizabeth SMITH and died October 6, 1856 in Trenton. He married (1) February 16, 1843 Mary RUE who died before 1849. He married (2) May 9, 1849 in NJ Henrietta A. MOORE
Children by first marriage born Hightstown, NJ:
    i- BREARLEY Samuel S. born November 28, 1843
    ii- BREARLEY Joseph R. born December 14, 1846
Children by second marriage:
    iii- BREARLEY Anna born July 20, 1850
    iv- BREARLEY Helen A. born October 29, 1851
    v- BREARLEY William Henry born August 23, 1854 in Trenton, married October 22, 1879 in Trenton Emily M. RUE

135- **TINDALL** Mercy (*Joseph Tindall, Abigail, Thomas, Jasper, John*) was born August 17, 1793 in Ewing, NJ daughter of Joseph **TINDALL** and Phebe **HENDRICKSON** and died December 18, 1845. She married ca 1809 William **WHITE** who was born February 24, 1784 in Shrewsbury, NJ son of John **WHITE** and Margaret **COOK** and died September 1, 1838 in Hackettstown, NJ.
Children born in Monmouth Co. NJ:

      i- **WHITE** Sarah born November 10, 1810 and died January 15, 1831. She married _____ **MARTIN**

      ii- **WHITE** Deborah born September 16, 1812 and died January 9, 1813

293-   iii- **WHITE** John born July 21, 1814

      iv- **WHITE** Huldah born December 28, 1816 and died January 2, 1845

      v- **WHITE** Penninah born January 18, 1819, died Albion, Mi. She married _____ **GROFF**

      vi- **WHITE** William born June 1, 1821 and died May 19, 1885. He married Elizabeth **MITCHELL**

      vii- **WHITE** Caroline born May 11, 1823 and died January 19, 1871. She married Benjamin **PALMER**

      viii- **WHITE** Joseph born April 2, 1825 and died July 4, 1873. He married Jane **SHARP**

294-   ix- **WHITE** Oziel born June 18, 1827

295-   x- **WHITE** Margaret born April 3, 1832

      xi- **WHITE** Mercy born December 26, 1829 and died October 8, 1901

      xii- **WHITE** James born June 14, 1837 and died September 28, 1838 in Monmouth, NJ.

136-   **GREEN** Thomas (*Elizabeth Tindall, Abigail, Thomas, Jasper, John*) was born ca 1781 in NJ son of Benjamin **GREEN** and Elizabeth **TINDALL** and died 1844. Spouse unknown
Children:

      i- **GREEN** Aaron born ca 1806

      ii- **GREEN** Benjamin born ca 1807 married Mary **PLEW** born ca 1811 in Ill.

      iii- **GREEN** Charles born ca 1808 married Anna **ROBBINS** born ca 1811

      iv- **GREEN** Mary I. born ca 1809 married _____ **WELLS**

      v- **GREEN** Rachel born ca 1810

      vi- **GREEN** Henry born ca 1811

      vii- **GREEN** Elizabeth born ca 1812

137-   **GREEN** Noah (*Elizabeth Tindall, Abigail, Thomas, Jasper, John*) was born ca 1788 in NJ son of Benjamin **GREEN** and Elizabeth **TINDALL**. He married Mary **LOUGHBURY** born ca 1790.
Children:

      i- **GREEN** James born ca 1809

      ii- **GREEN** Samuel born ca 1810 married _____ **EVERT**

      iii- **GREEN** Mary E. born ca 1811 married William **HUTCHINSON** born ca 1800 iv- GREEN Anna born ca 1812

138- GREEN Benjamin IV (*Elizabeth Tindall, Abigail, Thomas, Jasper, John*) was born ca 1789 in NJ son of Benjamin GREEN and Elizabeth TINDALL. He married Sarah LOUGHBURY born ca 1792.
Children:
   i- GREEN Sarah born ca 1814, married _____ DENSTON born ca 1807
   ii- GREEN Benjamin V. born ca 1815
   iii- GREEN John born ca 1816
   iv- GREEN Addison born ca 1817
   v- GREEN William born ca 1815

139- TINDALL Jesse (*Thomas Tindall, Abigail, Thomas, Jasper, John*) was born in 1812 in NJ son of Thomas TINDALL and Elizabeth HOWELL and died July 8, 1880 in Sycamore, De Kalb Co. Ill. He is listed in the 1880 census in Sycamore, De Kalb Co. Ill. age 68 born NJ with wife Mary age 65 born NY and children Betsey M. age 42 born in Mi., Orlando age 32 born Ill. and Carrie M. age 24 born Ill. Jesse is buried in S. Grove cemetery and wife Mary A. born July 20, 1814 and died December 31, 1905. Elizabeth Mahala (Betsey) born 1838 and died 1910 and Thomas J. born 1840 and died 1929 who was member of the 42nd Ill. Inf. in Civil War.
Known children:
   i- TINDALL Elizabeth Mahala born 1838 in Mi. and died 1910 in Sycamore, Ill.
   ii- TINDALL Thomas J. born 1840 and died 1929
   iii- TINDALL Orlando born ca 1848 in Ill.
   iv- TINDALL Carrie M. born ca 1856

140- TINDALL Enoch (*Thomas Tindall, Abigail, Thomas, Jasper, John*) was born July 13, 1819 in NJ son of Thomas TINDALL and Elizabeth HOWELL and died January 3, 1897 in Tecumseh, Mi. He is listed in the 1870 census in Tecumseh age 50 with wife Caroline and son Henry. In 1880 he is listed age 60 yrs with wife Caroline L. age 64 born Ct. and stepchildren born in Mi. Anna B. age 14, Carrie L. age 13 and Walter K. POWERS age 11.

141- SMITH James Laughlin (*Thomas H., Elijah, Thomas, Jasper, John*) was born ca 1808 in Tn. son of Thomas Hunt SMITH and Mary TABOR. He married (1) Alvira HAMRICK and (2) Jane MARTIN.
Children:
   i- SMITH George L. born 1834 in Ala., married January 3, 1856 Charlotte TODD.
   ii- SMITH Rosanna M. born June 18, 1836 and died Novermber 10, 1904 in Pontotoc Co.. She married (1) July 22, 1852 Ezekiel STAGGS and (2) March 4, 1855 Stephen PILCHER.
   iii- SMITH Susanna born April 10, 1838 and died August 10, 1905 in Pontotoc Co. Ms. She married September 8, 1857 James Elijah BROWNING
   iv- SMITH Cary Jane born June 3, 1840 and died December 24, 1910 in Pontotoc

40

Co. Ms. She married January 20, 1859 Jonathan Dewey **BROWNING**
v- **SMITH** James Laughlin born ca 1842, married October 16, 1865 Mary **TODD**
296-    vi- **SMITH** David Lofton born February 1844 in Ala.
vii- **SMITH** Sarah born ca 1846 in Ms.

142-    **SMITH** Burton Lytton (*Thomas H., Elijah, Thomas, Jasper, John*) was born 1810 in Tn. son of Thomas Hunt **SMITH** and Mary **TABOR**. He married July 21, 1829 in Ala. Sarah G. **WALKER** born February 26, 1812 in Tn.
Children:
i- **SMITH** Thomas Hunt born December 3, 1832 and died 1902 in Hot Springs, Ar. He married September 23, 1851 in Pontotoc Co. Mary **WARREN** born 1830 in Tn.
ii- **SMITH** Isaiah Walker born May 4, 1833 in Ala, buried Hot Springs, Ar.
iii- **SMITH** Susan Elizabeth born February 12, 1835 in Ala.

143-    **SMITH** Susannah T. (*Thomas H., Elijah, Thomas, Jasper, John*) was born 1813 in Tn. daughter of Thomas Hunt **SMITH** and Mary **TABOR** and died August 25, 1853 in Pontotoc Co. Ms. She married Jarret L. **BERRY** who was born ca 1805 in Clarke Co., Ga. son of William Green **BERRY** and Nancy **LINCECUM** and died November 15, 1865 in Augusta, Az. He married (2) July 18, 1854 Almeda **TIPPAH** born ca 1815 in Ga.
Children:
i- **BERRY** Alfred married Eva Sue ___
297-    ii- **BERRY** Resin Bowie born 1828 in Bibb Co. Ala.
298-    iii- **BERRY** Mary born 1832 in Bibb Co. Ala.
299-    iv- **BERRY** Burton Linton born October 31, 1836 in Winston Co. Ms.
300-    v- **BERRY** Thomas Hunt March 20, 1838 in Winston Co. Ms.
vi- **BERRY** Columbus born 1842 in Ms.
301-    vii- **BERRY** Serena born ca 1840 in Winston co. Ms.
302-    viii- **BERRY** Nancy Jane born ca 1844 in Pontotoc Co. Ms.
303-    ix- **BERRY** James Madison born February 21, 1847 in Ms.

144-    **SMITH** William Preston (*Thomas H., Elijah, Thomas, Jasper, John*) was born January 1822 in Russellville, Ar. son of Thomas Hunt **SMITH** and Mary **TABOR** and died May 21, 1892 in Union Co. Ms., buried New Albany cemetery. He married February 8, 1843 in Louisville, Ms. Permelia **JEFFRIES** who was born April 22, 1827 in Rome, Ga. daughter of Thomas **JEFFRIES** and Jane **FAGAN** and died December 8, 1882 in New Albany, Ms.
Children born in Ms.:
304-    i- **SMITH** Susan Arrena November 18, 1843
ii- **SMITH** Mary Jane born November 10/16, 1847
305-    iii- **SMITH** Thomas Hunt born January 13, 1850
iv- **SMITH** Nancy A. born February 19, 1852, married William Perry **TODD**
v- **SMITH** James L. born ca 1854
vi- **SMITH** William Preston born October 30, 1856
vii- **SMITH** Andrew Jackson born December 21, 1858, married (1) May 10, 1882 in

Union Co. Ms. Sally **SLOAN** and married (2) February 6, 1888 Dollie **SLOAN**.

   viii- **SMITH** Amanda born ca 1861

   ix- **SMITH** Beford Lee born ca 1864

145- **KNOX** Elijah Smith (*Cynthia, Elijah, Thomas, Jasper, John*) was born 1828 in Cannon, Tn. son of Joseph **KNOX** and Cynthia Ann **SMITH** and died April 7, 1863 at Battle of Shiloh, buried Shiloh National cemetery. He married August 2, 1849 Angelina **GAITHER** who was born September 4, 1830 in Cannon, Tn. daughter of Vincent **GAITHER** and Mary **STROUD** and died November 21, 1909 in Haslet, Tx.
Children born in Cannon, Tn.:

       i- **KNOX** Mary J. E. born June 1850

306-   ii- **KNOX** Thomas B. born April 1854

       iii- **KNOX** Cynthia

307-   iv- **KNOX** John Basil born June 1, 1860


146- **KNOX** Joseph A. (*Cynthia, Elijah, Thomas, Jasper, John*) was born 1834 in Cannon, Tn. son of Joseph **KNOX** and Cynthia Ann **SMITH**. He married April 22, 1864 in Cannon, Tn. Mrs. Elizabeth (?) **KNOX** born 1840 in Tn.
Children born in Cannon, Tn.:

       i- **KNOX** Cynthia born 1866

       ii- **KNOX** Mary J. born 1867

       iii- **KNOX** William A. born 1869

       iv- **KNOX** Nancy D. born 1871

       v- **KNOX** Ada born January 1870

       vi- **KNOX** Joseph Burton born August 28, 1878 and died September 29, 1903. He married Sally **BRANDON** who was born November 12, 1881 and died June 3, 1908 in Cannon, Tn. They are buried in Simpson cemetery.


147- **SMITH** Ann (*Absolom, John, Samuel, Jasper, John*) was born 1801 in NJ daughter of Absolom and Susannah **SMITH** and died January 18, 1879 in Brown Co. Ohio. She married Peter **MALOTT** who was born 1797 in Washington Co. Md. son of Theodore **MALOTT** and Ann **LANE** and died February 1849 in Sterling, Brown Co. Ohio.
Children born in Ohio:

308-   i- **MALOTT** Francis L. born 1823

       ii- **MALOTT** Lawner born March 16, 1825 and died February 17, 1901 in Crosstown, Oh. He married (1) November 18, 1850 Elizabeth Jane **BENHAM** born September 6, 1833 in Clermont Co. Ohio. He married (2) October 8, 1861 Melissa **KERSHKADDEN** and he married (3) October 17, 1865 Lucinda **FRYMAN** (divorced in 1878 and he married (4) March 9, 1878 Fidelia R. **CAMPBELL**

       iii- **MALOTT** Alpheus born January 26, 1830 and died July 25, 1883 in Ohio, buried Bloomrose cemetery. He married September 1, 1853 in Brown Co. Ohio Catherine **BALSER**

       iv- **MALOTT** Melissa born December 15, 1833 and died May 9, 1902. She married February 6, 1855 in Clermont Co. Ohio William N. **STEWARD** born October 14,

1835 in Ohio.

v- **MALOTT** Alvertus born 1836 and died April 21, 1865 in Washington, DC. He was with Co. C. 59th Reg. Oh. Inf.

148- **SMITH** John (*Absolom, John, Samuel, Jasper, John*) was born July 21, 1809 in Pa. son of Absolom and Susannah **SMITH** and died November 3, 1891 in Hancock, Ind. He married Harriet **THOMPSON** who was born July 7, 1813 in Ohio daughter of David and Rachel **THOMPSON** and died April 1, 1860 in Hancock, Ind. They are buried in Guillium cemetery.
One known child born Oaklandon, Ind.:
309-     i- **SMITH** Henry Nash born February 17, 1847

149-     **BILES** Elizabeth (*George Biles, Christian, Joshua, Jasper, John*) was born August 7, 1798 in Hope, NJ daughter of George and Mary **BILES** and died October 26, 1865 in Mexico, Ohio, buried Old Sycamore cemetery in Sycamore, Oh. She married August 17, 1815 in Warren Co. NJ Nathaniel **CORWIN** who was born December 17, 1789 in Chester, NJ probably son of Joseph **CORWIN** and Mary **WORTMAN** and died November 21,1860 in Hope, NJ, buried Free Union Church.
Known children:
          i- **CORWIN** Ann born 1818
310-     ii- **CORWIN** George S. born February 27, 1819
311-     iii- **CORWIN** William Biles born April 25, 1820
312-     iv- **CORWIN** Anthony 'Drake' born November 18, 1821
313-     v- **CORWIN** David (possible son) born 1822
314-     vi- **CORWIN** Joseph born February 16, 1823, married February 26, 1853 Tirza **GREEN**
          vii- **CORWIN** Mary born December 27, 1826 and died 1904 in Rochester, Mi. She married Mr. **DENNIS**
315-     viii- **CORWIN** Anna Alice born February 23, 1829 and died September 10, 1906 in Rochester, Mi.
316-     ix- **CORWIN** John B. born June 22, 1834 and died October 13, 1877 in Mexico, Ohio

150-     **BILES** William (*George Biles, Christian, Joshua, Jasper, John*) was born ca 1800 in Hope, NJ son of George and Mary **BILES** and died before 1841 in Hope. He married Anna (**HOWELL**) **ARMSTRONG** who was born ca 1804 in NJ and died after 1850. (could this be the Anna **BILES** wife of William L. who died in Sycamore, Ohio February 14, 1871 age 73 y 17 days and buried in Old Sycamore cemetery?)
Children born in Hope, NJ:
317-     i- **BILES** George born 1823
          ii- **BILES** Jane
          iii- **BILES** William II born ca 1825
318-     iv- **BILES** Elizabeth born 1826
          v- **BILES** Polly

319-    vi- **BILES** Electa Ann born 1830
       vii- **BILES** Rachel born ca 1839. She married John **KELLY** born ca 1838 in NJ
and had son Joseph W.

151-    **BILES** Anna (*George Biles, Christian, Joshua, Jasper, John*) was born in NJ
daughter of George and Mary **BILES**. She married June 20, 1822 Abraham **VLIET** who
was born February 20, 1797 in NJ son of Cornelius V. **VLIET** and Eleanor **MELICK** and
died February 1868.
Children:
320-    i- **VLIET** Margaret born March 10, 1825
321-    ii- **VLIET** William D. born January 24, 1829
322-    iii- **VLIET** Daniel September 13, 1833.

152-    **BILES** Jane (*George Biles, Christian, Joshua, Jasper, John*) was born 1810 in
Hope, NJ daughter of George and Mary **BILES** and died May 8, 1880 age 70 yrs 3 mos and
28 days. She married October 8, 1829 in Oxford, NJ John **CRUSON** (also spelled
**KRUSON**) who was born 1805 in Hope, NJ son of Jasper **KRUSON** and Nancy **ENGLE**
and died March 15, 1851. They are buried in the Hope Methodist cemetery.
Children:
       i- **KRUSON** Ellen married Mr. **COOK**
       ii- **KRUSON** Jacob born 1833
       iii- **KRUSON** Lizzie died 1855, married James **WEST**

153-    **BILES** Electa (*George Biles, Christian, Joshua, Jasper, John*) was born in NJ
daughter of George and Mary **BILES**. She married September 25, 1824 John C. **HAYES**.
One known child in Warren Co. NJ:
323-    i- **HAYES** Rebecca born August 24, 1826

154-    **BILES** Annanias (*George Biles, Christian, Joshua, Jasper, John*) was born in Hope,
NJ possible son of George and Mary **BILES**. He married in Hope, NJ July 10, 1841 Sarah
**ATTEN**.
One known child:
       i- **BILES** Mary Elizabeth born August 10, 1850/1

155-    **SMITH** Sally (*William, Joshua, Joshua, Jasper, John*) was born 1817 in Hector, NY
daughter of William H. **SMITH** and Catherine **LEONARD** and died in Fremont, NY before
1860. She married Harmon **NICHOLSON** born July 15, 1811 in Wayne Co. Pa. son of
Jonathan **NICHOLSON** born Glastonbury, Conn. and Elizabeth **SWINGLE** and died June
1890, leaving will. She was buried in Nicholson cemetery on Turnpike Rd. and no cemetery
records were found for Harmon, probably buried same place.
Children:
324-    i- **NICHOLSON** Harriet born November 22, 1836
325-    ii- **NICHOLSON** William Wesley born July 6, 1839
326-    iii- **NICHOLSON** Hulda born January 26, 1841

327-    iv- **NICHOLSON** Horatio born 1843

      v- **NICHOLSON** William W. born ca 1844

328-    vi- **NICHOLSON** Elmer M. or Egbert born 1846

Children by second marriage:

      i- **NICHOLSON** Harmon Randall born ca 1859 and died 1873

329-    ii- **NICHOLSON** Lillian Estelle July 15, 1865

330-    iii- **NICHOLSON** Emma L. born November 12, 1872


156-    **SMITH** Abram L. (*William, Joshua, Joshua, Jasper, John*) was born May 2, 1818 in Hector, NY son of William H. **SMITH** and Catherine **LEONARD** and died January 24, 1896. He married August 13, 1842 Minas Almira **NICHOLSON** who was born April 17, 1823 daughter of Jonathan **NICHOLSON** and Elizabeth **SWINGLE** and died December 26, 1903 in Hornellsville, NY. They are buried in the Fairview cemetery on the Turnpike Rd. in Hornellsville, NY

Children:

      i- **SMITH** Ira born June 18, 1843, served in Co. K. 107th Reg. NY Vol. Infantry. during the Civil War and died March 19, 1863 one month after returning home, buried in Fairview cemetery

      ii- **SMITH** George born March 31, 1845 and died June 4, 1845, buried in Fairview cemetery.

331-    iii- **SMITH** Lucinda born May 8, 1846

332-    iv- **SMITH** Alonzo born March 30, 1848

333-    v- **SMITH** Melissa born December 15, 1850

334-    vi- **SMITH** Rosalie born December 6, 1852

335-    vii- **SMITH** Flora born September 22, 1855

336-    viii- **SMITH** Hobart Clinton born April 18, 1859

337-    ix- **SMITH** Thadeus Benton February 15, 1861


157-    **SMITH** John L. (*William, Joshua, Joshua, Jasper, John*) was born February 2, 1820 in Hector, NY son of William H. **SMITH** and Catherine **LEONARD** and died 1903. He married Elsie Ann **GREGORY** born in Livingston Co. NY and moved to Harrison Valley, Pa. and died 1906. They are buried in White's Corners cemetery, Harrison Valley, Pa. One Known child:

338-    i- **SMITH** Levi born 1847 in Steuben Co. NY

Note: There may have been twins who died as infants and buried in the Johnson cemetery in Howard, NY


158-    **SMITH** Dennis T. (*Joshua Jr., Joshua, Joshua, Jasper, John* ) was born April 26, 1823 in Hector, NY son of Joshua **SMITH** Jr. and Lydia **CLARK** and died 1873. He married (1) Melissa (maiden name unknown) who was born 1819 and died 1849. He married (2) Marilla **LEWIS** born December 5, 1830 in Lawrence Corners, Pa. daughter of Peter **LEWIS** and Jane **VANDERPOEL** and died 1885, all buried in Lawrence Corners cemetery.

Children by first marriage:

i- SMITH Joshua born 1849 and died 1871, buried Lawrence Corners cemetery
ii- SMITH Horace born 1849 and died 1911, buried Lawrence Corners cemetery,
also Sarah born 1848, possibly his wife.
Children by second marriage:
   iii- SMITH Adelain born ca 1852
   iv- SMITH Debraella born ca 1854
339-   v- SMITH Eva Ann born January 3, 1858
   vi- SMITH Meade born ca 1860/67 moved to Melan, Pa., married Gertrude RICE
daughter of Miles David RICE and Henrietta SPOOR
   vii- SMITH Josephine born April 1857
   viii- SMITH Adelaide born ca 1875
   ix- SMITH Peter buried in Lawrence Corners cemetery son of Dennis (no dates)
   x- SMITH Mary O. daughter of Dennis died 1864, buried in Lawrence Corners
cemetery

159-   SMITH Philetus P. (*Joshua Jr., Joshua, Joshua, Jasper, John*) was born January
13, 1825 in Sullivan Twp. Pa. son of Joshua Smith Jr. and Lydia Clark and died September
11, 1905 in Mainesburg, Sullivan Twp. Pa. He married August 5, 1849 Roxane Emeline
SCOUTEN who was born March 1, 1826 in Kortwright, NY daughter of Abraham and
Elizabeth SCOUTEN and died February 10, 1900. They are buried in Mainesburg
cemetery.
Children:
340-   i- SMITH Lydia Elizabeth born January 26, 1851
341-   ii- SMITH Frances D. born April 15, 1853
342-   iii- SMITH Melissa E. born February 1855
   iv- SMITH Hosmer P. born ca 1856/7 (listed in the 1880 census in Athen, NY born
1857 and wife Elnora born 1859
343-   v- SMITH Flora E. born ca 1858/59
344-   vi- SMITH Jennie born March 1861
345-   vii- SMITH Lavina born March 1863
   viii- SMITH Joseph Hiram died young

160-   SMITH Ephraim Clark (*Joshua Jr., Joshua, Joshua, Jasper, John*) was born
January 1826 son of Joshua SMITH Jr. and Lydia CLARK and died November 2, 1909 in
Mainesburg, Pa. His wife Helen Angeline was born 1828 and died 1906, also buried there.
Note: 1880 census gives wife's name as Louisa born 1835
Children born Sullivan Twp. Pa.:
   i- SMITH Franklin born ca 1853
   ii- SMITH Chauncy born ca 1855
   iii- SMITH Ellen L. born ca 1856
   iv- SMITH Eliza born ca 1857
   v- SMITH Dennis Vaughn born January 1864, married Cora SMITH born 1873
daughter of Sanford SMITH and died in Wellsboro November 1890 (see #187)
   vi- SMITH Hannah born ca 1867

46

161-    SMITH Olive Rebecca (*Joshua Jr., Joshua, Joshua, Jasper, John*) was born April 11, 1835 in Sullivan Twp. Pa. daughter of Joshua SMITH Jr. and Lydia CLARK and died June 9, 1913 in Elk Run, Pa. She married (1) in 1856 Isaac YOUNG who was born ca 1833 and died April 8, 1864. She married (2) in 1872 Andrew W. SQUIRES (see #163).
Children by first marriage:
      i- YOUNG Gideon born ca 1857 (moved to Plainview, Neb)
      ii- YOUNG Edward J. born April 1860
      iii- YOUNG Hilsy born ca 1864 married Reuben SQUIRES
Children by second marriage:
      iv- SQUIRES Cora born 1866 and died 1877 in Sullivan Twp.
      v- SQUIRES Joshua J. born 1868 in Sullivan Twp. and died there May 28, 1879. He was shot by friend playing with gun.

162-    SMITH Diantha (*Joshua Jr., Joshua, Joshua, Jasper, John*) was born ca 1836 daughter of Joshua SMITH Jr. and Lydia CLARK and died in her 75th year, buried Roseville cemetery. She married Jason WATKINS.
One known child:
346-    i- WATKINS Mary Ellen (Ella) born April 22, 1860 in Rutland, Pa.

163-    SMITH Lydia (*Joshua Jr., Joshua, Joshua, Jasper, John*) was born ca 1846 in Sullivan Twp. Pa. daughter of Joshua SMITH Jr. and Diadama ROBLYER and died there 1870. She married March 12, 1865 in Sullivan Twp. Pa. Andrew W. SQUIRES who was born December 13, 1845 son of Judson SQUIRES and died January 14, 1927 in Sullivan Twp. Pa., buried Squire's cemetery. They had two children who died young. After she died, he married her sister Olive A. SMITH (see #161) who died June 6, 1913.

164-    SMITH David Thomas (*Charles, Joshua, Joshua, Jasper, John*) was born November 18, 1824 in Hector, NY son of Charles SMITH and Elizabeth THOMAS and died March 11, 1894 in Sullivan Twp. Pa. He married before 1846 Lucretia WELCH who was born February 15, 1821 in Sullivan Twp. Pa. daughter of Nathaniel WELCH and Nancy HAKES and died April 19, 1891. They are buried in Ames Hill cemetery.
Children:
347-    i- SMITH William Harrison born September 4, 1859
      ii- SMITH daughter

165-    SMITH Isaac (*Charles, Joshua, Joshua, Jasper, John*) was born June 1827 in Jackson. NY son of Charles SMITH and Elizabeth THOMAS and died July 22, 1892. He married Julia Ann WILSON who died December 24, 1902 age 74 yrs 6 mos 16 days. They are buried in Gray Valley cemetery.
Children:
      i- SMITH Julinette born January 9, 1848 and died November 4, 1897. She married Orson O. DODGE born April 28, 1847. They are buried in Gray Valley cemetery. They had daughter Josie M. born ca 1871
348-    ii- SMITH Maria born July 11, 1851

166- SMITH George (*Charles, Joshua, Joshua, Jasper, John*) was born December 29, 1832 in Jackson, NY son of Charles SMITH and Elizabeth THOMAS and died February 23, 1908 in Sullivan Twp. He married March 1, 1852 Mary Ann TEARS who was born June 15, 1832 daughter of Zopher TEARS and Lorinda COWAN of Sullivan Twp. Pa. and died January 17, 1908. They are buried in the Mainesburg cemetery.
Children:
349-    i- SMITH Josephine born ca 1854
350-    ii- SMITH Martha born 1854 and died 1918. She married Joseph H. DEWITT son of Caleb born 1846 and died 1912, buried Mainesburg cemetery. Listed in 1880 census with daughter Mary H. born 1878
        iii- SMITH Lydia born December 10, 1857 and died January 5, 1932. She married Frank P. CASE of Troy, Pa. born March 11, 1859 and died March 30, 1937. They are buried in Glenwood cemetery.
        iv- SMITH Ida M. born 1869 and died 1948. (see #186)

167-    SMITH Mary (*Charles, Joshua, Joshua, Jasper, John*) was born ca 1830/35 in Sullivan Twp. Pa. daughter of Charles SMITH and Elizabeth THOMAS and died 1880-1890. She married September 1, 1854 Artemus RUMSEY who was born November 1832 in Sullivan Twp. Pa. son of Seth RUMSEY and Jerusha KELTS and died April 22, 1905. They are buried in Mainesburg cemetery.
Children:
        i- RUMSEY Kate born ca 1869, married ____ INGULLAS and removed to Ca.
351-    ii- RUMSEY Charles Smith born March 22, 1861
        iii- RUMSEY Mary E. born ca 1861
        iv- RUMSEY Frances (possibly) born ca 1855/56

168-    RICHMOND Lois (*Anna, Joshua, Joshua, Jasper, John*) was born ca 1823 daughter of Isaac RICHMOND and Anna SMITH and died September 4, 1862. She married William Whitlock BRYANT born July 26, 1822 son of Ephraim BRYANT and Mary WOOD and died January 22, 1892. They are buried in Wood cemetery. He married (2) Mary REYNOLDS daughter of David REYNOLDS and Margaret RICHMOND
Children:
        i- BRYANT Jerome born 1850 in Tioga, Co. Pa. and died March 28, 1926, buried Oakwood cemetery . He married 1903 Stella BARNARD of Rushville, NY. No issue
        ii- BRYANT Antoinette born January 17, 1852 and died June 18, 1856
352-    iii- BRYANT Isaac born January 18, 1853
        iv- BRYANT Frank born April 26, 1857 and died January 3, 1875, buried Wood cemetery
        v- BRYANT Horace S. (possible son) born February 15, 1856 and died January 16, 1868, buried Wood cemetery

169-    RICHMOND Annanias (*Anna, Joshua, Joshua, Jasper, John*) was born August 25, 1824 son of Isaac RICHMOND and Anna SMITH and died May 23, 1910 in Richmond Twp. Pa. He married (1) Sally Ann TEARS who was born 1825 daughter of Zopher

TEARS and Lorinda COWAN and died May 25, 1868. He married (2) June 1, 1869 Hannah STRANGE who was born April 28, 1830 daughter of Marcus STRANGE and Hannah BURT and died August 24, 1898 and he married (3) October 11, 1899 Miss Charlotte L. BAILEY who was born February 22, 1841 and died February 1, 1916. They are buried in Prospect cemetery, Mansfield, Pa.
Children by first marriage:
353-     i- RICHMOND Mary E. born ca 1846
354-     ii- RICHMOND Viola A. born can 1848 in Tioga Co. Pa.
355-     iii- RICHMOND Amenzo born ca 1851 in Sullivan Twp. Pa.
356-     iv- RICHMOND Oscar H. born ca 1852 in Sullivan Twp. Pa.
357-     v- RICHMOND Delphine born ca 1856 in Sullivan Twp. Pa.
Children by second marriage:
358-     vi- RICHMOND Flora E. born ca 1870
         vii- RICHMOND Alice J. born ca 1871 died November 10, 1886 in Mansfield, Pa.
         viii- RICHMOND Nellie R. born ca 1874 and died January 4, 1956 in Milport, NY, buried Prospect cemetery in Mansfield, Pa. married (1) December 28, 1896 Jerome SPENCER and (2) Wilson GRACE
         ix- RICHMOND Bert W. born 1878 and died March 3, 1961 in Alfred, NY. He married ____ VAN NESS. Leaves sons Joseph C. of Chevy Chase, Md., Bert W. Jr. of Alfred and 4 grandchildren
         x- RICHMOND May born May 1880 nfi

170-     RICHMOND Albert T. (*Anna, Joshua, Joshua, Jasper, John*) was born March 9, 1827 in Hector, NY son of Isaac RICHMOND and Anna SMITH and died October 12, 1897 in Elk Run, Sullivan Twp. Pa. He married Sally SCOUTEN who was born 1830 in NY and died October 13, 1894. They are buried in Ames Hill cemetery.
Children:
359-     i- RICHMOND Isaac born February 1848
360-     ii- RICHMOND Sperry born 1850
         iii- RICHMOND Lucinda born ca 1851 married May 20, 1874 Francis G. REXFORD of Chautauqua, NY
         iv- RICHMOND Royal born ca 1853 nfi
361-     v- RICHMOND Dayton born ca 1855
         vi- RICHMOND Jehial ca 1857 nfi
         vii- RICHMOND infant daughter died September 12, 1860, buried Ames Hill cemetery

171-     RICHMOND Melissa (*Anna, Joshua, Joshua, Jasper, John*) was born 1829 in Pa. daughter of Isaac RICHMOND and Anna SMITH and died before 1896. She married James RUGGLES who was born December 12, 1827 in Vermont son of Orrin RUGGLES and Sally BEARDSLEY.
Children:
362-     i- RUGGLES Emma F. born ca 1853
363-     ii- RUGGLES Ella born July 30, 1857

iii- **RUGGLES** Jenett born ca 1850 and died before 1870

172- **RICHMOND** Obadiah (*Anna, Joshua, Joshua, Jasper, John*) was born May 19, 1832/33 in Sullivan Twp. Pa. son of Isaac **RICHMOND** and Anna **SMITH** and died February 1, 1907 in Sullivan Twp. Pa. He married (1) Sarah Eliza **BRADFORD** who was born May 22, 1832 in Pa. and died May 5, 1891. They are buried Mainesburg cemetery Mansfield, Pa. He married (2) ca 1897/98 Emma E. (unknown maiden name) who was born September 10, 1835 and died December 25, 1902. Children by first marriage:
      i- **RICHMOND** Frances born ca 1847/48
      ii- **RICHMOND** Ella born ca 1853
364-    iii- **RICHMOND** Mary Louisa born October 30, 1868
      iv- **RICHMOND** B. W. (male) born April 1876
      v- **RICHMOND** a son born ca 1887 died by 1900

173- **RICHMOND** Matilda (*Anna, Joshua, Joshua, Jasper, John*) was born ca 1835 in Sullivan Twp. Pa. daughter of Isaac **RICHMOND** and Anna **SMITH** and died April 17, 1891. She married by 1856 Warren **RUMSEY** born September 23, 1829 son of Seth S. **RUMSEY** and Jerusha **KELTS** of Sullivan Twp. Pa. and died February 13, 1907 age 78 by the hand of son Clarence, was struck on the head and found frozen in field near home. They are buried in Mainesburg cemetery.
Children:
365-    i- **RUMSEY** Julius born December 16, 1856
366-    ii- **RUMSEY** Barton born February 9, 1859 and died March 31, 1898, buried Mainesburg cemetery
      iii- **RUMSEY** Wilber born ca 1860, went west to Dakotas and married there
      iv- **RUMSEY** Emerson born August 1866 and died January 14, 1953 unmarried, buried Mainesburg cemetery
      v- **RUMSEY** Horace born 1868 and died 1908 unmarried, buried Mainesburg cemetery
      vi- **RUMSEY** Addie born November 1869, married September 29, 1888 Harvey J. **DAVIS** who was born ca 1868 and was killed in a RR accident in Canandaigua, NY May 4, 1889 age 21 years.
      vii- **RUMSEY** Nellie born 1873 and died 1934 unmarried, buried Mainesburg cemetery
      viii- **RUMSEY** Walter born 1875 and died January 1881, buried in Mainesburg cemetery
      ix- **RUMSEY** Clarence born ca 1876, married Myrtle (?) abandoned her and two daughters.

174- **RICHMOND** Elizabeth (Betsey) (*Anna, Joshua, Joshua, Jasper, John*) was born July 16, 1837 in Sullivan Twp. Pa. daughter of Isaac **RICHMOND** and Anna **SMITH** and died May 3, 1905. She married David **SLINGERLAND** who was born 1831 son of Tunis **SLINGERLAND** and Mary **BAKER** and died January 9, 1889. They are buried in Glenwood cemetery in Troy, Pa. She married (2) December 31, 1891 Israel A. **PIERCE**

who was born October 3, 1820 in Rehoboth, Mass. and died June 24, 1898. His first wife was Harriet G. BURGESS who died February 12, 1891 age 65 yrs.
Children:
     i- SLINGERLAND Bert born ca 1855 in Sullivan Twp. Pa. and died October 29, 1862, buried Glenwood cemetery
     ii- SLINGERLAND Elmer born May 4, 1863 and died March 14, 1904, buried Glenwood cemetery, had 1 son born December 21, 1903
367-     iii- SLINGERLAND Jennie Mae born May 1867 and died June 21, 1883
     iv- SLINGERLAND Herman born 1869 and died March 14, 1924
     v- SLINGERLAND Florence born ca 1873, married December 6, 1893 Isaac REDDINGTON born 1870 in Troy, Pa. son of Edmond and Maria L. REDDINGTON
368-     vi- SLINGERLAND Raymond Charles born ca 1882

175-    RICHMOND Malinda (*Anna, Joshua, Joshua, Jasper, John*) was born January 14, 1840 daughter of Isaac RICHMOND and Anna SMITH and died March 31, 1874 in Sullivan Twp. Pa., buried in Ames Hill cemetery. She married by 1859 Benjamin Franklin BEEBE.
Children:
     i- BEEBE Della born after June 1860
     ii- BEEBE Edgar died December 27, 1862 age 10 mos, 27 days

176-    RICHMOND Lyman (*Anna, Joshua, Joshua, Jasper, John*) was born February 13, 1844 in Sullivan Twp. Pa. son of Isaac RICHMOND and Anna SMITH and died May 6, 1896. He married December 1, 1863 Adeline HORTON who died 1914. They are buried Watson cemetery.
Children:
369-     i- RICHMOND Frederick born ca 1864
     ii- RICHMOND Eva M. born ca 1871 married September 1896 Earl BAILEY born 1872 of Binghamton, NY son of H. C. BAILEY

177-    SMITH Matilda (*Daniel T., Joshua, Joshua, Jasper, John*) was born 1818 in Tompkins, Co. NY daughter of Daniel T. SMITH and Sally HALL and died September 28, 1846 age 28 years 10 months and 20 days, buried in Reynoldsville, NY. She married January 1, 1842 David TABOR born July 31, 1815 in Rhode Island. He married (2) Margaret JOHNSON born ca 1805.
Children:
     i- TABOR Catherine born January 18, 1843 and died June 1, 1858, buried in Reynoldsville cemetery
     ii- TABOR Matilda born 1846 and died 1905 (see #180)

178-    SMITH Mary Elizabeth (*Daniel T., Joshua, Joshua, Jasper, John*) was born April 1, 1825 in Tompkins, Co. NY daughter of Daniel T. SMITH and Sally HALL and died February 23, 1892. She married William SHERMAN who was born September 1, 1818 in Albany, NY and died October 5, 1897 in Ward, Pa. They are buried in Webbs Mill

cemetery in Southport, NY.
Known children:
    i- SHERMAN Miner E. born September 7, 1845 and died May 10, 1916. He married Mary S. PEDRICK who was born May 25, 1845 daughter of John S. and Hannah M. PEDRICK and died November 25, 1879. They are buried in Webbs Mill cemetery in Southport, NY
    ii- SHERMAN Charles Henry born 1856 and died November 25, 1928 in Lamb's Creek, Pa., buried Prospect cemetery, 3 daughters.

179-    SMITH Susan M. (*Daniel T., Joshua, Joshua, Jasper, John*) was born September 21, 1832 in Tompkins, Co. NY daughter of Daniel T. SMITH and Sally HALL and died January 6, 1899. She married John Hall SWICK who was born in Seneca Co. NY December 13, 1816 son of Tunis SWICK and Phebe HALL and died January 5, 1903. They are buried in Jones cemetery in Hector, NY. He married (1) September 1838 Annis SECORD daughter of Josiah SECORD and Betsey HAUSNER. Annis died September 9, 1853/5 age 43 years 3 months 12 days, buried Jones cemetery in Perry City, NY.
Children by first marriage:
    i- SWICK Adelia C. born 1840 and died May 27, 1866. She married Benjamin FLETCHER born ca 1835. They had 1 child Elizabeth born ca 1865. He married (2) Sarah E. SLACK and removed to Clayton, Mi. by 1880.
    ii- SWICK William S. born ca 1849 and died June 14, 1878 age 28 years, 7 months and 2 days. He married Julia E. WESTCOTT who died January 30, 1878 age 28/29, both buried in Union cemetery in Valois, NY. They had 1 child Cora M. born December 5, 1874 who was living with John and Susan in 1880.
    iii- SWICK Schuyler G. died August 17, 1861 age 5 year 11 month 9 days, buried Jones cemetery
    iv- SWICK Horace born September 27, 1847 and died January 10, 1909. He maried Emily PROPER and had 1 daughter Mabel born April 19, 1900 in Hector.
Children by second marriage:
370-    v- SWICK Ida born December 28, 1861
    vi- SWICK Carrie born ca 1864 and died October 28, 1940. She married Dewitt C. SWICK who was born 1869 in Hector, NY son of George W. and Elcy SWICK and died June 14, 1931, buried in Jones cemetery.

180-    SMITH Nelson (*Daniel T., Joshua, Joshua, Jasper, John*) was born January 14, 1839 son of Daniel T. SMITH and Sally HALL and died October 14, 1890 (possibly in Catherine, NY). He married his cousin Matilda TABOR who was born September 28, 1846 daughter of David TABOR and Matilda SMITH and died November 8, 1905. (see #177). They are buried in Laurel Hill cemetery.
Children:
    i- SMITH Luella D. born October 22, 1873
    ii- SMITH Lillian born November 25, 1881 in Cayutaville

181-    SMITH Alexander Cumstock (*Jasper, Joshua, Joshua, Jasper, John*) was born

December 13, 1826 in Hector, NY son of Jasper **SMITH** and ELizabeth **HALL** and died April 17, 1895 in Sullivan Twp. Pa. He married October 18, 1849 Mary Abbott **BRADFORD** who was born April 13, 1828 in Bristol, RI daughter of Joseph Reynolds **BRADFORD** and Mary **MONROE** and died July 5, 1897 in Sullivan Twp. They are buried in Card cemetery.
Children:

    i- **SMITH** Linnaeus A.

    ii- **SMITH** Mary E. born October 7, 1854 and died April 1, 1896 married (1) Frank **AVERY** and (2) Sanford **SMITH**

    iii- **SMITH** Merton B.

    iv- **SMITH** L. Frank

    v- **SMITH** Mark J. died at age 14 years


182-    **SMITH** Lufannie (*Jasper, Joshua, Joshua, Jasper, John*) was born July 1, 1829 in Hector, NY daughter of Jasper **SMITH** and Elizabeth **HALL** and died April 8, 1895 in Ward, Tioga Co. Pa., buried State Rd. cemetery in Sullivan Twp. She married January 16, 1851 in Sullivan Twp. Pa. Solomon Henry **SMITH** who was born December 4, 1828 in Sullivan Twp. son of Rufus **SMITH** and Eunice Northrup **WILSON** and died May 17, 1896 in Canton, Bradford Co. Pa.
Children:

371-     i- **SMITH** Frances Elizabeth born July 12, 1852 in Sullivan Twp. Pa.

372-     ii- **SMITH** George Wesley born September 18, 1854 in Sullivan Twp.

373-     iii- **SMITH** Hulda Abigail born April 4, 1857 in Ward Twp.

374-     iv- **SMITH** Eunice Isabelle born June 16, 1863 in Ward Twp.

375-     v- **SMITH** Jasper Rufus born February 19, 1868 in Ward Twp.


183-    **SMITH** Hulda (*Jasper, Joshua, Joshua, Jasper, John*) was born December 16, 1833 in Sullivan Twp. Pa. daughter of Jasper **SMITH** and Elizabeth **HALL** and died January 8, 1899. She married Isaac **SQUIRES** who was born March 14, 1830 and died July 24, 1906. They are buried in Gray cemetery in Coventry, Pa.
Children:

376-     i- **SQUIRES** Ella born 1855

    ii- **SQUIRES** William J. born ca 1862


184-    **SMITH** Arad T. (*Jasper, Joshua, Joshua, Jasper, John*) was born August 2, 1839 in Sullivan Twp. Pa. son of Jasper **SMITH** and Elizabeth **HALL** and died 1890. He married March 22, 1859 Samantha **DOUD** who was born August 2, 1839 daughter of Ripley **DOUD** and died August 2, 1890 in Elmira, NY.
Known child:

    i- **SMITH** Phebe


185-    **SMITH** Lyman R. (*Jasper, Joshua, Joshua, Jasper, John*) was born June 1843 in Sullivan Twp. Pa. son of Jasper **SMITH** and Elizabeth **HALL** and died 1920, buried State Rd. cemetery. He married Charlotte E. **WELCH** who was born February 1846 in Sullivan

Twp. daughter of James WELCH and Rosilla RICH and died 1914. Unknown children.

186-    SMITH Mary Jane (*George, Joshua, Joshua, Jasper, John*) was born May 8, 1838 in Sullivan Twp. Pa. daughter of George F. SMITH and Keturrah Rebecca HODGES and died 1916 in Sulivan Twp. She married February 24, 1858 George SQUIRES who was born 1833 in Sullivan Twp. son of William Sturgis SQUIRES and Charlotte BURROWS and died 1905. They are buried in Gray Valley cemetery.
Children:
        i- SQUIRES Josephine L. born January 1861 and died June 9, 1947. She married December 31, 1878 Bert L. PALMER who was born June 1853 in Sullivan Twp. Pa. son of Lester PALMER and Adeline PROVIN and died 1930, both buried in Gray Valley cemetery
        ii- SQUIRES Burtis George born 1862 and died 1922. He married November 11, 1886 Ida May SMITH born August 1869 daughter of George SMITH and Mary A. TEARS in Sullivan Twp. and died 1948 (see #166). Their daughter Mary Josephine was born September 27, 1900 in Mansfield, Pa. and died in Wellsboro March 6, 1988. They are buried in Gray Valley cemetery.
        iii- SQUIRES Porter C. born 1868 and died 1944. He married Susan (unknown maiden name) who was born Ireland or Scotland
        iv- SQUIRES William Arthur born February 2, 1874 and died February 21, 1949 in Sullivan Twp. He married (1) in Nichols, NY June 8, 1898 L. Annah BOWEN who was born 1875 in/of Warren Ctr. Pa. and died 1906. He married (2) Stella CHAMBERLAIN

187-    SMITH Sally A. (*George, Joshua, Joshua, Jasper, John*) was born April 16, 1841 in Rutland Twp. Pa. daughter of George F. SMITH and Keturrah Rebecca HODGES and died June 11, 1871 in Sullivan Twp. Pa., buried Wood cemetery. She married November 24, 1860 Sanford Gaylord SMITH who was born December 13, 1838 in Rutland Twp. son of Morris SMITH and Matilda Carrie GAYLORD. He married (2) Emma Keturrah SMITH (see #68) and married (3) Mary Elizabeth SMITH and (4) Joanna CHAPMAN. Children of Sanford and Sally born Sullivan Twp. Pa.:
        i- SMITH son born August 29, 1861 and died same day
        ii- SMITH Carrie K. born June 18, 1863 and died in child birth February 18, 1885. The baby also died. She married George Eugene DOUD who was born 1864 son of Peleg DOUD and Mary KING and died 1934. They are buried in State Road cemetery.
        iii- SMITH Cora May born November 29, 1865 and died November 24, 1890 age 27 when child was 4 mos old, buried Mainesburg cemetery. She married December 25, 1886 in Covington, Pa. Dennis Vaughn SMITH who was born January 13, 1864 in Mainesburg, Pa. son of Ephraim Clark and Louisa SMITH and died March 25, 1954 in Columbia Town, Bradford Co. Pa. (see #160)
377-    iv- SMITH Frances Augusta born April 20, 1868
        v- SMITH Frederick E. born October 14, 1870 and died May 22, 1871, buried Wood cemetery
Child of Sanford and Emma Keturrah:
        i- SMITH Hobart M. born October 31, 1872 in Tioga Co. Pa. and died December 25, 1962 in Sylvania, Pa., buried Sylvania cemetery. He married (1) Delia (unknown

54

maiden name) and (2) July 1, 1894 Edith Ann **RICHMOND** (see #580).

188- **SMITH** Nehemiah (*George, Joshua, Joshua, Jasper, John*) was born June 27, 1844 in Rutland Twp. Pa. son of George F. **SMITH** and Keturrah Rebecca **HODGES**. He married before 1869 Francella Delilah **PALMER** born 1850 in Sullivan Twp. Pa. daughter of Mark Preston **PALMER** and Helen Angeline **SMITH**. Nehemiah lived in NY State in 1896
Children:

      i- **SMITH** Burt W. married Kate (unknown maiden name)
      ii- **SMITH** Lyman
      iii- **SMITH** Gladys
      iv- **SMITH** Helena
      v- **SMITH** Mark born 1869 in Sullivan Twp. Pa.
      vi- **SMITH** Fred M. born November 19, 1871 and died February 11, 1949 in Blossburg, Pa., buried Lawrence Corners. He married Nellie Delia **STONE** who was born March 17, 1883 daughter of David Waldo **STONE** and Emma **BRACE** and died June 19, 1901
      vii- **SMITH** Colie was born ca 1874 and died June 15, 1924 in Ward Twp. Pa. He married December 27, 1900 Margaret Jane **LOWERY** who was born May 23, 1875 in Scotland daughter of Campbell **LOWERY** and Mary Jane **SMITH** and died November 22, 1922 in Fallbrook, Pa. They are buried in State Rd. cemetery.

189- **SMITH** George Manley (*George, Joshua, Joshua, Jasper, John*) was born July 23, 1846 in Rutland Twp. son of George F. **SMITH** and Keturrah Rebecca **HODGES**. He married (1) Matilda **WILLIAMS** born 1844 and christened in Canton, Pa. He married (2) November 26, 1906 Ida M. **HAMMOND**.
Children by first marriage:
378-    i- **SMITH** Clarence Adelbert born 1869
      ii- **SMITH** Marion

190- **SMITH** Charles Wesley (*George, Joshua, Joshua, Jasper, John*) was born June 15, 1859 in Rutland Twp. Pa. son of George F. **SMITH** and Keturrah Rebecca **HODGES** and died August 15, 1904 of injuries in barn raising. He married ca 1880 Lucy **VAN NESS** born February 13, 1856 in Tioga Co. Pa. daughter of John **VAN NESS** and Louisa M. **WILSON** and died February 18, 1906. They are buried in Prospect cemetery in Mansfield, Pa.
Children:

      i- **SMITH** Rayburn born April 18, 1895, served in World War I, married Evelyn **HATCH**. She lived in Tonawanda, NY in 1966
      ii- **SMITH** Anson J. born 1898 and died 1962. He married Velma **CLARK** who was born 1905, lived Elmira, NY. They are buried in Prospect cemetery in Mansfield, Pa.

191- **SMITH** Frances Augusta (*George, Joshua, Joshua, Jasper, John*) was born August 3, 1855 in Rutland, Twp. Pa. daughter of George F. **SMITH** and Keturrah Rebecca

HODGES and died May 21, 1882 in Richmond Twp. Pa., buried State Rd. cemetery. She married Lucien H. DOUD who was born 1855 in Sullivan Twp. son of Peleg DOUD and Mary KING. He married (1) Helen R. SARLE daughter of George SARLE.
Children of Lucien and Frances:
   i- DOUD Howard L. born October 21, 1878, lived in Boston in 1898
   ii- DOUD Mary Augusta born May 14, 1882, lived Wellsburg, Pa. in 1898

192- SMITH Anna R. (*George, Joshua, Joshua, Jasper, John*) was born ca 1876 in Sullivan Twp. Pa. daughter of George F. SMITH and Amelia WILSON and died January 4, 1971 in Wellsboro, Pa. age 94 years. She married September 15, 1893 Wilson B. NILES who was born March 4, 1876 in Rutland Twp. Pa. son of Russell NILES and Delphia BARTLETT and died April 15, 1936 in Rutland Twp. They are buried in Watson cemetery.
One known child:
   i- NILES daughter who married Clarence BROWN

193- SMITH George F. Jr. (*George, Joshua, Joshua, Jasper, John*) was born ca 1870 in Rutland Twp. Pa. son of George F. SMITH and Amelia WILSON. He married Martha CRUM who was born ca 1879 in Rutland Twp. Pa. daughter of Edward CRUM and Florence VAUGHAN and died November 22, 1933 in Rutland Twp., buried Watson cemetery.
Known children:
379-  i- SMITH Ethel ca 1900.
   ii- SMITH Millie born 1903 and died 1999, married Freeman DIXON of Dundee, NY born 1907 and died March 14, 1973. They are buried in the Bradford cemetery in Bradford, NY.
380-  iii- SMITH Manley G. born November 28, 1898

194- SMITH Effie Sarah (*George, Joshua, Joshua, Jasper, John*) was born November 20, 1877 in Rutland Twp. Pa. daughter of George F. SMITH and Amelia WILSON. She married Merritt William SMITH who was born November 22, 1872 son of Lyman Burton SMITH and Catherine Francelia VAN NOCKEN and died July 1, 1945 age 72 yrs.
Children:
   i- SMITH Lee
   ii- SMITH Wilson N. born 1906 and died September 1, 1962 in Towanda, Pa. He married Eleanor (unknown maiden name) and had 2 sons Roe and Gerald

195- SMITH Ellen Jane (*Obadiah, Joshua, Joshua, Jasper, John*) was born ca 1849 in Tioga Co. Pa. daughter of Obadiah SMITH and Ann WELCH and died December 23, 1935 in Horseheads, NY. She married March 13, 1872 John W. STYRES who was born December 6, 1850 in Tompkins Co. NY son of William and Rachel STYRES and died June 3, 1923. They are buried in Gray Valley cemetery in Sullivan Twp. Pa.
Children:
   i- STYRES Effie who married Oley MASON and removed to Detroit, Mi.

ii- **STYRES** Cora born August 26, 1876 and died August 10, 1950 in Horseheads, NY. She married John C. **BOGARDUS** who died November 5, 1965 (?). They are buried in Woodlawn cemetery in Elmira, NY

iii- **STYRES** Bert who removed to Belona, NY or Geneva, NY and died there 1961. He married Lula G. **MASON**

iv- **STYRES** Nora born 1873 and died 1957, unmarried

(2 children died in childhood, one was Roy who was struck by lightning age 12 years)

196- **SMITH** Cornelius (*Obadiah, Joshua, Joshua, Jasper, John*) was born 1847 in Tioga Co. Pa. son of Obadiah **SMITH** and Ann **WELCH** and died September 10, 1931 in Mainesburg, Pa. age 84 years 2 months and 10 days, buried Gray Valley cemetery. He married March 10, 1869 Martha **SMITH** who was born ca 1836 and died November 17, 1929 in Mainesburg, Pa.

Children:

381-     i- **SMITH** Cora M. born 1871

      ii- **SMITH** Ada born ca 1877

197- **SMITH** Albert Obadiah (*Obadiah, Joshua, Joshua, Jasper, John*) was born December 1853 in Tioga Co. Pa. son of Obadiah **SMITH** and Ann **WELCH** and died 1936. He married Lucy Permelia **HULSLANDER** who was born September 1854 in Sullivan Twp. Pa. daughter of Thomas J. **HULSLANDER** and Eunice Ann **SQUIRES** and died April 13, 1923. They are buried in Gray Valley cemetery.

Known children:

      i- **SMITH** Walter born 1877 and died January 1923 (possibly married Lillian M. **GREY** on December 30, 1899)

      ii- **SMITH** Nellie who married John **HURLBURT**

198- **SMITH** Benjamin Schoonover (*Joshua, Platt, Joshua, Jasper, John*) was born September 15, 1804 in Walpack, NJ son of Joshua **SMITH** and Elizabeth **VAN AUKEN** and died April 20, 1876. He married December 25, 1826 Rachel **KING** who was born 1808 and died July 3, 1889. They are buried in Grove cemetery in Ulysses, NY.

Children:

382-     i- **SMITH** Betsey A. born 1830

      ii- **SMITH** Jeremiah born 1838 and died 1843, buried Quaker Settlement cemetery in Ulysses, NY

383-    iii- **SMITH** Reuben L. born January 30, 1846

199- **SMITH** Hannah (*Joshua, Platt, Joshua, Jasper, John*) was born 1806 in NJ or Ulysses, NY daughter of Joshua **SMITH** and Elizabeth **VAN AUKEN** and died May 22, 1888. She married John **DEREMER** who was born 1803 in Newark, NJ son of Abraham and Jane **DEREMER** and died July 9, 1880. They are buried in Grove cemetery.

Children born Tompkins Co. NY:

      i- **DEREMER** Irving born 1830 and died April 21, 1897, unmarried, buried Grove cemetery

384-    ii- **DEREMER** Elizabeth born October 13, 1833
385-    iii- **DEREMER** Martha born 1840

200-    **SMITH** Casperus Van Auken (*Joshua, Platt, Joshua, Jasper, John*) called Van Auken was born 1807 in Walpack, NJ son of Joshua **SMITH** and Elizabeth **VAN AUKEN**. He married Harriet (unknown maiden name) born Pa.
Children:
386-    i- **SMITH** John A. born 1836
        ii- **SMITH** Minerva born 1837
        iii- **SMITH** George born 1839
        iv- **SMITH** Louise born 1843
        v- **SMITH** Sarah born 1845
        vi- **SMITH** Charles H. born 1853
        vii- **SMITH** Ella B. born 1855

201-    **SMITH** Elijah (*Joshua, Platt, Joshua, Jasper, John*) was born February 11, 1811 in Walpack, NJ son of Joshua **SMITH** and Elizabeth **VAN AUKEN** and died November 3, 1870 in Grand Rapids, Mi. His first wife is unknown. He married (2) Charlotte **KNAPP** who was born October 12, 1824 daughter of Sylvester **KNAPP** and Lucy **FITCH** and died December 14, 1883. They moved to Wright Twp. Mi. They are buried in Quaker Settlement cemetery in Hector, NY.
Children by first marriage:
        i- **SMITH** Susan
        ii- **SMITH** Thomas Jefferson born February 12, 1839 and died February 26, 1864
Children by second marriage:
387-    iii- **SMITH** Sylvester K. born September 28, 1844 and died July 14, 1897
388-    iv- **SMITH** Antoinette born October 12, 1846
389-    v- **SMITH** Alice Amelia born July 26, 1854
390-    vi- **SMITH** Joshua Legrant born April 10, 1855
        vii- **SMITH** Clara Esther born January 10, 1861, married October 27, 1878 Henry **BODELL**
391-    viii- **SMITH** Horace D. born February 15, 1866

202-    **SMITH** George Washington (*Joshua, Platt, Joshua, Jasper, John*) was born April 17, 1814 probably in Tompkins Co. NY son of Joshua **SMITH** and Elizabeth **VAN AUKEN** and died February 12, 1900 in Buffalo, NY. He married January 16, 1834 Martha **WAGER** who was born March 30, 1817 daughter of James and Nancy **WAGER** and died October 11, 1894 in Buffalo.
Children:
        i- **SMITH** Mary Ann born 1835 and died before 1894
        ii- **SMITH** Christina born April 4, 1835 and died November 23, 1853. She married John B. **HICKS** born 1830 son of John B. and Corintha **HICKS** and died June 12, 1870. They are buried in Forest Lawn cemetery in Buffalo, NY
        iii- **SMITH** Dewitt C. born 1837 and died March 29, 1877

58

392-    iv- SMITH Clara M. born 1842

203-    SMITH Mary Ann (*Joshua, Platt, Joshua, Jasper, John*) was born 1820 in Tompkins Co. NY daughter of Joshua SMITH and Elizabeth VAN AUKEN and died ca 1860. She married John G. HURLBURT son of William HURLBURT and Sarah WESTBROOK as his second wife. His first wife was Eliza J. SMITH.
Children of John G. and Eliza J.;
        I- HURLBURT William H. born ca 1841
        ii- HURLBURT Daniel W. born ca 1843
        iii- HURLBURT Mary H. born ca 1846
        iv- HURLBURT Emma L. born ca 1849 in Ithaca, NY

204-    SMITH Horace David (*Joshua, Platt, Joshua, Jasper, John*) was born March 10, 1827 in Tompkins Co. NY son of Joshua SMITH and Elizabeth VAN AUKEN and died February 21, 1909 in Ithaca, NY. He married March 30, 1853 Margaret POTTER who was born October 3, 1828 and died January 29, 1906. They are buried in Hayt's cemetery in Ithaca, NY
Children:
393-        i- SMITH Flora E. born 1856
394-        ii- SMITH Horace Floyd born July 6, 1868

205-    VAN HORN Margaret (*Mary, Platt, Joshua, Jasper, John*) was born November 19, 1807 in Tompkins Co. NY daughter of George VAN HORN and Mary SMITH and died January 1, 1871. She married James R. KING who was born August 2, 1803 in Herkimer Co. NY and died September 30, 1885. They are buried in Mc Intyre Settlement cemetery.
Children born Tompkins Co.:
        i- KING Paulina born 1824 and died 1827
395-        ii- KING Lovina born 1828
396-        iii- KING Nelson V. born 1831
397-        iv- KING Mary E. born October 1, 1834 and died February 15, 1882
        v- KING George born 1837/8 and died 1839
398-        vi- KING Emma born 1840
399-        vii- KING Matilda born 1843
400-        viii- KING Cornelius born 1848

206-    VAN HORN Beniah (*Mary, Platt, Joshua, Jasper, John*) was born June 8, 1810 in Hector, NY son of George VAN HORN and Mary SMITH. He married May 26, 1853 in Hector Fanny Geru RODERICK born June 2, 1818 in Montreal, Canada. Unknown children

207-    VAN HORN Hannah (*Mary, Platt, Joshua, Jasper, John*) was born 1815 in Tompkins Co. NY daughter of George VAN HORN and Mary SMITH. She married John MOORE born ca 1811 and died about 1868.
Children:

i- **MOORE** Mary born ca 1832

ii- **MOORE** Catherine born 1836, married \_\_\_ **MORRIS**

ii- **MOORE** Albert born ca 1838

401-    iii- **MOORE** Oliver born January 1840

iv- **MOORE** Emma L. born ca 1850

208-    **VAN HORN** Matilda (*Mary, Platt, Joshua, Jasper, John*) was born 1818 in Hector, NY daughter of George **VAN HORN** and Mary **SMITH** and died 1850-60. She married Richard F. **CARLEY** born October 11, 1816 in Tompkins Co. NY and died October 29, 1891. They were living in Portage Co. Wis. by 1860. He married (2) Mary Jane **CHAPMAN** born July 7, 1832 in Barrington, Ill. daughter of Lewis and Lucy **CHAPMAN** and died December 29, 1899. They are buried in Plover Village cemetery.

Children by first wife:

402-    i- **CARLEY** Simeon born November 1839 in NY

403-    ii- **CARLEY** William born 1844 in NY

iii- **CARLEY** Emma born 1850 in Ill.

iv- **CARLEY** Henry S. born 1850 Ill.

Children by second wife:

v- **CARLEY** Frank born ca 1862

vi- **CARLEY** Andrew born ca 1865 and died May 18, 1948 in Portage Co. Wis., buried Plover Village cemetery.

209-    **VAN HORN** Oliver (*Mary, Platt, Joshua, Jasper, John*) was born October 5, 1821 in Hector, NY son of Simeon **VAN HORN** and Mary **SMITH** and died March 26, 1897. He married (1) Adeline **SMITH** born 1828 daughter of Robert P. **SMITH** and Elizabeth **MILLER** and died 1863 (see #76). He married (2) her sister Calista Matilda **SMITH** who died July 23, 1889. They were divorced April 21, 1868 and he married (3) Mary L. (unknown maiden name) who was born 1838 and died August 1908.

Children by first marriage:

i- **VAN HORN** Elizabeth born 1850 married June 6, 1867 Willard **INK** born ca 1848 son of John B. and Julia Ann **INK** of Hector, NY

ii- **VAN HORN** Ellen A. born 1852 and died 1865, buried Mc Intyre Settlement cemetery

iii- **VAN HORN** Robert P. born 1857 and died 1918, buried Mc Intyre Settlement cemetery (listed in 1880 census as Ross)

Child by third marriage:

iv- **VAN HORN** Eugenie born October 25, 1873 and died May 2 1887, buried Mc Intyre Settlement cemetery

210-    **VAN HORN** Angelina Adelia (*Mary, Platt, Joshua, Jasper, John*) was born 1827 in Hector, NY daughter of Simeon **VAN HORN** and Mary **SMITH** and died June 28, 1887. She married Reuben **CHAPMAN** who was born February 21, 1819 son of John **CHAPMAN** and Sarah **PIERCE** and died June 6/16, 1897 (death record gives date as June 6).

Children born Catherine, NY:

     i- **CHAPMAN** Mary Mariah born April 29, 1848 and died May 24, 1863
404-    ii- **CHAPMAN** Emma born January 1851
     iii- **CHAPMAN** Ann Eliza born 1853
405-    iv- **CHAPMAN** George W. born February 14, 1855
     v- **CHAPMAN** Delphine born 1861 married G. Munson **HALL** born 1858 son of
Munson **HALL** and Clara **JUDD**
406-   vi- **CHAPMAN** Elizabeth born 1866
     vii- **CHAPMAN** Edward
     viii- **CHAPMAN** Lida

211-    **VAN HORN** Anna Eliza (*Mary, Platt, Joshua, Jasper, John*) was born 1824 in
Hector, NY daughter of Simeon **VAN HORN** and Mary **SMITH** and died May 12, 1893.
She married Gilbert **CHAPMAN** who was born April 1827 son of John **CHAPMAN** and
Sarah **PIERCE** and died April 28, 1904 in Catherine, NY. They are buried in Laurel Hill
cemetery.
Children probably all in Catherine, NY:
407-    i- **CHAPMAN** Simeon born 1847
     ii- **CHAPMAN** Orsemus born 1850 and died July 19, 1863
408-   iii- **CHAPMAN** William M. born February 1854
     iv- **CHAPMAN** Melissa Jane born 1858 and died August 1, 1863
     v- **CHAPMAN** Ellen Ann died 1866 age 6 months

212-    **RICHARDS** Platt (*Johannah, Platt, Joshua, Jasper, John*) was born September 1809
in Tompkins Co. NY son of Nathaniel **RICHARDS** and Johannah **SMITH** and died March
24, 1868 in Ulysses, NY. His wife Elizabeth was born December 1809 and died July 15,
1865. They are buried in the Jacksonville cemetery.
Children:
409-    i- **RICHARDS** Mary Adeline born 1835
410-    ii- **RICHARDS** Melissa born June 6, 1837
411-   iii- **RICHARDS** Emeline born September 1839
412-    iv- **RICHARDS** Elizabeth born 1845
413-    v- **RICHARDS** Lafayette born 1849

213-    **RICHARDS** Benjamin (*Johannah, Platt, Joshua, Jasper, John*) was born September
20, 1810 son of Nathaniel **RICHARDS** and Johannah **SMITH** and died April 28, 1896. He
married Marian A. **STOWELL** who was born May 22, 1807 and died December 20, 1879.
They are buried in Smithboro cemetery in Smithboro, NY
Children:
414-    i- **RICHARDS** Mary Louisa born September 28, 1838
     ii- **RICHARDS** Hannah E. born 1841
     iii- **RICHARDS** Elias F. born September 18, 1844 and died May 2, 1865 in Civil
War, served in Co. I. 107th Reg. and 63rd Reg. and is buried in Smithboro cemetery.

214-    **RICHARDS** Alvah (*Johannah, Platt, Joshua, Jasper, John*) was born 1811 in

Tompkins Co. NY son of Nathaniel **RICHARDS** and Johannah **SMITH** and died in Greenwood, NY February 28, 1896. He married Hannah A. (unknown maiden name) born 1817. They are buried in W. Union cemetery in Jasper, NY
Children:
  i- **RICHARDS** Augustine born 1838
  ii- **RICHARDS** Isaac born 1845 and died December 31, 1848, buried in W. Union cemetery in Jasper, NY
  iii- **RICHARDS** Wilbur born 1848 and died April 10, 1887 age 34 yrs 4 mos 15 days, buried Jasper Village Cemetery in Jasper, NY. His daughter Hannah born 1880 and died September 29, 1881. He is listed in the 1880 census in Greenwood, NY with wife Gusta and children Emery born 1872, Bell born 1874 and Carrie born 1876
  iv- **RICHARDS** Lufanny born 1851
  v- **RICHARDS** Miriam born 1853
  vi- **RICHARDS** Andrew born 1860

215-  **RICHARDS** Hannah (*Johannah, Platt, Joshua, Jasper, John*) was born 1812 in Tompkins Co. NY daughter of Nathaniel **RICHARDS** and Johannah **SMITH** and died 1879 in Warren Co. NJ. She married Daniel **CUMMINS** who was born September 2, 1802 son of Christian **CUMMINS** and Mary **SMITH** and died 1873 in Warren Co. NJ.
Children:
415-    i- **CUMMINS** Nathaniel born ca 1831 in NY
  ii- **CUMMINS** Louisa born ca 1834, listed in 1880 census in Hackettstown, NJ James **JEFFERSON** born ca 1831 in NJ with wife Louisa born ca 1835 and son Lewis born ca 1863
  iii- **CUMMINS** Christian born ca 1839, listed in 1880 census in Independence, NJ born ca 1830 in NJ with wife Matilda born ca 1849 and brother Nelson born ca 1845
  iv- **CUMMINS** Nelson born ca 1845
  v- **CUMMINS** Jeremiah born ca 1846 died before 1879
  vi- **CUMMINS** Emeline born ca 1848, married ____ **SCHMEAL**
  vii- **CUMMINS** Daniel born ca 1854 and died before 1879
416-  viii- **CUMMINS** Andrew J. born ca 1859

216-  **RICHARDS** Robert (*Johannah, Platt, Joshua, Jasper, John*) was born June 13, 1815 in Tompkins Co. son of Nathaniel **RICHARDS** and Johannah **SMITH** and died in Windham Twp. Pa. December 29, 1897. He married (1) Elizabeth **ROE** who was born 1820 daughter of Samuel J. **ROE** and Sarah **MC CANN** and died July 20, 1847, buried Quaker Settlement cemetery. He married (2) March 8, 1848 Rebecca (**MORRIS**) **VOUGHT** who was born June 19, 1822 daughter of John V. and Polly **MORRIS** and died July 30, 1904, buried Windham cemetery. Her first husband was Nehemiah **VOUGHT**.
Children by first marriage:
  i- **RICHARDS** Nathaniel born 1837
417-  ii- **RICHARDS** Mary E. born 1839
Children by second marriage:
  iii- **RICHARDS** Louisa born 1850 (possibly married to Dallas E. **WATSON**

62

September 26, 1868)
    iv- RICHARDS Benjamin F. born 1852. Listed in the 1880 census in Windham,
Pa. with wife Mary born Pa. 1859 and son Floyd born 1880. Floyd married Edna
NICHOLS born 1894 and died July 11, 1980, buried Bumpville cemetery in Bradford Co.
Pa.
    v- RICHARDS George O. born 1857. He was civil Engineer on St. Paul,
Chicago, Milwaukee RR. nfi
    vi- VOUGHT Isaac born 1843 (stepson)
    vii- VOUGHT Charles born 1845 and died 1855 (stepson)

217-  RICHARDS Albert (*Johannah, Platt, Joshua, Jasper, John*) was born 1816 in
Tompkins Co. NY son of Nathaniel RICHARDS and Johannah SMITH and died November
1, 1892 in Covert, NY, buried Grove cemetery. He moved to Rome Twp. Pa. before 1870
and back to Hector, NY. He married (1) Harriet BONHAM who was born 1827 in Pa.
daughter of Andrew and Elizabeth BONHAM and died November 2, 1873, buried Bumpville
cemetery in Bradford Co. Pa. He married (2) Caroline (HORTON) CRISSY, her second
marriage, born September 1816 in Dutchess Co. NY daughter of T. P. HORTON and
Phebe CONROE and died September 10, 1912. She later married Benjamin WOODWARD
(see #220)
Children:
    i- RICHARDS Irene born 1844
    ii- RICHARDS George born 1846 and died September 23, 1873, buried Bumpville
cemetery.
418-  iii- RICHARDS Smith born 1849
419-  iv- RICHARDS Charles born 1859
    v- RICHARDS Eugene born 1864 and died 1933, buried Hayt's cemetery in
Ithaca, NY. He married Bessie May JOHNSON born 1867 in Hoopers Valley, Pa. daughter
of Thomas JOHNSON and Martha PRIMROSE

218-  RICHARDS Louisa M. (*Johannah, Platt, Joshua, Jasper, John*) was born 1822 in
Tompkins Co. NY daughter of Nathaniel RICHARDS and Johannah SMITH and died
October 24, 1886. She married Brunson KING who was born February 28, 1826 and died
August 28, 1886. They are buried in Grove cemetery.
Children:
420-  i- KING Hannah born May 2, 1846
421-  ii- KING Mary M. born 1850
422-  iii- KING Emily S. (Emma) born 1854
    iv- KING Jane Anne born 1868, married ____ ROWE of Ithaca

219-  RICHARDS William (*Johannah, Platt, Joshua, Jasper, John*) was born 1824 in
Tompkins co. NY son of Nathaniel RICHARDS and died October 6, 1904 in Pleasant
Valley, Pa. He married (1) Sarah GUILTNER who was born 1825 and died May 6, 1865.
They are buried in Grove cemetery in Trumansburgh, NY. He married (2) Harriet
RANDOLF born May 1836 and died 1917, buried on the EICHLOR lot in Bumpville

63

cemetery, Tioga Co. Pa.
Children:
423-    i- RICHARDS Alonzo born January 1845 in NY
424-    ii- RICHARDS Leroy born March 1852 in Bradford Co. Pa.    425-    iii-
RICHARDS Lyman William born 1861
        iii- RICHARDS Jessie born 1869 (adopted)

220-    WOODWARD Benjamin S. (*Keziah, Platt, Joshua, Jasper, John*) was born April
22, 1819 in Covert, NY son of Samuel WOODWARD and Keziah SMITH and died May 8,
1900. He married (1) Rachel Emeline RICHARDS who was born September 14, 1818
daughter of Nathaniel RICHARDS and Johannah SMITH and died August 30, 1892. (see
#73) They are buried in Grove cemetery in Trumansburg, NY. He married (2) in Hector,
NY age 74 Caroline (HORTON) RICHARDS born Dutchess Co. daughter of T. P.
HORTON and Phebe CONROE. (see #217)
Children:
        i- WOODWARD Albert R. born 1841 and died May 14, 1900. buried Grove
cemetery
        ii- WOODWARD Irving T. born December 1843 and died March 5, 1905, buried
Grove cemetery
        iii- WOODWARD Louisa S. born March 11, 1849 and died June 20, 1850, buried
Grove cemetery
        iv- WOODWARD George H. born January 4, 1850 and died March 26, 1850,
buried Grove cemetery
426-    v- WOODWARD William C. born 1853 and died July 28, 1912
        vi- WOODWARD Hermon S. born July 16, 1857 and died June 28, 1858, buried
Grove cemetery
427-    vii- WOODWARD Mary E. born October 1859
        viii- WOODWARD Frank B. born September 1862 and died March 29, 1910, buried
Grove cemetery

221-    SMITH Harriet A. (*Robert P., Platt, Joshua, Jasper, John*) was born 1833 in
Tompkins Co. NY daughter of Robert P. SMITH and Elizabeth MILLER and died in
Ulysses, NY September 7, 1902. She married Atmore ARNOLD who was born May 22,
1837 in Providence, RI son of Job W. and Phebe ARNOLD. They removed to Pt. Jarvis,
Delaware Co. NY. He died July 29, 1892, buried Arnold Burying Ground in Coventry, RI
One known child:
        i- ARNOLD Bell V. born ca 1859 and died January 11, 1912, found frozen to
death at Trumansburg, buried Grove cemetery

222-    VAN AUKEN Horace J. (*Lovina, Platt, Joshua, Jasper, John*) was born ca 1830 in
Tompkins Co. NY son of David VAN AUKEN and Lovina SMITH and died February 14,
1893 in Bushkill, Pa. He married July 3, 1881 in Jacksonville, NY Sarah Jane SHANNON
daughter of Clayton S. and Phebe D. SHANNON. Sarah married (1) William RILEY who
died July 17, 1876.

223- SMITH Alice Amelia (*Lafayette, Jasper, Joshua, Jasper, John*) was born May 1861 in Ulyssses, NY daughter of Lafayette SMITH and Lovina BORDEN and died May 25, 1921. She married March 24, 1887 George A. POPPINO who was born August 1858 son of Henry H. POPPINO and Mary BROWN and died September 11, 1921.
Children:
428- i- POPPINO Henry Lafayette (twin) born January 14, 1890
429- ii- POPPINO Harry Borden (twin) born January 14, 1890

224- SMITH Mary F. (*Lafayette, Jasper, Joshua, Jasper, John*) was born 1869 in Ulysses, NY daughter of Lafayette SMITH and Lovina BORDEN and died December 2, 1925. She married Henry W. WILSON who was born 1856 and died March 20, 1932. They are buried in Jones cemetery in Hector, NY. Unknown children

225- SMITH Elizabeth (*Obadiah, Obadiah, Joshua, Jasper, John*) was born April 5, 1818 daughter of Obadiah SMITH and Ann CULVER and died January 15, 1907. She married Ward S. MILLER who was born 1813 son of Ziba and Sally MILLER and died October 8, 1883. They are buried in Grove cemetery.
Children:
430- i- MILLER Judson H. born 1842
431- ii- MILLER William H. born 1848
iii- MILLER Charles H. born 1850 and died April 26, 1919. He married Elly HOLLIEN born 1894 and died 1983?
iv- MILLER Frank A. born March 1854 and died August 9, 1921. He married Della BROWN born 1865 and died 1929.
432- v- MILLER Olin born 1856
433- vi- MILLER Carrie L. born 1862

226- SMITH Berentha (*Obadiah, Obadiah, Joshua, Jasper, John*) was born October 10, 1830 daughter of Obadiah SMITH and Ann CULVER and died January 30, 1920, buried Grove cemetery. She married May 6, 1851 Jonathan GANOUNG who was born 1830 son of James GANOUNG and Eliza Ann JARVIS and died March 19, 1863 in Barkley Twp, Black Hawk Co. Iowa.
Children:
i- GANOUNG infant born April 4, 1853, died April 14, 1853
434- ii- GANOUNG Adeline born May 9, 1854

227- SMITH Gideon Osborne (*Obadiah, Obadiah, Joshua, Jasper, John*) was born ca 1836 in Tompkins Co. NY son of Obadiah SMITH and Ann CULVER and died March 3, 1924 in Odessa, NY. He was a physician. He married (1) Anna MALLORY who was born 1848 and died 1917 and he married (2) Charlotte MALLORY who was born 1848 and died 1917, both were daughters of Aaron E. MALLORY and Alice Genet BEARDSLEY. They are buried in Laurel Hill cemetery.
Children:
435- i- SMITH Alice M. born June 7, 1868

ii- SMITH Helen M. born 1880 and died 1962, unmarried

228-    SMITH Harris Irvin (*Obadiah, Obadiah, Joshua, Jasper, John*) was born 1838 son of Obadiah SMITH and Ann CULVER and died 1922. His wife Almina Nichols WHITNEY was born 1844 and died 1919. They are buried in Hayt's cemetery in Ithaca. Children listed in 1880 census:
    i- SMITH Carrie born ca 1870
    ii- SMITH Martha born ca 1876
    iii- SMITH Howard born ca 1878
    iv- SMITH Olin Whitney born October 17, 1884 (see #681)

229-    SMITH Francis Drake (*Annanias, Obadiah, Joshua, Jasper, John*) was born January 8, 1828 in Tompkins Co. NY son of Annanias SMITH and Anna DRAKE and died July 22, 1896 in Lansing, NY. He is buried in Ludlowville cemetery. He married October 25, 1855 in Chemung Co. Katherine BARNES who was born August 2, 1836 daughter of Jeremiah BARNES and Lena Ellen SWARTWOOD and died August 10, 1908.
Children:
436-    i- SMITH Monroe A. born January 8, 1857
        ii- SMITH Olin J. born August 21, 1858 and died February 22, 1871 in Van Etten, NY
437-    iii- SMITH Jessie Ruth born August 27, 1861
438-    iv- SMITH John Barnes born October 27, 1863
        v- SMITH Jay R. born September 11, 1865 and died February 24, 1871 in Van Etten, NY
439-    vi- SMITH Eleanor Elizabeth born April 12, 1867
440-    vii- SMITH Jeremiah Annanias born August 16, 1870
441-    viii- SMITH Gurnee B. born June 29, 1873 and died June 25, 1952. He married Ida SWAYZE
442-    ix- SMITH Frank O. born December 10, 1876 and died March 26, 1943. He married Viola PALMER. They were divorced.

230-    SMITH Melissa (*Robert T., Obadiah, Joshua, Jasper, John*) was born September 1831 in Tompkins Co. NY daughter of Robert T. SMITH and Hannah NORTON and died November 5, 1917. She married John R. BROWN of Jacksonville, NY who was born May 1832 son of James and Darinda BROWN and died July 7, 1914. They are buried in Hayt's cemetery.
Children born in Ulysses, NY:
        i- BROWN Adella B. born March 1865 and died March 27, 1929
443-    ii- BROWN Floyd J. born July 1867
        iii- BROWN Homer R. born 1872, removed to Buffalo, NY
444-    iv- BROWN Clarkson M. (Manley Clark) born February 20, 1875

231-    SMITH Jehiel (*Robert T., Obadiah, Joshua, Jasper, John*) was born September 15, 1834 in Tompkins co. NY son of Robert T. SMITH and Hannah Norton and died January 3,

1902. He married Mercy J. HUSON who was born February 18, 1837 daughter of Samuel HUSON and died January 31, 1908. They are buried in Hayt's cemetery.
Children:
      i- SMITH Eva born September 11, 1860 (blind), moved to Auburn, NY after parents died.
445-    ii- SMITH Lizzie A. born 1868

232-    SMITH Abigail (*Robert T., Obadiah, Joshua, Jasper, John*) was born September 6, 1836 daughter of Robert T. SMITH and Hannah NORTON and died in Willow Creek, NY September 15, 1905. She married February 8, 1860 Amos T. HOPKINS who was born December 26, 1832 son of Thomas and Caroline G. HOPKINS and died May 30, 1915. They are buried in Hayt's cemetery in Ithaca, NY
Children:
      i- HOPKINS Ella Mae born May 19, 1863 and died December 8, 1875, buried Hayt's cemetery
446-    ii- HOPKINS Milo C. born September 26, 1866
447-    iii- HOPKINS Fred born March 29, 1868
448-    iv- HOPKINS Nettie B. born July 27, 1873
449-    v- HOPKINS Thomas born January 2, 1877
450-    vi- HOPKINS Pearl born November 21, 1881

233-    SMITH William C. (*Clement, Obadiah, Joshua, Jasper, John*) was born November 20, 1831 in Covert, NY son of Clement H. SMITH and Lucy SAVAGE and died September 14, 1859. He married Didenia (or Cordella) ROBINSON
One child:
451-    i- SMITH Clement D. born 1855

234-    SMITH Elizabeth (*Clement, Obadiah, Joshua, Jasper, John*) was born 1836 in Covert, NY daughter of Clement H. SMITH and Lucy SAVAGE. She married Gabriel DRAKE born ca 1824 of S. Lansing, NY
Children:
      i- DRAKE Mary L. born ca 1860
      ii- DRAKE Charles C. born ca 1864
      iii- DRAKE Edmond born January 1870

235-    SMITH Alonzo (*Clement, Obadiah, Joshua, Jasper, John*) was born April 17, 1840 in Covert, NY son of Clement H. SMITH and Lucy SAVAGE February 18, 1917. He married in Ulysses, NY Samantha KING who was born June 5, 1842 daughter of Asaph and Jane KING and died August 25, 1907. They are buried in Grove cemetery.
Children:
452-    i- SMITH William B. born May 6, 1864
      ii- SMITH Darwin L. born July 25, 1867 and died November 21, 1921, married Cora BARDWELL who died April 28, 1947
      iii- SMITH Alice B. born May 12, 1870 and died May 14, 1937. She married

November 24, 1872 George **BAKER** who died September 2, 1916, buried Grove cemetery. They had 1 child Lucie S. born February 5, 1899. She married December 13, 1917 Edgar W. **MAYES** born ca 1897 and died January 16, 1935. They are buried in Grove cemetery. They had one child Doris Evelyn born November 16, 1921

    iv- **SMITH** Anna E. born September 3, 1872, married Arthur **QUEAL** who was born 1874 and died October 20, 1935. They are buried in Grove cemetery.

236- **SMITH** Julia M. (*Clement, Obadiah, Joshua, Jasper, John*) was born 1843 in Covert, NY daughter of Clement H. **SMITH** and Lucy **SAVAGE** and died November 29, 1918. She married October 7, 1874 Thomas **VANN** who was born December 23, 1813 son of Samuel **VANN** and Mary **BOUND** and died March 31, 1893. They are buried in Grove cemetery.
One child:
453-     i- **VANN** Fred born July 1, 1880

237- **SMITH** Laura A. (*Clement, Obadiah, Joshua, Jasper, John*) was born 1844 daughter of Clement H. **SMITH** and Lucy **SAVAGE** and died 1930. She married Henry **TURNER** a native of England who was born 1844 and died 1936. He served in Co. F. 9th H. Art. Vol. in Civil War. They are buried in Pine Grove cemetery in Ludlowville, NY
One known child:
    i- **TURNER** Helen born ca 1868 married ____ **RASBECK**

238- **SMITH** Frances (*Clement, Obadiah, Joshua, Jasper, John*) was born July 29, 1848 in Covert, NY daughter of Clement H. **SMITH** and Lucy **SAVAGE** and died March 30, 1876. She married Will C. **BROTHERTON** who was born 1851 and died December 19, 1898.
One child:
    i- **BROTHERTON** son born March 18, 1876 and died April 16, 1876

239- **SMITH** Gilbert Cole (*John T., Obadiah, Joshua, Jasper, John*) was born July 27, 1839 in Covert, NY son of John T. **SMITH** and Emeline **COLE** and died July 13, 1899. He married Lola **OURY** who was born 1852 daughter of William Sanders **OURY** and Inez **GARCIA**.
Children:
454-     i- **SMITH** Cornelius Cole born April 7, 1869
455-     ii- **SMITH** Gilbert Cole Jr. born November 24, 1870
    iii- **SMITH** Inez born 1873 married Henry **BARBER** and had son Henry A. J. born July 31, 1896
456-     iv- **SMITH** Emeline born 1874
457-     v- **SMITH** William Oury born 1876

240- **SMITH** Delos H. (*John T., Obadiah, Joshua, Jasper, John*) was born December 1841 in Covert, NY son of John T. **SMITH** and Emeline **COLE**. He married Martha Matilda **MC CURDY** born January 1850 daughter of ____ and Harriet **MC CURDY**. Lived

Tucson, Az. 1880
Children:
> i- SMITH F. Mc Curdy born 1872 in Cal.
> ii- SMITH Jessie A. born November 1877 in NM
> iii- SMITH Delos H. Jr. born May 1884 in NM

241-    SMITH Athena (*John T., Obadiah, Joshua, Jasper, John*) was born March 14, 1845 in Lodi, NY daughter of John T. SMITH and Emeline COLE and died February 18, 1909 in Monterey, Mass. She married William H. TUFTS born September 1849 in St. Louis, Mo. son of Almanza TUFTS and Sarah MELLEN.
Children:
> i- TUFTS Clara M. born April 1877 in Great Barrington, Mass., married September 20, 1900 Judson C. LOGAN of Westborough, Mass. born 1877 in Nova Scotia son of Rupert Judson LOGAN and Esther Fisher BURRS. Unknown children
> ii- TUFTS Emeline C. born September 15, 1879 in Washington, DC

242-    SMITH Emeline (*John T., Obadiah, Joshua, Jasper, John*) was born June 3, 1849 in Tompkins Co. NY daughter of John T. SMITH and Margaret GILMORE and died in Penn Yan, NY 1917. She married October 11, 1865 Wolcott COLE who was born February 28, 1849 in Jerusalem, NY son of John COLE and Jane GILMORE and died August 11, 1935 in Penn Yan, NY. He married (2) August 28, 1918 Janet MC MINN born 1881 in Penn Yan, NY daughter of Thomas MC MINN. They are buried in Lakeview cemetery.
Children by first marriage:
> i- COLE Albert A. born August 13, 1868 and died November 25, 1882, buried Lakeview cemetery
458-    ii- COLE Lewis M. born March 1870
> iii- COLE Herman born 1872, died May 15, 1920 in Geneva, NY
> iv- COLE Harman born July 14, 1872 and died September 12, 1873, buried Lakeview cemetery
459-    v- COLE Emma born ca 1875
> vi- COLE Wilkie born December 25, 1876 and died February 13, 1877, buried in Lakeview cemetery
460-    vii- COLE Wolcott Jr. born 1878 in Penn Yan, NY
> viii- COLE Carrie born July 15, 1880

243-    SMITH Herman Towne (*John T., Obadiah, Joshua, Jasper, John*) was born August 8, 1864 son of John T. SMITH and Margaret GILMORE and died April 6, 1944. He married Eva TAYLOR who was born June 13, 1875 daughter of _____ and Mary TAYLOR and died October 23, 1947. They are buried in Grove cemetery.
Children:
> i- SMITH Francis Wilbur born 1903 and died August 25, 1903 in Covert, NY, buried Grove cemetery
> ii- SMITH Marguerite born July 15, 1904 and died April 11, 1906 in Covert, NY,

buried in Grove cemetery

    iii- **SMITH** Edna May born December 7, 1906

461-    iv- **SMITH** Frank Taylor born March 12, 1909

    v- **SMITH** Marion Herman born March 5, 1912

462-    vi- **SMITH** Alfred John born January 30, 1913

244-    **SMITH** Mary Jane (*Joshua, Annanias, Joshua, Jasper, John*) was born 1817/9 in Tompkins Co. NY daughter of Joshua and Peggy **SMITH** and died in Athen, Pa. March 2, 1886. She married Ira M. **WOLCOTT** who was born 1819 and died December 14, 1897. He served in Co. C. 71st Reg. Pa Vol.

One child:

463-    i- **WOLCOTT** Tompkins Smith born July 1845

245-    **SMITH** Priscilla (*Joshua, Annanias, Joshua, Jasper, John*) was born 1811 in Enfield, NY daughter of Joshua and Peggy **SMITH** and died October 15, 1878 in Clinton Co. Mi. She married November 1, 1827 in Enfield, NY Alfred H. **LYON** who was born September 16, 1805 in Tompkins Co. son of Samuel **LYON** and Sarah **MERRITT** and died in Clinton Co. Mi. 1859. They are buried in the Bray cemetery in Bengel Twp. Mi.

Children born in Enfield, NY:

464-    i- **LYON** Lorenzo M. born September 27, 1828

    ii- **LYON** Ellen A. born 1831

465-    iii- **LYON** William H. born 1836

466-    iv- **LYON** Francis J. born April 10, 1838

467-    v- **LYON** Edward H. born April 13, 1843

    vi- **LYON** Lovina born 1848

246-    **SMITH** Lovina (*Joshua, Annanias, Joshua, Jasper, John*) was born July 9, 1813 in Tompkins Co. NY daughter of Joshua and Peggy **SMITH** and died November 27, 1887 in Bengal, Mi. She married Miles **GEORGIA** who was born December 13, 1812 son of Elijah and Hila Ann **GEORGIA** and died August 13, 1891 in Bengal Mi. They are buried in the Georgia cemetery in Bengal.

Children:

    i- **GEORGIA** Priscilla S. born 1838

468-    ii- **GEORGIA** Sarah C. born 1844

469-    iii- **GEORGIA** Schuyler born 1846 and died 1931

    iv- **GEORGIA** Clarissa born February 1, 1849 and died September 21, 1871, buried Georgia cemetery. She married Phillip **DAVID** and had 2 children Nora and Emerantha

470-    v- **GEORGIA** William W. born October 8, 1850

247-    **SMITH** Lewis Hartsough (*Joshua, Annanias, Joshua, Jasper, John*) was born October 9, 1816 in Ulysses, NY son of Joshua and Peggy **SMITH** and died November 28, 1890 in Newfield, NY. He married March 7, 1841 Mary Lewis **BRAGAW** who was born December 6, 1819 in Poughkeepsie, NY daughter of Samuel **BRAGAW** and Anna

COVENHOVEN and died November 18, 1871, buried Trumbull's Corners cemetery.
Children born in Newfield, NY:
471-     i- SMITH Margaret Anna born September 22, 1843
         ii- SMITH Edgar born 1846 and died September 17, 1848
472-    iii- SMITH Helen born December 25, 1847
473-    iv- SMITH Tompkins born January 7, 1851
474-     v- SMITH Elizabeth born December 15, 1859
         vi- SMITH Mary E. born 1860 and died March 29, 1864

248-    SMITH Daniel D. Tompkins (*Joshua, Annanias, Joshua, Jasper, John*) was born
1821 in Tompkins Co. NY son of Joshua and Peggy SMITH and died May 14, 1893. He
married Sarah GEORGIA who was born 1821 daughter of Elijah B. and Hila Ann
GEORGIA and removed to Bengal Twp. Mi. by 1860. Unknown children

249-    SMITH George Washington (*Peter, Annanias, Joshua, Jasper, John*) was born ca
1814 in Tompkins Co. NY son of Peter and Elizabeth SMITH and died May 30, 1872 in
Buffalo, NY. He married Maria Catherine HICKS who was born July 4, 1817 daughter of
John B. HICKS and Corintha PARSONS and died March 12, 1905. They are buried in
Forest Lawn cemetery in Buffalo, NY.
Children:
475-     i- SMITH Elizabeth C. born October 12, 1837
         ii- SMITH Edwin R. died June 8, 1861 age 7 yrs 7 mos.
        iii- SMITH Louisa M. died June 15, 1861

250-    SMITH Christina G. (*Peter, Annanias, Joshua, Jasper, John*) was born 1816 in
Tompkins Co. NY daughter of Peter SMITH and Elizabeth MOORE and died August 29,
1897 in Buffalo, NY. She married June 11, 1835 in Ulysses, NY Henry INMAN who was
born 1802 and died July 2, 1865. They are buried in Forest Lawn cemetery in Buffalo. She
married (2) ____ MC LANE.
Children born in Buffalo, NY:
         i- INMAN William H. born 1837 and died 1855
         ii- INMAN Maria E. born 1839
476-    iii- INMAN George H. born 1841

251-    SMITH William Henry (*Peter, Annanias, Joshua, Jasper, John*) was born 1826 in
Tompkins Co. NY son of Peter SMITH and Elizabeth MOORE and died December 1,
1868. His wife Emily A. was born 1828.
Children born probably in Buffalo, NY:
         i- SMITH Ella C. born 1851
         ii- SMITH Mary E. born 1853 married ____ GRIFFIN
        iii- SMITH Julia A. born 1858

252-    LANNING Gideon (*Nancy, Annanias, Joshua, Jasper, John*) was born 1827 in Pa.
son of Elias LANNING and Nancy SMITH and died August 29, 1908 in Ithaca, NY age 81

yrs 6 mos. His wife Julia C. was born 1841 and died 1918. They are buried in Hayt's cemetery, Ithaca.
Children:
477-    i- LANNING Nellie born ca 1876

253-    GANOUNG Lovisa (*Elizabeth, Annanias, Joshua, Jasper, John*) was born 1826 in Tompkins Co. NY daughter of Ezra GANOUNG and Elizabeth SMITH. She married John KENNEDY who was born November 30, 1819 in Tompkins Co. and died October 7, 1875, buried in Hayt's cemetery in Ithaca. She married (2) Joseph CASTERLINE.
One child:
        i- KENNEDY Marion C. born 1864, married _____ RAWSON and removed to Indianapolis, Ind.

254-    SMITH William Henry (*Benjamin, Annanias, Joshua, Jasper, John*) was born 1822 son of Benjamin SMITH and Charlotte GIBB and died October 14, 1908. His wife Lovina was born 1841 and died 1906 in Hillsdale, Mi. They are buried in Oak Grove cemetery.
One known child born Hillsdale, Mi.:
        i- SMITH Lottie L. who married _____ MARVIN

255-    SMITH John H. (*Benjamin, Annanias, Joshua, Jasper, John*) was born 1837 in Tompkins Co. NY son of Benjamin SMITH and Charlotte GIBB and died August 28, 1899 in Hillsdale, Mi., buried Oak Grove cemetery. He married Lucinda (unknown maiden name) born July 1840. She married (2) _____ NORTH
        i- SMITH Edward J. born ca 1863 in Ohio, moved to Clary, ND (from obit for father)
        ii- SMITH Kate born ca 1878, married _____ LENNON of Council Bluffs, ND

256-    SMITH James Tuttle (*Benjamin, Annanias, Joshua, Jasper, John*) was born ca 1847 in Tompkins Co. NY son of Benjamin SMITH and Charlotte GIBB and died April 1902 New Rockford, ND. He was buried in Oak Grove cemetery in Hillsdale, Mi. His first wife Martha A. was born December 29, 1844 and died November 17, 1868. His second wife Ellen was born May 1852 and died June 7, 1900. Unknown children.

257-    SUMMERTON Thomas L. (*Sally, Annanias, Joshua, Jasper, John*) was born in Enfield, NY February 18, 1829 son of John SUMMERTON and Sally SMITH. He married September 23, 1851 Mary Jane HARVEY born July 24, 1813 in Plainfield, NY daughter of Amasa HARVEY and Clara ACKLEY and died March 27, 1880.
Children possibley born in Catherine, NY:
478-    i- SUMMERTON Irettie born ca 1853
479-    ii- SUMMERTON Olive Rose born April 27, 1855
        iii- SUMMERTON Margrette born ca 1857
        iv- SUMMERTON Eldora born ca 1859
        v- SUMMERTON Elvira born ca 1859
        vi- SUMMERTON Mary L. born ca 1870

258- **SUMMERTON** Alonzo (*Sally, Annanias, Joshua, Jasper, John*) was born 1835 in Tompkins Co. NY son of John **SUMMERTON** and Sally **SMITH**. He is listed in the 1880 census in Clay, Winnebago Co. Wis. age 43 born NY and wife Pauline age 33 years. Children listed in 1880 census:

    i- **SUMMERTON** Frederick born ca 1865
    ii- **SUMMERTON** George W. born ca 1867
    iii- **SUMMERTON** Florence born ca 1868
    iv- **SUMMERTON** Daisy born ca 1870
    v- **SUMMERTON** Mary E. born ca 1872
    vi- **SUMMERTON** Lina born ca 1874
    vii- **SUMMERTON** Edward born ca 1877

259- **SUMMERTON** Nancy (*Sally, Annanias, Joshua, Jasper, John*) was born May 1839 in Enfield, NY daughter of John **SUMMERTON** and Sally **SMITH**. She married Samuel N. **FOWLER** born 1836, died before 1900.
Children:

    i- **FOWLER** Mary A. born 1861
    ii- **FOWLER** Nancy A. born June 1863, married Cassius **BREED** born June 1862.
They had daughter Alma **BREED** born May 1886 and were living in Moravia, NY in 1900

### Seventh Generation

260- **SKIRM** Charles Henry (*Eliza Fish, Sarah, John, John, Jasper, John*) was born July 29, 1832 in Ewing, NJ son of Abram **SKIRM** and Eliza **FISH** and died October 25, 1907. He married 1856 Elizabeth T. **WHITE** born ca 1836 in Lawrenceville, NJ daughter of Job **WHITE** and Mary C. **HOWELL**.
Children:
480-    i- **SKIRM** William H. born December 12, 1856
    ii- **SKIRM** Robert H. born April 30, 1860, married Annie **STOCKTON**
    iii- **SKIRM** Ferdinand R. born October 30, 1866 and died May 30, 1885
    iv- **SKIRM** Benjamin born June 3, 1869

261- **SKIRM** Ferdinand (*Eliza Fish, Sarah, John, John, Jasper, John*) was born April 30, 1836 in NJ son of Abram **SKIRM** and Eliza **FISH** and died May 13, 1885. Spouse unknown.
Known children:

    i- **SKIRM** Mary E. born September 1, 1863 and died November 14, 1863
    ii- **SKIRM** Lewis R. born April 9, 1865 and died February 7, 1866

262- **SMITH** James Henry (*Joseph Gardiner, Daniel, Jasper, John, Jasper, John*) was born March 16, 1805 in Littletown, NJ son of Joseph Gardiner **SMITH** and Mary **CASTERLINE** and died August 1887 in Westminister, Cal. He married April 4, 1833 in Pompton Plains, NJ Hannah **VAN WAGONER** who was born April 4, 1815 in Pompton Plains, NJ daughter of Halmagh Johannes **VAN WAGONER** and Hannah **VAN HOUTEN** and died October 26, 1901 in Provo, Utah. They are buried in Provo.
Children:
481-     i- **SMITH** Halma James born March 31, 1834
        ii- **SMITH** Josiah born April 9, 1836 and died May 1, 1914 in Orange Cal. He married (1) Sarah Jane **JOHNSON** born ca 1836 and married (2) ____ **AUDIE** born ca 1836
482-    iii- **SMITH** Hyrum born April 2, 1838
483-    iv- **SMITH** John born April 6, 1840
484-     v- **SMITH** Sarah Ann born September 11, 1842
485-    vi- **SMITH** Mary Emma born May 21, 1845
486-   vii- **SMITH** Joseph born January 11, 1848 in Salt Lake City
487-  viii- **SMITH** Hannah Eunice born June 8, 1852 in Big Cottonwood, Utah
        ix- **SMITH** James Henry Jr. born March 28, 1853 in Big Cottonwood, Utah and died January 6, 1889 in Provo, Utah
488-     x- **SMITH** Henry born May 19, 1854 in Big Cottonwood, Utah 489-        xi- **SMITH** William Edwin born September 5, 1857 in Big Cottonwood, Utah

263-    **BREARLEY** Caroline (*Mehitabel, Asher, Jasper, John, Jasper, John*) was born February 23, 1825 in NJ daughter of James **BREARLEY** and Mehitabel **SMITH** and died March 29, 1891. She married January 1847 David **LANNING** who was born 1819 in NJ son of Ralph **LANNING** and Mary **WYNKOOP** and died February 9, 1889 in Trenton, NJ. They are buried in the Presbyterian cemetery.
Children born in NJ:
        i- **LANNING** Mary E. born 1849 and died March 29, 1853
        ii- **LANNING** James B. born ca 1854 Mercer Co. NJ
        iii- **LANNING** Eveline born October 3, 1860
        iv- **LANNING** Eva born ca 1861 in Ewing Twp. NJ

264-    **BREARLEY** Charles (*Mehitabel, Asher, Jasper, John, Jasper, John*) was born November 4, 1822 in Lawrenceville, NJ son of James **BREARLEY** and Mehitabel **SMITH**. He married (1) July 7, 1849 Sarah **BURKE** born ca 1826 daughter of William **BURKE** and married (2) June 2, 1873 Annie B. **SLOAN**.
Child by first marriage:
        i- **BREARLEY** Elizabeth born October 3, 1852 and married Robert W. **KENNEDY**

265-    **BREARLEY** George (*Mehitabel, Asher, Jasper, John, Jasper, John*) was born ca 1824 in Lawrenceville, NJ son of James **BREARLEY** and Mehitabel **SMITH**. He married January 7, 1852 Jane Stevens **PHILLIPS** born October 29, 1827 in Lawrenceville, NJ daughter of James Armstrong **PHILLIPS** and Catherine **STEVENS** (see #130)

Children born in Trenton, NJ:

      i- **BREARLEY** Joseph G. born January 27, 1853 and married December 26, 1883 Julia A. **BARNES** of Philadelphia, Pa.

      ii- **BREARLEY** Mabel born March 14, 1855 and married September 23, 1879 George **HOTTEL** born ca 1843

      iii- **BREARLEY** Ellen born November 15, 1859 and married October 23, 1878 Roland **LLOYD** born ca 1845

490-    iv- **BREARLEY** Julia Florence born January 12, 1864

      v- **BREARLEY** Mary born May 17, 1866

      vi- **BREARLEY** Angeline L. born January 10, 1875

266-    **ANDERSON** Catherine (*Mary Clark, Hannah, Jasper, John, Jasper, John*) was born ca 1816 in NJ daughter of Joshua **ANDERSON** and Mary **CLARK**. She married February 25, 1835 Amos H. **REEDER** who was born March 2, 1810 son of Amos **REEDER** and Rachel **FOLWELL** and died April 12, 1898 in Ewing, NJ.

One known child:

      i- **REEDER** Alfred M. born February 19, 1836 in Ewing, NJ. He married (1) Margaret A. **COVERT** born ca 1840 and died before 1880. He married (2) Cornelia **JONES** born July 11, 1838 daughter of Enoch **JONES** and Margaret **HART**.

267-    **SCUDDER** Edward Wallace (*Jasper Scudder, Sarah, Jasper, John, Jasper, John*) was born August 11, 1822 in Scudder's Falls, NJ son of Jasper Smith **SCUDDER** and Mary Stillwell **REEDER** and died 1893. He married May 23, 1848 Mary Louisa **DRAKE** who was born November 30, 1823 and died January 20, 1890.

Children born in NJ:

      i- **SCUDDER** Edward D. born ca 1849, married Elizabeth **HEWITT**

      ii- **SCUDDER** Henry Darcy born ca 1851, married Marvina **DAVIS**

491-    iii- **SCUDDER** Wallace Mc Ilvaine born December 26, 1853

      iv- **SCUDDER** George D. born ca 1855, married Helen **DAMARIN**

      v- **SCUDDER** Mary born ca 1857

      vi- **SCUDDER** Louisa born ca 1858

268-    **MERSHON** Frances Shreve (*Samuel Mershon, Prudence, Jasper, John, Jasper, John*) was born March 31, 1828 in NJ daughter of Samuel D. **Mershon** and Mary **SHREVE** and died February 1, 1878. She married Randall **HUTCHINSON** who was born ca 1823 and died November 29, 1855. They are buried in Lawrence cemetery in Lawrenceville.

Children:

492-    i- **HUTCHINSON** Mary C. born ca 1848

493-    ii- **HUTCHINSON** Samuel born ca 1849

494-    iii- **HUTCHINSON** Henrietta born ca 1850

      iv- **HUTCHINSON** Nettie L. born ca 1856

      v- **HUTCHINSON** Randall born ca 1860 (in the 1880 census he was living with his sister Nettie L. **HUTCHINSON** born ca 1856)

269- **MERSHON** Louisa (*Samuel Mershon, Prudence, Jasper, John, Jasper, John*) was born March 17, 1832 in NJ daughter of Samuel D. **MERSHON** and Mary **SHREVE**. She married February 7, 1856 Edward P. **BREARLEY** born November 27, 1832 in NJ son of Harvey **BREARLEY** and Ann C. **MOORE**.
Children born in Lawrenceville, NJ:
    i- **BREARLEY** George J. born September 14, 1857. He married January 26, 1884 Madge **EWING** of Lawndate, Ill.
    ii- **BREARLEY** Samuel M. born February 10, 1860 and died in Rahway, NJ
    iii- **BREARLEY** Jasper M. born November 21, 1861
    iv- **BREARLEY** Juliet born ca 1863
    v- **BREARLEY** Edward S. born ca 1865
    vi- **BREARLEY** Louis G. born ca 1867

270- **PHILLIPS** William Wilson Lata (*George Phillips, Sarah, Joshua, John, Jasper, John*) was born ca 1830 in Lawrenceville, NJ son of George **PHILLIPS** and Abigail **KETCHAM**. He married (1) Margaret **MC KELWAY** born ca 1825 in Trenton, NJ daughter of John and Isabella **MC KELWAY** and he married (2) Meta **MC ALPINE** born in Pa. ca 1840 daughter of Alexander **MC ALPINE**.
Child by first marriage:
    i- **PHILLIPS** Isabella born ca 1862. She married Joseph **THOMPSON** born ca 1860 in May's Landing, NJ
Children by second marriage:
    i- **PHILLIPS** Helen born ca 1868
    ii- **PHILLIPS** William Wilson Lata Jr. born ca 1870
    iii- **PHILLIPS** Mc Alpine born ca 1872

271- **PHILLIPS** Ephraim (*George Phillips, Sarah, Joshua, John, Jasper, John*) was born ca 1832 in Lawrenceville, NJ son of George **PHILLIPS** and Abigail **KETCHAM**. He married Mary **MC CLURE** who was born ca 1840 and died before 1880.
Children:
    i- **PHILLIPS** William E. born ca 1857
    ii- **PHILLIPS** Walter S. born ca 1861
    iii- **PHILLIPS** George E. born ca 1864 (not in 1880 census)
495-    iv- **PHILLIPS** Robert Hazlett Cummings born ca 1865
    v- **PHILLIPS** Mary A. B. born ca 1867
    vi- **PHILLIPS** Emma B. born ca 1867

272- **FEASTER** Ephraim P. (*Mary Phillips, Sarah, Joshua, John, Jasper, John*) was born November 15, 1841 in Northumberland, Pa. son of David **FEASTER** and Mary **PHILLIPS** and died in Newtown, Pa. He married April 19, 1864 Elizabeth **MC MAKIN** born January 31, 1845 in Philadelphia, Pa. daughter of Joseph **MC MAKIN** and Elizabeth **SMITH**.
Children:
    i- **FEASTER** David born ca 1864
    ii- **FEASTER** Frank born ca 1865

iii- **FEASTER** Lizzie C. born ca 1866
iv- **FEASTER** Joseph born ca 1867
v- **FEASTER** Dora born ca 1868
vi- **FEASTER** Agnes born ca 1869
vii- **FEASTER** Beatrice born ca 1870

273- **SMITH** Edgar (*Charles, William, Joshua, John, Jasper, John*) was born ca 1868 in NJ son of Charles **SMITH** and Martha Hughes **SMITH**. He married Nellie **CASE** born ca 1870.
Children:
    i- **SMITH** Irving born ca 1891
    ii- **SMITH** Lalor born ca 1892

274- **SMITH** Charles H. (*Charles, William, Joshua, John, Jasper, John*) was born ca 1870 in NJ son of Charles **SMITH** and Martha Hughes **SMITH**. He married Harriet Cunningham **MAPLE** who was born ca 1876 in NJ daughter of Jefferson Roe **MAPLE** and Anna Mary **DEY** and died January 2, 1951.
    i- **SMITH** Stanley M. born Janaury 22, 1901 in Lawrenceville, NY, married Grace **UPDIKE** and had 2 children
    ii- **SMITH** Edgar Leroy born May 13, 1902, married November 17, 1920 Margaret (unknown maiden name)
    iii- **SMITH** Albert born September 1903
    iv- **SMITH** Jefferson Russell born September 23, 1904, married February 17, 1927 Mary **KERR**
    v- **SMITH** Charles Hartwell born December 9, 1906 (He and his wife adopted a son and named him Chris **SMITH**)
    vi- **SMITH** Elmer Norris born March 25, 1908
    vii- **SMITH** William Carleton born June 15, 1909 and died October 5, 1942
    viii- **SMITH** Hattie Cunningham born June 14, 1911 and died October 20, 1917
    ix- **SMITH** Eleanor May born August 19, 1914 and died Aptil 7, 1915
    x- **SMITH** Lester Raymond born May 7, 1916
    xi- **SMITH** Martha Lillian born November 15, 1917, married Robert W. **DAVIS**

275- **WOODS** Harry A. (*Amanda, William, Joshua, John, Jasper, John*) was born ca 1870 in Trenton, NJ son of James **WOODS** and Amanda **SMITH**. He married Ida H. **NEFF** born ca 1875 in Trenton, NJ daughter of William **NEFF** and Elizabeth **HENCKIN**.
One child:
    i- **WOODS** Harry James born ca 1896

276- **WOODS** Barton H. (*Amanda, William, Joshua, John, Jasper, John*) was born ca 1872 in NJ son of James **WOODS** and Amanda **SMITH**. He married Julia Ann **LINCOLN** born February 10, 1871 daughter of Geroge Dwight **LINCOLN** and Charlotte **VANDEVEER**.
One known child:

i- WOODS Lester Lincoln born ca 1899

277-    COOK Caroline Wyncoop (*Absolom Cook, Keziah, Joshua, John, Jasper, John*) was born ca 1843 in Pennington, NJ daughter of Absolom Price COOK and Margaret WYNKOOP.  She married September 17, 1867 Charles CRAVEN born January 26, 1843 son of James R. CRAVEN and Mary CORNELL.
Children born NJ:
    i- CRAVEN William born ca 1868 married Jennie GARNER born ca 1873 in Williamsport, Pa.
    ii- CRAVEN Abraham Lincoln born ca 1869
    iii- CRAVEN Thomas born ca 1870
    iv- CRAVEN Fred born ca 1871
    v- CRAVEN Samuel born ca 1872
    vi- CRAVEN Charles Edgar born ca 1885, married May 22, 1912 Elizabeth TAYLOR born ca 1887 and died December 3, 1973, 2 children

278-    COOK Amanda (*George Cook, Keziah, Joshua, John, Jasper, John*) was born January 2, 1844 in NJ daughter of George Rea COOK and Rebecca Elizabeth BLACKWELL.  She married Vincent PERRINE born ca 1844.
Children:
    i- PERRINE Norman born ca 1867, not listed in 1880 census
    ii- PERRINE Cora D. born ca 1869, married Jacob WETHERILL born ca 1866 in Monmouth Co. NJ
    iii- PERRINE Catherine born ca 1873

279-    COOK Thomas B. (*George Cook, Keziah, Joshua, John, Jasper, John*) was born May 18, 1847 in NJ son of George Rea COOK and Rebecca Elizabeth BLACKWELL.  He married Mary COLEMAN born ca 1852
Children:
    i- COOK George R. born 1870 in Hopewell, NJ, married Emma SMITH born 1872 (see #108)
    ii- COOK Ida May born ca 1876

280-    COOK Daniel Livingston (*George Cook, Keziah, Joshua, John, Jasper, John*) was born ca 1854 in NJ son of George Rea COOK and Rebecca Elizabeth BLACKWELL.  He married Elizabeth COOMBS born 1853
Children born NJ:
    i- COOK Mildred R. born ca 1875 married Addison STULTS born February 27, 1871 in Cranbury, NJ son of Jacob and Cornelia STULTS
    ii- COOK Sarah C. born ca 1877
    iii- COOK Merta S. born ca 1880

281-    COOK Hiram Augustus (*George Cook, Keziah, Joshua, John, Jasper, John*) was born ca 1861 in NJ son of George Rea COOK and Rebecca Elizabeth BLACKWELL.  He

married Carrie **SHANGLE** born October 6, 1854 daughter of Frederick **SHANGLE** Sr. and Catherine Amanda **UPDYKE**.
Children:
    i- **COOK** Frederick born ca 1878
    ii- **COOK** Hattie born ca 1879
    iii- **COOK** Alice born ca 1880
    iv- **COOK** Sadie born ca 1881
    v- **COOK** Reba born ca 1882
    vi- **COOK** George R. born ca 1883
    vii- **COOK** Carrie born ca 1884

282- **COOK** Emma Skillman (*Lewis Cook, Keziah, Joshua, John, Jasper, John*) was born February 11, 1853 in NJ daughter of Lewis D. **COOK** and died January 27, 1897. She married William W. **SMALLEY** who was born December 17, 1850 son of John **SMALLEY** and Elizabeth **WINDSOR** and died December 27, 1916 in Bound Brook, NJ. They are buried in Bound Brook Presbyterian cemetery. He was State Senator 1908-1916. He married (2) her sister Jessie **COOK** who was born January 21, 1870 and died March 25, 1928
Children:
    i- **SMALLEY** George Oakley born March 1885 and died January 16, 1956 in Boundbrook, NJ. He married May 15, 1912 Bertha Evelyn **EDGERTON** who was born October 8,. 1889 in Felton, Del. daughter of William Wallace **EDGERTON** and Sarah **HARDY** and died February 1973 in Bound Brook, NJ. They are buried in Mountain Ave. cemetery
    ii- **SMALLEY** Ethel C. born November 1883 and died 1957. She married John Clarence **MILLER** born 1879 and died 1951. They are buried in Mountain Ave. cemetery in Bound Brook, NJ.

283- **COOK** Charles Howell (*Edmund Cook, Keziah, Joshua, John, Jasper, John*) was born ca 1857 in Hopewell, NJ son of Edmund Burroughs **COOK** and Sarah D. **HOWELL**. He married Lucy **BRADY** born ca 1860 daughter of Henry **BRADY**
One known child:
    I- **COOK** Lucy born ca 1883

284- **COOK** George R. (*Edmund Cook, Keziah, Joshua, John, Jasper, John*) was born ca 1858 in Hopewell, NJ son of Edmund Burroughs **COOK** and Sarah D. **HOWELL** and died in Trenton, NJ. He married Mary **TAYLOR** born ca 1862 in Morrisville, Pa. daughter of Joseph **TAYLOR**.
Children:
    i- **COOK** Eleanor born ca 1885
    ii- **COOK** Horace born ca 1886
    iii- **COOK** Donald

285- **COOK** Edmund Dunham (*Edmund Cook, Keziah, Joshua, John, Jasper, John*) was

born ca 1859 in NJ son of Edmund Burroughs **COOK** and Sarah D. **HOWELL** and died
May 9, 1909. He married Margaret **PARSONS** born ca 1862.
Children:
    i- **COOK** Ruth
    ii- **COOK** Charlotte
    iii- **COOK** Edmund
    iv- **COOK** George
    v- **COOK** Margaret

286-   **LANNING** Jasper P. (*William Lanning, Jasper Lanning, Elizabeth, John, Jasper,
John*) was born 1842 in Tompkins Co. NY son of William **LANNING** and Rebecca H.
**TABOR**. He married Sarah E. **WALLENBECK** born ca 1848 daughter of Morgan
**WALLENBECK**.
Children:
    i- **LANNING** Thersa married D. J. **SMITH**
    ii- **LANNING** John born 1866 and died 1869, buried Rolfe cemetery
496-   iii- **LANNING** Lura born ca 1867
497-   iv- **LANNING** Anthela born 1869
498-   v- **LANNING** Charles Wesley born March 7, 1874 in Enfield. He was a Dr. and
lived in Herkimer, NY in 1948
499-   vi- **LANNING** Florence born 1876
500-   vii- **LANNING** Bertha born December 22, 1878
501-   viii- **LANNING** Edna Mae born 1881
502-   ix- **LANNING** Francis L. born 1883 in Enfield, NY

287-   **TUCKER** William (*Caroline Lanning, Jasper Lanning, Elizabeth, John, Jasper,
John*) was born 1841 in Enfield, NY son of Ezra **TUCKER** and Caroline **LANNING** and
died 1926. He married April 1863 Adelia **HOSNER** of Enfield. William is buried in Grove
cemetery with 2nd wife Mary **WARNER** born 1842 and died 1920.
Children by first marriage:
    i- **TUCKER** Carrie B. born 1866 (see #607)
    ii- **TUCKER** Adeline born 1871
    iii- **TUCKER** Olive born 1874 married John **RITEMORE** and had 1 child Delia
    iv- **TUCKER** Jennie born 1876

288-   **TUCKER** Mary Jane (*Caroline Lanning, Jasper. Lanning, Elizabeth, John, Jasper,
John*) was born 1839 in Enfield, NY daughter of Ezra **TUCKER** and Caroline **LANNING**.
She married (1) April 4, 1897 John **DOOLITTLE** who was born 1828 in Newfield, NY.
She married (2) Clarence **DICKENS** who was born March 27, 1852 in Catherine, NY son of
Robert **DICKENS** and Lydia **BEEBE**. He married (1) Hulda **DEPEW** who died March 19,
1887 and had 2 children Howard and Emily
    Children by Mary J.:
    i- **DOOLITTLE** Jay lived in Farmer, Seneca Co., married Carrie **BENNETT** and
had 2 children Oliver and Walter

    ii- **DOOLITTLE** Frank live in Farmer, Seneca Co. and married Mary **TURNER**, 2 children Lottie and Helen

    iii- **DOOLITTLE** Fred lived in Farmer, Seneca Co. and married Kate **WOOD**, 2 children Albert and Hazel

    iv- **DOOLITTLE** Edith married William **GRAVES** of Montour Falls, NY and had son Elmer

      v- **DOOLITTLE** Charles

     vi- **DOOLITTLE** Evelyn


289-    **PHILLIPS** Robert Phares (*Elizabeth Stevens, Thomas Stevens Jr., Catherine, Jasper Jr., Jasper, John*) was born November 17, 1837 in Princeton, NJ son of Benjamin Mershon **PHILLIPS** and Elizabeth **STEVENS**. He married Mary **MIDDLETON** born ca 1840 daughter of ____ and Ida L. **MIDDLETON**.
Children:

     i- **PHILLIPS** Nellie born ca 1868

    ii- **PHILLIPS** Catherine born ca 1871


290-    **PHILLIPS** Ellen (*Catherine Stevens, Thomas Stevens Jr., Catherine, Jasper Jr., Jasper, John*) was born February 18, 1829 in Lawrencevile, NJ daughter of James Armstrong **PHILLIPS** and Catherine **STEVENS**. She married Benjamin F. **JOHNSTON** born ca 1825 in Lawrenceville, NJ, served in Co. H. 21st NJ Vol. in Civil War
One known Child born in Lawrenceville, NJ:

503-    i- **JOHNSTON** Cornelia Phillips born ca 1850


291-    **SMITH** Peter Ten Eyck (*Benjamin, Israel Jr., Israel, Jasper, Jasper, John*) was born ca 1843 in NJ son of Benjamin Clark **SMITH** and Sarah **SUTTON**. He married Caroline Louise **TEN EYCK** born ca 1845 in Delaware.
Children born in Delaware:

     i- **SMITH** Julia born ca 1869

    ii- **SMITH** Gertrude born ca 1871

   iii- **SMITH** Horace born ca 1876

504-    iv- **SMITH** Caroline Louise born November 3, 1877

     v- **SMITH** Katherine born ca 1880


292-    **SMITH** Ella Maria (*Benjamin, Israel Jr., Israel, Jasper, Jasper, John*) was born October 14, 1847 in Philadelphia, Pa. daughter of Benjamin Clark **SMITH** and Sarah **SUTTON** and died 1908. She married in Philadelphia October 21, 1874 Charles **BOOTH** who was born 1842 and died September 15, 1892 in Lansdowne, Pa.
Children:

     i- **BOOTH** Lonita born ca 1876 in Pa.

    ii- **BOOTH** Elsie born September 17, 1879 in Md.

505-    iii- **BOOTH** Ella S. born July 25, 1882 in Wilmington, De. and died Phoenix, Arizona. She married Gideon T. **SMITHMAN** Jr.

293- **WHITE** John (*Mercy Tindall, Joseph Tindall, Abigail, Thomas, Jasper, John*) was born July 21, 1814 in Monmouth, NJ son of William **WHITE** and Mercy **TINDALL** and died February 7, 1884 in Hackettstown, NJ. He married January 31, 1835 in Monmouth Bethany S. **BIRD** who was born ca 1811 in NJ and died May 15, 1888.
Children born Monmouth Co. NJ:
506-      i- **WHITE** Sarah Clarissa born 1835
507-      ii- **WHITE** Hiram D. born June 9, 1837
        iii- **WHITE** William born ca 1839 and died 1920. He married Jennie A. **MARTIN** born 1846 and died 1928.
        iv- **WHITE** Fanny born ca 1842 and died 1922 in Hackettsvile, NJ. She married S. V. **FISHER** born NJ.
        v- **WHITE** Calarissa born ca 1846
        vi- **WHITE** Mercy born ca 1848 and died 1867 (of Linn Co. Mo.) married James **MARLATT** lived Pawnee Co. Ks. in 1880

294- **WHITE** Oziel (*Mercy Tindall, Joseph Tindall, Abigail, Thomas, Jasper, John*) was born June 18, 1827 in Monmouth, NJ son of William **WHITE** and Mercy **TINDALL** and died November 15, 1881 in Lamoille, Ill. His wife Minerva (unknown maiden name) was born ca 1831 in NJ.
Children born in Ill:
        i- **WHITE** George Marion born ca 1854
        ii- **WHITE** Elida R. born ca 1857
        iii- **WHITE** Charlie P. born ca 1859
        iv- **WHITE** Edson D. born ca 1868
        v- **WHITE** Persis born ca 1871

295- **WHITE** Margaret (*Mercy Tindall, Joseph Tindall, Abigail, Thomas, Jasper, John*) was born April 3, 1832 in Monmouth, NJ daughter of William **WHITE** and Mercy **TINDALL**. She married January 18, 1854 Joshua H. **CURTIS** of NJ.
Children born in NJ:
        i- **CURTIS** George Palmer born November 10, 1854. He married January 25, 1899 in NJ Mary Elizabeth **MUNSON** born NJ.
        ii- **CURTIS** Alice Eveline born July 22, 1856
        iii- **CURTIS** Joseph White born October 27, 1857. He married November 1, 1888 in NJ Sarah Dunn **BEATTY** of NJ.
        iv- **CURTIS** Albert Jehu born April 10, 1861 and died October 9, 1863
        v- **CURTIS** Frank Wallace born April 9, 1865. He married in NJ October 14, 1897 Alevia **HARTUNG** of NJ.

296- **SMITH** David Lofton (*James L., Thomas H., Elijah, Thomas, Jasper, John*) was born February 1844 in Ala. son of James Laughlin **SMITH** and Jane **MARTIN** and died August 23, 1912 in Conway Co. Ar. He married January 5, 1867 in Pontotoc, Ms. Susan Jane **BROWNING** who was born March 26, 1846 in Pontotoc Co. Ms. and died August 26, 1933 in Lollie, Ar., buried Conway Co.

82

Children:
    i- **SMITH** son
    ii- **SMITH** James Litton born 1867 and died 1947, married Mary L. **BROWNING**
508-   iii- **SMITH** George Martin born April 26, 1870 Pontotoc Co.
    iv- **SMITH** Nancy Jane born 1872, married Dempsy **HOOVER**
    v- **SMITH** John Thomas born 1874, married C. A. **LIPSCOMB**
    vi- **SMITH** Mary P. P. born 1877 and died 1949, married C. E. **WICKLIFFE**
    vii- **SMITH** Robert Bolden born 1882, married (1) Pearl **HOGAN** and (2) Ida **DAVIS**
    viii- **SMITH** Ira S. born 1885 and died 1946, married C. E. **HARVEY**
    ix- **SMITH** Walter Hamilton born 1888 and died 1950, married Minnie **BELK**

297-   **BERRY** Resin Bowie (*Susannah, Thomas H., Elijah, Thomas, Jasper, John*) was born 1828 in Bibb Co. Ala. son of Jarret L. **BERRY** and Susannah T. **SMITH** and died 1866 in Cotton Plant, Az. He married January 1, 1852 in Pontotoc Co., Ms. Christian **WARREN** who was born July 1832 in Tn.
Children:
    i- **BERRY** Susan S. born 1853 in Ms. married Thomas **WALDRON**
509-   ii- **BERRY** Joseph Henry born 1853 in Pontotoc Co. Ms.
    iii- **BERRY** Jarret E. born 1856 in Ms.

298-   **BERRY** Mary (*Susannah, Thomas H., Elijah, Thomas, Jasper, John*) was born 1832 in Bibb Co. Ala. daughter of Jarret L. **BERRY** and Susannah T. **SMITH** and died 1860 in Woodruff Co. Ark. She married April 4, 1852 in Pontotoc Co. Ms. Eli **STAGGS** who was born 1831 in Ala. and died August 1, 1866 in Woodruff Co. Ark.
Children:
    i- **STAGGS** Nancy J.
    ii- **STAGGS** Lewis
    iii- **STAGGS** Susan E. married December 19, 1876 in Woodruff Co. Ark. Elijah **SPRIGGS**
510-   iv- **STAGGS** George Birton born February 14, 1860

299-   **BERRY** Burton Litton (*Susannah, Thomas H., Elijah, Thomas, Jasper, John*) was born October 31, 1836 in Winston Co. Ms. son of Jarret L. **BERRY** and Susannah T. **SMITH** and died June 27, 1899 in Woodruff Co. Ar., buried Oddfellows cemetery. He married July 19, 1857 in Bayou Cache, Ar. Mary Jane **SELLERS** who was born September 6, 1843 in SC and died December 24, 1876. He married (2) March 18, 1877 in Augusta, Ar. Easter **CRAIG** who was born 1859 and died February 5, 1884. He married (3) October 19, 1884 in Woodruff Co. Ar. Mary Frances **HESS** who was born February 1865 in Ar. and died May 1930 in Memphis, Tx.
Children by first marriage born in Woodruff Co. Ark.:
511-   i- **BERRY** Martha J. born ca 1864
512-   ii- **BERRY** Willie A. born 1866
    iii- **BERRY** James Henry born November 9, 1869 and died December 21, 1963 in

83

Abilene, Tx. He married February 17, 1895 in Augusta, Ar. Lizzie **LANCASTER**
513- iv- **BERRY** Nannie May born October 18, 1871
v- **BERRY** Burton L. born August 20, 1874
vi- **BERRY** Elmore Jackson born November 27, 1876, married February 10, 1897 in Dallas, Tx. Willie M. **HARDWICK**
Children by second marriage born Mc Crory, Ark.:
514- vii- **BERRY** John Thomas born February 18, 1878
515- viii- **BERRY** Mary Elizabeth born January 1880 and died 1913 in Mc Crory, buried Oddfellows cemetery
Children by third marriage born Woodruff Co. Ark.:
516- ix- **BERRY** Burton E. born January 1886
x- **BERRY** Alfred born May 26, 1888
xi- **BERRY** Clayton Preston born March 4, 1890
xii- **BERRY** Ada born April 1892, married ____ **SMITH**
xiii- **BERRY** Eva Suzanne born February 28, 1894, married (1) Joseph **STRUDER** and (2) Ernest **SMITH**
xiv- **BERRY** infant buried in Oddfellows cemetery

300- **BERRY** Thomas Hunt (*Susannah, Thomas H., Elijah, Thomas, Jasper, John*) was born March 20, 1838 in Winston Co. Ms. son of Jarret L. **BERRY** and Susannah T. **SMITH** and died January 1, 1918 in Van Buren Co. Ar. He married Easter **STRACENER** who was born November 2, 1841 in Ala. and died April 26, 1886 in Wiville, Ar., buried in Stracener cemetery. He married (2) unknown and (3) Belle ____ born June 1850 in Ill.
Children by first marriage:
i- **BERRY** Elizabeth born ca 1889 in Ar.
ii- **BERRY** Mary E. born ca 1865 in Ar. married John B. **BEARD** born 1851 in Ar. and died 1890, had 1 daughter and 3 sons
iii- **BERRY** Georgia Ann born ca 1886
iv- **BERRY** Samuel
Children by second marriage:
v- **BERRY** Serena
vi- **BERRY** daughter
Children by third marriage:
vii- **BERRY** Myrtle born May 1892 in Ar.
viii- **BERRY** Walter born January 1896 in Ar.

301- **BERRY** Serena (*Susannah, Thomas H., Elijah, Thomas, Jasper, John*) was born ca 1840 in Winston Co. Ms. daughter of Jarret L. **BERRY** and Susannah T. **SMITH**. She married May 7, 1856 in Pontotoc Co. Ms. John Milton **STAGGS** born February 6, 1836.
Children:
i- **STAGGS** Mittie born ca 1856
ii- **STAGGS** Mary born ca 1861

302- **BERRY** Nancy Jane (*Susannah, Thomas H., Elijah, Thomas, Jasper, John*) was

born ca 1844 in Pontotoc Co. Ms. daughter of Jarret L. **BERRY** and Susannah T. **SMITH**. She married 1864 Eli **STAGGS** born 1831 in Ala. She married (2) in Woodruff Co. Ar. William T. **GILLIAM** born 1840 in Ala.
Children by first marriage born in Ar.:

      i- **STAGGS** Robert M. (twin) born March 10, 1866
517-    ii- **STAGGS** Florence Arminda (twin) born March 19, 1866

303-    **BERRY** James Madison (*Susannah, Thomas H., Elijah, Thomas, Jasper, John*) was born February 21, 1847 in Pontotoc, Co. Ms. son of Jarret L. **BERRY** and Susannah T. **SMITH** and died December 13, 1919 in Springfield, Ar., buried Springfield cemetery. He married January 17, 1869 in Woodruff Co. Ark. Nancy Emmaline **SELLERS** who was born July 26, 1851 in Tn. and died March 24, 1922 in Ark.
Children born in Ar.:

518-    i- **BERRY** William Andrew born November 16, 1871
      ii- **BERRY** Della M. born March 18, 1874 and died January 13, 1943 in Conway Co. Ar.
      iii- **BERRY** Minnie Ann born August 1, 1877 and died January 29, 1961 in Conway Co. Ar.
      iv- **BERRY** Julius born Mary 31, 1881 and died August 21, 1885 in Conway Co. Ar.
519-    v- **BERRY** James Walter born August 19, 1885
      vi- **BERRY** Alice E. born February 10, 1890, married February 1, 1920 Edward F. **CARROLL** who was born September 8, 1896 and died June 14, 1964. They had a son James born February 25, 1923 and died December 3, 1938

304-    **SMITH** Susan Arrena (*William P., Thomas H., Elijah, Thomas, Jasper, John*) was born November 18, 1843 in Louisville, Ms. daughter of William Preston **SMITH** and Permelia **JEFFRIES** and died August 14, 1919 in Desdemonia, Tx. She married March 14, 1860 in Pontotoc Co. Ms. John Hodges **WEATHERALL** who was born November 12, 1828 in Abbevile, SC son of James A. **WEATHERALL** and Frances Evelyn **HODGES** and died April 1, 1903 in Ellis Co. Tx.
Children born in Ms.:

520-    i- **WEATHERALL** William born March 25, 1861
      iii- **WEATHERALL** John Hodges Jr. June 9, 1863
521-    iv- **WEATHERALL** Georgia Ann Sarah Virginia born December 7, 1865
      v- **WEATHERALL** Permelia Malvina born June 10, 1868 and died May 1, 1898 in Blue Ridge Mts., Ms. She married Leroy **SNYDER** and had 3 children, John Hodges, Verda and Willie
      vi- **WEATHERALL** Mary Susan born October 28, 1870 and died October 10, 1932, married Clint **PRUITT** and had 2 children
      vii- **WEATHERALL** Nannie Mae born March 8, 1873 and died January 1, 1951 in Wawaka, Ok., married M. L. **BOREN**, 8 children
522-    viii- **WEATHERALL** James Thomas born August 10, 1875
523-    ix- **WEATHERALL** Carrie Amanda Lee born April 20, 1878

x- WEATHERALL Ethel Elizabeth March 23, 1883 Clifton, Tx. and died July 7, 1937 in Waco. Tx., married Jim GILMORE and had 5 children, William A., James H., Eugene, Mose Surf and Flossie

xi- WEATHERALL Hattie Ione born August 15, 1887, married Harry Leon KING and had son Clyde Clifton born August 16, 1917

305- SMITH Thomas Hunt *(William P., Thomas H., Elijah, Thomas, Jasper, John)* was born January 13, 1850 in Ms. son of William Preston SMITH and Permelia JEFFRIES and died August 8, 1923 in New Albany, Ms., buried in New Albany cemetery. He married Martha Meador JARVIS who was born November 1, 1856 in New Albany, Ms. daughter of Levi JARVIS and Aley Ann MEADOR and died March 23, 1906.
Children probably born in Ms.

    i- SMITH Hulet Sylvester born 1876 and died 1930. He married Elvira HAMRICK

    ii- SMITH Lola Gertrude born 1878, married Thomas CAMP

    iii- SMITH Lee Jarvis born 1880 and died 1930, married Ethel CRAWFORD

    iv- SMITH William Preston born August 1882, married Mary Lou ROPER

524-    v- SMITH Thomas Hendricks born July 1, 1885

    vi- SMITH Aley Ann Permelia born September 1887, married Fred LIPSCOMB

    vii- SMITH Martha Mae born February 1890, married Ervin L. SIMMONS

    viii- SMITH Robert Dewitt born November 1891, marred Ada WALKER

    ix- SMITH Arthur Wayne born June 22, 1895 and died June 20, 1902

    x- SMITH Carroll Grady born February 1898 and died Horeston, Tx., married Mary Caroline HUNT

306- KNOX Thomas B. *(Elijah Knox, Cynthia, Elijah, Thomas, Jasper, John)* was born April 1854 in Ar. son of Elijah Smith KNOX and Angelina GAITHER. He married Margaret E. (unknown maiden name) born 1860 in Tn.
Children born in Tn.:

    i- KNOX Burton born September 1881

    ii- KNOX Corn born November 1885

    iii- KNOX Lola born March 1887

    iv- KNOX William Joseph born November 1888

    v- KNOX Charles T. born January 1890

    vi- KNOX Elijah Smith born May 1894

    vii- KNOX John H. born 1896

    viii- KNOX Robert L. born 1897

    ix= KNOX David Alexander born April 1899

307- KNOX John Basil *(Elijah Knox, Cynthia, Elijah, Thomas, Jasper, John)* was born June 1, 1860 in Cannon, Tn. son of Elijah Smith KNOX and Angelina GAITHER and died January 12, 1948 in Harbor City, Cal. He married December 21, 1886 Lorena CARNAHAN who was born November 14, 1861 in Cannon, Tn. daughter of Newton Calvin CARNAHAN and Permelia J. AKERS and died December 7, 1941 in Harbor City, Cal.

Children:

  i- **KNOX** Elijah Smith born September 23, 1887 in Cannon
  ii- **KNOX** Edmond James born September 25, 1889 in Cannon
525- iii- **KNOX** Minnie Pearl born February 10, 1892 in Cannon
  iv- **KNOX** John Calvin born March 2, 1894 in Fannon, Tx.
  v- **KNOX** Willie Othella (twin) born August 30, 1898 in Iverson Hill, Tx.
  vi- **KNOX** Lillie May (twin) born August 30, 1898
  vii- **KNOX** Charles Raymond born December 5, 1900 in Iverson Hill, Tx.
  viii- **KNOX** Talmage born December 8, 1902 in Milford, Tx.

308- **MALOTT** Francis (*Ann, Absolom. John, Samuel, Jasper, John*) was born 1823 son of Peter **MALOTT** and Ann **SMITH**. He married July 5, 1846 in Brown Co. Ohio Margaret **MALOTT** born 1830 daughter of Theodore **MALOTT** and Hannah **WAITS**.
Child:
526- i- **MALOTT** Adnie born August 28, 1847 in Brown Co. Oh.

309- **SMITH** Henry Nash (*John, Absolom, John, Samuel, Jasper, John*) was born February 18, 1847 in Oaklanden, Ind. son of John **SMITH** and Harriet **THOMPSON** and died December 28, 1926 in Mc Cordsville, Ind. He married August 15, 1869 Olive **DUNHAM** who was born June 11, 1851 in Hancock Co. Ind. and died August 25, 1873. He married (2) March 22, 1874 Martha Elizabeth **SAMPLE** who was born May 15, 1851 in Noblesville, Ind. daughter of John S. **SAMPLE** and Ellen **SHERMAN** and died January 17, 1925 in Hancock Co. Ind. They are buried in the IOOF cemetery.
Children by first marriage born in Ind.:

  i- **SMITH** Ida B. born November 6, 1869
  ii- **SMITH** Orrin born January 5, 1872

310- **CORWIN** George S. (*Elizabeth Biles, George Biles, Christian, Joshua, Jasper, John*) was born February 27, 1819 in Hope, NJ son of Nathaniel **CORWIN** and Elizabeth **BILES** and died September 24, 1883 in Carry, Ohio. He married November 2, 1843 Elizabeth Ann **BLAIR** born April 20, 1824 in Blairstown, NJ and died November 9, 1897. They are buried in Old Sycamore cemetery in Sycamore, Ohio.
Children:

  i- **CORWIN** James B. born ca 1844 and died 1913, buried Old Sycamore cemetery in Sycamore, Ohio
  ii- **CORWIN** Almeda born June 24, 1848 and died 1919. She married Henry Harrison **PENNINGTON** who was born 1844 and died 1923 in Sycamore, Ohio. They are buried in Old Sycamore cemetery.
  iii- **CORWIN** daughter born May 22, 1850
  iv- **CORWIN** Adella born May 22, 1851 and died March 29, 1895. She married George W. **CROKER** born April 29, 1851. They are buried in Old Sycamore cemetery (no death date for George)
  v- **CORWIN** Mary born ca 1858

311-  **CORWIN** William B. *(Elizabeth Biles, George Biles, Christian, Joshua, Jasper, John)* was born ca 1820 in Hope, NJ son of Nathaniel **CORWIN** and Elizabeth **BILES**. He married Hulda **DENNIS** born ca 1822.
Children:
  i- **CORWIN** Sophia born May 20, 1850 married Will **JOHNSON**
  ii- **CORWIN** Emma Sevilla born April 5, 1856/7
  iii- **CORWIN** Lidia Ann born December 10, 1859/60

312-  **CORWIN** Anthony 'Drake' *(Elizabeth Biles, George Biles, Christian, Joshua, Jasper, John)* was born November 18, 1821 in NJ son of Nathaniel **CORWIN** and Elizabeth **BILES** and died October 2, 1908 in Rochester, Mi. He married February 12, 1842 in Warren Co. NJ Martha **KETCHAM** born NJ who probably died by 1870. He is listed in the 1880 census in Avon, Oakland Co. Mi. with wife Charlotte born ca 1849 in NJ
Children by first marriage born NJ:
  i- **CORWIN** Nathaniel born ca 1846
  ii- **CORWIN** Elizabeth born December 24, 1848/9
  iii- **CORWIN** Mandy married John **VLIET**
  iv- **CORWIN** George born ca 1852
Child by second marriage:
  v- **CORWIN** Josephine born 1871

313-  **CORWIN** David B. *(Elizabeth Biles, George Biles, Christian, Joshua, Jasper, John)* was born ca 1822 in Hope, NJ (possibly) son of Nathaniel **CORWIN** and Elizabeth **BILES**. He married Martha F. (unknown maiden name) born ca 1821.
Children:
  i- **CORWIN** Nathaniel born ca 1844
  ii- **CORWIN** Elizabeth born ca 1848

314-  **CORWIN** Joseph *(Elizabeth Biles, George Biles, Christian, Joshua, Jasper, John)* was born ca 1824 in Hope, NJ son of Nathaniel **CORWIN** and Elizabeth **BILES**. He married February 26, 1853 in Hope, NJ Tirsah **GREEN** born August 13, 1832 and died July 12, 1897 in Hope, NJ. They are buried in Free Union Methodist cemetery.
One known child:
  i- **CORWIN** Mary E. born December 2, 1853 and died January 11, 1939, buried Free Union Methodist cemetery

315-  **CORWIN** Anna Alice *(Elizabeth Biles, George Biles, Christian, Joshua, Jasper, John)* was born February 23, 1829 in Warren Co. NJ daughter of Nathaniel **CORWIN** and Elizabeth **BILES** and died September 10, 1906 in Rochester, Mi. She married John Stinson **HOWELL** who was born July 6, 1817 in Warren Co. NJ son of Levi **HOWELL** and Phebe **SMITH** and died September 1, 1906 in Rochester, Mi. They are buried in Mr. Avon cemetery in Rochester.
Children born Hope Twp. NJ:
  i- **HOWELL** Margaret born 1848/9

527-    ii- HOWELL Marquis De Lafayette born November 21, 1849
528-    iii- HOWELL William Biles born September 29, 1851
        iv- HOWELL Electa A. born September 29, 1851 and died February 15, 1924.
She married Frank PARKER and had a daughter Mary Elizabeth born November 28, 1875
and died in Hamilton, Ontario, Canada. She married Mr. St. John
        v- HOWELL Mary Elizabeth born 1853 in Hope, NJ and died June 23, 1947 .
She married 1886 Merwin J. TURRELL and resided in Ogemaw Co. Mi.
529-    vi- HOWELL Emma A. born 1856 in Hope, NJ
530-    vii- HOWELL Alice Levina born 1859 in Hope, NJ
        viii- HOWELL Franklin Anthony born 1869 in Utica, Mi. and died March 28, 1904
in Rochester, Mi. He married 1896 Effie MESSENGER
        ix- HOWELL Martha Elinor died infancy, buried Union cemetery in Hope Twp.
NJ


316-    CORWIN John B. (*Elizabeth Biles, George Biles, Christian, Joshua, Jasper, John*)
was born ca 1833 in Hope, NJ son of Nathaniel CORWIN and Elizabeth BILES. He
married Mary (unknown maiden name) ca 1853.
Known children:
        i- CORWIN daughter born February 10, 1854/5
        ii- CORWIN Mary born August 20, 1856/7


317-    BILES George W. (*William Biles, George Biles, Christian, Joshua, Jasper, John*)
was born ca 1823 in NJ son of William BILES and Anna ARMSTRONG and died July 6,
1906 in Sycamore, Ohio. He married December 25, 1847 in Warren Co. NJ Mary BLAIR
born Blairstown, NJ daughter of James BLAIR. She probably died before 1870. He is
listed in the 1880 census in Upper Sandusky, Ohio with wife Emily M. HUNT born ca 1833
Children by first marriage:
        i- BILES Sarah Ann born March 19, 1848/91849 in Hope, NJ
        i- BILES Mary Elizabeth born August 10, 1850/1
        iii- BILES William Clinton born August 9, 1850/1
        iv- BILES Anna Melinda born November 5, 1853
        v- BILES daughter born December 22, 1854/5
        vi- BILES Caroline born August 31, 1856/7
        vii- BILES Cora born 1860, buried in Sycamore cemetery, no date of death listed
        viii- BILES James died June 1, 1862 age 2 yrs 2 mos
        ix- BILES infant born April 7, 1864 and died same day
        x- BILES Paul died April 21, 1867
child by second marriage:
        xi- BILES Mary born 1871 in Mi.


318-    BILES Elizabeth (*William Biles, George Biles, Christian, Joshua, Jasper, John*) was
born 1826 in NJ daughter of William BILES and Ann (HOWELL) ARMSTRONG . She
married William BEATTY born ca 1826 in NJ.
Children:

i- **BEATTY** John born ca 1841
ii- **BEATTY** Mary born ca 1844
iii- **BEATTY** William W. born ca 1847
iv- **BEATTY** Electa S. born 1850

319- **BILES** Electa Ann (*William Biles, George Biles, Christian, Joshua, Jasper, John*) was born June 18, 1830 in Hope, NJ daughter of William **BILES** and Anna (**HOWELL**) **ARMSTRONG** and died September 28, 1849. She married January 27, 1849 James D. **LANTERMAN** who was born September 18, 1825 in Hope, NJ son of William **LANTERMAN** and Isabella **DILTZ** and died January 15, 1918. He married (2) December 29, 1853 Lucy Ann **RICE** who was born October 9, 1823 daughter of Abram **RICE** and Sarah **ROBB** and died June 1, 1911. They are buried in Cedar Ridge cemetery.
One child by first marriage:
　　　i- **LANTERMAN** Anna born 1856, married Andrew H. **HIBLER** and had 2 children Cornelia born ca 1876 and Andrew born ca 1878, listed in the 1880 cenus in Wyandot Co. Ohio.

320- **VLIET** Margaret (*Anna Biles, George Biles, Christian, Joshua, Jasper, John*) was born March 10, 1825 in NJ daughter of Abraham **VLIET** and Ann **BILES** and died December 5, 1903. She married December 1853 Jonathan **LUNDY** who was born January 14, 1828 son of David **LUNDY** and Sarah **WILDRICK** and died January 7, 1877. Children born Warren Co. NJ:
　　　i- **LUNDY** George Adams born August 22, 1853 and died 1923. His wife Sarah was born 1857 and died 1917. They are buried in Cedar Ridge cemetery
531-　　ii- **LUNDY** Sarah Ann born October 26, 1856
532-　　iii- **LUNDY** Julia Elizabeth born December 12, 1860
533-　　iv- **LUNDY** William Vliet born January 13, 1862

321- **VLIET** William (*Anna Biles, George Biles, Christian, Joshua, Jasper, John*) was born January 24, 1829 in Warren Co. NJ son of Abraham **VLIET** and Anna **BILES**. He married Elizabeth **DECKER**.
Children:
　　　i- **VLIET** John
　　　ii- **VLIET** George
　　　iii- **VLIET** Rosella

322- **VLIET** Daniel (*Anna Biles, George Biles, Christian, Joshua, Jasper, John*) was born September 13, 1833 in Warren Co. NJ son of Abraham **VLIET** and Anna **BILES**. He married October 23, 1860 Maria Ellen **AYERS** who was born July 24, 1838 in Cadington, NJ daughter of Robert **AYRES** and Malinda **CUMMINS** and died September 12, 1864. He married (2) Mary E. **DECKER** born ca 1848.
Child by first marriage:
　　　i- **VLIET** Arura born ca 1862
Children by second marriage:

ii- **VLIET** Rosa E. born ca 1868
iii- **VLIET** Abram born ca 1869
iv- **VLIET** Emma born ca 1871
v- **VLIET** Anna born ca 1876

323-    **HAYES** Rebecca (*Electa Biles, George Biles, Christian, Joshua, Jasper, John*) was born August 24, 1826 in Warren Co. NJ daughter of John C. **HAYES** and Electa **BILES** and died August 4, 1862 in Catlett, Va. She married October 4, 1845 in Hope, NJ Abraham Newman **HAZEN** who was born April 16, 1824 in Hardwick, NJ son of Levi Howell **HAZEN** and Elizabeth **NEWMAN** and died April 12, 1901 in Washington, DC. He married (2) unknown
Children:
        i- **HAZEN** Almeda born January 28, 1847 in Hope, NJ and died December 1922 in Washington, DC, unmarried
534-    ii- **HAZEN** Almatha born July 4, 1848 in Hope, NJ
535-    iii- **HAZEN** Ann Elizabeth born August 8, 1850 in Catlett Va.
536-    iv- **HAZEN** Eugenia born September 27, 1852 in Catlett, Va.
        v- **HAZEN** Irvin born Washington, DC died young
Child by his second marriage:
537-    vi- **HAZEN** Ernest Carroll born May 24, 1871 in Washington

324-    **NICHOLSON** Harriet (*Sally, William, Joshua, Joshua, Jasper, John*) was born November 22, 1836 in Hornellsville, NY daughter of Harmon **NICHOLSON** and Sally **SMITH**. She married (1) W. E. **SHAFFER** and married (2) March 18, 1854 Tryon **CROSS** who died before 1880. She died February 27, 1907 in Hornellsville, NY.
Children by second marriage:
        i- **CROSS** Huldah born 1856
        ii- **CROSS** Howard born 1861 and died 1916, buried Hope cemetery in Hornell
        iii- **CROSS** William born 1862

325-    **NICHOLSON** William Wesley (*Sally, William, Joshua, Joshua, Jasper, John*) was born July 6, 1839 in Fremont, NY son of Harmon **NICHOLSON** and Sally **SMITH** and died December 23, 1915. He married (1) Sarah Elizabeth **SHERBURN** who died August 8, 1866. He married (2) September 7, 1867 Cora **PRATT** who was born October 22, 1848 in Columbia Co. NY daughter of Ethan R. and Lucretia **PRATT** and died October 22, 1900 in Hornellsville, NY.
One child by second marriage:
        i- **NICHOLSON** Grace born 1879

326-    **NICHOLSON** Hulda (*Sally, William, Joshua, Joshua, Jasper, John*) was born January 26, 1841 in Fremont, NY daughter of Harmon **NICHOLSON** and Sally **SMITH** and died February 20, 1918 in Howard, NY. She married Harrison **RUSSELL** who was born ca 1839 possibly in Hector, NY son of Joel **RUSSELL** and Elinor **DOW** and died April 22, 1908 in Howard, NY.

Children:
538-  i- RUSSELL Harmon born February 17, 1864
539-  ii- RUSSELL Alice born February 8, 1866
      iii- RUSSELL Harrison Jr. born ca 1869/70
540-  iv- RUSSELL Anna D. born December 21, 1868
541-  v- RUSSELL Mary E. born February 13, 1871
542-  vi- RUSSELL Joel Dean born July 17, 1879

327-  NICHOLSON Horatio (*Sally, William, Joshua, Joshua, Jasper, John*) was born
April 30, 1843 in Fremont, NY son of Harmon NICHOLSON and Sally SMITH and died
June 29, 1911 in Hornellsville. He married Eliza FOWLER daughter of Edmond
FOWLER and Betsey GRAY. She died February 22, 1929 in Hornellsville, NY and they
are buried in Hope cemetery.
Children:
543-  i- NICHOLSON Edmund F. born ca 1869
      ii- NICHOLSON Gertrude born ca 1871

328-  NICHOLSON Elmer M./ Edgar (*Sally, William, Joshua, Joshua, Jasper, John*) was
born June 25, 1845 in Fremont, NY son of Harmon NICHOLSON and Sally SMITH and
died May 10, 1914 in Fremont, NY. He married (1) Mary V. CONKLIN who was born
April 27, 1851 daughter of Jacob CONKLIN and Mary REESE and died January 14, 1910
in Fremont, NY. He married (2) November 15, 1911 in Hornellsville, NY Alida PALMER
daughter of Gersham PALMER and Eunice BURDEN. They are buried in Mt. Pleasant
cemetery.
Children (possible):
      i- NICHOLSON Nellie born June 21, 1861, married ____ ROSS, and died July
21, 1911 in Hornellsville, NY
544-  ii- NICHOLSON Maria Antoinette born ca 1863
545-  iii- NICHOLSON Fannie S. born January 2, 1867 and died June 10. 1911 in
Hornellsville, NY. She married David Devillo WELD who was born 1863 and died 1931.
They are buried in Howard Village cemetery.
546-  iv- NICHOLSON Howard born ca 1869
547-  v- NICHOLSON Anna Laura born ca 1875

329-  NICHOLSON Lillian Estelle (*Sally, William, Joshua, Joshua, Jasper, John*) was
born ca 1866 in Fremont, NY daughter of Harmon NICHOLSON and Mary LOGHRY.
She married Phillip BURLINGHAM son of Charles BURLINGHAM and Martha
DEXTER.
One known child:
      i- BURLINGHAM Leah M. born August 4, 1894 and died May 15, 1919 in
Hornell, NY

330-  NICHOLSON Emma L. (*Sally, William, Joshua, Joshua, Jasper, John*) was born
November 12, 1872 in Fremont, NY daughter of Harmon NICHOLSON and Mary

92

LOGHRY and died May 25, 1936 in Hornellsville, NY. She married 1898 in Hornellsville Thomas B. MILLER born May 1871 and died 1912. They are buried in Nicholson cemetery.

331- SMITH Lucinda (*Abram, William, Joshua, Joshua, Jasper, John*) was born May 8, 1846 in Hornellsville, NY daugher of Abram L. SMITH and Almira NICHOLSON and died January 27, 1894 in S. Dakota, buried in Okojobo cemetery. She married March 25, 1867 in Howard, NY Richard TOWLE III born ca 1842 son of John D. TOWLE and Elizabeth A. ABER. He died at his daughter's in Pierre, S. Dakota leaving 3 sons and 1 daughter. He served in Civil War.
Known children:
  i- TOWLE Dorr born 1869 and died in Hornell, NY at Erie RR Station getting ready to leave for S. Dakota.
  ii- TOWLE Archie born 1877 and died January 4, 1879 in Hornellsville, NY
  iii- TOWLE Stella
Also 3 sons, not named

332- SMITH Alonzo (*Abram, William, Joshua, Joshua, Jasper, John*) was born March 30, 1848 in Hornellsville, NY son of Abram L. SMITH and Almira NICHOLSON and died November 23, 1929. He married (1) in June 1870 Electa FORMAN who was born April 6, 1854 daughter of Henry FORMAN and Ann ELLIS and died ca 1876. He married (2) Sarah SOUTHERBY born December 1857 daughter of John SOUTHERBY and Eliza DENSMORE and died 1930. They are buried in Nicholson cemetery.
Children by first wife:
548- i- SMITH Addie born March 17, 1871
549- ii- SMITH Nellie born September 22, 1872
550- iii- SMITH Ella born April 18, 1874
  iv- SMITH Flora born June 22, 1875 died young
  Children by second marriage:
551- v- SMITH Roscoe born 1878
552- vi- SMITH Alonzo Jr. born 1880
553- vii- SMITH Bertha born April 25, 1889

333- SMITH Melissa (*Abram, William, Joshua, Joshua, Jasper, John*) was born December 15, 1850 in Hornellsville, NY daughter of Abram L. SMITH and Almira NICHOLSON and died February 5, 1873, buried Nicholson cemetery. She married August 30, 1867 in Haskinsville, NY Martin LAKE who was born 1845 son of Israel and Emily LAKE and died 1897. He married (2) September 27, 1877 in Bath, NY Annie DAILEY of Fremont, NY.
Children:
  i- LAKE Annie born 1869 and died in Hornellsville, NY March 5, 1879
554- ii- LAKE Albert born 1871 and died 1961
  iii- LAKE Clara ?
One known child of Martin and Annie:

i- LAKE Vinton born 1878 and died in Hornellsville, NY February 25, 1879

334- SMITH Rosalie (*Abram, William, Joshua, Joshua, Jasper, John*) was born December 6, 1852 in Hornellsville, NY daughter of Abram L. SMITH and Almira NICHOLSON and died September 11, 1929. She married February 15, 1867 in Hornellsville, NY William TOWLE who was born December 7, 1840 in Howard, NY son of John TOWLE and Elizabeth A. ABER and died December 7, 1906. They are buried in Nicholson cemetery in Hornellsville.
Children:
555- i- TOWLE Lizzie born ca 1873
556- ii- TOWLE Edna born October 30, 1875

335- SMITH Flora (*Abram, William, Joshua, Joshua, Jasper, John*) was born September 22, 1855 in Hornellsville, NY daughter of Abram L. SMITH and Almira NICHOLSON and died March 31, 1917 in Canisteo, NY. She married September 20, 1873 in Alfred, NY George Washington FISHER who was born May 22, 1853 in Alfred, NY son of Cornelius FISHER and Catherine SEARLES and died November 27, 1928 in Canisteo. They are buried in Nicholson cemetery in Hornellsville, NY.
Children:
557- i- FISHER Clinton Darwin born June 1, 1874
558- ii- FISHER Alta May born March 1, 1876
iii- FISHER Rosa born in Virginia February 23, 1878 and died December 5, 1893 in Hornellsville, NY, buried in Fairview (Nicholson) cemetery.
559- iv- FISHER Arthur Abraham (twin) born October 1, 1881
560- v- FISHER Archie Cornelius (twin) born October 1, 1881
561- vi- FISHER Mildred B. born June 3, 1890

336- SMITH Hobart Clinton (*Abram, William, Joshua, Joshua, Jasper, John*) was born April 18, 1859 in Hornellsville, NY son of Abram L. SMITH and Almira NICHOLSON and died October 12, 1929 in Hornellsville. He married in Almond, NY April 18, 1883 Hannah Belle LEONARD born October 3, 1863 in Hornellsville, NY daughter of John LEONARD and Mary E. MEEKS and died September 19, 1934. They are buried in the Rural cemetery in Hornell, NY.
Children:
562- i- SMITH Lena Mary born June 18, 1884
563- ii- SMITH Edith Almira born December 14, 1885
iii- SMITH Carrie Mildred born November 22, 1891 and died in Horseheads, NY October 18, 1989, unmarried
564- iv- SMITH Frank Hobart born May 4, 1897

337- SMITH Thadeus Benton (*Abram, William, Joshua, Joshua, Jasper, John*) was born February 15, 1861 in Hornellsville, NY son of Abram L. SMITH and Almira NICHOLSON and died 1959 in Newburgh, NY. He married Ella BAKER who was born July 16, 1866 daughter of Nathan S. BAKER and Roxie ORDWAY of Canisteo, NY and

died 1950 in Newburgh, NY. He was a Doctor of medicine, surgeon and later a dentist in Cameron, NY and in Newburgh, NY. They are buried in Newburgh cemetery.
Children:
565-     i- SMITH E. Jay born July 23, 1890
         ii- SMITH Mildred born November 15, 1893, unmarried
         iii- SMITH Roxanna born August 11, 1904 and died in Newburg, NY November 1984, unmarried

338-    SMITH Levi (*John L., William, Joshua, Joshua, Jasper, John*) was born 1847 probably in Steuben Co. NY son of John L. SMITH and Elsie GREGORY and died 1922 in Harrison Valley, Pa. He married Caroline MARBLE who was born 1852 in Potter Co. Pa. and died 1922. They are buried in White's Corners cemetery.
One child:
        i- SMITH Myrtle born 1878, never married

339-    SMITH Eva Ann (*Dennis T., Joshua Jr., Joshua, Joshua, Jasper, John*) was born January 3, 1858 in Rutland Twp. Pa. daughter of Dennis T. SMITH and Marilla LEWIS and died October 14, 1919 in Plainview, Neb. She married February 2, 1879 in Tioga, Pa. Wilbur SQUIRES who was born May 7, 1850 in Sullivan Twp. Pa. son of Judson SQUIRES and died August 3, 1934 in Plainview, Neb. They are buried in Plainview. His first wife was Abbie Estelle SMITH who was born 1856 in Sullivan Twp. Pa. daughter of Albert Guthrie SMITH and Louisa MANSFIELD and died November 13, 1876 age 20, buried Smith cemetery in Sullivan Twp.
Children by second marriage:
566-    i- SQUIRES Hulda Marilla April 24, 1882 in Sullivan Twp.
567-    ii- SQUIRES Wilbur Glen born June 1, 1889 in Plainview

340-    SMITH Lydia Elizabeth or Elizabeth Lydia (*Philetus, Joshua Jr., Joshua, Joshua, Jasper. John*) was born January 26, 1851 in Sullivan Twp. Pa. daughter of Philetus P. SMITH and Roxane Emeline SCOUTEN and died January 23, 1916. She married (1) William Henry RUMSEY son of Isaac St. John RUMSEY who died 1877. She married (2) Barton RUMSEY who was born February 9, 1859 son of Warren and Matilda RUMSEY and died March 31, 1938. (see #366) They are buried in Mainesburg cemetery.
Children by first marriage:
568-    i- RUMSEY Minnie E. born 1870
        ii- RUMSEY Grace born July 1876, married Walter WRIGHT

341-    SMITH Frances D. (*Philetus, Joshua Jr. Joshua, Joshua, Jasper, John*) was born ca 1853 in Sullivan Twp. Pa. daughter of Philetus P. SMITH and Roxane Emeline SCOUTEN and died in Canton, Pa. 1929 age 76 years. She married Jonathan LEIBY who was born 1847 and died 1932. They are buried in Mainesburg cemetery.
Children:
        i- LEIBY Jennie born ca 1879 and died February 8, 1960 in Columbia Cross Rds., Pa. She married Arthur HAGAR of Troy, Pa.

569-    ii- **LEIBY** Hosmer P. born 1880, lived Morris, NJ. He married E. Blanche **MC CONNELL** and had one known child Christine Lillian born 1907
570-    iii- **LEIBY** Charles born 1885 (not in obit for Mother)
        iv- **LEIBY** Edith born January 1886
        v- **LEIBY** Pearl born 1890
571-    vi- **LEIBY** Arthur

342-    **SMITH** Melissa E. (*Philetus, Joshua Jr., Joshua, Joshua, Jasper, John*) was born February 11, 1855 in Sullivan Twp. Pa. daughter of Philetus P. SMITH and Roxane Emeline SCOUTEN. She married (1) February 20, 1878 Leander R. AUSTIN who was born June 28, 1831 son of Alvin Bolivar AUSTIN and Sally Drinkwater RUMSEY and died October 19, 1893. They are buried in Mainesburg cemetery. His first wife was Rebecca BROWN of Covington, Pa. who died 1876. Melissa married (2) Frank DAILEY born June 30, 1846.
One child:
        i- **AUSTIN** Ethel born February 10, 1892 and died 1930, buried Glenwood cemetery in Troy, Pa. married March 2, 1917 James **KENNEDY** son of Elmer **KENNEDY** and Minnie **STRAIGHTON**.

343-    **SMITH** Flora E.(*Philetus, Joshua Jr., Joshua, Joshua, Jasper, John*) was born ca 1858/59 in Sullivan Twp. Pa. daughter of Philetus P. SMITH and Roxane Emeline SCOUTEN and died in Lyons, NY. She married George Ingham **MAYNARD** who was born 1854 and died 1938, buried in Lock Berlin cemetery in Galen, NY.
One known child:
        i- **MAYNARD** Daisy born April 1884 and died January 13, 1899 buried Lock Berlin.

344-    **SMITH** Jennie A. (*Philetus, Joshua Jr., Joshua, Joshua, Jasper, John*) was born March 1861 in Sullivan Twp. Pa. daughter of Philetus P. SMITH and Roxane Emeline SCOUTEN and died February 14, 1901. She married ca 1882 Hubert E. **BARTLETT** born September 1859.
Children:
572-    i- **BARTLETT** Neva born July 1884
        ii- **BARTLETT** Charles born March 1886 and died 1951, married Belva **ROBBINS**
        iii- **BARTLETT** Melissa (Mittie) E. born December 1888, married Frank **RUMSEY** (see #365)
        iv- **BARTLETT** Ned E. born February 1890 and died 1937, married Maude **CASEY**
        Perhaps others

345-    **SMITH** Lavina (*Philetus, Joshua Jr., Joshua, Joshua, Jasper, John*) was born March 1863 in Sullivan Twp. Pa. daughter of Philetus P. SMITH and Roxane Emeline SCOUTEN. She married 1884/85 ____ **BAILEY** who deserted her. She married (2) ____ **SMITH**

Child:

    i- BAILEY Nelly born September 1886

346-    WATKINS Mary Ellen (Ella) (*Diantha, Joshua Jr. Joshua, Joshua, Jasper, John*) was born April 22, 1860 in Rutland, Pa. daughter of Jason WATKINS and Diantha SMITH and died November 3, 1926. She married July 3, 1879 Nathan BENSON of Roseville who was born 1856 son of Grandison BENSON and Jerusha A. RICE and died March 5, 1938. They are buried in Watson cemetery.
Children:
573-    i- BENSON Cora born
    ii- BENSON Colie born 1883 and died June 14, 1914
574-    iii- BENSON Bertha M. born November 27, 1884
575-    iv- BENSON Edith born 1887
    v- BENSON Pearl born 1895 and died May 2, 1989, married Fritz WHITE born 1895 and died April 14, 1980. They are buried in Watson cemetery. Their daughter Lucille married ___ DE CAMPLI
    vi- BENSON Ella

347-    SMITH William Harrison (*David Thomas, Joshua Jr., Joshua, Joshua, Jasper, John*) was born September 4, 1859 in Sullivan Twp. Pa. son of David Thomas SMITH and Lucretia WELCH and died January 2, 1939. He married Antoinette SQUIRES who was born November 19, 1863 daughter of William and Mary Anne SQUIRES and died September 26, 1925. They are buried in Gray Valley cemetery.
Child:
    i- SMITH Harry H. born February 21, 1893 and died January 26, 1930. His spouse is unknown, had one son Gordon

348-    SMITH Maria (*Isaac, Charles, Joshua, Joshua, Jasper, John*) was born July 11, 1851 in Sullivan Twp. Pa. daughter of Isaac SMITH and Julia Ann MOSHER and died July 18, 1897. She married Byron C. SMITH who was born January 15, 1849 in Chandlersburg, Pa. and died November 24, 1940 in Elmira, NY. He married (2) Ida KILGORE who was born 1864 daughter of Dunning KILGORE and died 1906. They are buried in Gray Valley cemetery. Also, Dunning SMITH buried with them born 1900 and died 1907, a son by second marriage.
Children by first marriage:
    i- SMITH Delbert C.
    ii- SMITH Ray I.
    iii- SMITH Ross C.

349-    SMITH Josephine (*George, Charles, Joshua, Joshua, Jasper, John*) was born ca 1854 in Tioga Co. Pa. daughter of George SMITH and Mary Ann TEARS and died 1931. She married November 20, 1873 Calvin H. DEWITT who was born October 29, 1853 Monore Co. Pa. son of Caleb DEWITT and died December 10, 1880. They are buried in Mainesburg cemetery.

Children:

    i- DEWITT Fannie born ca 1877 and died May 23, 1958. She married Dennis J. JOHNS who was born February 24, 1872 son of Charles and Addie JOHNS and died in a train accident in Corning, NY November 13, 1933. They had an adopted son Jack B.

    ii- DEWITT George C. born September 14, 1879 and died December 12, 1910, buried Mainesburg cemetery.

    iii- DEWITT Charles born October 12, 1884 and died 1916

    iv- DEWITT Jennie born 1886/7 and died August 16, 1959

    v- DEWITT Ethel born 1889

    vi- DEWITT Josephine born April 14, 1891 and died April 1978 in Cortland, NY hospital. She married Ernest M. PERKINS who died 1956 in Dryden, NY. They are buried in Willow Glen cemetery. They had 2 sons.

350-    SMITH Martha (*George, Charles, Joshua, Joshua, Jasper, John*) was born ca 1856 in Tioga Co. Pa. daughter of George SMITH and Mary Ann TEARS. She married Joseph H. DEWITT son of Caleb.

One known child:

    i- DEWITT Mary H. born ca 1878 and died March 18, 1897

351-    RUMSEY Charles Smith (*Mary, Charles, Joshua, Joshua, Jasper, John*) was born March 22, 1861 in Sullivan Twp. Pa. son of Artemus RUMSEY and Mary SMITH and died December 9, 1934 in Mainesburg, Pa. He married (1) January 1, 1886 May L. HAVEN who was born 1866 and died 1912. They are buried in Watson cemetery. He married (2) in 1926 Mrs. Carrie MC CONNELL of Richmond, Pa.

Children:

576-    i- RUMSEY Edith born January 1886

    ii- RUMSEY Pearl born 1891 and died 1988, buried in Watson cemetery. She married L. S. COOLIDGE

352-    BRYANT Isaac (*Lois Richmond, Anna, Joshua, Joshua, Jasper, John*) was born January 18, 1853 in Sullivan Twp. Pa. son of William BRYANT and Lois RICHMOND and died February 22, 1938 in Richmond Twp. Pa. He married March 31, 1893 Charity May AUSTIN daughter of Edmund AUSTIN and Ellen BURGESS and died age 82, buried in Oakwood cemetery in Mansfield.

Children:

    i- BRYANT Frank born February 6, 1895 and died December 1975, buried Oakwood cemetery. He married Mildred Esther BAILEY who was born May 21, 1895 in Sullivan Twp. daughter of Fred L. BAILEY and Cora A. STONE and died February 2, 1977 in Wellsboro

    ii- BRYANT Raymond born July 26, 1896 and died 1923

577-    iii- BRYANT Jay had a daughter Janet who was killed in auto accident age 15 mos.

    iv- BRYANT William married Jane Mary REYNOLDS

353-    RICHMOND Mary E. (*Annanias Richmond, Anna, Joshua, Joshua, Jasper, John*) was born ca 1846 in Sullivan Twp. Pa. daughter of Annanias RICHMOND and Sally Ann TEARS and died May 5, 1900. She married M. B. CLARK. nfi

354-     RICHMOND Viola A. (*Annanias Richmond, Anna, Joshua, Joshua, Jasper, John*) was born ca 1848 in Tioga Co. Pa. daughter of Annanias RICHMOND and Sally Ann TEARS. She married December 22, 1875/6 John W. BEACH of Richmond, Pa. They had a son born 1880.

355-     RICHMOND Amenzo A.(*Annanias Richmond, Anna, Joshua, Joshua, Jasper, John*) was born November 25, 1850 in Sullivan Twp. Pa. son of Annanias RICHMOND and Sally Ann TEARS and died April 8, 1904, buried Prospect cemetery in Mansfield, Pa. He married by June 1880 Clara (Carrie) Sophronia HULSLANDER who was born January 20, 1859 in Tioga Co. Pa. and died 1936, buried Gray Valley cemetery. No children mentioned in obit.

356-     RICHMOND Oscar H. (*Annanias Richmond, Anna, Joshua, Joshua, Jasper, John*) was born ca 1852 in Sullivan Twp. Pa. son of Annanias RICHMOND and Sally Ann TEARS and died 1900. He married (1) Ella VAN NESS born ca 1852 and died 1885. He married (2) 1897 Emily HOWE who was born Lackawanna Co. Pa. daughter of John C. HOWE and died December 25, 1902.
Children:
578-     i- RICHMOND Nettie
        ii- RICHMOND Bertha born ca 1874
        iii- RICHMOND Bert
        iv- RICHMOND Ray who died August 23, 1894 age 12 yrs 4 mos

357-     RICHMOND Delphine (*Annanias Richmond, Anna, Joshua, Joshua, Jasper, John*) was born ca 1856 in Sullivan Twp. Pa. daughter of Annanias RICHMOND and Sally Ann TEARS. She married December 24, 1882 Orson WILLIAMS.
Children born Sullivan Twp. Pa.:
        i- WILLIAMS daughter
579-     ii- WILLIAMS Lynn Annanias born January 4, 1889

358-     RICHMOND Flora E. (*Annanias Richmond, Anna, Joshua, Joshua, Jasper, John*) was born ca 1870 in Sullivan Twp. Pa. daughter of Annanias RICHMOND and Sally Ann TEARS. She married July 4, 1891 Morris H. SHEPARD who was born January 26, 1867 nr Elmira, NY son of Dayton SHEPARD and Angeline GARRISON and died December 9, 1936.
One known child:
        i- SHEPARD Ivah married Edward WALTON of Mainesburg, Pa. and had 2 children Edward Francis and Morris Shepard

359-     RICHMOND Isaac (*Albert Richmond, Anna, Joshua, Joshua, Jasper, John*) was born February 1848 in Sullivan Twp. Pa. son of Albert RICHOND and Sally SCOUTEN.

He married Margery **SMITH** who was born 1857 in Sullivan Twp. daughter of Charles **SMITH** and Sally **CHANDLER**.
Children:

    i- **RICHMOND** Harry L. born ca 1872 and died January 1881
    ii- **RICHMOND** Colin R. born 1875
    iii- **RICHMOND** Florence Alta born 1878
    iv- **RICHMOND** Ruel Irwin born 1881 and died 1973
    v- **RICHMOND** Ina M. born 1883 and died 1970

360-    **RICHMOND** Sperry (*Albert Richmond, Anna, Joshua, Joshua, Jasper, John*) was born 1850 in Sullivan Twp. Pa. son of Albert and Sally **RICHMOND** and died 1920. He married Sarah **KELTS** who was born 1855 daughter of Sobrine **KELTS** and Susan **MIDDAUGH** and died 1933, buried Upper Gillette cemetery in S. Creek Bradford Co. Pa.
Children:

    i- **RICHMOND** son died September 1881 in Chandlersburg, Pa.
    ii- **RICHMOND** Clyde of Friendship, NY
    iii- **RICHMOND** Lee of Gillette, Pa. married ____ **DAVIS**
    iv- **RICHMOND** Alberta married ____ **BREWER** of Wellsburg

361-    **RICHMOND** Dayton (*Albert Richmond, Anna, Joshua, Joshua, Jasper, John*) was born ca 1855 in Sullivan Twp. Pa. son of Albert **RICHMOND** and Sally **RICHMOND** and was buried in Woodlawn cemetery in Elmira, NY June 6, 1931. He married Mrs. Rosebell **SANFORD**.
Children from 1880 census:

    i- **SANFORD** Sarah born ca 1875, stepdaughter, married Frank **BUCK** born ca 1864 and had children Flossie, Leland, Howard and Kathryn
580-    ii- **RICHMOND** Edith Ann born June 29, 1878

362-    **RUGGLES** Emma (*Melissa Richmond, Anna, Joshua, Joshua, Jasper, John*) was born ca 1855 in Tioga Co. Pa. daughter of James **RUGGLES** and Melissa **RICHMOND** and died May 18, 1913 age 58 yrs. She married L. Smith **PALMER** born ca 1848 and died in Troy, Pa. age 78, buried Glenwood cemetery.
Children:

    i- **PALMER** Clarence born ca 1874 of Willard, NY
    ii- **PALMER** Edith G. born ca 1876, married ____ **COREY**

363-    **RUGGLES** Ella L. (*Melissa Richmond, Anna, Joshua, Joshua, Jasper, John*) was born July 30, 1857 in Sullivan Twp. Pa. daughter of James **RUGGLES** and Melissa **RICHMOND** and died September 19, 1918. She married Edgar Fremont **CONGDON** who was born April 6, 1857 son of Simon **CONGDON** and Diantha **COVERT** and died June 1940. They are buried in Gillette cemetery.
Children:
581-    i- **CONGDON** Henry Earl born September 29, 1880
    ii- **CONGDON** Smith born August 2, 1882 and died September 19, 1884, buried

100

Upper Gillette cemetery
582-    iii- CONGDON Lynn born August 14, 1884
583-    iv- CONGDON Ray born January 11, 1886
584-    v- CONGDON James Bert born March 1, 1888
        vi- CONGDON Blanche born August 1895 and died November 19, 1975. She
married September 24, 1913 Albert Raymond DOUGLAS who was born February 28, 1890
and died 1958. They removed to Cal.
585-    vii- CONGDON Hazel Emma born September 27, 1897
        viii- CONGDON Ella May born June 7, 1898 in Wells, Pa.

364-    RICHMOND Mary Louisa (*Obadiah Richmond, Anna, Joshua, Joshua, Jasper,
John*) was born October 30, 1868 daughter of Obdiah RICHMOND and Sarah Elizabeth
BRADFORD and died May 15, 1935. She married 1886 Earnest A. SEYMOUR who was
born September 15, 1865 son of G. W. and Ellen M. SEYMOUR and died March 6, 1948,
buried Mainesburg cemetery.
One known child:
        i- SEYMOUR Donald A. born August 20, 1909 in Mainesburg, Pa. and died
January 28, 1978 of a self inflicted gunshot to his head. He was a veteran of World War II.
        ii- SEYMOUR George of Flint, NY
        iii- SEYMOUR Stanley of Mainesburg, Pa., married ____ WELCH daughter of
Fred WELCH
        iv- SEYMOUR Doris married ____ BULLARD

365-    RUMSEY Julius (*Matilda Richmond, Anna, Joshua, Joshua, Jasper, John*) was born
December 16, 1856 in Sullivan Twp. Pa. son of Warren RUMSEY and Matilda
RICHMOND and died October 8, 1956. He married December 17, 1876 Electa SCOUTEN
who was born December 12, 1856 daughter of Ira Brown SCOUTEN and Mary Jane
SEELEY and died May 2, 1920. They are buried in Mainesburg cemetery
Children:
        i- RUMSEY Burt Ira born October 19, 1876 and died April 16, 1898, buried
Mainesburg cemetery
        ii- RUMSEY Frank Henry born July 18, 1882 and died August 16, 1974. He
married Melissa E. (Mittie) BARTLETT (see #344) born December 1888 grand-daughter of
Philetus P. SMITH and died December 2, 1964.

366-    RUMSEY Barton (*Matilda Richmond, Anna, Joshua, Joshua, Jasper, John*) was
born February 9, 1859 in Sullivan Twp. Pa. son of Warren RUMSEY and Matilda
RICHMOND and died March 31. 1938 in Richmond Twp. He married 1891 Lydia
Elizabeth (Smith) RUMSEY born January 26, 1850 widow of William H. RUMSEY (see
#340) and daughter of Philetus P. SMITH and Roxane Emeline SCOUTEN. She died
January 23, 1916 in Sullivan Twp. Pa. He married (2) Viola (CLEVELAND) HARVEY.
Children:
        i- RUMSEY Walter born September 24, 1892 and died July 5, 1984. He married
1916 Iva May MOORE in Fairmont, W. Virginia.

367- **SLINGERLAND** Jennie May (*Elizabeth Richmond, Anna, Joshua, Joshua, Jasper, John*) was born May 1867 daughter of David **SLINGERLAND** and Elizabeth **RICHMOND**. She married Shepard Silas **COSPER** who was born August 1864 in Pa. son of Daniel J. **COSPER** and Lucy **KIFF**.
Children:
586-     i- **COSPER** Florence Jane born April 8, 1867 in Alba, Pa.
587-     ii- **COSPER** Helen M. born June 1870
         ii- **COSPER** Lucy B. born February 1890 in Canton, Pa.
         iii- **COSPER** Daniel born Jul 1894 in Canton, Pa.
         iv- **COSPER** son born May 24, 1903

368- **SLINGERLAND** Raymond Charles (*Elizabeth Richmond, Anna, Joshua, Joshua, Jasper, John*) was born 1882 son of David **SLINGERLAND** and Elizabeth **RICHMOND** and died 1931 in Sayre, Pa. He married Bessie Mae **MAC BLANE** who was born August 26, 1899 in Ward Twp. Pa. daughter of Robert **MAC BLANE** and Janet **STEWART** and died March 9, 1929 in Troy Hospital, buried Fulton St. cemetery in Elmira, NY with infant son Raymond who was born March 9, 1929 and died April 25, 1929.
Children:
         i- **SLINGERLAND** Isaac lived Alliance, Ohio
         ii- **SLINGERLAND** Wilbur married Betty **FOUST**
         iii- **SLINGERLAND** Florence
         iv- **SLINGERLAND** Marjorie married William **KING** son of Mrs. Roy **LENNON**
of San Francisco and resided in Birmingham, Ala.
         v- **SLINGERLAND** Robert D. born 1907 and died May 27, 1988. He married
Mildred M. **MERRITT** born 1911. They are buried in Glenwood cemetery with children Raymond, Jo Ann, Robert and Rudy.

369- **RICHMOND** Frederick (*Lyman Richmond, Anna, Joshua, Joshua, Jasper, John*) was born ca 1864 in Sullivan Twp. Pa. son of Lyman **RICHMOND** and Adeline **HORTON**. He married Jessie **NILES**.
One known child:
         i- **RICHMOND** Mayme (or Ethel) born November 22, 1884 and married Henry C.
**STONE** who was born August 9, 1880 and died June 28, 1919

370- **SWICK** Ida Augusta (*Susan, Daniel, Joshua, Joshua, Jasper, John*) was born December 28, 1861 in Hector, NY daughter of John Hall **SWICK** and Susan M. **SMITH** and died January 14, 1946. She married March 4, 1882 in Hector Charles Lamont **VORHEES** who was born September 2, 1856 in Nile, NY son of Jacob **VOORHEES** and Emeline **SWICK** and died April 6, 1932 in Hector, NY. They are buried in Jones cemetery.
Children born in Hector, NY:
588-     i- **VORHEES** Susie May born May 30, 1885
589-     ii- **VORHEES** William Edwin born December 10, 1887
590-     iii- **VORHEES** Carrie Ethel born November 23, 1896

371- **SMITH** Frances Elizabeth (*Lufannie, Jasper, Joshua, Joshua, Jasper, John*) was born July 12, 1852 in Sullivan Twp. Pa. daughter of Solomon Henry **SMITH** and Lufannie **SMITH** and died March 31, 1928. She married October 8, 1874 George Dudley **MOORE** who was born November 6, 1855 in Armenia, Bradford Co. Pa. son of Israel **MOORE** and Harriet **KIFF** and died March 30, 1939 in Armenia. They are buried in Park cemetery in Canton, Pa.
Children born in Armenia, Pa.:

     i- **MOORE** Owen Israel born August 25, 1877 and died July 29, 1948 in Canton, Pa. He married Nina **INGERICK** who was born December 20, 1880 in Charleston Twp. Pa. daughter of George F. **INGERICK** and Minnie **IVES** and died October 1, 1950 in Canton, Pa. They are buried in Grover cemetery, Bradford Co. Pa.

     ii- **MOORE** Hulda Blanche born September 22, 1880 and died February 21, 1896

     iii- **MOORE** Edith Elizabeth born May 22, 1882 and died July 2, 1948 in Canton, Pa. She married Willard R. **CEASE** who was born 1874 son of Nelson Prince **CEASE** and Margaret **EATON** and died April 9, 1926. They are buried in Park cemetery, Canton, Pa.

372- **SMITH** George Wesley (*Lufannie, Jasper, Joshua, Joshua, Jasper, John*) was born September 18, 1854 in Sullivan Twp. Pa. son of Solomon Henry **SMITH** and Lufannie **SMITH** and died December 3, 1929, buried Gray cemetery. He married (1) March 2, 1874 Zylphia Ann **INGALLS** who was born 1849 in Richmond Twp. Pa. daughter of Erastus and Elizabeth **INGALLS** and died 1919 in Covington, Pa. He married (2) in 1925 Ella P. **BRIGGS** who was born 1857 in Sullivan Twp. Pa. daughter of John **BRIGGS** and died January 9, 1936 in Mansfield, Pa., buried Propect cemetery. Her first husband was George C. **MC CONNELL** by whom she had 2 children.

373- **SMITH** Hulda Abigail (*Lufannie, Jasper, Joshua, Joshua, Jasper, John*) was born April 4, 1857 in Ward Twp. Pa. daughter of Solomon Henry **SMITH** and Lufannie **SMITH** and died May 30, 1928 in Williamsport, Pa. She married October 12, 1874 Thomas Paul **FURMAN** who was born July 15, 1850/4 in Columbia, Bradford Co. Pa. son of Alfred **FURMAN** and Elizabeth Jane **GUSTIN** and died June 2, 1927, buried in Park cemetery in Canton, Pa.
One known child:

     i- **FURMAN** Alfred born 1876

374- **SMITH** Eunice Isabelle (*Lufannie, Jasper, Joshua, Joshua, Jasper, John*) was born June 16, 1863 in Ward Twp. Pa. daughter of Solomon Henry **SMITH** and Lufannie **SMITH** and died August 4, 1933 in Kingston, NY. She married (1) January 1, 1880 John Nathan **LANDON** who was born February 9, 1855 in Union Twp. Pa. son of Ezra and Nancy A. **LANDON** and died December 10, 1910. They are buried in Mt. Pleasant cemetery in Shavertown, Pa. She married (2) October 12, 1910 in Sayre, Pa. James Kearney **CAREY** who was born October 9, 1864 and died September 21, 1949. Unknown children

375- **SMITH** Jasper Rufus (*Lufannie, Jasper, Joshua, Joshua, Jasper, John*) was born February 19, 1868 in Ward Twp. Pa. son of Solomon Henry **SMITH** and Lufannie **SMITH**

and died November 6, 1907 in Ward Twp. Pa. He married December 23, 1887 Charlotte **HERON** who was born May 4, 1867 in East Wrenton, Durham Co. England daughter of John **HERON** and died February 22, 1947 in Richmond Twp. Pa. They are buried in State Rd. cemetery in Sullivan Twp. She married (2) August 7, 1910 Franklin SMITH.
Children by second marriage:

   i- **SMITH** Gladys Louise born July 7, 1911 and died January 24, 1983 in Blossburg, Pa.

   ii- **SMITH** Edna married ____ **BURR** of Bath, NY

   iii- **SMITH** Laureen married ____ **STICKLES** of Lowman, NY

376- **SQUIRES** Ella (*Hulda, Jasper, Joshua, Joshua, Jasper, John*) was born 1855 in Sullivan Twp. Pa. daughter of Isaac **SQUIRES** and Hulda **SMITH** and died 1939. She married September 15, 1886 Elisha Rich **ORVIS** who was born February 28, 1842 son of Eleazer **ORVIS** and Celestia **RICH** and died April 20, 1918. They are buried in Gray Valley cemetery.
Children:

   i- **ORVIS** William born October 19, 1890, married September 6, 1911 Sadie K. MC CONNELL. He married (2) Daisy L. (unknown maiden name) born 1893 and died 1984. They are buried in Gray Valley cemetery.

591- ii- **ORVIS** Esther born March 30, 1896

377- **SMITH** Frances Augusta (*Sally, George, Joshua, Joshua, Jasper, John*) was born April 20, 1868 daughter of Sanford Gaylord **SMITH** and Sally A. **SMITH** and died January 26, 1894 in Rutland Twp. Pa. She married 1891 John Ulysses **FROST** who was born February 11, 1862 son of Selah **FROST** and Matilda **WILSON** and died December 22, 1927 in Blossburg hospital, buried Watson cemetery. He married (2) Myrtle **BOUGHTON** daughter of Henry **BOUGHTON**.
Children:

   i- **FROST** Bertha who married Frank **JENKINS**

592- ii- **FROST** Martha born May 23, 1901

378- **SMITH** Clarence Adelbert (*George M., George, Joshua, Joshua, Jasper, John*) was born 1869 son of George Manley **SMITH** and Matilda **WILLIAMS** and died January 25, 1932 in Troy, Pa., buried Glenwood cemetery. He married October 5, 1893 Mary **BALLARD** who was born August 1869 in Sullivan Twp. Pa. daughter of Adelbert **BALLARD** and Frances R. **NASH**.
Child:

   i- **SMITH** Leon J. was born April 29, 1896 in Mainesburg, Pa. and died February 17, 1895, buried Glenwood cemetery in Troy, Pa. (spouse unknown) had 2 children LaRancie of Wilmington, Del. and Beatrice who married George **PEPPER** of Columbia Cross Rds. Pa.

379- **SMITH** Ethel (*George F. Jr., George F., Joshua, Joshua, Jasper, John*) was born ca 1900. She married (1) Ray **CUMMINGS** and married (2) ____ **FIELDS**.

104

One known child:
593-    i- CUMMINGS Jerald Lewis born August 4, 1923

380-    SMITH Manley G. (*George Jr., George, Joshua, Joshua, Jasper, John*) was born November 28, 1898 son of George SMITH Jr. and Martha CRUMB and died January 15, 1973 in Wellsboro, Pa., buried in Watson cemetery. He married Ora B. STONE who was born July 7, 1901 in Byrd Creek, Pa. daughter of Fred STONE and Edith COOK and died April 26, 1984 in Wellsboro, Pa., buried Job's Corners. She married (2) Perry GAIGE who died February 5, 1979. age 82 yrs.
Children:
        i- SMITH Marion who married Robert GEE of Wellsboro
594-    ii- SMITH Vivian G. married Morris COLEGROVE of Nelson

381-    SMITH Cora M. (*Cornelius, Obadiah, Joshua, Joshua, Jasper, John*) was born June 17, 1871 in Tioga Co. Pa. daughter of Cornelius SMITH and Martha SMITH and died January 19, 1913. She married March 26, 1892 Elmer E. UPDYKE who was born 1872 and died 1948. They are buried in Gray Valley cemetery.
Child:
        i- UPDYKE Charlotte born 1895 and died April 13, 1971, married Glen T. BRACE who was born 1900 and died 1988. They are buried Gray Valley cemetery

382-    SMITH Betsey A. (*Benjamin S., Joshua, Platt, Joshua, Jasper, John*) was born 1830 in Tompkins Co. NY daughter of Benjamin Schoonover SMITH and Rachel KING and died 1912. She married Richard PHILLIPS born 1825 probably son of Augustus and Maria T. PHILLIPS. They are buried in Grove cemetery.
One known child:
        i- PHILLIPS Anna born August 26, 1869 and died August 30, 1869, buried Hayt's cemetery in Ithaca near Augustus and Maria T.

383-    SMITH Reuben L. (*Benjamin S., Joshua, Platt, Joshua, Jasper, John*) was born January 23, 1846 in Tompkins Co. NY son of Benjamin Schoonover SMITH and Rachel KING and died October 20, 1920, buried Grove cemetery. He married (1) Kate M. (unknown maiden name) born 1848 and married (2) Kathleen W. (unknown maiden name)
Child by first marriage:
        i- SMITH Fred P. born 1868
Children by second marriage:
        ii- SMITH Richard L. born 1899?
        iii- SMITH Catherine

384-    DEREMER Elizabeth (*Hannah, Joshua, Platt, Joshua, Jasper, John*) was born October 13, 1833 in Tompkins Co. NY daughter of John DEREMER and Hannah SMITH and died January 23, 1920 in Ithaca, NY. She married Isaiah COLE who was born 1826 son of Tunis and Margritt COLE and died April 7, 1880. They are buried in Grove cemetery.

Children:
595-     i- COLE John born March 31, 1859 and died June 28, 1859, buried Grove
cemetery
         ii- COLE Irving born 1861 and died 1931, unmarried, buried Grove cemetery
596-    iii- COLE Grant born July 1864
         iv- COLE Walter born March 4, 1866 and died January 22, 1884, buried Grove
cemetery

385-    DEREMER Martha (*Hannah, Joshua, Platt, Joshua, Jasper, John*) was born 1840
in Tompkins Co. NY daughter of John DEREMER and Hannah SMITH and died February
28, 1892, buried Grove cemetery. She married John FULMER.
Children:
597-     i- FULMER Grace born August 1867
598-    ii- FULMER Fanny born 1868

386-    SMITH John A. (*Van Auken, Joshua, Platt, Joshua, Jasper, John*) was born ca 1834
in Tompkins Co. NY son of Casperus Van Auken and Harriet SMITH. He married
Emarentha (unknown maiden name) born ca 1841 and was living in Darien, NY by 1870.
Children:
         i- SMITH Elmer born ca 1862
         ii- SMITH George born ca 1867

387-    SMITH Sylvester Knapp (*Elijah, Joshua, Platt, Joshua, Jasper, John*) was born
September 28, 1844 in Tompkins Co. NY son of Elijah SMITH and Charlotte KNAPP and
died July 14, 1897. He removed to Buffalo, NY where he married Julia HARRIS. She
died in Meade Co. SD and he married (2) February 26, 1883 in Kent Co. Mi. Ida
WHIPPLE who was born July 17, 1859 in Casanovia, Mi. daughter of David and Harriet
WHIPPLE. They lived Cottonwood, SD. Ida married (2) September 27, 1900 Elsworth
BOWMAN.
One known child by second marriage:
         i- SMITH Minnie born February 22, 1884

388-    SMITH Antoinette (*Elijah, Joshua, Platt, Joshua, Jasper, John*) was born October
12, 1846 in Tompkins Co. NY daughter of Elijah SMITH and Charlotte KNAPP and died of
an accidental overdose of morphine February 26, 1887. She married 1874 Herman VAN
ANTWERP and lived Grand Rapids, Mi.
Children:
         i- VAN ANTWERP Pearl B. born May 2, 1875
         ii- VAN ANTWERP George born April 6, 1878
         iii- VAN ANTWERP Edward born 1880
         iv- VAN ANTWERP Fred born 1885

389-    SMITH Alice Amelia (*Elijah, Joshua, Platt, Joshua, Jasper, John*) was born July
26, 1854 in Tompkins Co. NY daughter of Elijah SMITH and Charlotte KNAPP and died

June 22, 1871 at her daughter's in Chicago, Ill. She married February 22, 1871 Irving J.
GOODENOW who was born April 10, 1871 in Rush, NY son of Horatio GOODENOW
and Evelyn HOYT and died January 11, 1937 in Chicago, Ill., buried Casanovia, Mi.
Children:
599-      i- GOODENOW Fannie born December 1873 in Wisconsin
600-      ii- GOODENOW Ralph J. born November 1879 in Mi.
          iii- GOODENOW Maude born August 21, 1881 in Saginaw Co. Mi. and died
February 24, 1901
599-      iv- GOODENOW Harold Elijah born August 1888 in Mi.

390-    SMITH Joshua Lagrant (*Elijah, Joshua, Platt, Joshua, Jasper, John*) was born April
10, 1855 in Tompkins Co. NY son of Elijah SMITH and Charlotte KNAPP and died
March 20, 1916 in Cedar Co. Neb. He married January 1887 Flora MC CALLISTER/ MC
NEAL. They had no children but adopted a son Elmer PARK.

391-    SMITH Horace Dewitt (*Elijah, Joshua, Platt, Joshua, Jasper, John*) was born
February 15, 1866 in Tompkins Co. NY son of Elijah SMITH and Charlotte KNAPP and
died October 13, 1929 in Newaygo Co. Mi. He married June 30, 1886 in Grand Rapids,
Mi. Birdella Lavinna PUTNAM who was born May 28, 1866 daughter of Truman S.
PUTNAM and Harriet A. WHIPPLE of Sackett's Harbor, NY and died March 14, 1956.
They are buried in Chubbuck's cemetery in Kent Co. Mi.
Children:
          i- SMITH Lottie Harriet born January 30, 1888 in Grand Rapids, Mi. and died
1956 in Birmingham, Ala. She married January 30, 1910 in Kent City, Mi. Algeth
CARLSON
600-      ii- SMITH Edith Viola born May 18, 1891 and died August 6, 1950
          iii- SMITH Allie May born August 17, 1893 and died February 14, 1968
          iv- SMITH William Alden born August 11, 1898 in Kent City, Mi. and died
October 8, 1974. He married Grace Mary BREWER.

392-    SMITH Clara M. (*George W., Joshua, Platt, Joshua, Jasper, John*) was born 1842
daughter of George Washington SMITH and Martha WAGER and died October 25, 1913 in
Jamestown, NY, buried Forest Lawn cemetery in Buffalo, NY. She married Philo
BALCOM born 1842.
Children:
          i- BALCOM Mattie W. born June 30, 1962 and died July 26, 1964 in Buffalo,
NY, buried Forest Lawn cemetery
602-      ii- BALCOM Harrison C. born March 1864
603-      iii- BALCOM Frederick H. born 1870

393-    SMITH Flora E. (*Horace D., Joshua, Platt, Joshua, Jasper, John*) was born 1856
in Tompkins Co. NY daughter of Horace David SMITH and Margaret POTTER and died
1919. She married Andrew CRAWFORD who was born 1853 son of Eliza and died 1927.
They are buried in Hayt's cemetery in Ithaca, NY. Unknown children

394- **SMITH** Horace Floyd (*Horace D., Joshua, Platt, Joshua, Jasper, John*) was born July 6, 1868 in Tompkins Co. NY son of Horace D. **SMITH** and Margaret **POTTER** and died January 1, 1930. He married Ida Bell **WALKER** who was born September 18, 1871 daughter of Alexander **WALKER** and Margaret **SMITH** and died October 2, 1961. They are buried in Hayt's cemetery in Ithaca, NY.
Children:
604-     i- **SMITH** Horace Walker born March 14, 1897
ii- **SMITH** Harry Andrew born January 10, 1901
iii- **SMITH** Charles Bill born January 12, 1912 and died February 20, 1993. He married Marguerite **SCHROEDER** who was born January 8, 1915 in Ithaca, NY daughter of Mervyn C. **SCHROEDER** and Nellie Marguerite **JENKS**.

395- **KING** Lovina (*Margaret Van Horn, Mary, Platt, Joshua, Jasper, John*) was born 1828 in Hector, NY daughter of James B. **KING** and Margaret **VAN HORN**. She married Artemus F. (or John F.) **JACKSON** born 1825. (found in 1880 census in Veteran, NY, called John F.)
Children:
i- **JACKSON** Martha born ca 1846
ii- **JACKSON** Andrew born December 2, 1849 and died 1902, buried Laurel Hill cemetery, also his wife Tressa **NEWBERRY** born March 10, 1856 and died May 13, 1909, son Harold C. **JACKSON** born July 21, 1900, died March 28, 1901 and Artemus E. born 1875 died 1965 with wife Ina B. born 1883 and died September 16, 1962
iii- **JACKSON** James Marion born ca 1852
iv- **JACKSON** Ann B. born ca 1854
v- **JACKSON** Ellen S. born ca 1857 (possibly a daughter Ida M. age 29 born in Orange, NY daughter of Ellen S. Jackson who married James **WAINWRIGHT** November 4, 1908 in Watkins, NY)
vi- **JACKSON** Annie May born ca 1863
vii- **JACKSON** Cornelius born 1869

396- **KING** Nelson V. (*Margaret Van Horn, Mary, Platt, Joshua, Jasper, John*) was born 1831 in Hector, NY son of James B. **KING** and Margaret **VAN HORN**. He married Mahala **VAN HORN** who was born 1835 and died 1917 in Ulysses, NY
Children:
605-     i- **KING** Eva Jane born 1853
ii- **KING** George Hampton born 1856
iii- **KING** Clara Adell born August 19, 1850

397- **KING** Mary Ellen (*Margaret Van Horn, Mary, Platt, Joshua, Jasper, John*) was born October 1, 1834 in Hector, NY daughter of James B. **KING** and Margaret **VAN HORN** and died February 15, 1882. She married James M. **ROLOSON** who was born October 3, 1826 and died October 3, 1889, buried Mc Intyre Settlement cemetery.
Children:
i- **ROLOSON** Emma J. born 1851

ii- **ROLOSON** James Myron born 1854

606- iii- **ROLOSON** Alice S. born 1856 married September 11, 1881 Frank D. **ATWATER** of Horseheads, NY

iv- **ROLOSON** Georgianna born September 1859 and died May 1914. She married March 31, 1882 Alvah **SAXTON** of Newfield, NY who was born January 1851 son of John A. and Lovira **SAXTON** and died June 15, 1930. They are buried in Laurel Hill cemetery. One known child Alice M. born September 1884

398- **KING** Emma (*Margaret Van Horn, Mary, Platt, Joshua, Jasper, John*) was born 1840 in Hector, NY daughter of James B. **KING** and Margaret **VAN HORN** and died October 5, 1884. She married Asa **BEARDSLEY** born 1840 son of John **BEARDSLEY** and Martha **MC CANN**.

Children born in Hector, NY:

i- **BEARDSLEY** Elmer E. born 1861 and died September 11, 1884, killed by falling tree in Hector, NY

607- ii- **BEARDSLEY** Frank J. born 1864

iii- **BEARDSLEY** Maggie S. born 1868

iv- **BEARDSLEY** Martha E. born 1874

v- **BEARDSLEY** Hattie B. born ca 1876

399- **KING** Matilda Jane (*Margaret Van Horn, Mary, Platt, Joshua, Jasper, John*) was born 1843 in Hector, NY daughter of James B. **KING** and Margaret **VAN HORN** and died in Montour Falls, NY May 15, 1912, buried Laurel Hill cemetery in Catherine. (stone reads February 15, 1912, possible errorin reading). She married Leander F. **STRONG** born 1844/5 in Geneva, NY son of Larue Perine **STRONG** and Amanda Jane **REYNOLDS** and died July 18, 1923, buried Laurel Hill cemetery.

Children:

i- **STRONG** Pauline Druscilla born 1867 and died 1949. She married James **SICKLER** born July 1950. They had daughter Jennie M. born November 1886

ii- **STRONG** Leander F. Jr. (had 2 sons John and Ortha)

iii- **STRONG** Lizzie B. born 1889 married Fred W. **ALDRICH** born 1888 and had son Leroy born 1905

iv- **STRONG** Marion removed to Lamar, Mo.

400- **KING** Cornelius (*Margaret Van Horn, Mary, Platt, Joshua, Jasper, John*) was born 1848 in Hector, NY son of James B. **KING** and Margaret **VAN HORN** and died May 6, 1888. He married February 18, 1871 in Watkins, NY Josephine **CHAPMAN** who was born 1853 daughter of James **CHAPMAN** and Rhoda **BOYER** and died 1975, buried Mitchell cemetery. He married (2) Cora **SAXTON** born 1856 and died July 23, 1914, buried Mitchell cemetery.

Child by first marriage:

i- **KING** Joseph died 1875 age 6 months

Child by second marriage:

ii- **KING** Ernest born 1879 and died March 6, 1936. He married January 31, 1906

Julia A. MC CARTHY born 1885 daughter of Lawrence MC CARTHY and Julia ARANCE and died July 17, 1923, buried in Burdette, NY.

401-    MOORE Oliver (*Hannah Van Horn, Mary, Platt, Joshua, Jasper, John*) was born January 1840 in Tompkins Co. NY son of John MOORE and Hannah VAN HORN and died about 1905. He married Mary (unknown maiden name) born January 1851. They were living in Medina, NY in 1880.
Children:
        i- MOORE Luella born 1874 married ___ PARKER
        ii- MOORE Rolland born 1875 (lived Glen Falls or Plattsburg, NY in 1908)
        iii- MOORE Grace E. born October 1876, married ___ SHANTZ and lived in Rochester, NY
        iv- MOORE Oliver O. Jr. born April 1879, lived Elboron, NJ
        v- MOORE Irene S. born January 1889

402-    CARLEY Simeon (*Matilda Van Horn, Mary, Platt, Joshua, Jasper, John*) was born 1839 in Tompkins Co. NY son of Richard F. CARLEY and Matilda VAN HORN and died 1908 in Portage Co. Wis. He married Angeline NEWBY who was born ca 1848 in Canada and died January 26, 1921. They are buried in Liberty Corners cemetery.
Children:
        i- CARLEY Hugh born 1868 and died 1879
        ii- CARLEY Cora born 1869 and died 1883, buried in Liberty Corners Cemetery
        iii- CARLEY Minnie born December 20, 1872 and died November 3, 1956, buried Plover Village cemetery. She married Lewis A. PRECOURT son of Joseph and Rosina PRECOURT
        iv- CARLEY Lillie born ca 1875
        v- CARLEY S. Earl born December 9, 1880 and died June 14, 1959

403-    CARLEY William (*Matilda Van Horn, Mary, Platt, Joshua, Jasper, John*) was born 1844 in Tompkins Co. NY and died 1916 in Portage Co. Wis. He married (1) Elizabeth (unknown maiden name). He married (2) Belle (unknown maiden name) born 1855 and died 1891. They are buried Plover Village cemetery.
Children by 1st marriage:
608-    i- CARLEY Simeon W. born September 1869 and died 1941
609-    ii- CARLEY Elmer born 1872
Children by second marriage:
        iii- CARLEY Pearl Lenore born April 1883 and died June 26, 1954. She married Forest BOURN born 1884 son of Algia and Alice.
        iv- CARLEY Guy E. born July 31, 1894 and died 1963. He married Dorothy BACHUS who was born 1898 and died November 22, 1937. They are buried in Plover cemetery.

404-    CHAPMAN Emma (*Angelina A. Van Horn, Mary, Platt, Joshua, Jasper, John*) was born January 1851 in Schuyler Co. NY daughter of Reuben CHAPMAN and Angelina

Adelia **VAN HORN** and died March 6, 1927. She married Jerome B. **HALL** who was born December 1850 and died November 1, 1918. No issue. They are buried in Laurel Hill

405- **CHAPMAN** George W. (*Angelina A. Van Horn, Mary, Platt, Joshua, Jasper, John*) was born February 14, 1855 in Catherine, NY son of Reuben **CHAPMAN** and Angelina Adelia **VAN HORN** and died June 19, 1908. He married Elizabeth Delphine **HALL** who was born February 18, 1861 (cemetery stone reads 1863) in Schuyler Co. NY daughter of Lyman **HALL** and Elizabeth **WILBUR** and died November 21, 1924. They are buried in Laurel Hill cemetery.

Children:
610-     i- **CHAPMAN** Arminda born July 9, 1877
611-     ii- **CHAPMAN** George Willis born April 1800
         iii- **CHAPMAN** Clarence born 1883

406- **CHAPMAN** Elizabeth (*Angelina A. Van Horn, Mary, Platt, Joshua, Jasper, John*) was born 1866 in Schuyler Co. NY daughter of Reuben **CHAPMAN** and Angelina Adelia **HALL** and died November 30, 1943. She married (1) William **HALL** and (2) George **FOSTER**

Children by first marriage:
         i- **HALL** William Jr.
         ii- **HALL** Harry
         iii- **HALL** Grace Adelia born 1887 and died 1941 in Dundee, NY. She married Daniel **RAPLEE** who was born September 1882 son of Elmer E. **RAPLEE** and Mary **WHEELER** and died 1942 in Dundee, NY. They had 3 sons and 1 daughter
         iv- **HALL** Ella who married ____ **LEVIN** and (2)____ **DOLAN**. They had son Edward **DOLAN** who married Thelma **VAN LONE** daughter of Floyd **VAN LONE** and Fanny **SNYDER**

407- **CHAPMAN** Simeon (*Anna Eliza Van Horn, Mary, Platt, Joshua, Jasper, John*) was born 1847 in Schuyler Co. NY son of Gilbert **CHAPMAN** and Anna Eliza **VAN HORN** and died July 1, 1912. He married (1) September 27, 1871 Emma **WELLS** who was born July 29, 1854 in Newfield, NY daughter of Nelson and Mary **WELLS** and died May 8, 1885. He married (2) Anna **MC FADDEN** of Philadelphia.

Children by first marriage:
612-     i- **CHAPMAN** William Bert born 1873. He had 2 children Richard who died young and Winifred of Athens, Pa.
613-     ii- **CHAPMAN** Clarence Lavern born June 28, 1880 and died 1945, buried Laurel Hill cemetery in Catherine, NY. His wife Mabelle G. was born 1877 and had daughter Ruth who married and removed to Nutley, NJ.

408- **CHAPMAN** William M. (*Anna Eliza Van Horn, Mary, Platt, Joshua, Jasper, John*) was born February 1, 1854 in Schuyler Co. NY son of Gilbert **CHAPMAN** and Ana Eliza **VAN HORN** and died April 2, 1941 in Catherine, NY. He married (1) Julia A. **MISNER** who was born December 2, 1849 daughter of Abraham and Delilah **MISNER** and died

January 22, 1897 in Catherine, NY. He married (2) Edith **GILLAM** born 1876 and died 1961. They are all buried in Laurel Hill cemetery.
Child by first marriage:
614-  i- **CHAPMAN** Kenneth born 1900

409-  **RICHARDS** Mary Adeline (*Platt Richards, Johannah, Platt, Joshua, Jasper, John*) was born 1835 in Ulysses, NY daughter of Platt and Elizabeth RICHARDS. She married (1) Andrew **HARRINGTON** who was born 1837. He served in the 157th Reg., was a POW in Civil War, paroled and died in Army Hospital in Baltimore October 11, 1862. She married (2) Robert **WHITCOMB** born 1831 son of Ira Medes **WHITCOMB** and Fanny **BURNHAM**. He was adjudged insane and sent to Willard in September 1883, released and living with daughter Hattie in Ithaca in 1910.
Children by first marriage:
  i- **HARRINGTON** Charles born 1857
  ii- **HARRINGTON** Ida Bell born 1864 (probably should be 1860 since Father died in 1862
Children by second marriage:
  iii- **WHITCOMB** Lucy born 1866
  iv- **WHITCOMB** Adell born 1873
615-  v- **WHITCOMB** Hattie M. born September 1874

410-  **RICHARDS** Melissa (*Platt Richards, Johannah, Platt, Joshua, Jasper, John*) was born June 6, 1837 in Ulysses, NY daughter of Platt and Elizabeth RICHARDS and died at daughter's in Phelps, NY September 24, 1917. She married William **DIMMICK** who was born 1831 son of Daniel and Rebecca **DIMMICK** and died April 4, 1892. They are buried in Grove cemetery.
Children born in Ulysses, NY:
616-  i- **DIMMICK** George born 1853
617-  ii- **DIMMICK** Eliza E. born May 1856
  iii- **DIMMICK** Rebecca born August 20, 1857 and died April 23, 1873, buried Grove cemetery
618-  iv- **DIMMICK** Frank born 1860
619-  v- **DIMMICK** John W. born 1862
  vi- **DIMMICK** Harriet born May 1865
  vii- **DIMMICK** Cora M. born August 1867, married Harry **BEACHAM** born 1861 of Auburn, NY
620-  viii- **DIMMICK** William born 1870
621-  ix- **DIMMICK** Estelle born August 1873
622-  x- **DIMMICK** Adelbert born 1876

411-  **RICHARDS** Emeline (*Platt Richards, Johannah, Platt, Joshua, Jasper, John*) was born September 1839 in Ulysses, NY daughter Platt and Elizabeth RICHARDS and died March 30, 1915. She married Daniel **FRAZIER** who was born 1839 and died November 18, 1918. He came from England to US in 1849/51. They are buried in Grove cemetery.

Children:
623-    i- FRAZIER Samuel born 1866
        ii- FRAZIER Fred born August 1868
624-    iii- FRAZIER Charles born October 26, 1871
625-    iv- FRAZIER Carrie L. born September 1873
        v- FRAZIER Mary born about February 1873 died young

412-    RICHARDS Elizabeth (*Platt Richards, Johannah, Platt, Joshua, Jasper, John*) was born October 18, 1845 in Tompkins Co. NY daughter of Platt and Elizabeth RICHARDS and died October 30, 1897 in Trumansburg, NY. She married Emerson SPICER who was born October 5, 1845 son of Benjamin SPICER and Phebe Ann DIMMICK and died April 16, 1923. He served in Co. F. 5th NY Heavy Artillery. They are buried in Grove cemetery.
Children:
626-    i- SPICER Mary E. born November 3, 1867
        ii- SPICER Alice M. born August 16, 1872
627-    iii- SPICER Elizabeth born May 24, 1876

413-    RICHARDS Lafayette (*Platt Richards, Johannah, Platt, Joshua, Jasper, John*) was born 1849 in Tompkins Co. NY son of Platt and Elizabeth RICHARDS and died in Ulysses, NY June 21, 1928. He married Ellen (unknown maiden name) who was born 1856 and died May 4, 1925. They are buried in Grove cemetery.
Children:
628-    i- RICHARDS Eugene born February 1872
629-    ii- RICHARDS Nellie born October 1875
630-    iii- RICHARDS Clarence born 1881

414-    RICHARDS Mary Louisa (*Benjamin Richards, Johannah, Platt, Joshua, Jasper, John*) was born September 28, 1838 in Smithboro, NY daughter of Benjamin RICHARDS and Marian STOWELL and died June 25, 1893 in Tioga Co. NY. She married John Milton WHITCOMB who was born August 1833 son of Ira Medes WHITCOMB and Fanny BURNHAM and died 1909 in Smithboro, NY
Children:
631-    i- WHITCOMB Benjamin Richards born September 29, 1861
632-    ii- WHITCOMB Forman Elmer (twin) born July 24, 1866
633-    iii- WHITCOMB Herman Edwin (twin) born July 24, 1866
634-    iv- WHITCOMB Warren Milton born October 4, 1870
635-    v- WHITCOMB Gurdon Allen born October 9, 1872
        vi- WHITCOMB Nathaniel John born February 13, 1878. He married Maud HOUGH who was born 1887 and died 1959

415-    CUMMINS Nathaniel (*Hannah Richards, Johannah, Platt, Joshua, Jasper, John*) was born November 21, 1832 in Tompkins Co. NY son of Daniel CUMMINS and Hannah RICHARDS. He married Amanda (unknown maiden name) who was born ca 1843 in NJ

and died 1921
Children:
    i- CUMMINS Viola June born ca 1859 (dumb)
    ii- CUMMINS Anna (or Hannah) born ca 1865 (dumb)
    iii- CUMMINS Isaiah born ca 1870
    iv- CUMMINS Alameda born ca 1871
    v- CUMMINS Grant died in Independence, NJ February 21, 1899 age 23y 11m
and 9 days, buried Pequest cemetery
    vi- CUMMINS Sevilla born ca 1877

416-    CUMMINS Andrew J. (*Hannah Richards, Johannah, Platt, Joshua, Jasper, John*)
was born ca 1859 in NJ and died in Independence, NJ February 21, 1912 age 79, buried in
Pequest cemetery in Independence, NJ with wife Elizabeth who died October 26, 1912 age
79 yrs. and children:
    i- CUMMINS Alvey B. died October 5, 1880 age 24y 13 days
    ii- CUMMINS D. Walter died June 1, 1881 age 25y 8m 17 days
    iii- CUMMINS Lizzie died April 27, 1888 age 23y 3m 16 days

417-    RICHARDS Mary E. (*Robert Richards, Johannah, Platt, Joshua, Jasper, John*) was
born 1839 in Tompkins Co. NY daughter of Robert RICHARDS and Elizabeth ROE and
died October 29, 1924. She married Daniel VAN LONE who was born July 22, 1836 and
died March 10, 1910. They are buried in Tioga Point cemetery.
Children:
636-    i- VAN LONE Frank E. born January 25, 1858
    ii- VAN LONE Lizzie V. born 1866, married B. E. HEATH

418-    RICHARDS Smith (*Albert Richards, Johannah, Platt, Joshua, Jasper, John*) was
born 1849 in Tompkins Co. NY son of Albert RICHARDS and Harriet BONHAM and died
December 6, 1912 in Trumansburgh, NY, buried Grove cemetery. His wife Julia E.
(unknown maiden name) was born ca 1850.
One known child:
637-    i- RICHARDS Hattie O. born ca 1876 in Trumansburg, NY

419-    RICHARDS Charles (*Albert Richards, Johannah, Platt, Joshua, Jasper, John*) was
born 1859 in Tioga Co. Pa. son of Albert RICHARDS and Harriet BONHAM. His wife
Ella M. (unknown maiden name was born ca 1858.
One known child:
    i- RICHARDS Harry E. born ca 1889 and died 1925, buried Bumpville cemetery.
Listed in 1910 census with wife Emily D. age 18 and son Alton S. age 11 mos.

420-    KING Hannah (*Louisa M. Richards, Johannah, Platt, Joshua, Jasper, John*) was
born May 2, 1846 in Tompkins Co. NY daughter of Brunson KING and Hannah KING and
died June 16, 1901. She married February 8, 1862 Ira VAN ORDER who was born May
22, 1837 in Ithaca, NY son of Henry VAN ORDER and Belinda NORTH and died

114

December 2, 1912 in Ithaca, NY.
Children:
    i- **VAN ORDER** Edgar S. born 1863 and died February 7, 1919 in Detroit, Mi.,
left wife Ada and son Stanley S. born 1885 and Ira who moved to Warsaw, NY
    ii- **VAN ORDER** Henry B. born 1868. He had wife Agnes and daughter Beatrice
B. They removed to Detroit, Mi.
    iii- **VAN ORDER** Arthur born 1863 and died before 1912
    iv- **VAN ORDER** William Jerome born 1876, moved to Syracuse

421-    **KING** Mary M. (Almeda) (*Louisa M. Richards, Johannah, Platt, Joshua, Jasper,
John*) was born 1850 in Tompkins Co. NY daughter of Brunson **KING** and Louisa M.
**RICHARDS** and died June 18, 1891, buried Grove cemetery. She married Thomas
**GALLOUP** of Covert, NY born 1841 son of Perry Willis **GALLOUP** and Hannah **NORTH**
and died in Geneva, NY July 18, 1899. His first wife was Harriet (unknown maiden name)
by whom he had one child.
Child by second marriage:
    i- **GALLOUP** Carrie married ____ **LIGHT**

422-    **KING** Emily S. (Emma) (*Louisa M. Richards, Johannah, Platt, Joshua, Jasper,
John*) was born 1854 in Tompkins Co. NY daughter of Brunson **KING** and Louisa M.
**RICHARDS** and died 1886, buried Grove cemetery. She married Crecque **WOLVERTON**
who was born July 14, 1852 and died September 19, 1926.
Children:
638-    i- **WOLVERTON** Ora May born June 1877
        ii- **WOLVERTON** Charles

423-    **RICHARDS** Alonzo (*William Richards, Johannah, Platt, Joshua, Jasper, John*) was
born January 1845 in Tompkins Co. NY son of William **RICHARDS** and Sarah
**GUILTNER** and died 1917 in Bradford Co. Pa. He married Martha (unknown maiden
name) born August 1844 and died 1955? They are buried in Bumpville cemetery.
Children born Bradford Co. Pa.:
    i- **RICHARDS** Carrie born 1869 married Wallace **MERRILL** and had son Charles
A. born May 30, 1896 in Bumpville, Pa. and died September 27, 1980 in Sayre, Pa. He
married (1) Alberta **LINDSAY** born 1900 and died 1946 and married (2) Helen D.
**LINDSAY** born 1900 daughter of Eugene **LINDSAY** and Della **ELLIOTT** and died August
22, 2000. They are buried in Tioga Point cemetery.
    ii- **RICHARDS** William born 1873

424-    **RICHARDS** Leroy (*William Richards, Johannah, Platt, Joshua, Jasper, John*) was
born March 1852 in Bradford Co. Pa. son of William **RICHARDS** and Sarah **GUILTNER**
and died 1913. He married Lucinda **EICHLOR** who was born 1855 and died 1932. They
are buried in the Rome cemetery in Rome Twp. Pa.
One known child:
    i- **RICHARDS** Alma born February 1882, married George **HILL** born March 1878

425- **RICHARDS** Lyman William (*William Richards, Johannah, Platt, Joshua, Jasper, John*) was born 1861 in Bradford Co. Pa. son of William **RICHARDS** and Sarah **GUILTNER**. He is listed in the 1880 census in Litchfield, Pa. with wife Pama born 1861. In the 1910 census he is listed with wife A. I. born 1868 and children:

    i- **RICHARDS** Floyd born 1892 (In Bumpville cemetery there is listed Edna (**NICHOLS**) **RICHARDS** wife of Floyd born November 6, 1894 and died July 11, 1980.

    ii- **RICHARDS** Letha M. born 1902

    iii- **RICHARDS** Daisy A. born 1905

426- **WOODWARD** William C. (*Benjamin Woodward, Keziah, Platt, Joshua, Jasper, John*) was born 1853 in Tompkins Co. NY son of Benjamin **WOODWARD** and Keziah **SMITH** and died July 28, 1912. He married Mary (unknown maiden name) born 1852. Children:

    i- **WOODWARD** Larue born 1871

    ii- **WOODWARD** Lucy born 1872

    iii- **WOODWARD** Charles born 1874

    iv- **WOODWARD** Mary born 1877

    v- **WOODWARD** Herman born 1878 and died November 1878, buried Grove cemetery

427- **WOODWARD** Mary E. (*Benjamin Woodward, Keziah, Platt, Joshua, Jasper, John*) was born October 1859 in Tompkins Co. NY daughter of Benjamin S. **WOODWARD** and Rachel Emeline **RICHARDS** and died 1937. She married January 20, 1881 Arthur M. **HARRIS** of Lansing, NY who was born November 1857 and died February 5, 1934 in Ithaca
Children:

    i- **HARRIS** Nathaniel R. born 1881

    ii- **HARRIS** Albert W. born November 1882

    iii- **HARRIS** Jennie M. born September 1886 married ____ **LINDERMAN**. (Possibly the Genevieve **LINDERMAN** who died April 25, 1983 age 93 yrs and William **LINDERMAN** who died April 17, 1951 age 68 yrs. They are buried in Grove cemetery lot #1076

    iv- **HARRIS** Arthur M. Jr. born October 1891

    v- **HARRIS** Emma married ____ **TEETER**

428- **POPPINO** Henry Lafayette (*Alice Amelia, Lafayette, Jasper, Joshua, Jasper, John*) was born January 14, 1890 in Ulysses, NY twin son of George A. **POPPINO** and Alice Amelia **SMITH** and died December 21, 1953, buried Jones cemetery, no stone. He married Olive (unknown maiden name)
Children:

    i- **POPPINO** George removed to Pocotello, Idaho

    ii- **POPPINO** Donald removed to Orangevale, Ca.

    iii- **POPPINO** Neva married ____ **HAMMOND** and removed to Orangevale, Ca.

116

429- **POPPINO** Harry Borden (*Alice Amelia, Lafayette, Jasper, Joshua, Jasper, John*) was born January 14, 1890 in Ulysses, NY twin son of George A. **POPPINO** and Alice Amelia **SMITH** and died January 27, 1962 in Trumansburg, NY, buried Jones cemetery. He married January 14, 1914 in Hector, NY Bertha L. **ROLFE** who was born April 16, 1890 daughter of Harold **ROLFE** and Sarah **RUSSELL** and died August 28, 1987. One child:
639-     i- **POPPINO** Edna Sarah born April 4, 1921

430- **MILLER** Judson H. (*Elizabeth, Obadiah, Obadiah, Joshua, Jasper, John*) was born 1842 son of Ward S. **MILLER** and Elizabeth **SMITH** and died March 2, 1917. He married Sarah A. **GOULD** who was born 1846 and died 1918. They are buried in Grove cemetery. Children:
         i- **MILLER** Nettie
        ii- **MILLER** William

431- **MILLER** William H. (*Elizabeth, Obadiah, Obadiah, Joshua, Jasper, John*) was born 1848 son of Ward S. **MILLER** and Elizabeth **SMITH** and died February 19, 1929 in Covert, NY. He married 1874 Emma **HAWKS** who was born October 12, 1854 daughter of George W. and Elizabeth E. **HAWKS** and died August 15, 1886 in Covert, NY. He married (2) Anna **WOLMINGTON** born 1859 and died 1934. They are buried in Grove cemetery.
Children:
640-     i- **MILLER** Bert born February 24, 1881
        ii- **MILLER** Fred
       iii- **MILLER** Hugh born 1886 and died 1953, married Lulu (unknown maiden name)
        iv- **MILLER** Bessie
also listed in 1880 census in Ithaca, NY daughters Margaret born 1878 and Ruth born 1880

432- **MILLER** Olin (*Elizabeth, Obadiah, Obadiah, Joshua, Jasper, John*) was born 1856 in Tompkins Co. NY son of Ward S. **MILLER** and Elizabeth **SMITH** and died 1929. He married Nettie **KERST** who was born 1866 daughter of John **KERST** and Adeline **DECKER** and died 1908. They are buried in Grove cemetery.
Children:
641-     i- **MILLER** Adelaide Elizabeth born December 1889
642-    ii- **MILLER** J. Edwin born July 1895

433- **MILLER** Carrie (*Elizabeth, Obadiah, Obadiah, Joshua, Jasper, John*) was born 1862 daughter of Ward S. **MILLER** and Elizabeth **SMITH** and died 1939. She married Allen **CURTIS** who was born 1857 son of Hiram and Lydia **CURTIS** and died May 4, 1924. They are buried in Grove cemetery.
Children:
         i- **CURTIS** Martha born 1902 and died December 6, 1961, buried in Grove cemetery.
643-    ii- **CURTIS** Millard C. born 1904

434-    GANOUNG Adeline (*Berentha, Obadiah, Obadiah, Joshua, Jasper, John*) was born May 9, 1854 in Tompkins Co. NY daughter of Jonathan GANOUNG and Berentha SMITH and died December 30, 1927. She married George Dawson MASON who was born December 20, 1852 adopted son of Edwin MASON and Sarah WRIGHT and died July 27, 1911. They are buried in Grove cemetery.
Children:
644-    i- MASON Flora Elizabeth born August 21, 1975
645-    ii- MASON Herman J. born January 14, 1883

435-    SMITH Alice M. (*Gideon, Obadiah, Obadiah, Joshua, Jasper, John*) was born in Odessa, NY daughter of Gideon SMITH and Anna MALLORY and died September 16, 1964 in Los Angeles, Cal. She married January 27, 1892 Herbert LYON.
Children:
        i- LYON Maynard S. born May 7, 1893
        ii- LYON J. Gordon

436-    SMITH Monroe A. (*Francis, Annanias, Obadiah, Joshua, Jasper, John*) was born January 8, 1857 in Lansing, NY son of Francis Drake SMITH and Katherine BARNES and died November 1918. He married March 1893 Hattie A. CREBBS born 1872.

437-    SMITH Jessie Ruth (*Francis, Annanias, Obadiah, Joshua, Jasper, John*) was born August 27, 1861 in Tompkins Co. NY daughter of Francis Drake SMITH and Katherine BARNES and died March 18, 1939. She married in 1882 Eugene MOREY born 1857.
Children:
        i- MOREY Paul
        ii- MOREY Harry born 1894 and died in France 1918, buried N. Lansing cemetery, Lansing, NY. He was member of Bat. B. 334th Field Art. 187th Div.

438-    SMITH John Barnes (*Francis, Annanias, Obadiah, Joshua, Jasper, John*) was born October 27, 1863 son of Francis Drake SMITH and Katherine BARNES and died April 13, 1947. He married Esther Elizabeth KNEESHAW who was born October 12, 1868 in Tompkins Co. NY daughter of John KNEESHAW and Fanny PRATT and died in Ithaca, NY July 29, 1935. They are buried in Lakeview cemetery in Ithaca.
Children:
646-    i- SMITH Olin J. born November 11, 1886
647-    ii- SMITH Gertrude Katherine born October 27, 1890
648-    iii- SMITH Harold Rockwell born June 13, 1895
649-    iv- SMITH Raymond Frank born February 14, 1898 Genoa, NY
650-    v- SMITH Ralph born December 8, 1900
651-    vi- SMITH Stanley I. born September 4, 1902

439-    SMITH Eleanor Elizabeth (*Francis, Annanias, Obadiah, Joshua, Jasper, John*) was born April 12, 1867 in Tompkins Co. NY daughter of Francis Drake SMITH and Katherine BARNES and died April 14, 1940. She married July 12, 1902 in Tompkins Co. Walter D.

**HUNT** who was born 1863 in Tompkins Co.
One child:
652-      i- **HUNT** Ethel Katherine born August 30, 1903

440-      **SMITH** Jeremiah Annanias (*Francis, Annanias, Obadiah, Joshua, Jasper, John*) was born August 16, 1870 in Van Etten, NY son of Francis Drake **SMITH** and Katherine **BARNES** and died September 27, 1949 in Ludlowville, NY. He married Lillian May **SWAYZE** who was born in Ludlowville, NY daughter of Theodore Lydell **SWAYZE** and Sarah Araminta **DAVIS** and died January 14, 1945 in Ludlowville. They are buried in Lansingville cemetery.
One child:
653-      i- **SMITH** Robert Francis born May 24, 1899

441-      **SMITH** Gurnee B. (*Francis, Annanias, Obadiah, Joshua, Jasper, John*) was born June 29, 1873 in Van Etten, NY son of Francis Drake **SMITH** and Katherine **BARNES** and died June 25, 1952. He married Ida **SWAYZE** born ca 1875 in Lake Ridge, NY. No issue

442-      **SMITH** Frank O. (*Francis, Annanias, Obadiah, Joshua, Jasper, John*) was born December 10, 1876 in Van Etten, NY son of Francis Drake **SMITH** and Katherine **BARNES** and died March 26, 1943. He married 1901 Viola **PALMER** born 1880. They were divorced.

443-      **BROWN** Floyd J. (*Melissa, Robert T., Obadiah, Joshua, Jasper, John*) was born July 1867 in Ulysses, NY son of John R. **BROWN** and Melissa **SMITH** and died 1934. He married Mary L. (unknown maiden name) born January 1869 and died 1903. They are buried in Hayt's cemetery in Ithca, NY
One child:
          i- **BROWN** Alice born August 1890 and died 1977. She married Howard **MILLER** who was born 1884 son of Edward B. and Frances S. **MILLER** and died 1949. They are buried in Lakeview cemetery in Interlaken, NY.

444-      **BROWN** Manly Clarkson (*Melissa, Robert T., Obadiah, Joshua,, Jasper, John*) was born February 20, 1875 in Jacksonville, NY son of John R. **BROWN** and Melissa **SMITH** and died November 13, 1962 in Ithaca, NY. He married March 15, 1899 in Trumansburg, NY Florence Maria **TICHENOR** who was born August 12, 1877 in Hector, NY daughter of William Jewett **TICHENOR** and Lovisa Tamson **PRATT** and died August 9, 1947 in Ulysses, NY. They are buried in Grove cemetery.
Children born Jacksonville, NY:
          i- **BROWN** William Roland born March 19, 1900, married January 8, 1925 Anna **QUACKENBUSH** who died 1962 in Scotia, NY
654-      ii- **BROWN** John Raymond born February 19, 1901
655-      iii- **BROWN** Elma Beatrice born June 19, 1902
          iv- **BROWN** Theodore born 1903 and died February 14, 1904
656-      v- **BROWN** Frederick Tichenor born March 11, 1910

vi- **BROWN** Henrietta Melissa born February 16, 1914 and died December 26, 2004 in Ithaca, NY, unmarried

445- **SMITH** Lizzie *(Jehiel, Robert T., Obadiah, Joshua, Jasper, John)* was born 1868 in Ulysses, NY daughter of Jehiel **SMITH** and Mercy **HUSON**. She married Frank **MATTOCKS** born 1855 of Pa. They lived in Corning, NY.
Children:
    i- **MATTOCKS** Ruth A. born 1897
    ii- **MATTOCKS** Ralph S. born 1899
    iii- **MATTOCKS** Magram? born 1902

446- **HOPKINS** Milo C. *(Abigail, Robert T., Obadiah, Joshua, Jasper, John)* was born September 26, 1866 son of Amos T. **HOPKINS** and Abigail N. **SMITH**. He married Alma **ADAMS** and was living in Santa Cruz, Cal. in 1905.
Children:
    i- **HOPKINS** Irma B. born 1892
    ii- **HOPKINS** George C. born 1899
    iii- **HOPKINS** Theodore A. born 1903

447- **HOPKINS** Fred *(Abigail, Robert T., Obadiah, Joshua, Jasper, John)* was born March 29, 1868 son of Amos T. **HOPKINS** and Abigail N. **SMITH** and was killed in Ithaca, NY September 25, 1902. He married Bertie **ATWATER** who was born 1870 and died November 27, 1891. They are buried in Grove cemetery. Unknown any children.

448- **HOPKINS** Nettie B. *(Abigail, Robert T., Obadiah, Joshua, Jasper, John)* was born July 27, 1873 daughter of Amos T. **HOPKINS** and Abigail N. **SMITH**. She married George **BARTO** born 1888.
Children:
    i- **BARTO** Irene born 1916
    ii- **BARTO** William born ca 1918

449- **HOPKINS** Thomas *(Abigail, Robert T., Obadiah, Joshua, Jasper, John)* was born January 1877 son of Amos T. **HOPKINS** and Abigail N. **SMITH** and died August 18, 1950 in Jacksonville, NY. He married Mary **HUSON** born 1877 and died September 12, 1940. They are buried in Grove cemetery.
Children:
    i- **HOPKINS** Esther married ___ **DONALDSON** of Branchport, NY
    ii- **HOPKINS** Alfred H.

450- **HOPKINS** Pearl *(Abigail, Robert T., Obadiah, Joshua, Jasper, John)* was born November 21, 1881 daughter of Amos T. **HOPKINS** and Abigail N. **SMITH** and died April 10, 1955. She married William Thomas **VANN** who was born August 9, 1874 son of George Howe **VANN** and Mary Elizabeth **WARD** and died July 5, 1949. They are buried in Grove cemetery.

Children:
657-    i- VANN Kenneth born June, 19, 1902
658-    ii- VANN Dorothy born May 14, 1904
        iii- VANN Robert born May 14, 1904 and died March 21, 1927
659-    iv- VANN Harold born December 11, 1920

451-    SMITH Clement D. (*William, Clement, Obadiah, Joshua, Jasper, John*) was born 1855 in Tompkins Co. NY son of William C. SMITH and Didinia (or Cordella) ROBINSON and died 1935. He married Adah R. BROWN who was born 1859 and died July 17, 1928. He is buried in Hayt's cemetery in Ithaca, NY
Children:
660-    i- SMITH Laura Mae born May 1875
        ii- SMITH Burnice A. born 1880
        iii- SMITH Avery D.

452-    SMITH William B. (*Alonzo, Clement, Obadiah, Joshua, Jasper, John*) was born May 6, 1864 son of Alonzo SMITH and Samantha KING and died February 24, 1932, buried in Grove cemetery. He was living in Brooklyn, NY in 1907, He married (1) Ida ALLEN and married (2) Barbara BOHN.
Children:
        i- SMITH Mabel S. born February 20, 1886 and died November 10, 1964, married
____ CORNELL
        ii- SMITH A. Hazel born January 22, 1888 and died December 1969/70
        iii- SMITH Isley A. born January 5, 1891 and died December 22, 1930

453-    VANN Fred Samuel (*Julia M., Clement, Obadiah. Joshua, Jasper, John*) was born July 1, 1880 in Tompkins Co. NY son of Thomas VANN and Julia M. SMITH and died September 20, 1959. He married May 3, 1914 Mabel Rebecca ARMSTRONG who was born June 17, 1889 daughter of Miles and Alida ARMSTRONG of Newfield, NY and died July 11, 1955.
Children:
        i- VANN Ivan Fred died infancy
661-    ii- VANN Carl Wilbert born December 26, 1916
662-    iii- VANN Alvin Gilbert born January 7, 1921

454-    SMITH Cornelius Cole (*Gilbert C., John T., Obadiah, Joshua, Jasper, John*) was born April 7, 1869 in Covert, NY son of Gilbert Cole SMITH and Lola OURY and died January 10, 1936. He married (1) December 22, 1896 Frances Agnes GRAHAM who died February 27, 1909 and he married (2) Kathleen CROWLEY who was born July 25, 1880 and died October 15, 1959.
Children by first marriage:
663-    i- SMITH Gilbert Cole born November 1, 1897
        ii- SMITH James Graham born September 27, 1900
Children by second marriage:

iii- **SMITH** Cornelius Cole Jr. born July 18, 1913, married Grace **MANTEL**
iv- **SMITH** Alice Crowley born July 16, 1916 and died May 23, 1961. She married John **RANDOLPH**

455- **SMITH** Emeline (*Gilbert C., John T., Obadiah, Joshua, Jasper, John*) was born 1874 daughter of Gilbert C. **SMITH** and Lola **OURY**. She married Pegram **WHITWORTH** who was born August 5, 1871 son of William Thomas **WHITWORTH** and Laura Alexander **PEGRAM**. He was a graduate of West Point in 1894.
One child:
    i- **WHITWORTH** Pegram October 9, 1909 in Mansfield, La.

456- **SMITH** Gilbert Cole Jr. (*Gilbert C., John T., Obadiah, Joshua, Jasper, John*) was born November 20, 1870 in Covert, NY son of Gilbert Cole **SMITH** and Lola **OURY** and died November 26, 1921. He married June 15, 1903 Anita Veronica **PHILLIPS** born 1887 daughter of George R. **PHILLIPS** and Rosa **MILLS** and died 1959.
Children:
664-    i- **SMITH** Anita born April 22, 1905
    ii- **SMITH** Phillips born 1910

457- **SMITH** William Oury (*Gilbert C., John T., Obadiah, Joshua, Jasper, John*) was born 1876 son of Gilbert C. **SMITH** and Lola **OURY**. He married Annette **WILSON**.
One known child:
    i- **SMITH** Mary married ____ **SIMS**

458- **COLE** Lewis M. (*Emeline, John T., Obadiah, Joshua, Jasper, John*) was born March 1870 in Yates Co. NY son of Wolcott **COLE** and Emeline **SMITH** and died June 30, 1933. He married Mary E. (Minnie) E. **WILLIAMSON** born 1883 in Hamilton, Ontario, Canada daughter of Robert **WILLIAMSON** and Ellen **ROONEY** and died February 14, 1961 in Yates Co. They are buried in Lakeview cemetery.
One child:
    i- **COLE** Delphina born 1904 and died 1977, married Howard V. **TYLER** born 1901. No issue

459- **COLE** Emma (*Emeline, John T., Obadiah, Joshua, Jasper, John*) was born ca 1875 in Jerusalem, NY daughter of Wolcott **COLE** and Emeline **SMITH** and died October 11, 1934 in Binghamton, NY. She married Oscar **GRISWOLD** who was born 1875 in Milo, NY son of Sylvester Thomas **GRISWOLD** and Ann **SPINK** and died December 10, 1960. They are buried in Lakeview cemetery.
Children:
    i- **GRISWOLD** Howard born Penn Yan, NY, married (unknown spouse) and had 1 child born September 1924 in Binghamton, NY
665-    ii- **GRISWOLD** Oscar Cole born August 7, 1900
666-    iii- **GRISWOLD** Margaret born May 25, 1902
    iv- **GRISWOLD** Albert born July 26, 1910 in Penn Yan, NY and died June 1982 in

122

New Ipswich, NH

460- COLE Wolcott Jr. (*Emeline, John T., Obadiah, Joshua, Jasper, John*) was born in 1878 in Penn Yan, NY son of Wolcott COLE amd Emeline SMITH and died 1940 in Penn Yan. He married August 10, 1904 Jennie GRISWOLD born February 1885 in Penn Yan.
child:
      i- COLE Elwood married Genevieve COLE born January 24, 1905 daughter of Thomas COLE and Emma SPINK

461- SMITH Frank Taylor (*Herman T., John T., Obadiah, Joshua, Jasper, John*) was born March 12, 1909 in Tompkins Co. NY son of Herman Towne SMITH and Eva TAYLOR and died February 1, 1996. He married April 4, 1931 Gladys STRICKLAND who was born November 24, 1911 daughter of William STRICKLAND and Ida COLORS and died August 6, 1991.
Children (twins):
667-   i- SMITH Dorothy born August 10, 1941
     ii- SMITH Kenneth born August 10, 1941, unmarried

462- SMITH Alfred John (*Herman T., John T., Obadiah, Joshua, Jasper, John*) was born January 30, 1913 in Hector, NY son of Herman Towne SMITH and Eva TAYLOR and died August 11, 1994. He married November 25, 1948 Vivian GAUNT who was born February 4, 1924 daughter of John Jefferson GAUNT and Edna Elizabeth GERMAIN and died January 8, 1984. They are buried in Grove cemetery.
Children:
     i- SMITH Marsha E. born October 25, 1949
668-   ii- SMITH Richard Alan born June 18, 1951
     iii- SMITH Raymond Geoffrey born February 26, 1953
669-   iv- SMITH Sheila Rose born February 14, 1956

463- WOLCOTT Tompkins Smith ( *Mary Jane, Joshua, Annanias, Joshua, Jasper, John*) was born 1845, possibly in Athens, Pa. son of Ira M. WOLCOTT and Mary Jane SMITH and died 1916. He married (1) Margaret (unknown maiden name) who was born 1854 and he married (2) Anna Elizabeth HOBLER born August 1850.
One child:
     i- WOLCOTT Alice M. born 1883

464- LYON Lorenzo M. (*Priscilla, Joshua, Annanias, Joshua, Jasp559er, John*) was born in Enfield, NY son of Alfred H. LYON and Priscilla SMITH and died January 25, 1923 in Carson City, Mi. He married in Dewitt, Mi. December 27, 1854 Eliza JONES born in Enfield, NY August 24, 1837 daughter of Edward JONES and Lois CLARK and died November 14, 1911 in Carson City, Mi.
Children born Mi.:
     i- LYON George H. born 1858
670-   ii- LYON Fidelia born August 20, 1860

iii- **LYON** Alice born ca 1863
iv- **LYON** Ellen born ca 1865
v- **LYON** Edward born ca 1868

465-  **LYON** William H. (*Priscilla, Joshua, Annanias, Joshua, Jasper, John*) was born in Enfield, NY in 1836 son of Alfred H. **LYON** and Priscilla **SMITH**. He married Matilda **BRAY** born ca 1836 in Canada.
Children:
  i- **LYON** Luther born 1860
  ii- **LYON** May born 1866

466-  **LYON** Francis J. (*Priscilla, Joshua, Annanias, Joshua, Jasper, John*) was born April 10, 1838 in Enfield, NY son of Alfred H. **LYON** and Priscilla **SMITH** and died May 2, 1891 in Clinton Co. Mi. He married Biancy **MORSE** who was born 1854 daughter of Hudson S. **MORSE** and died 1921. They are buried in the Bray cemetery Bengal Twp. Mi.
Children:
  i- **LYON** Oramel G. born 1876
  ii- **LYON** Carrie B. born 1879

467-  **LYON** Edward H. (*Priscilla, Joshua, Annanias, Joshua, Jasper, John*) was born April 13, 1843 in Enfield, NY son of Alfred H. **LYON** and Priscilla **SMITH** and died February 27, 1917 in Clinton Co. Mi. He married January 21, 1866 in St. John, Mi. Sarah Jane (unknown maiden name).
Children:
  i- **LYON** Lelie (twin) born March 15, 1869 and died October 13, 1869, buried Bray cemetery in Bengal, Mi.
  ii- **LYON** Lee (twin) born March 15, 1869 and died March 28, 1870, buried Bray cemetery.
  iii- **LYON** Eva born ca 1868
  iv- **LYON** Bertha born ca 1874

468-  **GEORGIA** Sarah Kosiah (*Lovina, Joshua, Annanias, Joshua, Jasper, John*) was born 1844 Enfield, NY (or in Clinton Co. Mi.) daughter of Miles **GEORGIA** and Lovina **SMITH**. She married Byron C. **DAVID** born December 16, 1836 in Bath, NY son of Alpha **DAVID** and Mary **COMPTON**.
Children born Clinton Co. Mi.:
671-    i- **DAVID** Miles Riley born March 29, 1863
672-    ii- **DAVID** Frank E. born 1864
    iii- **DAVID** Scotfield Matson born 1865
    iv- **DAVID** Lewis S. born 1870
673-    v- **DAVID** Eva C. born 1872
    vi- **DAVID** Lovina Georgia born December 19, 1874
    vii- **DAVID** Ora V. born January 8, 1881 and died December 12, 1956. He married Mabel Maud **SPIKE** who was born June 9, 1883 in Ontario, Canada daughter of William

Bryan **SPIKE** and Sarah Eliza **PURDY** and died January 22, 1962 in Kalamazoo, Mi.
    viii- **DAVID** Lenora (Nora) G. born 1882
    ix- **DAVID** Roy G. born 1886

469-     **GEORGIA** Schuyler (*Lovina, Joshua, Annanias, Joshua, Jasper, John*) was born 1847 in NY State son of Miles **GEORGIA** and Lovina **SMITH** and died December 18, 1931 in Bengal Twp. Mi. He married August 5, 1873 in Ingham, Mi. Aseneth **BRAY** who was born March 5, 1857 in Wentworth, Ontario, Canada daughter of Israel M. **BRAY** and Charlotte **WOOD** and died February 21, 1934 in Bengal Twp. They are buried in Mt. Rest cemetery, St. Johns, Mi.
Children born Clinton Co. Mi.:
674-     i- **GEORGIA** Fred Dudley born 1875
675-     ii- **GEORGIA** Mark Lewis born 1877
676-     iii- **GEORGIA** Tyler R. born May 8, 1879

470-     **GEORGIA** William W. (*Lovina, Joshua, Annanias, Joshua, Jasper, John*) was born October 8, 1850 in Tompkins Co. NY son of Miles **GEORGIA** and Lovina **SMITH** and died January 25, 1891 in Bath, Mi. He married Sarah J. **SUTTON** who was born 1845 in Ohio daughter of William A. and Sarah J. **SUTTON** and died May 18, 1895 in Bath, Mi. They are buried in Georgia cemetery in Bengal, Mi.
Children:
    i- **GEORGIA** Clara A. born 1875
    ii- **GEORGIA** Roma 1880

471-     **SMITH** Margaret Ann (*Lewis H., Joshua, Annanias, Joshua, Jasper, John*) was born September 20, 1843 in Enfield, NY daughter of Lewis Hartsough **SMITH** and Mary Lewis **BRAGAW** and died February 5, 1909. She married Henry Sanford **FREESE** who was born November 9, 1836 in Trumbull's Corners, NY son of Simon **FREESE** and Mary **WOLBERT** and died March 4, 1912. They are buried in Trumbull's Corners cemetery.
Children:
    i- **FREESE** Minnie born July 23/24, 1868 and died August 16, 1868, buried Trumbull's Corners cemetery
677-     ii- **FREESE** Myrtle Louise born August 30, 1869
678-     iii- **FREESE** Willard Smith born September 15, 1873
679-     iv- **FREESE** Lewis Orville born November 9, 1875
680-     v- **FREESE** Mary Edith born August 19, 1878

472-     **SMITH** Helen (*Lewis H., Joshua, Annanias, Joshua, jasper, John*) was born 1847 in Tompkins Co. NY daughter of Lewis Hartsough **SMITH** and Mary Lewis **BRAGAW**. She married in Ithaca, NY June 1, 1882 William **EMLEY** who was born 1840 son of Charles and Mary **EMLEY**.
Children:
    i- **EMLEY** Anna M. born 1884
681-     ii- **EMLEY** Ella Lelah born 1888 (see #228)

473-	SMITH Tompkins (*Lewis H., Joshua, Annanias, Joshua, Jasper, John*) was born
January 7, 1851 in Tompkins Co. NY son of Lewis Hartsough SMITH and Mary Lewis
BRAGAW and died July 9, 1884. He married Mary Elizabeth SMITH born 1852 in NY.
Children:
   i- SMITH Fannie born February 27, 1873 and died November 17, 1875
   ii- SMITH Ralph D. born 1877 and died 1961
   iii- SMITH Louie born February 19, 1884 and died February 4, 1885

474-	SMITH Elizabeth (*Lewis H., Joshua, Annanias, Joshua, Jasper, John*) was born
December 15, 1859 in Tompkins Co. NY daughter of Lewis Hartsough SMITH and Mary
Lewis BRAGAW and died 1943. She married Fred TILTON who was born 1856 and died
1929. They are buried in Hayt's cemetery in Ithaca, NY.
Children:
682-	 i- TILTON Laura B. born 1881
683-	 ii- TILTON Walter born 1883
684-	 iii- TILTON Grace born 1886
   iv- TILTON Ralph F. born 1893 and died July 20, 1981 (see #677)

475-	SMITH Elizabeth Corintha (*George W., Peter, Annanias, Joshua, Jasper, John*) was
born July 1837 daughter of George W. SMITH and Maria C. HICKS and died November
14, 1926. She married (1) Samuel B. SMITH who was born 1842 son of Jonathan SMITH
and died September 29, 1864. She married (2) November 6, 1867 in Buffalo, NY Brenton
D. BABCOCK born October 2, 1830 in Adams, NY son of William BABCOCK and Alvira
GAYLORD and died January 10, 1906. He served one year as mayor of Cleveland. They
are listed in the 1880 census (called Prentice Babcock) living in Cleveland, Ohio with son
Frank E. age 11 years born Canada and Maria C. SMITH age 63 yrs. as mother-in-law.

476-	INMAN George H. (*Christina G., Peter, Annanias, Joshua, Jasper, John*) was born
1841 son of Henry INMAN and Christina G. SMITH and died in Buffalo, NY May 26,
1876. His wife Mary W. died in Buffalo June 29, 1926. They are buried in Forest Lawn
cemetery.
One known child:
685-	 i- INMAN Cora born 1875

477-	LANNING Nellie (*Gideon Lanning, Nancy, Annanias, Joshua, Jasper, John*) was
born February 1876 in Ithaca, NY daughter of Gideon and Julia C. LANNING and died
1963, buried Hayt's cemetery in Ithaca. She married Chester D. LEONARD who was born
August 1868 son of James and Hannah LEONARD. They removed to Arizona.
Children:
686-	 i- LEONARD Ward born March 1898

478-	SUMMERTON Irettie (*Thomas L. Summerton, Sally, Annanias, Joshua, Jasper,
John*) was born 1853 daughter of Thomas L. SUMMERTON and Mary Jane HARVEY and
died 1949 in Tioga Co. NY. She married July 25, 1878 in Van Etten, NY Winton E.

126

WILLIAMS who was born 1848 and died 1917. They are buried in Barton Methodist Church cemetery in Barton, NY.
One known child:
  i- WILLIAMS Lewis Elmer born July 25, 1878 in Van Etten, NY and died June 25, 1958. His wife Cora L. Myra WILLIAMS was born 1881 daughter of George WILLIAMS and Harriette GOLDEN and died January 3, 1913

479- SUMMERTON Olive Rose (*Thomas L. Summerton, Sally, Annanias, Joshua, Jasper, John*) was born April 27, 1855 daughter of Thomas L. SUMMERTON and Mary Jane HARVEY and died in Tioga Co. NY January 28, 1918. She married July 11, 1882 Wesley Freeman ACKLEY who was born July 11, 1859 in E. Smithfield, Pa. son of Alexander Washington ACKLEY and Lydia Jane BURLINGAME and died October 16, 1930. They are buried in Lockwood cemetery in Tioga.
Children born in Lockwood, NY:
687- i- ACKLEY Walter Freeman born July 11, 1883
  ii- ACKLEY Clara Rose born February 10, 1885 and died March 16, 1885
  iii- ACKLEY Harry Dumont born February 13, 1886 and died March 12, 1886
688- iv- ACKLEY Mary Luella born November 13, 1887
689- v- ACKLEY Alvah Charles born December 18, 1890
  vi- ACKLEY Thomas Lewis born July 17, 1892 in Pa. and died September 17, 1892
  vii- ACKLEY Edna May born September 13, 1894 and died January 25, 1895
  viii- ACKLEY Cecil Lavern born November 25, 1896 and died October 15, 1993 married October 19, 1914 Sarah E. HOFFMAN born November 1, 1896 and died January 5, 1992 in Waverly
690- ix- ACKLEY Marion Weeks born ca 1901
691- x- ACKLEY Clifford Weeks born ca 1904

### Eighth Generation

480- SKIRM William H. (*Charles Skirm, Eliza Fish, Sarah, John, John, Jasper, John*) was born December 12, 1856 in NJ son of Charles Henry SKIRM and Elizabeth T. WHITE and died January 15, 1905. He married Helen PICKLE born ca 1860 in NJ daughter of Baltus PICKLE and Elizabeth HOLCOMB.
One known child:
  i- SKIRM Elizabeth born ca 1880 and married Chester A. WATERS born ca 1878 and had 2 children

481- SMITH Halma James (*James, Joseph, Daniel, Jasper, John, Jasper, John*) was born March 30, 1834 in Newark, NJ son of James SMITH and Hannah VAN WAGONER and died December 7, 1927 in Santa Ana, Cal. He married October 9, 1859 in Salt Lake City,

Utah Ann Booth **BOLTON** who was born August 15, 1840 in Woodbury, NY daughter of Curtis Edwin **BOLTON** and Rebecca B. **BUNKER** and died March 6, 1905 in Provo, Utah. He married (2) May 8, 1907 Elizabeth **DUKE** who was born May 9, 1864 in Provo, Utah daughter of Jonathan O. **DUKE** and Sarah **THOMPSON** and died October 19, 1919 in Provo.
Children born in Provo, Utah:
692-    i- **SMITH** Ann Gertrude May 28, 1860
693-    ii- **SMITH** Halma Bolton born January 28, 1862
        iii- **SMITH** Sarah Rebecca born September 18, 1864 and died February 27, 1865 in Provo, Utah
        iv- **SMITH** James Edwin born September 13, 1865 and died August 4, 1940 in Bakersfield, Cal.
694-    v- **SMITH** Emma Luella born April 2, 1869
        vi- **SMITH** John Curtis born July 9, 1871 and died January 13, 1894 in Provo, Utah
        vii- **SMITH** Charles Henry born April 21, 1873 and died June 6, 1873 in Provo, Utah
695-    viii- **SMITH** Alpheus Jackson born January 21, 1875
696-    ix- **SMITH** Edith May born March 9, 1877

482-    **SMITH** Hyrum (*James, Joseph, Daniel, Jasper, John, Jasper, John*) was born April 2, 1838 in Pompton, NJ son of James Henry **SMITH** and Hannah **VAN WAGONER** and died December 13, 1914 in Provo, Utah. He married ca 1870 Julia A. **HUNTSMAN** who was born December 21, 1851 in Coucil Bluffs, Iowa daughter of William J. **HUNTSMAN** and Elizabeth Amanda **PRAETER** and died December 19, 1935 in Huntington Park, Cal.
Children:
697-    i- **SMITH** Hyrum born October 29, 1872
        ii- **SMITH** Don born March 12, 1875

483-    **SMITH** John (*James, Joseph, Daniel, Jasper, John, Jasper, John*) was born April 27, 1840 in Pompton, NJ son of James Henry **SMITH** and Hannah **VAN WAGONER** and died April 27, 1899 in Colton, Utah. He married December 24, 1879 in Provo, Utah Julia Ett **BOWEN** who was born June 23, 1854 in Council Bluffs, Iowa and died September 11, 1934 in Roosevelt, Utah.
Children born in Provo, Utah:
        i- **SMITH** infant born 1880 and died in infancy
        ii- **SMITH** Catherine born August 14, 1882 and died October 29, 1940
        iii- **SMITH** Hannah Sophronia born July 12, 1884 and died November 21, 1920 in Provo
        iv- **SMITH** John Mervyn born October 10, 1886 and died October 31, 1971 in Tulare, Cal.
698-    v- **SMITH** Albert Harry born August 17, 1888
699-    vi- **SMITH** James Hastings born June 24, 1891
        vii- **SMITH** infant born November 8, 1892 died same day

viii- **SMITH** William Henry born August 8, 1895

484- **SMITH** Sarah Ann (*James, Joseph, Daniel, Jasper, John, Jasper, John*) was born September 11, 1842 in Pompton, NJ daughter of James Henry **SMITH** and Hannah **VAN WAGONER** and died February 13, 1866 in Provo, Utah. She married March 1861 Enoch Alpheus **CLARK** who was born May 11, 1838 in Farwest, Mo. son of John W. **CLARK** and Marla **BURR** and died October 28, 1914 in Salt Lake City, buried in Draper, Utah. Children:

700-    i- **CLARK** Enoch Alpheus born October 22, 1864 in Springville, Utah.

701-    ii- **CLARK** James Henry born November 8, 1865 and died February 10, 1919 in Provo, Utah

485- **SMITH** Mary Emma (*James, Joseph, Daniel, Jasper, John, Jasper, John*) was born May 21, 1845 in Pompton, NJ daughter of James Henry **SMITH** and Hannah **VAN WAGONER** and died February 11, 1901 in Elks, Nev. She married in 1863 in Provo, Utah Alpeus Alonzo **CONOVER** who was born June 12, 1842 in Hancock, Ill. son of Peter Wilson **CONOVER** and Eveline **GOLDEN** and died July 13, 1908 in Elks, Nev. Children:

i- **CONOVER** Vera born July 31, 1872 in Elks, Nev. and died February 13, 1962 in Long Beach, Cal., married 1910 Harry **GARRITY** born November 14, 1872 and died December 12, 1928. She married (2) ____ **BODDY** born ca 1870 of Long Beach, Cal.

ii- **CONOVER** Nettie E. born January 1873 in Elks, Nev.

iii- **CONOVER** Hannah Evelyn born February 14, 1879 in Elks

iv- **CONOVER** Eva born ca 1881 in Nevada and died October 27, 1943 in Long Beach, Cal., buried Sunnyside mauseleum. She married (1) 1910 Frank C. **SHAW** and (2) April 19, 1919 Zeno Lafayette **HEMPHILL** who died April 14, 1966

486- **SMITH** Joseph (*James, Joseph, Daniel, Jasper, John, Jasper, John*) ws born January 11, 1848 in Pompton, NJ son of James Henry **SMITH** and Hannah **VAN WAGONER** and died January 28, 1922 in Provo, Utah, buried Provo. He married (1) May 1891 in Provo Isabel Lucinda **PACE** who was born December 6, 1856 in Provo (or Norton, Ks.) daughter of William Byron **PACE** and Epsy Jane **WILLIAMS** and died November 6, 1906 in Provo. He married (2) August 1, 1912 in Provo Louise **MANGUM** born ca 1847. Children by first marriage born in Provo, Utah:

i- **SMITH** Edna Elvira born July 22, 1882 in Provo, Utah and died April 12, 1910

702-    ii- **SMITH** Joseph William born November 17, 1884

iii- **SMITH** James Henry born September 13, 1886 and died January 5, 1928 in Silver City, Utah

iv- **SMITH** Franklin born January 18, 1888 and died February 2, 1889 in Provo

v- **SMITH** Zella Nora born March 29, 1890 and died July 1976 in Los Angeles, Cal.

vi- **SMITH** Ralph Byron born August 9, 1892

487- **SMITH** Hannah Eunice (*James, Joseph, Daniel, Jasper, John, Jasper, John*) was born June 8, 1852 in Big Cottonwood, Utah daughter of James Henry SMITH and Hannah VAN WAGONER and died June 13, 1931 in Monarch, Mt. She married December 24, 1871 in Provo John Andrew CROFF born February 10, 1843 in Northfield, Ohio son of William C. CROFF and Julia Ann BOUGHEY and died July 14, 1907 in Monarch, Mt. Children:

    i- CROFF John Arthur born March 19, 1872 in Eureka, Utah and died October 22, 1942

    ii- CROFF Geneva born March 7, 1874 in Eureka

    iii- CROFF Emma Ella born August 16, 1875 in Eureka and died 1942

    iv- CROFF Benjamin B. born March 31, 1876 in Eureka

    v- CROFF Myrtle B. born April 2, 1878 in Eureka and died 1946 in Belt Park, Monarch, Mt.

    vi- CROFF William born ca 1880 in Eureka

    vii- CROFF Maurice born May 24, 1886 in Cascade, Mt.

    viii- CROFF Elmer born June 17, 1888 in Cascade, Mt. and died November 10, 1951

488- SMITH Henry (*James, Joseph, Daniel, Jasper, John, Jasper, John*) was born May 19, 1854 in Big Cottonwood, Utah son of James Henry SMITH and Hannah VAN WAGONER and died July 27, 1926 in Provo, Utah. He married January 2, 1878 in Provo, Utah Alveretta Henrietta CONOVER who was born May 5, 1862 in Provo daughter of Peter W. CONOVER and Mary Jane MC CARROLL and died February 12, 1937 in Provo. Children:

    i- SMITH Henry Van born April 16, 1880

    ii- SMITH Wilson Josiah born January 18, 1882 in Provo and died July 16, 1936

703-    iii- SMITH Martha Ella born October 8, 1884

    iv- SMITH Jesse Lawrence born October 17, 1891 and died September 18, 1959

    v- SMITH Albert James born October 26, 1889 and died July 15, 1960

489- SMITH William Edwin (*James, Joseph, Daniel, Jasper, John, Jasper, John*) was born September 5, 1857 in Big Cottonwood, Utah son of James Henry SMITH and Hannah VAN WAGONER and died July 12, 1924 in Salt Lake City. He married in Provo, Utah Alisetta Harriet CONOVER who was born May 5, 1862 in Provo daughter of Peter W. and M. J. CONOVER and died September 27, 1937 in Provo. He married (2) Hannah PETERSON born April 18, 1880 and died March 31, 1943. They had 1 daughter who married Vern Leroy WHITING.

490- BREARLEY Julia Florence (*George Brearley, Mehitabel, Asher, Jasper, John, Jasper, John*) was born January 12, 1864 in Trenton, NJ daughter of George BREARLEY and Jane Stevens PHILLIPS. She married October 18, 1888 Joseph Ellis STEVENSON born April 9, 1856 in Freehold, NJ son of Alfred STEVENSON and Isabel MC KNIGHT. Children:

    i- STEVENSON Jean Phillips born May 14, 1890

    ii- STEVENSON William Linford born May 7, 1891

130

iii- STEVENSON Sarah Smith born June 20, 1893
iv- STEVENSON Horace Newton born July 1, 1897
v- STEVENSON Isabelle Mc Knight born July 8, 1902

491- SCUDDER Wallace Mc Ilvaine (*Edward Scudder, Jasper Scudder, Sarah, Jasper, John, Jasper, John*) was born December 26, 1853 in NJ son of Edward Wallace SCUDDER and Mary Louisa DRAKE and died 1931. He married (1) Ida QUIMBY who was born August 1, 1855 daughter of James Moses QUIMBY and Hannah SWAYZE and died January 30, 1903. He married (2) Gertrude WITHERSPOON who was born ca 1860 in Buffalo, NY and died July 28, 1953 in NJ.
Children by first marriage:
　　i- SCUDDER Edward Wallace born 1882 and died February 19, 1953 in Islamadora, Fl. He married Katherine (unknown maiden name) and had 1 son
　　ii- SCUDDER Wallace Mc Ilvaine born ca 1884
　　iii- SCUDDER Antoinette Quimby born 1886 and died 1958

492- HUTCHINSON Mary C. (*Frances Mershon, Samuel Mershon, Prudence, Jasper, John, Jasper, John*) was born ca 1848 in NJ daughter of Randall HUTCHINSON and Frances Mershon. She married George C. CUBBERLY Jr. born ca 1846 son of George.
Children:
　　i- CUBBERLY William M. born ca 1876 and married Margaret FORD born ca 1872
　　ii- CUBBERLY Elmer born ca 1880
　　iii- CUBBERLY Harry born ca 1881

493- HUTCHINSON Samuel (*Frances Mershon, Samuel Mershon, Prudence, Jasper, John, Jasper, John*) was born ca 1849 in NJ son of Randall HUTCHINSON and Frances MERSHON. He married Elizabeth MEYERS born ca 1853. (in the 1880 census he is listed in Lawrenceville, NJ born ca 1849 with wife Julia HUTCHINSON and son Raymond HUTCHINSON born ca 1880.

494- HUTCHINSON Henrietta (*Frances Mershon, Samuel Mershon, Prudence, Jasper, John, Jasper, John*) was born ca 1850 in NJ daughter of Randall HUTCHINSON and Frances MERSHON. She married Thomas B. DE COU born ca 1845.
Children:
　　i- DE COU Edith born ca 1872
　　ii- DE COU Emily born ca 1873

495- PHILLIPS Robert Hazlett Cummings (*Ephraim Phillips, George Phillips, Sarah, Joshua, John, Jasper, John*) was born ca 1869 in Burlington, NJ son of Ephriam PHILLIPS and Mary MC CLURE. Spouse unknown
Children born in Trenton, NJ:
　　i- PHILLIPS Margaret born ca 1894
　　ii- PHILLIPS George Eldridge born ca 1895, married Mary READING born ca

1900. They had 2 children

   iii- **PHILLIPS** William E. born ca 1896

   iv- **PHILLIPS** Mary born ca 1897, married George W. **MANNING**

   v- **PHILLIPS** James Walter born ca 1898, married Sarah **LARRIMER** born ca 1900. They had 3 children

   vi- **PHILLIPS** Robert Hazlett Cummings born ca 1899, married ____ **LANNING** and had 1 child.

496-   **LANNING** Lura (*Jasper P. Lanning, William Lanning, Jasper Lanning, Elizabeth, John, Jasper, John*) was born ca 1866 in Tompkins Co. NY daughter of Jasper P. **LANNING** and Sarah E. **WALLENBECK**. She married July 15, 1884 in Dryden, NY Albert A. **QUAIL** who was born 1858 son of William **QUAIL** and Sarah **SWARTS**. Unknown children.

497-   **LANNING** Anthela (*Jasper P. Lanning, William Lanning, Jasper Lanning, Elizabeth, John, Jasper, John*) was born 1868 in Tompkins Co. NY daughter of Jasper P. **LANNING** and Sarah E. **WALLENBECK** and died in Willseyville, NY September 12, 1948. She married November 8, 1889 Arthur E. **DYKEMAN** who was born June 22, 1863 in Candor, NY son of Orin Franklin **DYKEMAN** and Betsey **BOGARDUS** and died February 10, 1948 in Willseyville, NY.
Children:

   i- **DYKEMAN** Charlie born February 12, 1891, probably died before 1948, not mentioned in Mother's obit

   ii- **DYKEMAN** Esther born April 2, 1892 and married O. V. **COLLINS** and removed to Wheeling WV.

   iii- **DYKEMAN** Blanche born July 30, 1894 and married William **DICKERSON**, lived Trumansburg in 1948

   iv- **DYKEMAN** Lois born January 9, 1900 and married John **LEACH**, lived Ithaca, NY in 1948

   v- **DYKEMAN** daughter who married T. O. **MC MAHON**, lived in Trumansburg in 1948

498-   **LANNING** Charles Wesley (*Jasper P. Lanning, William Lanning, Jasper Lanning, Elizabeth, John, Jasper, John*) was born March 7, 1874 in Enfield, NY son of Jasper P. **LANNNING** and Sarah E. **WALLENBECK** and died April 18, 1956. His wife Aminda (unknown maiden name) was born May 28, 1888 and died 1962.
Children born in Enfield, NY

   i- **LANNING** Charles Wesley lived Danbury, Ct.

   ii- **LANNING** daughter who married Harold T. **MOORE** and removed to Clayton, NY

   iii- **LANNING** daughter who married Donald G. **WILSON** and removed to Rochester, NY

   iv- **LANNING** daughter who married Horton C. **MOSHER** and removed to Scotia, NY

499- **LANNING** Florence (*Jasper P. Lanning, William Lanning, Jasper Lanning, Elizabeth, John, Jasper, John*) was born 1876 in Tompkins Co. NY daughter of Jasper P. **LANNING** and Sarah E. **WALLENBECK**. She married (1) Leigh **HUNT** and married (2) Edward **MILLER**.
Child by first marriage:
    i- **HUNT** Margaret who married ____ **VARGO**, 2 children
Children by second marriage:
    ii- **MILLER** Lillian
    iii- **MILLER** Paul

500- **LANNING** Bertha (*Jasper P. Lanning, William Lanning, Jasper Lanning, Elizabeth, John, Jasper, John*) was born December 22, 1878 daughter of Jasper P. **LANNING** and Sarah E. **WALLENBECK**. She married December 27, 1902 Frank William **PENCILLE** who was born February 2, 1868 in Lockport, NY and died there May 16, 1947.
One child:
    i- **PENCILLE** Orville Lanning born March 24, 1904 married June 30, 1923 Elizabeth **DINSMORE** who died 1924. They had a daughter who married (2) ____ **ZEH** and had 2 children. He married (2) Rita **BURNS** and had 8 children

501- **LANNING** Edna Mae (*Jasper P. Lanning, William Lanning, Jasper Lanning, Elizabeth, John Jasper, John*) was born 1881 daughter of Jasper P. **LANNING** and Sara E. **WALLENBECK** and died May 19, 1915 in Enfield, NY. She married December 4, 1900 Albert **SCHEBER** who was born 1876 in Germany and died May 7, 1963.
Children:
    i- **SCHEBER** Ellsworth born November 14, 1901 and died February 21, 1984, married Lena **SHERWOOD** and divorced
    ii- **SCHEBER** Lola born September 29, 1905 and died December 2, 1980
    iii- **SCHEBER** Florence Ethel born November 2, 1907 amd died August 26, 2000. She married Grant **WILSON** born August 22, 1903 and died March 15, 1980, had a daughter, married ____ **LETTERER**

502- **LANNING** Frances L. (*Jasper P. Lanning, William Lanning, Jasper Lanning, Elizabeth, John, Jasper, John*) was born 1883 in Enfield, NY daughter of Jasper P. **LANNING** and Sarah E. **WALLENBECK** and died August 12, 1904. She married Elmer Clarence **RUMSEY** who was born 1878 in Enfield, NY son of Harrison Edgar and Emma **RUMSEY** and died July 7, 1954. They are buried in Woodlawn cemetery in Newfield, NY. He married (2) March 29, 1927 Evangeline **PURDY** born August 12, 1889 in Newfield, NY
Children born in Newfield, NY:
    i- **RUMSEY** Harlan Clarence born April 5, 1906 and died November 9, 1992 in Eustis, Fl., buried Woodlawn cemetery in Newfield, NY. He married (1) Mildred A. **CARPENTER** and had 1 child, married (2) ____ **PARKER** and had 1 child
704-    ii- **RUMSEY** Donald Howard born July 16, 1911

503- **JOHNSTON** Cornelia Phillips (*Ellen Phillips, Catherine Stevens, Thomas Stevens*

*Jr., Catherine, Jasper Jr., Jasper, John)* was born ca 1850 in Lawrenceville, NJ daughter of Benjamin F. JOHNSTON and Ellen PHILLIPS. She married June 17, 1880 Robert Ayres MESSLER born July 12, 1855 in Mercerville, NJ son of James MESSLER and Sarah Jemima AYRES.
Children born in Trenton, NJ:
> i- MESSLER Benjamin Edmund born November 29, 1882
> ii- MESSLER James Stevens born January 12, 1885
> iii- MESSLER Mary Johnston born November 14, 1893

504-    SMITH Caroline Louise *(Peter, Benjamin, Israel Jr., Israel, Jasper, Jasper, John)* was born November 3, 1877 in Delaware daughter of Peter Ten Eyck SMITH and Caroline Louise TEN EYCK and died December 16, 1956 in Northridge, Cal. She married Charles Clark LAWTON who was born September 14, 1876 in Philadelphia, Pa. son of William J. LAWTON and Fanetta CLARK and died May 7, 1955 in Glendale, Cal. They are buried in Forest Lawn Memorial Park.
Children:
705-    i- LAWTON Carolyn Louise born January 28, 1902 in Del.
Children born in Los Angeles Co. Cal.
        ii- LAWTON Charles Clark Jr. born April 6, 1904, married Irene THOMPSON born 1910 and died 1970
        iii- LAWTON Gertrude S. born July 1, 1910, married Louis GROCE
        iv- LAWTON Robert C. born April 4, 1913
        v- LAWTON Katherine born September 7, 1916, married Chester Arthur GOSS

505-    BOOTH Ella S. *(Ella Marie, Benjamin, Israel Jr., Israel, Jasper, Jasper, John)* was born July 25, 1882 in Wilington, Del. daughter of Charles BOOTH and Ella Marie SMITH and died in Phoenix, Ar. She married Gideon T. SMITHETON Jr. born ca 1864.

506-    WHITE Sarah Clarissa *(John White, Mercy Tindall, Joseph Tindall, Abigail, Thomas, Jasper, John)* was born 1835 in NJ daughter of John WHITE and Bethany S. BIRD and died 1898. She married September 11, 1856 Coursen Henry ALBERTSON who was born March 26, 1833 son of Samson ALBERTSON and Abbie S. COURSEN and died January 7, 1913.
Children born Great Meadows, NJ:
706-    i- ALBERTSON Emily Frances born February 17, 1857
707-    ii- ALBERTSON John White born December 20, 1858
708-    iii- ALBERTSON Kerr Freeman born February 12, 1860
709-    iv- ALBERTSON Anna Bird born March 15, 1863
710-    v- ALBERTSON William Coursen born March 27, 1865
711-    vi- ALBERTSON Milton Hoagland born March 10, 1869
712-    vii- ALBERTSON Jennie Clarissa born October 18, 1871
        viii- ALBERTSON Charles Edwin born May 14, 1873 and died September 18, 1873
        ix- ALBERTSON Bertha White born November 10, 1875 and died September 27,
1877

507-   **WHITE** Hiram D. (*John White, Mercy Tindall, Joseph Tindall, Abigail, Thomas, Jasper, John*) was born June 9, 1837 in Monmouth Co. NJ son of John **WHITE** and Bethany S. **BIRD** and died 1926 in Beattsville, NJ. He married Theodosia **MARTIN** who was born 1839 and died 1892.
Children:
> i- **WHITE** Elizabeth M. born 1864 and died 1871
> ii- **WHITE** William W. born 1877 and died 1878

508-   **SMITH** George Martin (*David L., James L., Thomas H., Elijah, Thomas, Jasper, John*) was born April 26, 1870 in Pontotoc Co. Ms. son of David Lofton **SMITH** and Susan Jane **BROWNING** and died July 17, 1943 in Conway Co. Ar. He married November 5, 1898 in Preston Nannie Della **HOPPER** who was born January 3, 1881 and died March 17, 1957 in Conway Co. Ar.
Children:
> i- **SMITH** Marvin Homer born 1901 and died 1963, married Grace **SEAGO**
> ii- **SMITH** Gladys Leona
> iii- **SMITH** Garland Lester born May 7, 1906 in Conway Co. and died August 26, 1959 in Little Rock, Az. He married July 25, 1925 in Little Rock Harriet Elizabeth **CLARK** and had 2 children
> iv- **SMITH** Dolphus Edward born 1909 and died 1982
> v- **SMITH** daughter
> vi- **SMITH** daughter
> vii- **SMITH** daughter

509-   **BERRY** Joseph Henry (*Resin B. Berry, Susannah, Thomas H., Elijah, Thomas, Jasper, John*) was born March 30, 1853 in Pontotoc Co. Ms. son of Resin Bowie **BERRY** and Christian **WARREN** and died July 22, 1933 in Shady Grove, Ms. He married (1) Mary Etta Dyson **RUTLEDGE** and (2) February 14, 1874 M. A. **MC KAOWN** who was born June 25, 1856 in Sulphur Springs, Ms. and died May 9, 1897 in Ms. He married (3) May 27, 1901 M. A. Dyson **TODD**.
Children by second marriage:
> i- **BERRY** Laura L. born February 21, 1878 in Marshall Ms. and died December 25, 1908 in Hurricane, Ms. She married June 2, 1901 James Franklin **MC NEELEY**.
> ii- **BERRY** Jessie M. born February 11, 1880 in Marshall, Ms. and died February 25, 1959 in Hurricane, Ms. She married February 2, 1904 E. Z. **CAPLES**.
> iii- **BERRY** Mary Elizabeth born January 26, 1882 in Marshall, Ms. and died May 6, 1933 in Hurricane, Ms. She married February 8, 1905 Luther **MC CAIN**.
> iv- **BERRY** Nancy D. born December 5, 1884 in Logan Co. Az. She married January 27, 1902 Garvin **RUSSELL**.
> v- **BERRY** Bonnie C. born July 2, 1887 in Johnson Co. Az. She married February 15, 1905 Arthur **KIDD**
> vi- **BERRY** Thomas H. born May 3, 1890 in Pototoc Co. Ms. and died March 29, 1899
> vii- **BERRY** William A. born May 27. 1893 in Pontotoc Co. Ms. and died June 28,

1947. He married October 1912 Ather Lee **DOWDY**.
twin girls born October 29, 1896 and died same day

510- **STAGGS** George Birton (*Mary Berry, Susannah, Thomas H., Elijah, Thomas, Jasper, John*) was born was born February 14, 1860 in Jackson Co. Ar. son of Eli **STAGGS** and Mary **BERRY**. He married January 29, 1882 in Conway Co. Ar. Anna Josephine **THOMPSON** who was born 1858 in Jackson Co. Ar. and died July 14, 1899 in Opello, Ar. Children born in Woodruff Co. Ar.:
713-      i- **STAGGS** Mildred May born May 28, 1884
714-      ii- **STAGGS** George Lewis born July 8, 1886
            iii- **STAGGS** Carl born October 18, 1888 and died October 30, 1888
            iv- **STAGGS** James Birten born January 4, 1890 and died October 4, 1890
715-      v- **STAGGS** Walter Columbus born April 1, 1892
716-      vi- **STAGGS** William Robert born August 3, 1894
717-      vii- **STAGGS** Charles H. born August 23, 1896

511- **BERRY** Martha J. (*Burton L. Berry, Susannah, Thomas H., Elijah, Thomas, Jasper, John*) was born ca 1864 in Ar. daughter of Burton Litton **BERRY** and Mary Jane **SELLERS** and died 1903. She married (1) January 16, 1879 George **STUART** born ca 1857 in Ms. and married (2) Luther Henry **LONG** born ca 1856 in NC.
Children:
            i- **STUART** Lillie May born January 13, 1879 in Deview, Ar.
            ii- **STUART** William Archer born September 17, 1883 in Gray's Sta. Ar. and died after 1912 in Anson, Tx., buried Abilene, Tx.. He married in Anson Betty C. **BLACK**, 1 daughter

512- **BERRY** Willie A. (*Burton L. Berry, Susannah, Thomas H., Elijah, Thomas, Jasper, John*) was born 1866 in Ar. daughter of Burton Litton **BERRY** and Mary Jane **SELLERS** and died in Brownsfield, Tx. She married September 24, 1884 in Woodruff Co. Ar. J. W. **COLLIER**.
Children:
            i- **COLLIER** Fay
            ii- **COLLIER** Ernest
            iii= **COLLIER** Roy
            iv- **COLLIER** Mabel

513- **BERRY** Nannie May (*Burton L. Berry, Suaannah, Thomas H., Elijah, Thomas, Jasper, John*) was born October 18, 1871 in Woodruff Co. Ar. and died December 21, 1963 in Woodruff Co. Ar., buried Oddfellows cemetery. She married (1) Walter **BARBER** and married (2) December 27, 1893 in Mc Crory, Ar. James Alfred **MILLER**.
Child by first marriage:
            i- **BARBER** Mildred
Children by second marriage:
            ii- **MILLER** Versie

136

iii- **MILLER** Onia Cleo born September 4, 1898 and died October 1968 in Mc Crory, Ar. She married April 2, 1919 in Woodruff Co. James Marberry **CHAPPELL** born January 21, 1889

    iv- **MILLER** James Bernice born November 23, 1900 and died February 4, 1964

514-  **BERRY** John Thomas (*Burton L. Berry, Susannah, Thomas H., Elijah, Thomas, Jasper, John*) was born February 18, 1878 in Mc Crory, Ar. son of Burton Litton **BERRY** and Easter **CRAIG** and died December 4, 1968 in Abilene, Tx. He married (1) Mollie L. **THOMAS** who was born 1878 in Ar. and died April 29, 1907. He married (2) June 27, 1909 in Anson, Tx. Virginia Sarina Anne **BILLINGSLEY** who was born April 24, 1876 in Booneville, Ms. and died August 1, 1974 in Abilene, Tx. They are buried in Cedar Hill cemetery.
Children by first marriage:
    i- **BERRY** Lehmon
    ii- **BERRY** Willard born ca 1900 in Ar. married Lavern ____
    iii- **BERRY** Lehman
Children by second marriage:
    iv- **BERRY** Burton Billingsley born September 12, 1910 in Anson, Tx. and died December 2, 1962 in Abilene, Tx.
    v- **BERRY** son married Sarah Zelma **DILL** born April 12, 1918 in Abilene, Tx. and died June 17, 1993 in Gr. Prairie, Tx.
    vi- **BERRY** daughter

515-  **BERRY** Mary Elizabeth (*Burton L. Berry, Susannah, Thomas H., Elijah, Thomas Jasper, John*) was born January 1880 in Mc Crory, Ar. daughter of Burton Litton **BERRY** and Easter **CRAIG** and died 1913 in Mc Crory, buried Oddfellows cemetery. She married June 7, 1903 in Mc Crory William Benjamin **WISE** who was born November 10, 1879 in Mc Crory and died October 8, 1960 in Royal Oak, Mi., buried Woodman cemetery.
Children:
    i- **WISE** Jefferson Davis born March 14, 1904 and died June 17, 1982 in El Paso, Tx. He married July 4, 1931 in Lawton, Ok. Jewell Theus **FULLER** born 1913 in Marlow, Ok. and died 1997
    ii- **WISE** Eugene born 1906 in Mc Crory and died 1920
    iii- **WISE** Howard Taft born October 30, 1908 and died December 14, 1987 in Troy, Mi. He married ____ **BLAZINA** and had 3 children
    iv- **WISE** Annie Penn born 1910 and died 1913

516-  **BERRY** Burton E. (*Burton L. Berry, Susannah, Thomas H., Elijah, Thomas, Jasper, John*) was born January 1886 in Ar. son of Burton L. **BERRY** and Mary Frances **HESS** and died 1967 in Corpus Christi, Tx., buried Oddfellows cemetery. He married December 30, 1906 in Riverside, Ar. Elizabeth **GIPSON** born 1886 in Tn. and died 1973 in Kerrville, Tx.
Children:
    i- **BERRY** Alton
    ii- **BERRY** Roy

iii- **BERRY** Otis born October 1908 and died 1973. He had 1 son (spouse unknown)

iv- **BERRY** daughter

517- **STAGGS** Florence Arminda (*Nancy J. Berry, Susannah, Thomas H., Elijah, Thomas, Jasper, John*) was born March 10, 1866 in Augusta, Ar. daughter of Eli **STAGGS** and Nancy Jane **BERRY** and died 1935 in Cal. She married December 22, 1887 William Webster **BATES** born November 25, 1860 in Newton, Ga. and died August 13, 1926 in Eldorado, Ok.

Children:

i- **BATES** Willie Lea born October 27, 1888 in Newport, Ar. She married Green Fred **DANIELL** who was born April 1883 in Ga. and died September 3, 1923 in Windling, Ore. They had son Jesse Frederick and a daughter

ii- **BATES** Jesse Earl born October 31, 1891 in Crawford, Tx

iii- **BATES** Ada Pearl born June 1894 in Tx. and married Fritz **FITZGERALD**

iv- **BATES** Nora Minnie born October 7, 1897 in Goldwaite, Tx. and died March 15, 1918

v- **BATES** Chancy C. born August 23, 1900 in Eldorado, Ok. and died September 3, 1900

vi- **BATES** Robert Webster (spouse unknown) had 1 son

vii- **BATES** Albert

718- viii- **BATES** Beaulah Beatrice born June 1, 1907 in Eldorado

518- **BERRY** William Andrew (*James M. Berry, Susannah, Thomas H., Elijah, Thomas, Jasper, John*) was born November 16, 1871 in Ar. son of James Madison **BERRY** and Nancy Emeline **SELLERS** and died May 10, 1943 in Ar. He married in 1900 Katherine Ristice **CURETON** born February 9, 1877 in Tn. and died 1957 in Conway Co. Ar.

Children:

i- **BERRY** William Madison married (1) ___ **FERGUSON** (2) ___ **MC CLOSKEY** and (3) Duvall **TOWNSEND**

ii- **BERRY** Hugh born January 23, 1908 and died June 3, 1911

iii- **BERRY** Annie Lea born May 29, 1910 and died November 26, 1911

iv- **BERRY** son married ___ **THURMAN** and had 2 children

v- **BERRY** daughter married Aphi **RIDGEWAY** born July 22, 1873 and died 1898 in Conway Co. Ar. They had a son Carlton born November 1897 and died 1900 in Conway Co.

519- **BERRY** James Walter (*James M. Berry, Susannah, Thomas H., Elijah, Thomas, Jasper, John*) was born August 19, 1885 in Ar. son of James Madison **BERRY** and Nancy Emeline **SELLERS** and died December 12, 1959 in Seminole, Ok. He married Myrtle **HAWKINS** who was born August 1, 1887.

Children:

i- **BERRY** Syble Wyoma born January 18, 1910 and died 1955. She married (1) January 8, 1936 James H. **COLE** and had 1 son. She married (2) Eudie S. **GROSS**

ii- **BERRY** daughter

520- **WEATHERALL** William Preston (*Susan Arrens, William P., Thomas H., Elijah, Thomas, Jasper, John*) was born March 25, 1861 in New Albany, Ms. son of John Hodges **WEATHERALL** and Susan Arrens **SMITH** and died August 3, 1948 in Eastland, Tx. He married Almadore **BARRETT** born San Augustine, Tx.
Children:

    i- **WEATHERALL** James Preston
    ii- **WEATHERALL** Mary
    iii- **WEATHERALL** Stella

521- **WEATHERALL** Georgia Anna Sarah Virginia (*Susan Arrens, William P., Thomas H., Elijah, Thomas, Jasper, John*) was born October 28, 1870 in New Albany, Ms. daughter of John Hodges **WEATHERALL** and Susan Arrens **SMITH** and died in Ok. She married James Thomas **DEAN**.
Children:

    i- **DEAN** Carl married Verda **SNYDER** and had 3 children, Peter, Susan and Carl
    ii- **DEAN** Evie
    iii- **DEAN** Susan
    iv- **DEAN** John
    v- **DEAN** James
    vi- **DEAN** Lee

522- **WEATHERALL** James Thomas (*Susan Arrens, William P., Thomas H., Elijah, Thomas, Jasper, John*) was born August 10, 1875 in New Albany, Ms. son of John Hodges **WEATHERALL** and Susan Arrens **SMITH** and died June 21, 1937 in Waco, Tx. He married (1) Alma **COOK** and (2) Sarah Mattie **SPAIN** who was born August 24, 1884 in Decatur, Ala. and died November 20, 1970 in Grove Hill.
Children:

    i- **WEATHERALL** Minnie born May 6, 1897 and died June 5, 1967 in Waxahachie, Tx.
    ii- **WEATHERALL** William Claude born August 18, 1894, married (1) Hazel Pauline **BARKER** (2) Minnie Lucille **MORRIS**, 2 children and married (3) Willie Frances **MORRIS** born April 16, 1919 in Lone Cedar, Tx. He had 3 children that died at birth
    iii- **WEATHERALL** Robert Edward born February 21, 1907
    iv- **WEATHERALL** Lila Gertrude born July 27, 1909 and died February 10, 1935 in Longview, Tx., buried Grace Hill cemetery

523- **WEATHERALL** Carrie Amanda Lee (*Susan Arrens, William P., Thomas H., Elijah, Thomas, Jasper, John*) was born April 20, 1878 in New Albany, Ms. daughter of John Hodges **WEATHERALL** and Susan Arrens **SMITH** and died June 30, 1955 in Oklahoma City, Ok. She married November 15, 1896 in Ennis, Tx. Robert Ernest **BOREN** born February 22, 1874 in Reager Springs, Tx. and was murdered in Paoli, Ok. September 9, 1932. They are buried in Paoli cemetery.
Children born in Ellis Co. Tx.:

    i- **BOREN** Loray Arrena born September 26, 1897 and died January 1900 in

Reagor Springs, Tx.

    ii- **BOREN** Ralph Elliot born March 10, 1900, married Jimmie **COLBERT**

    iii- **BOREN** Ferrell Celeste born March 23, 1902 and died October 1, 1961 in Norman, Ok. She married April 20, 1929 James Victor **CONOVER** born October 12, 1901 in Windham, Tx. son of James Patrick **CONOVER** and Mary Elizabeth **HOLLADAY** and died December 7, 1988 in Norman, Ok. 2 children

    iv- **BOREN** James Clyde born September 13, 1904 and died March 1987 in Norman, Ok. He married July 1, 1928 in Oklahoma City Leta L. **SHEPARD** who was born March 10, 1909 and died January 4, 1977. They had 2 sons

    v- **BOREN** Willie Katherine August 23, 1907 and died March 3, 1996 in Norman, Ok. She married June 30, 1933 in Oklahoma City Ralph William **KELLY** who was born April 5, 1907 in Gibbs, Mo. and died May 19, 1978 in Norman, Ok., 1 son

    vi- **BOREN** Martha Sue born December 23, 1909 and died in Norman, Ok. She married Silas M. **VAWTER** and had 1 daughter

    vii- **BOREN** Robert Laverle born 1913, married Hazel J. **FLORENCE** and had 2 daughters

    viii- **BOREN** Mark Latimer born May 11, 1916, married May 10, 1951 Ruth Mc Laughlin **BROOKS**

524-   **SMITH** Thomas Hendricks (*Thomas H., William P., Thomas H., Elijah, Thomas, Jasper, John*) was born July 1, 1885 in New Albany, Ms. son Thomas Hunt **SMITH** and Martha Meador **JARVIS** and died April 22, 1962 in Memphis, Tn. He married Mable C. **LIPSCOMB** who died September 10, 1979, buried Memphis Gardens.
Children:

    i- **SMITH** Paul born 1907 and died 1966 in Memphis, Tn.

    ii- **SMITH** Alton Lee born July 22, 1908 in Memphis, Tn., married October 31, 1931 Eugenia **ANDERSON**, 2 daughters

    iii- **SMITH** Milton born March 8, 1912 and died 1973 in Memphis, Tn., married _____ **KIMBRELL** and had 5 children

525-   **KNOX** Minnie Pearl (*John B. Knox, Elijah Knox, Cynthia. Elijah, Thomas, Jasper, John*) was born February 10, 1892 in Cannon, Tn. daughter of John Basil **KNOX** and Lorena **CARNHAHAN** and died February 26, 1941 in Santa Maria, Cal. She married John Gordon **MELTON** who was born August 10, 1889 in Rockwell, Tx. son of James B. **MELTON** and Sarah Elizabeth **LOONEY** and died September 27, 1971 in Harbor City, Cal.
Children:

    i- **MELTON** John Ronald born March 24, 1912 in Hall Tx. and died April 27, 1967 in Cal.

719-   ii- **MELTON** Mary Helen born November 15, 1913 in Tx.

    iii- **MELTON** J. B. born January 24, 1917 in Hall, Tx.

526-   **MALOTT** Adnie (*Francis L. Malott, Ann, Absolom, John, Samuel, Jasper, John*) was born August 28, 1847 in Brown Co. Ohio daughter of Francis L. and Margaret

MALOTT and died December 7, 1911 in Milford Twp. Ill. She married April 5, 1865 in Marathon, Ohio Isaac H. SCOTT who was born 1843 in Brown Co. Ohio son of Isaac SCOTT and died January 28, 1897 in Iroquois Co. Ill. He served in Co. B. 48th Ohio Inf.
Children:
720-    i- SCOTT Sidney Ann born June 1866 in Clermont Co. Ohio
721-    ii- SCOTT Lillian B. born October 3, 1868 in Brown Co. Oh.
722-    iii- SCOTT John born September 6, 1872 in Brown Co. Oh.
723-    iv- SCOTT Margaret L. born September 16, 1875 in Brown Co.
        v- SCOTT Gula Esta born May 28, 1881, died July 4, 1882
        vi- SCOTT Dora L. born March 31, 1886 in Iroquois Co. Ill. and died April 15, 1965 in Hoopeston, buried Amity cemetery
        vii- SCOTT Walter F. born September 5, 1888 in Ash Grove Twp, Iroquois Co. Ill., lived Cal.

527-    HOWELL Marquis De Lafayette (*Anna A. Corwin, Elizabeth Biles, George Biles, Christian, Joshua, Jasper, John*) was born November 21, 1849 in Hope, Twp. NJ son of John Stinson HOWELL and Anna Alice CORWIN and died July 12, 1918 in Chicago, Ill., buried Mt. Greenwood cemetery in Chicago. He married February 4, 1874 Helen Leach SUMMERS who died before 1900.
Known children:
        i- HOWELL Floyd Wilbur born January 2, 1876
724-    ii- HOWELL Albert Summers born April 17, 1879
        iii- HOWELL Clyde John born October 14, 1885, buried Mt. Greenwood cemetery

528-    HOWELL William Biles (*Anna A. Corwin, Elizabeth Biles, George Biles, Christian, Joshua, Jasper, John*) was born September 29, 1851 in Hope Twp. NJ son of John Stinson HOWELL and Anna A. CORWIN and died March 31, 1935 in Rochester, Mi. He married February 23, 1881 in Avon Twp, Mi. Alice Beckwith NEWBERRY who was born June 18, 1859 in Avon Twp. daughter of Milo P. and Mary E. NEWBERRY and died March 29, 1924 in Rochester, Mi. They are buried in Mt. Avon cemetery in Rochester, Mi.
Children born Avon Twp. Mi.:
725-    i- HOWELL Maybelle born November 18, 1881
726-    ii- HOWELL Chester Arthur born April 4, 1883
727-    iii- HOWELL Anna Alice born October 16, 1887
728-    iv- HOWELL John Stinson born April 20, 1891
729-    v- HOWELL Milo Max born July 18, 1897 and died June 26, 1959 in Rochester.
730-    vi- HOWELL Leah Ruth born April 20, 1901 and died July 16, 1978 in Rochester Hill, Mi.

529-    HOWELL Emma A. (*Anna Corwin, Elizabeth Biles, George Biles, Christian, Joshua, Jasper, John*) was born 1856 in Hope, NJ daughter of John Stinson HOWELL and Anna CORWIN and died October 4, 1906 in Grand Rapids, Mi. She married (1) Mr. PRATT (2) George FELLOWS and married (3) James CHIPMAN.
Children by second marriage:

i- FELLOWS Boyd
ii- FELLOWS Ida May

530-    HOWELL Alice Lavina (*Anna Corwin, Elizabeth Biles, George Biles, Christian, Joshua, Jasper, John*) was born 1859 in Hope, NY daughter of John Stinson HOWELL and Anna CORWIN and died October 1, 1940 in Knox, Ind.  She married Charles MOORE
Children:
    i- MOORE Elmer born ca 1884
    ii- MOORE John born ca 1886

531-    LUNDY Sarah Ann (*Margaret Vliet, Anna Biles, George Biles, Christian, Joshua, Jasper, John*) was born October 26, 1856 in Warren Co. NJ daughter of Jonathan LUNDY and Margaret VLIET and died after January 3, 1920.  She married December 31, 1878 Albert Sylvester RAUB who was born January 4, 1852 in Warren Co. NJ son of Jacob Butts RAUB and Rachel Diltz LANTERMAN and died June 18, 1905 in Blairstown, NJ.  They are buried in Cedar Ridge cemetery.
One known child:
731-    i- RAUB Charles J. born June 2, 1882 in NJ.

532-    LUNDY Julia Elizabeth (*Margaret Vliet, Anna Biles, George Biles, Christian, Joshua, Jasper, John*) was born December 12, 1860 in Warren Co. NJ daughter of Jonathan LUNDY and Margaret VLIET and died May 10, 1902.  She married John Alvey BIRD who was born August 22, 1854 in Warren Co. NJ son of Thomas Stewart BIRD and Elizabeth LANTERMAN and died January 20, 1900.  They are buried in Brick Union cemetery in Blairstown, NJ.

533-    LUNDY William Vliet (*Margaret Vliet, Anna Biles, George Biles, Christian, Joshua, Jasper, John*) was born January 13, 1862 in Warren Co. NJ son of Jonathan LUNDY and Margaret VLIET and died January 29, 1926 in Ramseyville, NJ.  He married ca 1887 Elizabeth ACKLEY born ca 1866 who died January 29, 1926 in Ramseyville, NJ
One known child:
    i- LUNDY George Ackley born January 1888

534-    HAZEN Almatha (*Rebecca Hayes, Electa Biles, George Biles, Christian, Joshua, Jasper, John*) was born July 4, 1848 in Hope, NJ daughter of Abraham Newman HAZEN and Rebecca HAYES.  She married July 26, 1840 in Baltimore, Md. Francis Thomas MORRISON who was born March 16, 1848 in Baltimore, Md. and died May 20, 1884 in Allegany, Pa.
Children:
    i- MORRISON Charles Francis born June 8, 1872 in Allegany, Pa.  He married July 26, 1898 in Washington, DC Daisy Adell HAYNES born October 1, 1874 in Nashville, Tn.  No issue
    ii- MORRISON William Walter born June 19, 1874 in Allegany, Pa.  He married July 24, 1898 Minnie Virginia GRAY who was born April 4, 1876 in Dumfries, Va.

daughter of Charles Francis **GRAY** and Mary Catherine **BRAWNER**. They had 1 child
iii- **MORRISON** Harry born December 10, 1876 in Allegany, Pa. He married January 12, 1899 Emma M. **FASTNAUGHT**.
iv- **MORRISON** Annetta born December 2, 1878, married Will **REESE**

535- **HAZEN** Ann Elizabeth (*Rebecca Hayes, Electa Biles, George Biles, Christian, Joshua, Jasper, John*) was born August 8, 1850 in Catlett, Va. daughter of Abraham Newman **HAZEN** and Rebecca **HAYES**. She married in Washington DC January 10, 1877 Theodore **MITCHELL** who was born January 1852 son of George **MITCHELL** and Elizabeth **HORNBAKER**
Child:
i- **MITCHELL** Meda Addie born May 2, 1891 in Dumfries, Va. and married William **LIEISHEARS**

536- **HAZEN** Eugenia (*Rebecca Hayes, Electa Biles, George Biles, Christian, Joshua, Jasper, John*) born September 27, 1852 in Catlett, Va. daughter of Abraham Newman **HAZEN** and Rebecca **HAYES**. She married in Washington, DC November 17, 1880 Jerry Milton **HEPBURN** who was born January 20, 1852 in Washington, DC son of Peter **HEPBURN** and Mary **YOUNG**. They resided Indian Head, Md.
Children:
i- **HEPBURN** Mabel Irene born May 5, 1882. She married in Baltimore, Md. August 12, 1907 Charles Francis **CAMPBELL** who was born July 2, 1878 in Washington, DC son of John Alfred **CAMPBELL** and Molly Ann **HEATH**. They had 1 child.
ii- **HEPBURN** Arthur Wesley born January 10, 1884. He married September 19, 1906 Mary Theresa **WHITE** who was born September 4, 1885 in Washington, DC daughter of William Joseph **WHITE** and Ann **HARPER**. One daughter Margaret Isabella born November 18, 1907 in Washington, DC

537- **HAZEN** Ernest Carroll (*Rebecca Hayes, Electa Biles, George Biles, Christian, Joshua, Jasper, John*) was born May 24, 1871 in Washington, DC son of Abraham Newman **HAZEN** and Rebecca **HAYES**. He married September 1906 in Washington, DC Evalyne Martina **ALLEN** born September 4, 1885 in Norfolk, Va. daughter of Richard Marion **ALLEN** and Annie Lillian **PERINE**.
Children:
i- **HAZEN** Elmer Allen born January 11, 1896 and died February 22, 1896
ii- **HAZEN** Ethel Mildred born January 3, 1897. She married September 16, 1915 in Alexandria, Va. William John **BELL** born April 14, 1897 in Washington DC son of William Alexander **BELL** and Ella **BALL**
iii- **HAZEN** Grace born April 10, 1898 in Washington DC

538- **RUSSELL** Harmon (*Hulda Nicholson, Sally, William, Joshua, Joshua, Jasper, John*) was born February 17, 1864 in Fremont, NY son of Harrison **RUSSELL** and Hulda **NICHOLSON**. He married Cora M. (maiden name unknown) who was born January 1868. One child:

i- **RUSSELL** Ethel C. born November 1886, resided NY City and Philadelphia, Pa.

539- **RUSSELL** Alice (*Hulda Nicholson, Sally, William, Joshua, Joshua, Jasper, John*) was born February 8, 1867 in Fremont, NY daughter of Harrison **RUSSELL** and Hulda **NICHOLSON** and died 1930. She married March 20, 1891 in Fremont James **VAN KEUREN** who was born May 15, 1847 in Fremont son of Tcherick P. **VAN KEUREN** and Eleanor B. **SPAULDING** and died 1931. They are buried in Howard cemetery.
Children:
732-    i- **VAN KEUREN** Ila born February 7, 1900
      ii- **VAN KEUREN** Frank born 1902 and died 1986

540- **RUSSELL** Anna D. (*Hulda Nicholson, Sally, William, Joshua, Joshua, Jasper, John*) was born December 21, 1868 in Fremont, NY daughter of Harrison **RUSSELL** and Hulda **NICHOLSON** and died April 15, 1919 in Hornellsville, NY. She married December 21, 1886 in Fremont, NY Francis Marion **BURDETT** who was born June 26, 1860 in S. Dansville, NY son of Paul **BURDETT** and Mary A. **CURRY** and died February 4, 1931 in Hornell, NY, both buried in Howard cemetery.
Children born in Fremont, NY:
      i- **BURDETT** Paul S. born July 4, 1889 and died January 29, 1890
      ii- **BURDETT** Alice born April 17, 1891 and died January 3, 1892
733-   iii- **BURDETT** Donald Sawyer born September 22, 1893
734-   iv- **BURDETT** Joel Dean born August 12, 1896
735-   v- **BURDETT** Pauline Hulda born May 25, 1898
      vi- **BURDETT** George W. born February 29, 1900 and died July 29, 1901
736-   vii- **BURDETT** Murray Roscoe born March 24, 1902
737-  viii- **BURDETT** Beatrice Kathleen born July 6, 1904
738-   ix- **BURDETT** Roy Francis born August 16, 1906
739-   x- **BURDETT** Abby Lena born December 6, 1907
740-   xi- **BURDETT** James Wilson born December, 29 1912

541- **RUSSELL** Mary Elsie (*Hulda Nicholson, Sally, William, Joshua, Joshua, Jasper, John*) was born February 13, 1871 in Fremont, NY daughter of Harrison **RUSSELL** and Hulda **NICHOLSON** and died December 5, 1930 in Fremont, NY. She married November 9, 1889 Murray Charles **BURDETT** (also called Charles M.) who was born June 19, 1858 in S. Dansville, NY son of Paul S. **BURDETT** and Mary **CURRY** and died October 12, 1933 in Fremont, NY
Children:
741-   i- **BURDETT** Elmer Paul May 19, 1891 in Howard, NY
742-   ii- **BURDETT** Shirley Russell was born February 19, 1893
743-  iii- **BURDETT** Mary Wadsworth born September 30, 1894
744-   iv- **BURDETT** Ethel Vance born September 7, 1900
745-   v- **BURDETT** Charles Kenneth born April 25, 1904

144

542-   **RUSSELL** Joel Dean (*Hulda Nicholson, Sally, William, Joshua, Joshua, Jasper, John*) was born in Fremont, NY July 17, 1879 son of Harrison **RUSSELL** and Hulda **NICHOLSON** and died 1946.  He married ca 1900 Nellie **MOORE** who was born April 2, 1878 daughter of Henry **MOORE** and Martha **HOBER** and died June 15, 1951 in Fremont. Children:
746-   i- **RUSSELL** Harold H.
747-   ii- **RUSSELL** Harrison

543-   **NICHOLSON** Maria Antoinette (*Egbert Nicholson, Sally, William, Joshua, Joshua, Jasper, John*) was born ca 1863 daughter of Egbert **NICHOLSON** and Clarissa **LOGHRY** and died 1931. She married March 25, 1886 in Hornellsville, NY Curt D. **RANGER** who was born 1865 son of Henry R. **RANGER** and Betsey **BENNETT** and died 1946.  They are buried in Hope cemetery.
One known child:
      i- **RANGER** Bernice born June 5, 1902 (see #733)

544-   **NICHOLSON** Fannie S. (*Egbert Nicholson, Sally, William, Joshua, Joshua, Jasper, John*) was born January 2, 1867 daughter of Egbert **NICHOLSON** and Clarissa **LOGHRY** and died in Hornellsville, June 10, 1911.  She married May 15, 1890 in Hornell, NY David Devilo **WELD** who was born 1863 in Fremont, NY son of Eli T. **WELD** and Emma **BARDEEN** and died 1931.  They are buried in Howard cemetery.

545-   **NICHOLSON** Howard (*Egbert Nicholson, Sally, William, Joshua, Joshua, Jasper, John*) was born ca 1869 in Fremont, NY son of Egbert **NICHOLSON** and Clarissa **LOGHRY**.  He married September 16, 1891 in Hornell, NY Dora **BRASTED** born ca 1873 in Howard, NY daughter of Martin **BRASTED** and Emily **SAXTON**.

546-   **NICHOLSON** Anna Laura (*Egbert Nicholson, Sally, William, Joshua, Joshua, Jasper, John*) was born ca 1875 daughter of Egbert **NICHOLSON** and Clarissa **LOGHRY**. She married November 2, 1898 in Hornellsville, NY John H. **MOORE** son of Oliver **MOORE** and Margaret **HAUBER**.

547-   **NICHOLSON** Edmund F. (*Horatio Nicholson, Sally, William, Joshua, Joshua, Jasper, John*) was born ca 1869 son of Horatio **NICHOLSON** and Eliza **FOWLER**.  He married May 6, 1924 in Hornell, NY Bertha M. **NICHOLS** daughter of Jesse L. **NICHOLS** and Edith **SWAIN**

548-   **SMITH** Addie (*Alonzo, Abram, William, Joshua, Joshua, Jasper, John*) was born March 17, 1871 in Hornellsville, NY daughter of Alonzo **SMITH** and Electa **FORMAN** and died 1965.  She married November 3, 18__ Martin **CONDERMAN** probably son of Jacob and Sarah **CONDERMAN** born ca 1864
Children:
748-   i- **CONDERMAN** Gordon S. born December 10, 1891
749-   ii- **CONDERMAN** Ethel born 1893

549- SMITH Nellie (*Alonzo, Abram, William, Joshua, Joshua, Jasper, John*) was born September 22, 1872 in Hornellsville, NY daughter of Alonzo SMITH and Electa FORMAN and died 1959. She married Herbert Vern ROBERTS born 1872 son of William ROBERTS and died 1948. They are buried in Stephens Mills cemetery.
Children born in Hornellsville, NY:
750-      i- ROBERTS Mernie born September 22, 1891
751-      ii- ROBERTS Florence Janet born July 22, 1893
752-      i- ROBERTS Hazel Belle born July 25, 1895
753-      ii- ROBERTS Gertrude Mae born October 26. 1903 N. Hornell

550- SMITH Ella (*Alonzo, Abram, William, Joshua, Joshua, Jasper, John*) was born June 22, 1875 in Hornellsville, NY daughter of Alonzo SMITH and Electa FORMAN and died in Corning, NY December 12, 1937. She married October 6, 1890 in Hornellsville, NY George S. COOPER son of Philetus COOPER and Jane BRANK.
One known child:
         i- COOPER Francis J. born 1902 and died 1938, buried in Nicholson cemetery in Hornellsville.

551- SMITH Roscoe (*Alonzo, Abram, William, Joshua, Joshua, Jasper, John*) was born 1878 in Hornellsville, NY son of Alonzo SMITH and Sarah SOUTHERBY and died 1965 in Hornellsville, NY. He married Edna MESICK who was born 1884 daughter of Charles MESICK and Lydia Adelia TOWLE and died 1958. They are buried in the Nicholson cemetery in Hornellsville.
One child:
         i- SMITH Charles Albert born 1916 married in Bath, NY July 14, 1960 Lillian MERCELL daughter of William MERCELL and Ida CLEVELAND

552- SMITH Alonzo Jr. (*Alonzo, Abram, William, Joshua, Joshua, Jasper, John*) was born 1880 in Hornellsville, NY son of Alonzo SMITH and Sarah SOUTHERBY and died 1953 in Alfred, NY. He married Pearl JOHNSON who was born 1881 and died 1961.
Children:
754-      i- SMITH Clifford born January 25, 1905
755-      ii- SMITH Mildred born 1914

553- SMITH Bertha (*Alonzo, Abram, William, Joshua, Joshua, Jasper, John*) was born April 25, 1889 in Hornellsville, NY daughter of Alonzo SMITH and Sarah SOUTHERBY and died March 15, 1876 She married March 4, 1906 David GRIFFIN who was born September 13, 1888 in Wayne Co. NY son of Robert GRIFFIN and Josephine HUDSON and died January 1949.
Children:
756-      i- GRIFFIN Arthur Wendell born November 29, 1908
757-      ii- GRIFFIN Lyle David born March 22, 1910
758-      iii- GRIFFIN Anna Elizabeth born June 13, 1914
759-      iv- GRIFFIN Bernice Loretta born May 19, 1924

760-     v- GRIFFIN Luella Arline born March 15, 1927

554-     LAKE Bert (*Melissa, Abram, William, Joshua, Joshua, Jasper, John*) son of Martin
LAKE and Melissa SMITH married Della EMERY.
Children:
          i- LAKE Raymond
          ii- LAKE Charles

555-     TOWLE Lizzie (*Roselia, Abram, William, Joshua, Joshua, Jasper, John*) born ca
1873 in Hornellsville or Howard, NY daughter of William TOWLE and Roselia SMITH.
She married June 10/27, 1894 Alonzo HAMMER Jr. who was born 1868 son of Alonzo and
Susannah HAMMER and died 1911. No issue.

556-     TOWLE Edna C. (*Roselia, Abram, William, Joshua, Joshua, Jasper, John*) was
born October 30, 1875 in Hornellsville, NY or Howard, NY daughter of William TOWLE
and Roselia SMITH and died May 11, 1922 in Hornellsville, NY She married in
Hornellsville February 23, 1897 Leo FRANKLIN of Haskinsville, NY born ca 1876 son of
Joseph FRANKLIN and Clarissa BARTHOLOMEW.
Known Children:
          i- FRANKLIN Cora
          ii- FRANKLIN Weston

557-     FISHER Clinton Darwin (*Flora, Abram, William, Joshua, Joshua, Jasper, John*)
was born June 1, 1874 in Hornellsville, NY son of George W. FISHER and Flora SMITH
and died October 2, 1958. He married June 27, 1894 Laura Lanah HAMMER born April
1872 and died 1960 age 87 yrs. They are buried in Hillside cemetery in Canisteo, NY
Children:
761-     i- FISHER Norman F. born April 25, 1896
762-     ii- FISHER Donald L. born December 22, 1902
          iii- FISHER Edith born 1911 and died 1914, buried Turnpike cemetery
          iii- FISHER Bernice L. (Knight) born 1913 adopted by Clinton and Lanah Fisher
married June 22, 1940 in Canisteo, NY Paul B. VANDERHOEFF son of Glen H.
VANDERHOEFF and Ethel TERRIBURY

558-     FISHER Alta (*Flora, Abram, William, Joshua, Joshua, Jasper, John*) was born
March 1, 1876 in Hornellsville, NY daughter of George W. FISHER and Flora SMITH and
died May 1, 1981 in Canisteo, NY at age 105 years. She married February 15, 1894
Sherman Grant BEATTIE who was born 1866 in Hornellsville NY son of Thomas
BEATTIE and Amanda HENDERSHOT and died February 11, 1952 in Canisteo, NY.
They are buried in Hope cemetery. Children:
763-     i- BEATTIE Leo Milton born September 17, 1895 in Elmira
764-     ii- BEATTIE Isabel G. born September 10, 1897 in Hornell
765-     iii- BEATTIE Ina Gladys born April 9, 1901 in Hornellsville

**559-** **FISHER** Arthur Abraham (*Flora, Abram, William, Joshua, Joshua, Jasper, John*) was born October 1, 1881 in Hornellsville, NY twin son of George W. **FISHER** and Flora **SMITH** and died April 22, 1972 in Daytona Beach, Florida. He married April 19, 1905 in Hornellsville, NY Mabel **HAMMOND** daughter of James **HAMMOND** and Abbie **FRANKLIN**.
Children:
    i- **FISHER** Eunice born 1906 in Hornellsville, NY
    ii- **FISHER** Edith E. born March 12, 1911 and died January 13, 1914 in Hornell, NY, buried Turnpike cemetery
    iii- **FISHER** Emma W. married June 30, 1925 in Hornellsville, NY Ernest **BROWN** son of Edmond **BROWN** and Edith **BENHAM**

**560-** **FISHER** Archie Cornelius (*Flora, Abram, William, Joshua, Joshua, Jasper. John*) was born October 31, 1881 in Hornellsville, NY twin son of George W. **FISHER** and Flora **SMITH** and died January 27, 1983 in Lancaster, Pa. He married April 19, 1905 Martha **BUCHANAN** who was born February 18, 1888 in NJ and died January 1974 in Brooklyn, NY. He was living in Brooklyn, NY in 1972.
One known child:
    i- **FISHER** Mildred born 1907 and died 1995/96

**561-** **FISHER** Mildred B. (*Flora, Abram, William, Joshua, Joshua, Jasper, John*) was born June 3, 1890 in Hornellsville, NY daughter of George W. **FISHER** and Flora **SMITH** and died November 18, 1918. She married April 2, 1910 Floyd E. **TODD** who was born April 29, 1887 in Hartsville, NY son of Alexander **TODD** and Lucy **HENRY**. They are buried in Center cemetery in Hartsville, NY (no death date for Floyd)
Children:
    i- **TODD** Gladys born March 3, 1911 and died July 1986 in Corning, NY. She married 1930 Ellsworth **SICK** born December 27, 1908 and died April 1984 in Almond, NY
    ii- **TODD** F. Roberta born 1918 in Hornell, NY

**562-** **SMITH** Lena Mary (*Hobart, Abram, William, Joshua, Joshua, Jasper, John*) was born June 18, 1884 in Hornellsville, NY daughter of Hobart Clinton **SMITH** and Hannah Belle **LEONARD** and died June 12, 1967 in Hornell, NY. She married (1) April 24, 1907 Merton **GATES** who was born January 6, 1871 in Chatham, Pa. son of Addison G. **GATES** and Adeline **BUTLER** and died 1929. She married (2) October 26, 1932 Walter **ROBERTS** who was born April 1875 in Fremont, NY son of Erwin **ROBERTS** and died September 21, 1951, buried Rural cemetery in Hornell, NY with first wife. Lena is buried with her first husband in the Butler Hill cemetery, Knoxville, Pa. Walter's first wife Harriett died March 1929.
One child adopted:
**766-**    i- **GATES** Pauline born October 13, 1916
Note: Walter and Harriet had a daughter Cecil born 1906 and died 1982, married Fred **BENEDICT** born 1904 and died 1983. No issue

148

563- **SMITH** Edith Almira (*Hobart, Abram, William, Joshua, Joshua, Jasper, John*) was born December 14, 1885 in Hornellsville, NY daughter of Hobart Clinton **SMITH** and Hannah Belle **LEONARD** and died March 8, 1973. She married April 26, 1911 Delevan Russell **BUTLER** who was born March 1887 son of Franklin **BUTLER** and Polly **SEELEY** and died December 4, 1975. They are buried in the Butler Hill cemetery in Knoxville, Pa.
Children:
767-    i- **BUTLER** Milton Hobart born August 31, 1912
    ii- **BUTLER** Merlin Ross born April 4, 1916 and died May 1940 in an automobile accident less than five miles from home.
768-    iii- **BUTLER** Esther Belle born February 3, 1919

564- **SMITH** Frank Hobart (*Hobart, Abram, William, Joshua, Joshua, Jasper, John*) was born May 4, 1897 in Hornellsville, NY son of Hobart Clinton **SMITH** and Hannah Belle **LEONARD**. He married November 18, 1919 in Howard, NY Charlotte (Lottie) Maud **BOSSARD** daughter of William D. **BOSSARD** and Sarah A. **ALLEN**. He died September 15, 1951 in Howard, NY and she married (2) Michael **CANELLA** She died March 15, 1985 in Hornell, NY and they are buried in the Rural cemetery in Hornell.
Children:
769-    i- **SMITH** Ernest Glen born September 13, 1920 in Hornellsville, NY
770-    ii- **SMITH** Mary Louise born May 30, 1928 in N. Hornell, NY

565- **SMITH** E. Jay (*Thadeus, Abram, William, Joshua, Joshua, Jasper, John*) was born July 23, 1890 probably in Canisteo, NY son of Thadeus Benton **SMITH** and Ella **BAKER** and died February 27, 1987 in St. Cloud, Fl. He married (1) Betty (unknown maiden name) and married (2) Edith (unknown maiden name) who was born May 18, 1899 and died June 1995 in St. Cloud. No issue of either marriage.

566- **SQUIRES** Hulda Marilla (*Eva Ann, Dennis T., Joshua Jr. Joshua, Joshua, Jasper, John*) was born April 24, 1882 in Sullivan Twp. Pa. daughter of Wilbur **SQUIRES** and Eva Ann **SMITH** and died November 27, 1957 in Tuscon, Az. She married April 20, 1905 Franklin J. **LARSON** who was born January 19, 1883 in Plainview, Neb. son of John and Christina **LARSON** and died August 28, 1947 in Plainview. They are buried in Plainview, Neb.
Children:
    i- **LARSON** Naomi married ____ **MILLNITS**
    ii- **LARSON** Kenneth F.
    iii- **LARSON** Meade E.

567- **SQUIRES** Wilbur Glenn (*Eva Ann, Dennis T., Joshua Jr., Joshua Joshua, Jasper, John*) was born June 1, 1888 in Plainview, Neb. son of Wilbur **SQUIRES** and Eva Ann **SMITH** and died November 13, 1959 in Butte, Mt. He married 1911 Anna Augusta **KYRISS** in Bazile Mills, Neb. Unknown children

568- **RUMSEY** Minnie (*Lydia E, Philetus, Joshua Jr., Joshua, Joshua, Jasper, John*) was

born 1869 in Tioga Co. Pa. daughter of William Henry RUMSEY and Lydia Elizabeth SMITH and died 1948, buried Mainesburg cemetery. She married March 5, 1890 Leander Emery AUSTIN who was born 1868 in Sullivan Twp. Pa. son of Jesse W. AUSTIN and Hannah C. WATKINS and died 1940. They are buried in Mainesburg cemetery.
Child:

      i- AUSTIN Leah Grace born August 1, 1894 and died April 12, 1956. She married Herman R. DIAL who was born August 13, 1890 and died November 18, 1940. They are buried in Mainesburg cemetery.

569-    LEIBY Hosmer Philetus *(Frances D., Philetus, Joshua Jr., Joshua, Joshua, Jasper, John)* was born 1880 in Tioga Co. Pa. son of Jonathan LEIBY and Frances D. SMITH and died 1961 in Mansfield, Pa., buried Oakwood cemetery. He married (1) Lena SMITH born 1885. He married (2) June 7, 1905 E. Blanche MC CONNELL daughter of George MC CONNELL and Ella BRIGGS. She was found dead in cistern with rope around her neck at State College, Pa. age 56 having committed suicide.
Children:

      i- LEIBY George of Millboro, Pa.
      ii- LEIBY Glenn
      iii- LEIBY Christina Lillian born 1907, married Carl SELLICK

570-    LEIBY Charles *(Frances D., Philetus, Joshua Jr., Joshua, Joshua, Jasper, John)* was born 1885 in Tioga Co. Pa. son of Jonathan LEIBY and Frances D. SMITH and died 1975. He married Ruhamah WHITAKER who was born 1885 and died 1938. They are buried in Mainesburg cemetery.
One known child:

      i- LEIBY Dorothy born April 25, 1911 in Covington, Pa. and died November 22, 1998 in Wellsboro, Pa. She married March 25, 1932 Claude R. COONS who was born 1902 son of Harry L. COONS and Lorinda S. PACKARD and died November 22, 1998 in Wellsboro, Pa. They had twins that were stillborn.

571-    LEIBY Arthur *(Frances D., Philetus, Joshua, Jr., Joshua, Joshua, Jasper, John)* was born ca 1872 in Tioga Co. Pa. son of Jonathan LEIBY and Frances D. SMITH and died January 4, 1947 in Veteran, NY, buried Woodlawn cemetery in Elmira, NY Spouse unknown.
Children:

      i- LEIBY Elsie married ___ FREAS, lived Binghamton, NY
      ii- LEIBY daughter married Raymond WATKINS of Columbia Cross Rds., Pa.
771-      iii- LEIBY Frances died 1980

572-    BARTLETT Neva *(Jennie, Philetus, Joshua Jr. Joshua, Joshua, Jasper, John)* was born July 1884 in Tioga Co. Pa. daughter of Hubert BARTLETT and Jennie SMITH and died 1963. She married in 1905 Albert Ulysses CHAMBERLAIN who was born July 26, 1880 in Rutland Twp. Pa. son of Thomas CHAMBERLAIN and Susan SMITH and died December 6, 1927.

Children:

    i- CHAMBERLAIN Carl born April 28, 1908 and died 1971 in a car tractor-trailer accident nr Williamsport, Pa. He married Bertha DUNN and had 2 children, Greta and Harold.
772-    ii- CHAMBERLAIN Harold B.
(Note: Susan Smith Chamberlain was born January 26, 1858 daughter of Albert and Martha Smith and married Thomas Chamberlain)

573-    BENSON Cora (*Ellen (Ella) Watkins, Diantha, Joshua Jr., Joshua, Joshua, Jasper, John*) was born March 28, 1881 in Snedecker, Pa. daughter of Nathan BENSON and Ellen (Ella) WATKINS and died November 25, 1972, buried Pennsdale cemetery in Bodines, Pa. She married Robert BASTIAN who died before 1968.
Children:
773-    i- BASTIAN Robert E. born February 28, 1902 Ralston, Pa.
    ii- BASTIAN Pearl who married Thornton L. WOODWARD of Warren Mi.
    iii- BASTIAN Charles K. of Ralston, Pa.
    iv- BASTIAN Arthur S. of Ralston, Pa.
774-    v- BASTIAN Ella married Roy BURLEIGH
    vi- BASTIAN Daniel died in Italy during World War II

574-    BENSON Bertha (*Ellen (Ella) Watkins, Diantha, Joshua Jr., Joshua, Joshua, Jasper, John*) was born November 27, 1884 in Tioga Co. Pa. daughter of Nathan BENSON and Ellen (Ella) WATKINS and died February 1, 1976 in Troy, Pa. She married Lewis H. BROWN who died May 29, 1973 in Troy, Pa., buried Greenwood cemetery.
Children:
    i- BROWN Dorothy who married Verle EIGHMEY or Troy, Pa.
    ii- BROWN Rexford of Wellsboro, Pa.
    iii- BROWN Corey of Columbia Cross Roads, Pa.

575-    BENSON Edith L. (*Ellen (Ella) Watkins, Diantha, Joshua Jr., Joshua, Joshua, Jasper, John*) was born 1887 in Tioga Co. Pa. daughter of Nathan BENSON and Ellen (Ella) WATKINS and died March 2, 1962. She married (1) Mark J. MC CLURE who was born 1887 son of Lorenzo and Mary MC CLURE and died 1938. They are buried in Watson cemetery. She married (2) Arthur J. REDDING.
Children by first marriage:
775-    i- MC CLURE Lee W. born 1911 and died April 7, 1986. He married Maria EHLERS born 1898 and died September 13, 1990
    ii- MC CLURE Louise born 1912 and died 1973. She married Gerald KENNEDY. One known child Lois Ann died infancy, buried in Watson cemetery with mother.

576-    RUMSEY Edith (*Charles Rumsey, Mary, Charles, Joshua, Joshua, Jasper, John*) was born January 1, 1886 in Sullivan Twp. Pa. daughter of Charles RUMSEY and May L. HAVEN and died September 29, 1972. She married Frank C. CHAMBERLAIN who was born January 5, 1888 son of Thomas CHAMBERLAIN and Susan SMITH and died from self inflicted gunshot wound August 17, 1933. He was Sheriff in Tioga Co. They are buried in Mainesburg cemetery.

Children:

776-    i- **CHAMBERLAIN** Maurice born October 21, 1917

ii- **CHAMBERLAIN** Lawrence married Pauline **SEAGER** daughter of Paul K. and Ina **SEAGER** of Waverly

iii- **CHAMBERLAIN** Clifton

iv- **CHAMBERLAIN** Hugh born November 1920 and died March 28, 1941, buried Watson cemetery

577-    **BRYANT** Jay (*Isaac Bryant, Lois Richmond, Anna, Joshua, Joshua, Jasper, John*) married Edith M. **JENKINS** who died in Mansfield, Pa. March 29, 1989, buried Oakwood cemetery.

Children:

i- **BRYANT** Emma married Keith F. **SWEELEY** who was born October 3, 1923 in Rutland, Pa. son of Fred **SWEELEY** and Cora **LEISINGRING** and died October 27, 1987. They had 4 children, Roger married Susan, James married Emily, Phyllis married Martin **CURRAN** and Linda who married Joel **CLAWSON**.

ii- **BRYANT** Madeline who married ___ **WHITTAKER**

iii- **BRYANT** Janet who died in auto accident age 15 mos.

578-    **RICHMOND** Nettie (*Oscar Richmond, Annanias Richmond, Anna, Joshua, Joshua, Jasper, John*) was born in Tioga Co. daughter of Oscar **RICHMOND** and Ella **VAN NESS**. She married John Wesley **SHERMAN** born 1843 son of Seth and Catherine **SHERMAN**
Children born Richmond Twp. Pa.:

i- **SHERMAN** Carlton born November 27, 1896 and died January 7, 1970, buried in Forest Lawn cemetery, wife Lydia buried November 18, 1982 age 97 years

777-    ii- **SHERMAN** Lyle B. born January 14, 1897

778-    iii- **SHERMAN** Oscar born November 11, 1911 in Sullivan Twp. 779-    iv- **SHERMAN** Florence born January 21, 1906

579-    **WILLIAMS** Lynn Annanias (*Delphine Richmond, Annanias Richmond, Anna, Joshua, Joshua, Jasper, John*) was born January 4, 1889 in Sullivan Twp. Pa. son of Orson **WILLIAMS** and Delphine **RICHMOND** and died January 14, 1965. He married (1) August 25, 1915 Jennie **CONNELLY** who was born May 31, 1895 in Covington, Pa. daughter of George W. **CONNELLY** and died October 18, 1930. They are buried in Prospect cemetery. He married (2) January 23, 1935 Doris Loretta **CONNELLY** who was born August 27, 1904 in Covington, Pa. and died 2002, buried Welsh Settlement cemetery.

Children:

i- **WILLIAMS** Nellie married Louis N. **TEARS**

ii- **WILLIAMS** Ermel born July 8, 1923 in Mansfield, Pa. and died August 25, 1994 in Troy, Pa., buried Glenwood cemetery. She married Phillip R. **SPENCER**

580-    **RICHMOND** Edith Ann (*Dayton Richmond, Albert Richmond, Anna, Joshua,*

*Joshua, Jasper, John*) was born June 29, 1878 in Sullivan Twp. Pa. daughter of Dayton **RICHMOND** and Rosebell **SANFORD** and died 1965. She married (1) July 1, 1894 Hobart M. **SMITH** (see #187) and married (2) September 3, 1900 Leon Elmo **CARD** who was born 1879 and died 1962. They are buried in Card cemetery.
Child by first marriage:
780-　　i- **SMITH** Morris born ca 1895
Children by second marriage:
　　　ii- **CARD** Winnie (twin) born April 9, 1901
　　　iii- **CARD** Wayne (twin) born April 9, 1901
　　　iv- **CARD** Lillian M. born August 13, 1902
　　　v- **CARD** Merrill Elmo born September 17, 1903 and died February 3, 1963, buried Card cemetery
　　　vi- **CARD** Hilda married Charles **FRISBEE**
　　　vii- **CARD** Fanny married ____ **BROWN**
781-　viii- **CARD** Rachel married James Manley **DARROW**
　　　ix- **CARD** Catherine married ____ **DENGLE**
　　　x- **CARD** Gertrude married Theodore **MINER**
　　　xi- **CARD** Geraldine married ____ **JOHNSON**, lived Ohio
　　　xii- **CARD** Emma married Theodore **PITT**
　　　xiii- **CARD** Joseph Bradford born October 9, 1913 and died May 28, 1973, buried Card cemetery
　　　xiv- **CARD** Damon born 1901 and died 1976, buried Elmwood cemetery in Caton, NY, also son Damon Jr. born 1933 and died 1987
　　　xv- **CARD** Fenton died in Elmira, NY February 2, 1980. He married Adelaide **CALPUS** who died May 20, 1985. They are buried in Woodlawn cemetery in Elmira.

581-　　**CONGDON** Henry Earl (*Ella Ruggles, Melissa Richmond, Anna, Joshua, Joshua, Jasper, John*) was born September 29, 1880 in Troy, Pa. son of Edgar Fremont **CONGDON** and Ella **RUGGLES** and died 1971. He married (1) March 26, 1902 Mayme DeEtta **SAWDY** who was born January 14, 1883 and died August 12, 1956. They are buried in Upper Gilette cemetery. He married (2) Evelyn **DALTON**.
Children by first marriage:
782-　　i- **CONGDON** Fayette Edgar born October 8, 1906
　　　ii- **CONGDON** Eloise born February 4, 1914 and died 1929

582-　　**CONGDON** Lynn (*Ella Ruggles, Melissa Richmond, Anna, Joshua, Joshua, Jasper, John*) was born August 14, 1884 son of Edgar Fremont **CONGDON** and Ella **RUGGLES** and died 1961. He married April 24, 1907 Belle Vorhees **OLDROYD** who was born September 2. 1885 in Wells Twp. Pa. daughter of Mason G. **OLDROYD** and Loretta Vorhees **NEWTON** and died December 26, 1988 in Troy Pa., buried Gillette cemetery. Unknown children

583-　　**CONGDON** Ray (*Ella Ruggles, Melissa Richmond, Anna, Joshua, Joshua, Jasper, John*) was born January 11, 1886 in Troy, Pa. son of Edgar Fremont **CONGDON** and Ella

RUGGLES and died July 20, 1968. He married December 14, 1905 Frances SITZER who was born November 28, 1883 and died February 10, 1954.
One known child:
    i- CONGDON Harold born October 29, 1906

584-    CONGDON James Bert (*Ella Ruggles, Melissa Richmond, Anna, Joshua, Joshua, Jasper, John*) was born March 1, 1888 in Troy, Pa. son of Edgar Fremont CONGDON and Ella RUGGLES and died March 10, 1974 in Ridgebury Twp. Pa. He married (1) July 1, 1908 Edna QUEAL who was born February 17, 1887 daughter of James Gordon QUEAL and Mary Jane TICKNER and died April 9, 1925. He married (2) March 1, 1928 Louise Edna TEARS who was born May 11, 1902 daughter of Adelbert TEARS and Nellie QUEAL and died 1969, buried Upper Gillette cemetery.
Children by first marriage:
    i- CONGDON Bernice
    ii- CONGDON Edgar Porter born April 12, 1914 and was killed in action in the Phillipines January 24, 1942, served in Co. C. 31st Inf. He is buried in Lower Gillette cemetery.
    iii- CONGDON Marie
    iv- CONGDON Pauline

585-    CONGDON Hazel Emma (*Ella Ruggles, Melissa Richmond, Anna, Joshua, Joshua, Jasper, John*) was born September 27, 1897 daughter of Edgar Fremont CONGDON and Ella RUGGLES and died July 11, 1980 in Elmira, NY. She married September 27, 1919 Lewis Edward DIX who was born November 6, 1895 in Rutland Twp., Pa. son of Charles Edward DIX and Dora May CANEDY and died November 7, 1971 in Elmira, NY.
Children:
    i- DIX Delecia married ____ GREENO
    ii- DIX Rosalyn married Charles MARK of Riverview, Fl.
    iii- DIX E. Larue moved to Washington, DC
    iv- DIX Donald moved to Horseheads, NY

586-    COSPER Florence Jane (*Jennie M. Slingerland, Elizabeth Richmond, Anna, Joshua, Joshua, Jasper, John*) was born April 8, 1867 in Alma, Pa. daughter of Shepard Silas COSPER and Jennie May SLINGERLAND and died March 6, 1966 in Canton, Pa. She married September 18, 1890 in Canton, Pa. Willard H. DUNBAR who was born ca 1863 in Canton son of Alvin T. and Isabella DUNBAR.
Children:
    i- DUNBAR Helen married ____ SECHRIST lived Woodbridge, NY
    ii- DUNBAR Percy resided Owego, NY
    iii- DUNBAR Ivan Cosper born December 18, 1899 in Canton, Pa. and resided in Binghamton, NY
    iv- DUNBAR Clifford Lee born October 22, 1902 in Canton, Pa. and died 1974, resided Ithaca, NY. He married Carrie SEELEY who was born 1902 and died 1985. They are buried in Glenwood cemetery in Troy, Pa.

587-    COSPER Helen M. (*Jennie M. Slingerland, Elizabeth Richmond, Anna, Joshua, Joshua, Jasper, John*) was born June 1870 daughter of Shepard Silas COSPER and Jennie Mae SLINGERLAND and died 1945. She married by 1896 Perry D. FREEMAN who was born March 1868 in Pa. son of Henry Watson FREEMAN and Bell DOUGLAS and died 1946. They are buried in Alba cemetery, Canton Twp. Pa.
Children:
        i- FREEMAN Dwight H. married Geraldine BELLOWS who was born February 6, 1917 in Leroy Twp. Bradford Co. Pa. daughter of Luther John BELLOWS and Jennie Melissa HOAGLAND and died June 18, 1992 in Sayre, Pa.
        ii- FREEMAN Eloise I. born February 1896

588-    VORHEES Susie May (*Charles Vorhees, Susan, Daniel, Joshua, Joshua, Jasper, John*) was born May 30, 1885 in Hector, NY daughter of Charles Lamont VORHEES and Ida Augusta SWICK and died July 12, 1939 in Hector. She married (1) Fred POTTER who was born August 7, 1884 in Potterbrook, Pa. son of Norman POTTER and Caroline SCOTT and died January 29, 1916. She married (2) Frank WHEELER born ca 1881 in Hector.
Children by first marriage born in Hector, NY:
783-      i- POTTER Ralph Frederick born August 13, 1910
          ii- POTTER Charles Henry born February 3, 1909 and married Evelyn CRESTER
784-    iii- POTTER Leon Arthur born August 5, 1912 married Josephine VOSSLER and had 2 sons
          iv- POTTER Claude born April 8, 1916 and died May 18, 1916
Child by second marriage born in Hector, NY
785-      i- WHEELER Jay

589-    VORHEES William Edwin (*Charles Vorhees, Susan, Daniel, Joshua, Joshua, Jasper, John*) was born December 10, 1887 in Hector, NY son of Charles VORHEES and Ida Augusta SWICK and died October 16, 1861 in Montour, NY, buried Union cemetery in Hector. He married in Hector, NY August 12, 1908 Theresa Stillwell SWICK who was born July 1, 1789 in Hector, NY daughter of Arthur Eugene SWICK and Mary Adelia STILLWELL and died August 30, 1972.
Children born in Hector, NY:
          i- VORHEES Gladys
          ii- VORHEES Keith Charles born October 22, 1910 and died February 2, 1968
          iii- VORHEES Clifford
          iv- VORHEES Dewitt
          v- VORHEES Harold
          vi- VORHEES son living
          vii- VORHEES son living
          viii- VORHEES son living
786-      ix- VORHEES Lyle Robert born March 29, 1918
          x- VORHEES Frederick Arthur born March 2, 1920
          xi- VORHEES son living

xii- **VORHEES** son living
xiii- **VORHEES** son living
xiv- **VORHEES** Ronald Clyde born July 17, 1930 and died July 26, 1930
xv- **VORHEES** Russell Lee born October 28, 1931 and died April 23, 1949

590- **VORHEES** Carrie Ethel (*Charles Vorhees, Susan, Daniel, Joshua, Joshua, Jasper, John*) was born November 23, 1896 in Hector, NY daughteer of Charles Lamont **VORHEES** and Ida Augusta **SWICK** and died September 12, 1977. She married Lee **BARNES** born ca 1892.

591- **ORVIS** Esther (*Ella Squires, Hulda, Jasper, Joshua, Joshua, Jasper, John*) was born March 30, 1896 in Tioga Co. Pa. daughter of Elisha **ORVIS** and Ella **SQUIRES** and died 1985. She married Frederick L. **STRANGE** who was born 1899 and died January 3, 1979 in Elmira, NY. They are buried in Gray Valley cemetery.
Children:
    i- **STRANGE** Ella married Chester **MANTIE** and removed to Albuquerque, NM. They had 2 daughters Carol and Lorraine and 2 sons Steven and Allen
    ii- **STRANGE** Rosalyn married Clarence **FLEMING** of Elmira, NY. They had 2 children Laura and David born September 26, 1913

592- **FROST** Martha (*Frances Augusta, Sally, George, Joshua, Joshua, Jasper, John*) was born May 23, 1901 in Rutland, Pa. daughter of John Ulysses **FROST** and Frances Augusta **SMITH** and died May 6, 1986. She married Rev. Orey **CRIPPEN** of Tioga, Pa. who was born November 5, 1889 son of Osmer **CRIPPEN** and Ada Ann **REDFIELD** and died November 7, 1979 in Broad Acres Nursing Home in Wellsboro, Pa. They are buried in Watson cemetery.
Children:
    i- **CRIPPEN** Phyllis who married Rex **FAULKNER** born February 9, 1916 in Sandusky, NY and died April 29, 1980 in Tioga, Pa.
    ii- **CRIPPEN** Ada married Richard **DE GEUS** of Middletown, NY son of George **DE GEUS** and Gladys **NEWBERRY**

593- **CUMMINGS** Jerald Louis (*Ethel, George F. Jr., George F., Joshua, Joshua, Jasper, John*) was born August 4, 1923 in Lawrence Corners, Pa. son of Ray **CUMMINGS** and Ethel **SMITH** and died June 13, 1994 in Interlaken, Fl., buried in Watson cemetery in Roseville, Pa. He married Marie **CLEVELAND**.
Children:
    i- **CUMMINGS** Joyce M. married Dale L. **HOWEY** and they had a daughter Anna Marie **HOWEY**
    ii- **CUMMINGS** Linda Lee born 1954 and died March 19, 1957 in Corning, NY, buried Watson cemetery in Roseville, Pa.

594- **SMITH** Vivian (*Manley, George Jr., George, Joshua, Joshua, Jasper, John*) was born in Tioga Co. Pa. daughter of Manley G. **SMITH** and Martha **CRUMB** and died

156

September 1, 1999 in Wellsboro, Pa. She married Morris Dean COLEGROVE who was born September 11, 1921 in Lawrence Twp. Pa. son of Dean Alfred COLEGORVE and Edna WEST and died January 3, 2002 in Soldiers and Sailors Hospital in Wellsboro, buried in Evergreen cemetery.
Children:
     i- COLEGROVE Carl died 1992
    ii- COLEGROVE Alfred D. of Mansfield, Pa.

595-   COLE Grant (*Elizabeth Deremer, Hannah, Joshua, Platt, Joshua, Jasper, John*) was born July 1864 in Ulysses, NY son of Isaiah COLE and Elizabeth DEREMER and died April 28, 1933. He married Margaret W. (unknown maiden name) born September 1871.
Children:
791-   i- COLE Walter W. born December 1892
    ii- COLE Mildred A. born March 1894, married ___ MINTZ

596-   FULMER Grace (*Martha Deremer, Hannah, Joshua, Platt, Joshua, Jasper, John*) was born August 1867 in Ontario, Canada daughter of John FULMER and Martha DEREMER and died May 2, 1913 in Trumansburg, NY. She married in Willow Grove, NY October 9, 1889 Ezra YOUNG Jr. who was born 1862 son of Ezra YOUNG and Marietta WILLIS and died 1946. They are buried in Grove cemetery.
Children:
792-   i- YOUNG Ezra Lawrence Jr. born January 1891
    ii- YOUNG Margaret Winifred born October 1893

597-   FULMER Fanny (*Martha Deremer, Hannah, Joshua, Platt, Joshua, Jasper, John*) was born 1868 probably in Ontario, Canada daughter of John FULMER and Martha DEREMER and died June 17, 1897, buried Grove cemetery. She married at Willow Grove, NY January 1, 1900 Charles DAVIS of Enfield, NY born 1862 and died 1953. They are buried in Grove cemetery. Also buried there are Anne Maude DAVIS born 1870 and died 1933 and James O. DAVIS born 1900 and died 1921. possibly a second marriage.
One known child:
    i- DAVIS Lucy born 1897 and died 1950

598-   GOODENOW Fannie (*Alice A., Elijah, Joshua, Platt, Joshua, Jasper, John*) was born December 1873 in Wis. daughter of Irving J. GOODENOW and Alice Adelia SMITH. She married Robert I. WHITE born June 1874 in Mi.
Children:
    i- WHITE Alice I. born February 1899 in Kent Co. Mi.
    ii- WHITE Robert I. born December 28, 1908 in Elgin, Ill.
    iii- WHITE Nada born 1911 in Elgin, Ill.

599-   GOODENOW Ralph J. (*Alice A., Elijah, Joshua, Platt, Joshua, Jasper, John*) was born November 1879 in Mi. son of Irving J. GOODENOW and Alice Adelia SMITH. He married Janet E. CADREIRX (spelling) daughter of Isadore.

Children born Grosse Point Mi.:

    i- **GOODENOW** Alice E. born 1913

    ii- **GOODENOW** Ralph J. Jr. born 1915

    iii- **GOODENOW** Lorraine J. born 1918

600-   **GOODENOW** Harold Elijah (*Alice A., Elijah, Joshua, Platt, Joshua, Jasper, John*) was born August 1888 in Mi. son of Irving J. GOODENOW and Alice Adelia SMITH and died December 1932 in Los Angeles, Cal. He married Mildred Frances BARCHEUS born September 21, 1891 in Howell, Mi. daughter of George Thomas BACHEUS and Georgeanne BUCHANCE and died July 1987 in Palm Springs, Cal.

Children:

    i- **GOODENOW** Harold J. born Februay 13, 1917 in Oakland, Cal. and died December 1986 in Rancho Mirage, Cal. He was treasurer of Southern Cal. Gas Co. He married Mona **RODGERS** and had 3 children

    ii- **GOODENOW** Donald Irving was born April 16, 1920 in Berkley, Cal and died March 4, 1999 in Rancho Mirage, Cal. He was managing Editor of the Herald Examiner (Hearst Corp.) He married Grace Marie **STEDMAN** born August 17, 1921 daughter of Venice George **STEDMAN** and Josephine **LONGO**. They had 2 children

601-   **SMITH** Edith Viola (*Horace, Elijah, Joshua, Platt, Joshua, Jasper, John*) was born in Grand Rapids, Mi. May 18, 1891 daughter of Horace D. SMITH and Birdella Lavinna PUTNAM and died August 5, 1950 in Grand Rapids, buried Ashley cemetery. She married William James LESSITER who was born December 5, 1874 son of Henry LESSITER and Margaret Ann WEEKS and died February 17, 1965.

Children:

    i- **LESSITER** Margaret Arlene born December 25, 1917 in Grattan, Mi. married in Belding September 6, 1941 Orville J. **BUSH**

    ii- **LESSITER** Ruby Minnie born July 23, 1919

    iii- **LESSITER** Wayne Jay born February 9, 1924

    iv- **LESSITER** Nancy Jane born January 30, 1928, married April 21, 1951 Theodore Martin **WOOD**

    v- **LESSITER** Priscilla Beth born December 16, 1930

602-   **BALCOM** Harrison C. (*Clara M., George W., Joshua, Platt, Joshua, Jasper, John*) was born March 1864 in Buffalo, NY son of Philo BALCOM and Clara M. SMITH and died November 29, 1905 in Brooklyn, NY. He married Mary Lee PERKINS who was born November 1869 and died May 14, 1952. They are buried in Forest Lawn cemetery in Buffalo.

One known child:

    i- **BALCOM** Marion born June 1891

603-   **BALCOM** Frederick H. (*Clara M., George W., Joshua, Platt, Joshua, Jasper, John*) was born 1870 in Buffalo, NY son of Philo BALCOM and Clara M. SMITH. He married Fanny Louise CLINT who was born 1870 and died July 4, 1907. They are buried

in Forest Lawn cemetery in Buffalo, NY.
Children:
       i- **BALCOM** an infant who died December 27, 1900
      ii- **BALCOM** Frederick Jr. died infancy June 28, 1907

**604-**   **SMITH** Horace Walker (*Horace F., Horace D., Joshua, Platt, Joshua, Jasper, John*) was born March 14, 1897 in Tompkins Co. NY son of Horace F. **SMITH** and Ida Belle **WALKER** and died March 13, 1966, buried Grove cemetery. He married April 30, 1824 Ruth **HARVEY** who was born Arpil 12, 1892 daughter of Benjamin and Catherine **HARVEY** and died May 19, 1980.
One child:
790-      i- **SMITH** Harvey W. born November 7, 1925

**605-**   **KING** Eva Jane (*Nelson King, Margaret Van Horn, Mary, Platt, Joshua, Jasper, John*) was born 1853 in Tompkins Co. NY daughter of Nelson **KING** and Mahala **VAN HORN** and died 1919. She married Frank M. **DENSON** born April 23, 1851 son of Herman B. **DENSON** and Elmira Gennett **MALLOTT**. They are buried in Hector Union cemetery (no death date for Frank). He died April 1941 in Binghamton, NY
One known child:
      I- **DENSON** Eva Dell born after 1880

**606-**   **ROLOSON** Alice Irene (*Mary Ellen King, Margaret Van Horn, Mary, Platt, Joshua, Jasper, John*) was born February 9, 1857 daughter of James M. **ROLOSON** and Mary Ellen **KING** and died April 9, 1931. She married Frank Dwight **ATWATER** born October 25, 1859 son of Willis Goodyear **ATWATER** and Catherine **SNYDER** and died February 27, 1944, buried Woodlawn cemetery in Elmira, NY.
Children:
      i- **ATWATER** Cora Ann died August 1, 1974, buried Woodlawn cemetery in Elmira, NY
      ii- **ATWATER** Bertha Grace married Luciano **SALVAGGIO** who died August 29, 1959
      iii- **ATWATER** Clara Catherine died 1987, married Gordon H. **SHEELY** who died July 18, 1974
      iv- **ATWATER** Agnes Alice died January 29, 1940 married Frank **MANNING** who died April 14, 1927, buried Woodlawn cemetery
      v- **ATWATER** Mildred Eleanor February 24, 1983, married (1) Robert **BLAISDELL** and married (2) Phillip G. **COWLEY** who died April 21, 1992. They are buried in Woodlawn cemetery.
Note: dates from Woodlawn cemetery are burial dates

**607-**   **BEARDSLEY** Frank J. (*Emma King, Margaret Van Horn, Mary, Platt, Joshua, Jasper, John*) was born 1864 son of Asa **BEARDSLEY** and Margaret **VAN HORN**. He married Carrie B. **TUCKER** born 1864. (see #287) They are buried in the Mechlinburg cemetery.

Children:
  i- BEARDSLEY Robert W. born 1888 and died 1918
  ii- BEARDSLEY Herbert W. born ca 1889
  iii- BEARDSLEY Olive born 1894

608- CARLEY Simon W. (*William Carley, Matilda Van Horn, Mary, Platt, Joshua, Jasper, John*) was born September 1869 in Portage Co. Wis. son of William and Belle CARLEY and died 1941. He married Naira C. BENNETT who was born 1869 probably the daughter of Jay and Jemima BENNETT and died May 20, 1941. They are buried in Forest cemetery.
One known child:
  i- CARLEY Lawrence H. born January 3, 1896

609- CARLEY Elmer (*William Carley, Matilda Van Horn, Mary, Platt, Joshua, Jasper, John*) was born 1872 in Portage Co. Wis. son of William and Belle CARLEY and died 1942. His wife Esther (unknown maiden name) was born 1876 and died 1940, buried Plover Village cemetery.
Known children:
  i- CARLEY Florence Amy born January 12, 1897
  ii- CARLEY Ina M. born November 3, 1898

610- CHAPMAN Arminda (*George W. Chapman, Angelina Van Horn, Mary, Platt, Joshua, Jasper, John*) was born July 9, 1877 in Schuyler Co. daughter of George W. CHAPMAN and Elizabeth Delphine HALL and died April 10, 1908, buried Laurel Hill cemetery. She married Thomas MALONEY born June 1874.
Children:
  i- MALONEY Floyd
  ii- MALONEY Donald
  iii- MALONEY Minnie E. born April 6, 1908, married Addison CHAMBERLAIN born 1901 and died 1949. They had son Donald who was born November 10, 1928 and died December 15, 1928. They are buried in Laurel Hill cemetery.

611- CHAPMAN George Willis (*George W. Chapman, Angelina Van Horn, Mary, Platt, Joshua, Jasper, John*) was born April 1880 in Schuyler Co. son of George W. CHAPMAN and Elizabeth Delphine HALL and died November 15, 1955, buried Laurel Hill cemetery. His first wife unknown. He married (2) Grace NEWTON daughter of Charles NEWTON Louise HENRY.
Child by first marriage:
  i- CHAPMAN Lyle
Child by second marriage:
  ii- CHAPMAN Melvin Newton born January 16, 1924 and died April 13, 1978, buried Laurel Hill cemetery, also his baby died March 4, 1952 age 15 days

612- CHAPMAN William Burt (*Simeon Chapman, Anna Eliza Van Horn, Mary, Platt,*

*Joshua, Jasper, John*) was born 1873 son of Simeon **CHAPMAN** and Emma **WELLS** and died December 21, 1903 in Catherine, NY, buried Laurel Hill cemetery. Unknown spouse
Children:
>   i- **CHAPMAN** Richard
>   ii- **CHAPMAN** Winifred

613-   **CHAPMAN** Clarence Lavern (*Simeon Chapman, Anna Eliza Van Horn, Mary, Platt, Joshua, Jasper, John*) was born June 28, 1880 in Schuyler Co. NY son of Simeon **CHAPMAN** and Emma **WELLS** and died 1945, buried Laurel Hill cemetery. He married Mabelle G. (unknown maiden name) born 1877. They are buried in Laurel Hill cemetery.
One known child:
>   i- **CHAPMAN** Ruth married and removed to Nutley, NJ

614-   **CHAPMAN** Kenneth (*William Chapman, Anna Eliza Van Horn, Mary, Platt, Joshua, Jasper, John*) was born 1900 in Schuyler Co. NY son of William **CHAPMAN** and Julia **MISNER** and died March 29, 1962 in Catherine, NY. He married Margaret **SMITH** who was born 1903 daughter of Floyd **SMITH** and Mary **HALPIN** and died 1981. They are buried in Laurel Hill cemetery.
One known child:
>   i- **CHAPMAN** William Keith born 1930, wife Gloria Dawn M. born 1932 are buried in Laurel Hill cemetery, no death dates

615-   **WHITCOMB** Hattie B. (*Mary A. Richards, Platt Richards, Johannah, Platt, Joshua, Jasper, John*) was born September 1874 in Tompkins Co. NY daughter of Robert **WHITCOMB** and Mary Adeline **RICHARDS**. She married George **KISOR** born September 1863
Children:
>   i- **KISOR** Jennie born November 1883
>   ii- **KISOR** Clinton D. born October 1889

616-   **DIMMICK** George (*Melissa Richards, Platt Richards, Johannah, Platt, Joshua, Jasper, John*) was born 1853 in Ulysses, NY son of William **DIMMICK** and Melissa **RICHARDS**. He married November 13, 1877 Hattie T. **HADLEY** born 1877 and removed to Albion, Mi. after 1880. Unknown children

617-   **DIMMICK** Eliza E. (*Melissa Richards, Platt Richards, Johannah, Platt, Joshua, Jasper, John*) was born May 1856 in Ulysses, NY daughter William **DIMMICK** and Melissa **RICHARDS**. She married Warren H. **RUSSELL** born December 1855.
One known child:
>   i- **RUSSELL** Willard H. born June 1879 in Ulysses, NY

618-   **DIMMICK** Frank (*Melissa Richards, Platt Richards, Johannah, Platt, Joshua, Jasper, John*) was born 1860 in Ulysses, NY son of William **DIMMICK** and Melissa **RICHARDS** and died August 1, 1927. He married Cora **DAGGETT** who was born

September 1860 and died 1942. They are buried in Grove cemetery.
Children born in Trumansburg, NY:
> i- DIMMICK Dorsey
793- ii- DIMMICK Eva born June 1883 and died May 14, 1969
> iii- DIMMICK Clinton born July 1885 and died at Tompkins Co. Hospital 1925,
married Edith DURLING born 1888 and died 1948
794- iv- DIMMICK Mabel born July 22, 1888 and died 1912
795- v- DIMMICK Clark born August 1890 and died 1956
> vi- DIMMICK George born September 1892 and died April 13, 1893
> vii- DIMMICK Harry born March 1894 and died 1957, moved to Kennett Square,
Pa.
796- viii- DIMMICK Francis born September 1895
797- ix- DIMMICK Dorothy born March 1897
> x- DIMMICK Frank Townsend born June 1899 and died 1902
> xi- DIMMICK Daisy May born 1901 and died 1902

619-    DIMMICK John W. (*Melissa Richards, Platt Richards, Johannah, Platt, Joshua, Jasper, John*) was born 1862 in Ulysses, NY son of William DIMMICK and Melissa RICHARDS and died May 30, 1907 in Ithaca, NY, buried in Grove cemetery. He married (1) unknown and married (2) Minnie SEARS who was born January 1867 daughter of Absolom P. and Laura SEARS and died July 30, 1912 in Geneva, NY. She married (2) Thomas MANION.
Children:
> i- DIMMICK Harry died September 26, 1887 age 5 months
> ii- DIMMICK Raymond born June 1891
> iii- DIMMICK Laura born July 1894
> iv- DIMMICK Howard born July 1898

620-    DIMMICK William (*Melissa Richards, Platt Richards, Johannah, Platt, Joshua, Jasper, John*) was born 1870 in Ulysses, NY son of William DIMMICK and Melissa RICHARDS and died July 26, 1951 at Leonard's Nursing Home in Ithaca, NY, buried Grove cemetery. He married April 23, 1892 Stella BREWER born December 1868 daughter of Benjamin and Sarah BREWER.
Children:
> i- DIMMICK infant died March 21, 1894
> ii- DIMMICK Sarah born May 1895 buried Grove cemetery

621-    DIMMICK Estelle (*Melissa Richards, Platt Richards, Johannah, Platt, Joshua, Jasper, John*) was born August 1873 in Ulysses, NY daughter of William DIMMICK and Melissa RICHARDS. She married March 22, 1892 Otis BLAIN born December 1869 son of Amos BLAIN and Harriet BOND.
One known child:
> I- BLAIN Harold O. born November 1893

622- **DIMMICK** Adelbert (*Melissa Richards, Platt Richards, Johannah, Platt, Joshua, Jasper, John*) was born 1876 in Ulysses, NY son of William **DIMMICK** and Melissa **RICHARDS** and died in Trumansburg, NY June 28, 1908. He married Sarah E. **HENNESSEY** born September 1872 daughter of Daniel and Margaret **HENNESSEY**.
One known child:

    i- **DIMMICK** Nelson

623- **FRAZIER** Samuel (*Emeline Richards, Platt Richards, Johannah, Platt, Joshua, Jasper, John*) was born 1866 in Tompkins Co. NY son of Daniel **FRAZIER** and Emeline **RICHARDS** and died in Trumansburg, NY January 2, 1955. He married June 29, 1889 Dessie Demund **CURRY** who was born May 25, 1871 at Froggy Point, Cayuga Co. NY daughter of George V. **CURRY** Elizabeth MC **MILLAN** and died 1946. They are buried in Grove cemetery. Samuel was in the Army in WWI.
Children:

    i- **FRAZIER** Frank born July 15, 1890 and died February 4, 1891
798-  ii- **FRAZIER** George Daniel born July 16, 1892
    iii- **FRAZIER** William born February 22, 1901 and died February 22, 1901

624- **FRAZIER** Charles (*Emeline Richards, Platt Richards, Johannah, Platt, Joshua, Jasper, John*) was born August 1870 in Tompkins Co. son of Daniel **FRAZIER** and Emeline **RICHARDS** and died January 5, 1916. He married Margaret L. **SHINDLEDECKER** who was born 1873 in Md. and died in Ulysses, NY December 26, 1926. She married (2) John L. **ERNST** born ca 1874.
Children:

799-  i- **FRAZIER** Fred P. born March 11, 1902
    ii- **FRAZIER** Ethel died July 20, 1903 age 3 weeks
    iii- **FRAZIER** Emily born March 1906 died same month
    iv- **FRAZIER** Elizabeth died May 18, 1914 age 8 days

625- **FRAZIER** Carrie L. (*Emeline Richards, Platt Richards, Johannah, Platt, Joshua, Jasper, John*) was born September 1875 in Tompkins Co. daughter of Daniel **FRAZIER** and Emeline **RICHARDS** and died March 30, 1910. She married Everal **CHURCH** born 1866 son of Elisha and Mary J. **CHURCH**.
Children:

800-  i- **CHURCH** Margaret Hattie born 1910
    ii- **CHURCH** Wilbur born 1913

626- **SPICER** Mary (*Elizabeth Richards, Platt Richards, Johannah, Platt, Joshua, Jasper, John*) was born November 3, 1867 in Tompkins Co. NY daughter of Emerson **SPICER** and Elizabeth **RICHARDS** and died April 5, 1916 in Ulysses, NY. She married Alfred **HOLFORD** of Hector, NY who died December 14, 1961 age 84 yrs.
One known child:

    i- **HOLFORD** Ethel born ca 1906 and died November 13, 1936 married Frank **MANHEIM** who was born 1901 and died November 9, 1971. They are all buried in Grove cemetery.

627-    **SPICER** Elizabeth (*Elizabeth Richards, Platt Richards, Johannah, Platt, Joshua, Jasper, John*) was born May 24, 1876 in Tompkins Co. NY daughter of Emerson **SPICER** and Elizabeth **RICHARDS**. She married Clarence **CRETSER** who was born April 20, 1876 in Tompkins Co. son of Solomon and Anna **CRETSER** of Erin, NY.
Children probably born Tompkins Co.:
      i- **CRETSER** Paul E. born April 15, 1900 and died August 5, 1998, married (1) Phyllis **POWELL** and (2) Edith G. **TAYLOR** born Toronto, Canada daughter of Henry **TAYLOR** and Emma **GREEN** and died April 24, 1972
      ii- **CRETSER** Arland born July 18, 1903 and died September 30, 1986, married August 2, 1934 Gwendoline **POWELL** daughter of John **POWELL** who died February 2, 1996 age 90 yrs.
      iii- **CRETSER** Mildred born January 2, 1906 and died January 8, 1888, married Herman C. **FRANTZ** and had son Jack who died 1993 age 54 and left 2 children
      iv- **CRETSER** Iva born March 23, 1908, married Raymond **PIPER** and had son Donald
      v- **CRETSER** Evelyn born February 3, 1910, married Charles **POTTER**, no issue
      vi- **CRETSER** Clarence Donald born April 24, 1912 married Hilda **SPAULDING** and had 2 children David and Richard

628-    **RICHARDS** Eugene (*Lafayette Richards, Platt Richards, Johannah, Platt, Joshua, Jasper, John*) was born February 1872 in Ulysses, NY son of Lafayette and Ellen **RICHARDS** and died August 1, 1953. He married Sarah (unknown maiden name) who was born February 1877 and died 1931. They are buried in Grove cemetery.
Children:
      i- **RICHARDS** Mildred born 1904, buried in Grove cemetery
      ii- **RICHARDS** Walter L. born 1907 and died 1984

629-    **RICHARDS** Nellie (*Lafayette Richards, Platt Richards, Johannah, Platt, Joshua, Jasper, John*) was born October 1875 in Ulysses, NY daughter of Lafayette and Ellen **RICHARDS**. She married December 13, 1892 Adelbert **CHEESMAN** born January 1872 in Genoa, NY. They lived in Groton, NY in 1900.
One known child:
      i- **CHEESMAN** Florence A. born November 1894

630-    **RICHARDS** Clarence (*Lafayette Richards, Platt Richards, Johannah, Platt, Joshua, Jasper, John*) was born 1881 in Tompkins Co. NY son of Lafayette and Ellen **RICHARDS** and died November 30, 1946. He married Edith (unknown maiden name) born 1885.
Children born in Ithaca, NY:
      i- **RICHARDS** Thelma born 1907, married Morris **GERMAN**
      ii- **RICHARDS** Gertrude born 1910 and died May 10, 1965. She married Fred L. **VANDERBURG** born May 10, 1907 son of Frank **VANDERBURG** and Anna **DENNISTON**.

164

Note: An obituary for Ellen M. (ABEL) BRONG who died October 2, 1952 in Ithaca leaves daughters Thelma GERMAN and Gertrude VANDERBURG. She is buried in Grove cemetery.

631- WHITCOMB Benjamin (*Mary L. Richards, Benjamin Richards, Johannah, Platt, Joshua, Jasper, John*) was born September 29, 1861 son of John Milton WHITCOMB and Mary Louisa RICHARDS and died 1938 in Waverly, NY. He married Minnie E. SMITH who was born 1869 and died 1957. They are buried in Nichols cemetery in Waverly. Children born in Smithboro, NY:
> i- WHITCOMB Leon Wiswell born January 30, 1891 in Smithboro, NY and died February 11, 1966. He married Elizabeth B. KING who was born 1888 and died 1961. They are buried in Nichols cemetery.
> ii- WHITCOMB Percy E. born December 9, 1892
> iii- WHITCOMB Howard M. born July 8, 1896

632- WHITCOMB Forman Elmer (*Mary L. Richards, Benjamin Richards, Johannah, Platt, Joshua, Jasper, John*) was born July 24, 1866 probably in Tioga Co. NY son of John Milton WHITCOMB and Mary L RICHARDS and died 1945 in Smithboro, NY. He married November 8, 1891 Marion Josephine TUTHILL who was born November 21, 1874 and died 1923 in Smithboro, NY. They are buried Smithboro cemetery. Children born Smithboro:
> i- WHITCOMB Ethel May born August 9, 1892 and died May 20, 1897
> ii- WHITCOMB Carroll T. buried Smithboro no dates
> iii- WHITCOMB Mary born January 30, 1896

633- WHITCOMB Hermon E. (*Mary L. Richards, Benjamin Richards, Johannah, Platt, Joshua, Jasper, John*) was born July 24, 1866 probably in Tioga Co. NY son of John Milton WHITCOMB and Mary L. RICHARDS. He married November 19, 1890 Stella Lucy SMITH born August 15, 1872. They lived in Union Twp. Broome Co. NY. Children:
> i- WHITCOMB Losey Arnold born February 18, 1893
> ii- WHITCOMB Marguerite Evelyn born April 19, 1896

634- WHITCOMB Warren Milton (*Mary L. Richards, Benjamin Richards, Johannah, Platt, Joshua, Jasper, John*) was born October 4, 1870 probably in Tioga Co. NY son of John Milton WHITCOMB and Mary L. RICHARDS. He married May 10, 1896 Clara Elaine BIDWELL born August 10, 1873 possibly the daughter of Hexford and Ellen BIDWELL of Binghamton, NY. Children:
> i- WHITCOMB Francis Bidwell born January 22, 1897
> ii- WHITCOMB Harold Milton born January 27, 1899

635- WHITCOMB Gurdon Allen (*Mary L. Richards, Benjamin Richards, Johannah, Platt, Joshua, Jasper, John*) was born October 9, 1872 probably in Tioga Co. NY son of

John Milton **WHITCOMB** and Mary L. **RICHARDS** and died 1946. He married November 7, 1897 Leona **HURLBUT** who was born June 9, 1879 daughter of L. A. and Ann **HURLBUT** of Fremont, NY and died 1937. They are buried in Smithboro cemetery in Smithboro, NY.
Children:
  i- **WHITCOMB** Lester A. born October 20, 1899 and died 1986
  ii- **WHITCOMB** Judd E. born March 13, 1903

636-   **VAN LONE** Frank E. (*Mary E. Richards, Robert Richards, Johannah, Platt, Joshua, Jasper, John*) was born 1858 in Bradford Co. Pa. son of Daniel **VAN LONE** and Mary E. **RICHARDS** and died 192_. He married December 10, 1880 May F. **NEWHAND** who was born October 1, 1857 daughter of William **NEWHAND** and Emily **MC FARLANE**.
Children:
  i- **VAN LONE** Karl F. born 1881 and died 1913
  ii- **VAN LONE** Lizzie May Ione born August 7, 1885
  iii- **VAN LONE** Nathaniel R. born April 19, 1888

637-   **RICHARDS** Hattie O. (*Smith Richards, Albert Richards, Johannah, Platt, Joshua, Jasper, John*) was born in Tompkins Co. daughter of Smith and Julia E. **RICHARDS**. She married February 24, 1892 Arthur C. **NORTH** born 1874 in Ulysses, NY possibly the son of George W. and Mary A. **NORTH**. and died January 4, 1937, buried Grove cemetery.
Children:
  i- **NORTH** Grace D. born 1893
  ii- **NORTH** George W. born 1896
  iii- **NORTH** Pearle born 1900
(note: One daughter married Martin **JONES** of Lansing, NY)

638-   **WOLVERTON** Ora May, (*Emily S. King, Louisa M. Richards, Johannah, Platt, Joshua, Jasper, John*) was born June 1877 in Tompkins Co. NY daughter of Creque **WOLVERTON** and Emily S. **KING**. She married Fayette **DEWEY** who was born April 1879 son of Eugene V. **DEWEY** and Cornelia **BARTHOLOMEW** and died August 6, 1907, buried Grove cemetery with parents.
Children:
  i- **DEWEY** Mary M. born June 1899
  ii- **DEWEY** Charles K. born December 1899, (spouse unknown) had 2 children Mildred and Kenneth

639-   **POPPINO** Edna Sarah (*Harry B. Poppino, Alice Amelia, Lafayette, Jasper, Joshua, Jasper, John*) was born September 4, 1921 in Tompkins Co. NY daughter of Harry Borden **POPPINO** and Bertha **ROLFE** and died July 18, 1962 in a car accident. She married October 1, 1938 Seymour **RATHBUN** who was born 1924 son of Glenn **RATHBUN** and Emma **MEAD** and died August 25, 1998. They are buried in Grove cemetery.
Children :

801-    i- **RATHBUN** Ruth Edna born October 27, 1939
802-    ii- **RATHBUN** Keith Morris born June 12, 1941
803-    iii- **RATHBUN** Glenn Harry born September 1, 1942
        iv- **RATHBUN** David Arthur died October 1944 in infancy
804-    v- **RATHBUN** Paul Eugene born February 16, 1947
805-    vi- **RATHBUN** Carol Lynn born September 18, 1957

640-    MILLER Bert (*William H. Miller, Elizabeth, Obadiah, Obadiah, Joshua, Jasper, John*) was born February 24, 1881 son of William H. MILLER and Emma HAWKS and died August 18, 1966 in Ithaca, NY. His wife Bess (unknown maiden name) was born 1889 and died 1970. They are buried in Grove cemetery.
Children:
        i- MILLER Margaret born 1910, married ___ HODGES
806-    ii- MILLER Edwin C. born 1912
        iii- MILLER Edith born 1917 married Russell HARRIS (lived Poestenkill, NY)
        iv- MILLER Richard born September 1918 (lived Perry, NY)

641-    MILLER Adelaide Elizabeth (*Olin Miller, Elizabeth, Obadiah, Obadiah, Joshua, Jasper, John*) was born ca 1889 in Ulysses, NY daughter of Olin MILLER and Nettie KERST and died May 24, 1951, buried in Grove cemetery. She married George A. REYNOLDS.
Children:
        i- REYNOLDS John O. born 1912 and died March 26, 1970, buried in Grove cemetery
        ii- REYNOLDS Carl B. born 1914 and died June 17, 1979, buried in Grove cemetery
        iii- REYNOLDS Charles R. born ca 1915
        iv- REYNOLDS Ruth born ca 1919
        v- REYNOLDS Doris born ca 1920
        vi- REYNOLDS Frank M. born ca 1921
        vii- REYNOLDS Lida born ca 1922
        viii- REYNOLDS James E. born ca 1924

642-    MILLER John Edwin (*Olin Miller, Elizabeth, Obadiah, Obadiah, Joshua, Jasper, John*) was born July 1895 in Ulysses, NY son of Olin MILLER and Nettie KERST and died June 26, 1932. He married Joanna MC CARTHY who was born 1895 and died 1948. They are buried in Grove cemetery.
Children:
        i- MILLER John Edwin Jr. born 1917 and died 1990, buried in Grove cemetery.
He married Gertrude HOLLIEN born 1923
        ii- MILLER Julia Frances

643-    CURTIS Millard C. (*Carrie Miller, Elizabeth, Obadiah, Obadiah, Joshua, Jasper, John*) was born 1902 son of Allen CURTIS and Carrie MILLER and died 1943. He

married Mildred J. (unknown maiden name) born 1898 and died 1955. They are buried in Grove cemetery.
One child:
    i- CURTIS Mary Jean born 1930 and died 1931, buried Grove cenetery.

644- MASON Flora Elizabeth (*Adeline Ganoung, Berentha, Obadiah, Obadiah, Joshua, Jasper, John*) was born August 21, 1875 in Tompkins Co. NY daughter of George Dawson MASON and Adeline GANOUNG and died November 8, 1950. She married October 4, 1897 Herbert Leslie MC LALLEN who was born May 1, 1876 and died January 1, 1946. They are buried in Grove cemetery.
Children:
    i- MC LALLEN Georgia May born May 3, 1899 and died April 26, 1991. She married Rev. Levi W. LUNN born December 5, 1879 in England and died April 15, 1960. No issue
    ii- MC LALLEN John J. born August 19, 1902 and died October 1, 1903, buried in Grove cemetery
807-    iii- MC LALLEN Levi Herbert born May 6, 1906
808-    iv- MC LALLEN Raymond Mason born November 24, 1912

645- MASON Herman J. (*Adeline Ganoung, Berentha, Obadiah, Obadiah, Joshua, Jasper, John*) was born January 14, 1883 in Tompkins Co. NY son of George Dawson MASON and Adeline GANOUNG and died September 15, 1908. He married December 30, 1903 Georgianna BOND who was born January 23, 1880 daughter of Joseph BOND and Rachel EVERTS and died January 4, 1963. They are buried in Grove cemetery.
One child:
809-    i- MASON Mary Evelyn born June 21, 1907

646- SMITH Olin J. (*John B., Francis, Annanias, Obadiah, Joshua, Jasper, John*) was born November 11, 1886 in NY state son of John B. SMITH and Esther Elizabeth KNEESHAW and died May 1, 1970 in Hornell, NY. He married in Corning, NY November 24, 1915 Edna Esther BROKAW who was born July 24, 1888 daughter of Stephen BROKAW and Ellen Elvira NICHOLSON and died February 18, 1977 in Hornell, NY. They are buried in Rural cemetery in Hornell.
Children born in Hornell, NY:
810-    i- SMITH Esther Ellen born September 20, 1916
811-    ii- SMITH Rodney Olin born February 19, 1922
    iii- SMITH Richard Steven born April 22, 1925 married Jane and lived in Florida

647- SMITH Gertrude Katherine (*John B., Francis, Annanias, Obadiah, Joshua, Jasper, John*) was born October 27, 1890 in NY State daughter of John B. SMITH and Esther Elizabeth KNEESHAW and died May 23, 1973 in Waverly, NY. She married Fred STORM born in Rochester, NY June 7, 1897 and died May 4, 1997 in Penn Yan, NY
Children:
812-    i- STORM Jane J. born November 6, 1926

813-    ii- **STORM** John S. born November 18, 1928
        iii- **STORM** daughter who married Robert W. **MC LAUGHLIN** born September 1,
1926 in Rawlatt, Pa.  5 children

648-    **SMITH** Harold Rockwell (*John B., Francis, Annanias, Obadiah, Joshua, Jasper,
John*) was born June 13, 1895 in NY State son of John B. **SMITH** and Esther Elizabeth
**KNEESHAW** and died August 12, 1959. He married June 25, 1917 Arlene (unknown
maiden name).
Children:
        i- **SMITH** Shirley
        ii- **SMITH** Rockwell
        iii- **SMITH** Betty

649-    **SMITH** Raymond Frank (*John B., Francis, Annanias, Obadiah, Joshua, Jasper,
John*) was born February 14, 1898 in Genoa, NY son of John B. **SMITH** and Esther
Elizabeth **KNEESHAW** and died July 12, 1973 in Ithaca NY. He married June 18, 1919
Bernice Louisa **HAVENS** who was born November 8, 1896 in Enfield, NY and died May
16, 1975 in Ithaca, NY.
Children:
815-    i- **SMITH** Raymond F. Jr. born December 23, 1926
816-    ii- **SMITH** Phyllis Jean born April 7, 1928

650-    **SMITH** Ralph (*John B., Francis, Annanias, Obadiah, Joshua, Jasper, John*) was
born December 8, 1900 in NY State son of John B. **SMITH** and Esther Elizabeth
**KNEESHAW** and died March 1, 1968 in Ithaca, NY. He married in Detroit, Mi. February
28, 1920 Esther A. **ROE** who was born in Candor, NY November 1, 1900 daughter of
Horace Maltby **ROE** and Zelpha Aldora **JACKSON** and died August 6, 1892 in
Westminster, Ca., buried Candor, NY.
One child:
817-    i- **SMITH** Eldora Jane born April 8, 1925

651-    **SMITH** Stanley I. (*John B., Francis, Annanias, Obadiah, Joshua, Jasper, John*) was
born September 4, 1902 in Lansing, NY son of John B. **SMITH** and Esther Elizabeth
**KNEESHAW** and died February 12, 1973. He married Alberta **CORWIN** who was born
May 1, 1904 and died March 12, 1982. They are buried in Willow Glen cemetery in
Dryden, NY.
One child:
        i- **SMITH** Robert

652-    **HUNT** Ethel Katherine (*Eleanor E., Francis, Annanias, Obadiah, Joshua, Jasper,
John*) was born August 30, 1903 in NY state daughter of Walter D. **HUNT** and Eleanor
Elizabeth **SMITH**. She married June 24, 1925 Claud V. **PARSONS** born November 12,
1901
One child:

818-	i- **PARSONS** John Walter born July 30, 1932

653-	**SMITH** Robert Francis (*Jeremiah, Francis, Annanias, Obadiah, Joshua, Jasper, John*) was born May 24, 1899 in NY State son of Jeremiah Annanias SMITH and Lillian May SWAYZE and died November 14, 1946 in Ludlowville, NY, buried Lansingville cemetery. He married Florence K. (unknown maiden name) born 1900, buried Lansingville cemetery, no death dates.

654-	**BROWN** John Raymond (*Manly Clarkson Brown, Melissa, Robert T., Obadiah, Joshua, Jasper, John*) was born February 19, 1901 in Jacksonville, NY son of Manly Clarkson BROWN and Florence Maria TICHENOR and died March 27, 1982. He married August 23, 1921 Helen SMITH who was born October 2, 1903 and died May 1990. They are buried in Grove cemetery.
Children:
	i- **BROWN** Jeannette born March 14, 1922, married (1) John **BERGLAND** and married (2) Arthur **HYLAND**
	ii- **BROWN** Phyllis born May 16, 1923 in Ithaca, NY and died September 1976, married Harry **MC QUIRE**
	iii- **BROWN** John born February 21, 1931, married Marion **POYER**

655-	**BROWN** Elma Beatrice (*Manly Clarkson Brown, Melissa, Robert T., Obadiah, Joshua, Jasper, John*) was born June 19, 1902 in Jacksonville, NY daughter of Manly Clarkson BROWN and Florence Maria TICHENOR and died August 25, 1977. She married June 28, 1922 in Ulysses, NY Fred Merle TOWNSEND who was born April 23, 1897 in Day Mills, Mi. and died February 10, 1960 in Owosso, Mi.
Children:
	i- **TOWNSEND** Florence Jane born May 15, 1924 in Melrose, Mi. She married William Nelson **COFFEY** who was born July 28, 1921 and died October 22, 1945.
	ii- **TOWNSEND** Theodore Paul born June 25, 1932 in Ann Arbor, Mi. He married June 26, 1953 Rosemary **WILLIAMSON** who was born August 20, 1932 in Flint, Mi.

656-	**BROWN** Frederick Tichenor (*Manly Clarkson Brown, Melissa, Robert T., Obadiah, Joshua, Jasper, John*) was born March 11, 1910 in Ulysses, NY son of Manly Clarkson BROWN and Florence Marie TICHENOR and died July 21, 1984. He married November 23, 1935 Edith Iona **REYNOLDS** who was born April 9, 1913 in Penn Yan, NY and died February 24, 1982. They are buried in Grove cemetery.
Children:
	i- **BROWN** Manly Clarkson born October 16, 1936 in Penn Yan, NY, married (1) November 16, 1957 Judy Ann **HERITAGE** born May 29, 1939 and married (2) Frances Carol **HOCKEY**
819-	ii- **BROWN** Howard Frederick born April 10, 1938 in Cortland, NY.

657-	**VANN** Kenneth (*Pearl Hopkins, Abigail, Clement, Obadiah, Joshua, Jasper, John*) was born June 19, 1902 son of William Thomas **VANN** and Pearl **HOPKINS**. He married

R. TWITCHELL.
Children:
      i- VANN Alice
      ii- VANN Hester

658-    VANN Dorothy (*Pearl Hopkins, Abigail, Clement, Obadiah, Joshua, Jasper, John*) was born May 14, 1904 daughter of William Thomas VANN and Pearl HOPKINS and died May 13, 1987. She married Charles A. HALSTEAD who was born 1904 and died November 7, 1977. They are buried in Grove cemetery in Ulysses, NY.
Children:
      i- HALSTEAD Shirley
      ii- HALSTEAD Jerome
      iii- HALSTEAD Sandra
      iv- HALSTEAD James

659-    VANN Harold (*Pearl Hopkins, Abigail, Clement, Obadiah, Joshua, Jasper, John*) was born December 11, 1920 son of William Thomas VANN and Pearl HOPKINS. He married J. YARGA.
Children:
      i- VANN Robert
      ii- VANN Joan

660-    SMITH Laura Mae (*Clement D., William, Clement, Obadiah, Joshua, Jasper, John*) was born May 5, 1875 in Tompkins Co. NY daughter of Clement D. SMITH and Adah BROWN and died September 9, 1921. She married William TAGGART born ca 1867 possibly in Newfield, NY son of William TAGGART and Margaret HODGES and died 1947. They are buried in Woodlawn cemetery in Newfield, NY.
Children:
820-    i- TAGGART Cecil
821-    ii- TAGGART Mabel born 1904
822-    iii- TAGGART Robert born 1909 and died 1962, buried Woodlawn cemetery in Newfield, NY

661-    VANN Carl Wilbert (*Fred Vann, Julia M., Clement, Obadiah, Joshua, Jasper, John*) was born December 26, 1916 son of Fred VANN and Mabel Rebecca ARMSTRONG and died November 14, 2002. He served in World War II. He married May 25, 1946 Bertha Elizabeth NEWMAN who was born October 27, 1920 in Buffalo, NY daughter of Ernest T. and Selma NEWMAN and died March 30, 2002. They are buried in Grove cemetery in Ulysses, NY
Children:
823-    i- VANN Mark Newman born February 5, 1952
824-    ii- VANN Bruce Carl born February 14, 1953

662-    VANN Alvin Gilbert (*Fred Vann, Julia M., Clement, Obadiah, Joshua, Jasper,*

*John*) was born January 7, 1921 son of Fred **VANN** and Mabel Rebecca **ARMSTRONG**. He married June 1949 Olive **ADAMS** who was born May 10, 1928.
Children:
825-     i- **VANN** Linda born September 9, 1951
          ii- **VANN** Robert born February 9, 1956
826-     iii- **VANN** Kathy born August 26, 1958
          iv- **VANN** Gary born June 13, 1962
          v- **VANN** Susan born February 28, 1966

663-     **SMITH** Gilbert Cole (*Cornelius, Gilbert C., John T., Obadiah, Joshua, Jasper, John*) was born November 29, 1897 son of Cornelius Cole **SMITH** and Frances Agnes **GRAHAM** and died October 31, 1967. He married Louise (unknown maiden name) born October 18, 1910 and married (2) Marjorie Helen (unknown maiden name) born March 18, 1907.
Child by first marriage:
827-     i- **SMITH** James G. born November 7, 1932
Child by second marriage:
828-     ii- **SMITH** Frances born June 16 1946

664-     **SMITH** Anita (*Gilbert C., Gilbert C., John T., Obadiah, Joshua, Jasper, John*) was born April 22, 1905 daughter of Gilbert Cole **SMITH** and Anita Veronica **PHILLIPS** and died January 2, 1992. She married September 15, 1927 Edward **PETER** who was born December 23, 1904 son of Edward Compton **PETER** and Mary Gordon **VINSON** and died 1953.
Children:
829-     i- **PETER** Edward C. II born May 8, 1929
          ii- **PETER** Phillips Smith Sr. born January 24, 1932, married (1) Patitia **OSIUS** and married (2) Jania Jane **HUTCHINS**
          iii- **PETER** Nancy Vinson born May 31, 1937, married 1958 David Alden **BRUBAKER**

665-     **GRISWOLD** Oscar Cole (*Emma Cole, Emeline, John T., Obadiah, Joshua, Jasper, John*) was born August 7, 1900 in Penn Yan, NY son of Oscar **GRISWOLD** and Emma **COLE** and died May 5, 1971 in Jackson, Mi. He married July 2, 1924 in Cortland, NY Mildred **JENNINGS** who was born November 20, 1900 in Cortland, NY and died January 1994 in Jackson, Mi.
Children: (note: one was born September 1924)
          i- **GRISWOLD** Barbara
          ii- **GRISWOLD** Eloise

666-     **GRISWOLD** Margaret (*Emma Cole, Emeline, John T., Obadiah, Joshua, Jasper, John*) was born May 25, 1902 in Penn Yan, NY daughter of Oscar **GRISWOLD** and Emma **COLE** and died July 4, 1975. she married (1) Charles **FRUDD** of Yakima, Wa. who was born February 28, 1899 and died February 26, 1953. She married (2) September 14, 1954

Carl **CARLSON** of Jamestown, NY
Children by first marriage:
830-     i- **FRUDD** Eugene born August 9, 1924
         ii- **FRUDD** daughter
         iii- **FRUDD** Harry
         iv- **FRUDD** Charles
         v- **FRUDD** Robert
         vi- **FRUDD** daughter


667-    **SMITH** Dorothy (*Frank T., Herman T., John T., Obadiah, Joshua, Jasper, John*)
was born August 10, 1941 daughter of Frank Taylor **SMITH** and Gladys **STRICKLAND**.
She married Richard **ARDEN** born October 9, 1941 son of Raymond **ARDEN** and Doren
**HEATHWAITE**.
Children:
831-     i- **ARDEN** Carol born September 16, 1964
832-     ii- **ARDEN** Robert born January 23, 1968


668-    **SMITH** Richard Alan (*Alfred J., Herman T., John T., Obadiah, Joshua, Jasper,
John*) was born June 18, 1951 son of Alfred John **SMITH** and Vivian **GAUNT**. He married
February 2, 1972 Beverly **CORNISH** born February 2, 1953 daughter of Kenneth
**CORNISH** and Alice **CONNELLY**.
Children:
         i- **SMITH** Riqui Alliene born July 1, 1973
         ii- **SMITH** Traci Lou born March 14, 1977


669-    **SMITH** Shiela Rose (*Alfred J., Herman T., John T., Obadiah, Joshua, Jasper,
John*) was born February 14, 1956 daughter of Alfred John **SMITH** and Vivian **GAUNT**.
She married December 26, 1978 Lawrence L. **WOODWORTH** born July 12, 1952 son of
Nelson **WOODWORTH** and Anne **MORGAN**. They live in Hector, NY
One child:
         i- **WOODWORTH** James Paul born January 4, 1976


670-    **LYON** Fidelia (*Lorenzo Lyon, Priscilla, Joshua, Annanias, Joshua, Jasper, John*)
was born August 20, 1860 in Clinton Co. Mi. daughter of Lorenzo **LYON** and Eliza **JONES**
and died November 1938 n Hastings, Mi. She married Charles Benjamin **WHITAKER** born
October 2, 1855 in Argentine, Mi. son of Charles **WHITAKER** and Lydia **STURGIS** and
died October 6, 1932 in Hastings, Mi.
One known child born Waterloo, Mi.:
833-     i- **WHITAKER** Nellie Grace born August 17, 1887


671-    **DAVID** Miles Riley (*Sarah Georgia, Lovina, Joshua, Annanias, Joshua, Jasper,
John*) was born March 29, 1863 in Mi. son of Byron Compton **DAVID** and Sarah Kosiah
**GEORGIA** and died 1930. He married (1) April 13, 1884 in Clinton Co. Mi. Alice Adelia
**GILLETT** who was born August 18, 1864 daughter of Charles A. **GILLETT** and Edna

Calara **HOLCOMB** and died 1928. He married (2) November 26, 1891 Avis **BEAM** born 1861 in Mi. daughter of Asa P. **BEAM** and Mary Eliza **SKINNER** and married (3) Jennie Blanche **OSTRANDER** who died August 19, 1943.
Child by first marriage:
834-    i- **DAVID** Lora Agnes born July 1, 1886
Child by second marriage:
    ii- **DAVID** Miles Donovan born ca 1893 and died March 26, 1898 in Lafayette, Mi.
Child by third marriage:
    iii- **DAVID** Frank Morris born 1910 and died February 24, 1966 in Charlotte, Mi.

672-    **DAVID** Frank E (*Sarah Georgia, Lovina, Joshua, Annanias, Joshua, Jasper, John*) was born 1864 in Mi. son of Byron C. **DAVID** and Sarah Kosiah **GEORGIA** and died February 24, 1966 in Charlotte, Mi. He married in Gratiot, Co. Mi. Maud **HIPKONS**.
Children:
835-    i- **DAVID** Floyd
836-    ii- **DAVID** Archie born 1893 in Gratiot Co. Mi.

673-    **DAVID** Eva C. (*Sarah Georgie, Lovina, Joshua, Annanias, Joshua, Jasper, John*) was born September 25, 1871 in Clinton Co. Mi. daughter of Byron C. **DAVID** and Sarah **GEORGIA**. She married April 24, 1897 Francis A. **SENSABAUGH** who was born December 25, 1857 in Cayuga Co. NY son of Peter H. **SENSABAUGH** and Mary **BRIGDEN** and died 1905. His first wife was Louisa **MOORE** born April 8, 1858 in Steuben Co. NY by whom he had 6 children.
Children:
    i- **SENSABAUGH** Ithiel L.
    ii- **SENSABAUGH** Ernest C.

674-    **GEORGIA** Fred Dudley (*Schuyler Georgia, Lovina, Joshua, Annanias, Joshua, Jasper, John*) was born 1875 in Clinton Co. Mi. son of Schuyler **GEORGIA** and Aseneth **BRAY**. He married September 13, 1893 in Clinton Co. Mi. Caddie **BROWN** who was born February 6, 1873 in Bingham Twp. Mi. daughter of Joseph **BROWN** and died March 17, 1949 in Tampa, Fl.
One known child:
837-    i- **GEORGIA** Hazel

675-    **GEORGIA** Mark Lewis (*Schuyler Georgia, Lovina, Joshua, Annanias, Joshua, Jasper, John*) was born 1877 in Clinton Co. Mi. son of Schuyler **GEORGIA** and Aseneth **BRAY** and died April 1, 1911. He married Hattie **BROWN**.
Children:
    i- **GEORGIA** Lois married Herman J. **MATTER**
    ii- **GEORGIA** Glenn born May 12, 1901 in Bingham Twp. Mi. and died January 19, 1917

676-    **GEORGIA** Tyler R. (*Schuyler Georgia, Lovina, Joshua, Annanias, Joshua, Jasper,*

*John*) was born May 8, 1879 in Clinton Co. Mi. son of Schuyler **GEORGIA** and Aseneth **BRAY** and died June 17, 1944 in Clinton Co. He married September 14, 1889 Edna **PLOWMAN** who died December 1919 in Bengal Twp. Mi. He married (2) October 5, 1921 Josephine M. **BRAY** who was born May 16, 1893 in Thornapple daughter of Joseph Corwin **BRAY** and died November 1963 in Mi.

Child by second marriage:

    i- **GEORGIA** Maxine born 1923 who married Herman **ADDINGTON** and had 2 children Rebecca and Debra Lee

677-    **FREESE** Myrtle Eloise (*Margaret Anna, Lewis H., Joshua, Annanias, Joshua, Jasper, John*) was born August 30, 1869 in Tompkins Co. NY daughter of Henry Sanford **FREESE** and Margaret Ann **SMITH** and died February 26, 1970, buried Hayt's cemetery. She marrried September 3, 1890 Charles E. **FISH** who died 1893.

Children:

838-    i- **FISH** Helen Elma born June 9, 1892
839-    ii- **FISH** Wesley Elwood born August 15, 1896

678-    **FREESE** Willard Smith (*Margaret Anna, Lewis H., Joshua, Annanias, Joshua, Jasper, John*) was born September 15, 1873 in Tompkins Co. NY son of Henry Sanford **FREESE** and Margaret Ann **SMITH** and died October 30, 1928. He married June 15, 1910 Helen M. **GRAY** who was born June 20, 1873 daughter of David **GRAY** and Mary Caroline **DOTY** and died February 22, 1844. They are buried in Trumbull's Corners cemetery.

Children:

    i- **FREESE** Howard Gray born April 29, 1911 and died age 1 month
840-    ii- **FREESE** Mary Edith born November 28, 1913

679-    **FREESE** Lewis Orville (*Margaret Anna, Lewis H., Joshua, Annanias, Joshua, Jasper, John*) was born November 9, 1875 in Enfield, NY son of Henry Sanford **FREESE** and Margaret Anna **SMITH** and died March 16, 1941 in Ithaca, NY. He married June 29, 1902 Elizabeth Josephine **DUNSTER** who was born March 9, 1875 daughter of Alfred **DUNSTER** and Josephine **COOPER** and died October 14, 1937. They are buried in Hayt's cemetery in Ithaca, NY

Children born in Enfield, NY:

841-    i- **FREESE** Myrtle May born May 10, 1903
842-    ii- **FREESE** Cora Luella born May 30, 1907
    iii- **FREESE** Helen Margaret born November 24, 1912

680-    **FREESE** Mary Edith (*Margaret Anna, Lewis H., Joshua, Annanias, Joshua, Jasper, John*) was born August 10, 1878 in Enfield, NY daughter of Henry Sanford **FREESE** and Margaret Ann **SMITH** and died December 2/3, 1978. She married June 29, 1899 Luther Stevens **TEETER** who was born May 8, 1872 in Enfield, NY son of Henry Duane **TEETER** and Harriet Salome **STEVENS** and died June 1, 1957 in Ithaca, NY.

Children:

    i- **TEETER** Raymond Henry born May 27, 1900 and killed by falling tree March

23, 1923 in Ithaca, NY, buried Hayt's cemetery
843-    ii- **TEETER** Ann Margaret born March 20, 1902 in Newfield, NYT and died February 21, 1980 in Lakeland, Fl.

681-    **EMLEY** Ella Lelah (*Helen, Lewis H., Joshua, Annanias, Joshua, Jasper, John*) was born 1888 in Tompkins Co. NY daughter of William **EMLEY** and Helen **SMITH**. She married December 20, 1926 Olin Whitney **SMITH** who was born October 17, 1884 son of Harris Irvin **SMITH** and Almina Nichols **WHITNEY** and died November 17, 1966 in Ithaca, NY. (see #228)
Children:
        i- **SMITH** Olin W. Jr. born June 15, 1918, married March 18, 1942 Patricia **CAIN** and moved to Bowling Green, Ohio and died February 7, 1989
        ii- **SMITH** Herman Emley born August 14, 1920 and removed to Long Beach, Cal.

682-    **TILTON** Laura B. (*Elizabeth, Lewis H., Joshua, Annanias, Joshua, Jasper, John*) was born 1881 in Tompkins Co. NY daughter of Fred **TILTON** and Elizabeth **SMITH** and died 1978. She married Charles **SHEFFIELD** who was born 1879 in Enfield, NY son of John and Charlotte **SHEFFIELD** and died 1955. They are buried in Hayt's cemetery in Ithaca, NY
Children:
        i- **SHEFFIELD** Charles
        ii- **SHEFFIELD** Ernest who died February 1968, buried Hayt's cemetery
        iii- **SHEFFIELD** Clifford
        iv- **SHEFFIELD** Alice died January 17, 1917 age 4 mos. buried Hayt's cemetery
        v- **SHEFFIELD** Walter died July 15, 1914 age 5 days, buried Hayt's cemetery

683-    **TILTON** Walter (*Elizabeth, Lewis H., Joshua, Annanias, Joshua, Jasper, John*) was born 1883 in Tompkins Co. NY son of Fred **TILTON** and Elizabeth **SMITH**. He married Anna **BAKER** born 1884
Children:
        i- **TILTON** Theodore born 1901, married Polly **NEWHART**
        ii- **TILTON** Albert born 1902 and died July 25, 1985, married Alice **HOWORTH**
        iii- **TILTON** Clarence born 1902
        iv- **TILTON** Frederick born 1905, married Blanche ROLFE

684-    **TILTON** Grace (*Elizabeth, Lewis H., Joshua, Annanias, Joshua, Jasper, John*) was born 1886 in Tompkins Co. NY daughter of Fred **TILTON** and Elizabeth **SMITH** and died 1978. She married Perry **WILLIAMS** (or Percy who was born 1880 and died 1966 son of Charles and Sadie **WILLIAMS**. They are buried in Hayt's cemetery in Ithaca, NY.
Children:
        i- **WILLIAMS** Howard
        ii- **WILLIAMS** Gladys
        iii- **WILLIAMS** Lawrence (poss. buried in Grove cemetery who died November 7, 1959 age 49 yrs.)

iv- WILLIAMS Richard buried Hayt's cemetery, no dates

685-    INMAN Cora (*George H. Inman, Christina G., Peter, Annanias, Joshua, Jasper, John*) was born 1875 in Buffalo, NY daughter of George H. and Mary W. INMAN and died there August 3, 1956. She married Harry Thomas GALE who was born 1865 in Indianna son of Henry H. and Caroline F. GALE and died March 23, 1917 in Buffalo. They are buried in Forest Lawn cemetery. Unknown children

686-    LEONARD Ward (*Nellie Lanning, Gideon Lanning, Nancy, Annanias, Joshua, Jasper, John*) was born March 1888 son of Chester LEONARD and Nellie LANNING. He married Jenny MITCHELL daughter of Daniel and Nellie MITCHELL.
Children:
  i- LEONARD Marion
  ii- LEONARD Louise married ____ WATT

687-    ACKLEY Walter Freeman (*Olive Rose Summerton, Thomas Summerton, Sally, Annanias, Joshua, Jasper, John*) was born July 11, 1883 in Lockwood, NY son of Wesley Freeman ACKLEY and Olive Rose SUMMERTON and died June 28, 1951 in Spencer, NY. He married December 24, 1908 Clara May HOWELL who was born ca 1888 and died February 1925. They are buried in Lockwood cemetery, Tioga Co.
Children:
844-    i- ACKLEY Homer Howell born September 25, 1908
  ii- ACKLEY Robert who married Ruby BOSSARD
  iii- ACKLEY Lois Vivian born September 12, 1912 and died ca 1930
  iv- ACKLEY child died infancy
  v- ACKLEY child died infancy
  vi- ACKLEY Lester born July 1918

688-    ACKLEY Mary Luella (*Olive Rose Summerton, Thomas Summerton, Sally, Annanias, Joshua, Jasper, John*) was born November 13, 1887 in Lockwood, NY daughter of Wesley Freeman ACKLEY and Olive Rose SUMMERTON and died September 28, 1948, buried Trumansburg, NY. She married November 13, 1905 Raymond Eugene BAKER who was born November 14, 1878 and died January 23, 1952.
Children:
  i- BAKER Shirley H.
  ii- BAKER Mildred
  iii- BAKER Lawrence born ca 1915
  iv- BAKER Grace
  v- BAKER Stanley
  vi- BAKER Lyle Weeks
  vii- BAKER Edna

689-    ACKLEY Alvah Charles (*Olive Rose Summerton, Thomas Summerton, Sally, Annanias, Joshua, Jasper, John*) was born December 18, 1890 in Lockwood, NY son of

Wesley Freeman **ACKLEY** and Olive Rose **SUMMERTON** and died November 9, 1972 in Packer Hospital, Sayre, Pa. He married December 18, 1913 Bertha Emelia **MEISSNER** who was born July 23, 1892 in Fond Du Lac, Wis. daughter of Theodore **MEISSNER** and Caroline Wilhelmina **WAGNER** and died November 29, 1965 in Lockwood, NY. They are buried in Lockwood cemetery. He married (2) Margaret Julia **MALLORY** daughter of George **MALLORY** and Lottie **HANCOCK**.

Children:

845-    i- **ACKLEY** Charles William born March 31, 1915 in Lockwood, NY and died February 7, 2004 in Springville, NY, buried Prospect cemetery in Sidney, Delaware Co. NY. He married ____ **TRIPP** and had 2 children.

ii- **ACKLEY** Florence Emelia born January 19, 1918 and died January 12, 2003. She married Donald **SUFFERN**

iii- **ACKLEY** Alice Jane married Donald **CHANDLER** of Waverly

690-    **ACKLEY** Marion Weeks (*Olive Rose Summerton, Thomas Summerton, Sally, Annanias, Joshua, Jasper, John*) was born ca 1901 in Lockwood, NY daughter of Wesley Freeman **ACKLEY** and Olive Rose **SUMMERTON** and died August 11, 1960 in Vaverly, NY, buried Lockwood cemetery. She married Arthur Theodore **MEISSNER**.

Children:

i- **MEISSNER** Llewellyn
ii- **MEISSNER** Clifton

691-    **ACKLEY** Clifford S. (*Olive Rose Summerton, Thomas Summerton, Sally, Annanias, Joshua, Jasper, John*) was born ca 1900 son of Wesley Freeman **ACKLEY** and Olive Rose **SUMMERTON** and died by drowning in Skaneateles Lake April 13, 1955 while fishing. (news item in Syracuse Herald) He married Elsie K. (unknown maiden name) who was born May 16, 1895 in Stevensville, Pa. and died May 30, 1995 in Syracuse, NY, buried White Chapel Memory Gardens in Dewitt, NY. She had 2 children by first marriage.

## Ninth Generation

692-    **SMITH** Ann Gertrude (*Halma, James, Joseph, Daniel, Jasper, John, Jasper, John*) was born May 29, 1860 in Salt Lake City, Utah daughter of Halma James **SMITH** and Ann Booth **BOLTON** and died May 9, 1928 in Salt Lake City. She married (1) ____ **COLLIER** born ca 1856 in Provo, Utah and married (2) October 27, 1896 in Provo David Henry **LOVELESS**.

Children by second marriage born Provo, Utah:

i- **LOVELESS** Edith Louella born October 26, 1897. She married Martin Joseph **ARMSTRONG** and had son Vernon Martin who was born December 6, 1914 in Provo, Utah and married October 2, 1936 in Orange, Cal. Hazel May **MORROW** born March 26,

1916 in Villa Park Cal. They had 1 daughter and 1 son

    ii- LOVELESS Carl Edwin born September 15, 1904, married in Park City, Utah Sybil WORKMAN born March 19, 1905 daughter of Dee and Rose WORKMAN. He married (2) May 8, 1945 Dorthea HICKS born October 2, 1918 in Clinton, Utah daughter of James HICKS and Dorthea MC KEAN. He had 2 sons by first marriage and 1 son by second marriage,

693-    SMITH Halma Bolton (*Halma, James, Joseph, Daniel, Jasper, John, Jasper, John*) was born January 28, 1862 in Provo, Utah son of Halma James SMITH and Ann Booth BOLTON and died May 31, 1939 in Garden Grove, Cal. He married (1) February 1, 1887 Florena CLARK who was born September 7, 1869 in Springville, Utah daughter of Davis CLARK and Georgianna Eliza SPENCE and died December 13, 1897. He married (2) October 26, 1901 Allie May DIMOND and married (3) April 29, 1909 Nettie Lenzie PARKER.

Children by first marriage born in Springville, Utah:

846-    i- SMITH Eugenia Abigail born November 19, 1888
847-    ii- SMITH Claude Halma born November 30, 1890
    iii- SMITH Melvin born November 28, 1891 and died December 7, 1891
    iv- SMITH Thelma born November 16, 1893 and died October 31, 1951
848-    v- SMITH Georgianna Edith born September 23, 1895
    vi- SMITH Clark Rean born November 27, 1896, married Harriet HARRISON

Children by second marriage:

    vii- SMITH Elbert Lucius born August 18, 1909 in Provo, Utah and married November 25, 1947 Lida La Feuse MITCHELL born May 20, 1911 in Garden Grove, Cal. daughter of John Carlos MITCHELL and Nancy Anna EATON. They had 1 son and 1 daughter

    viii- SMITH Clara Elizabeth born March 21, 1912 in Santa Ana, Cal. and married January 17, 1955 John George BAERG born June 1, 1912 in Escondido, Cal. son of George John BAERG and Christine NICHOL. They had 1 son and 1 daughter.

694-    SMITH Emma Luella (*Halma, James, Joseph, Daniel, Jasper, John, Jasper, John*) was born April 2, 1869 in Provo, Utah daughter of Halma James SMITH and Ann Booth BOLTON and died January 30, 1950 in Bell, Cal. She married in 1890 Daniel Preston KELLOGG who was born April 17, 1868 in Provo, Utah and died 1945.

695-    SMITH Alpheus Jackson (*Halma, James, Joseph, Daniel, Jasper, John, Jasper, John*) was born January 21, 1875 in Provo, Utah son of Halma James SMITH and Ann Booth BOLTON and died April 27, 1951 in Santa Ana, Cal. He married June 14, 1922 Zella Laveve GARDNER who was born August 22, 1887 in Spanish Rock, Utah daughter of Serenus GARDNER and Josephine HANSEN.

696-    SMITH Edith May (*Halma, James, Joseph, Daniel, Jasper, John, Jasper, John*) was born March 9, 1877 in Provo, Utah daughter of Halma James SMITH and Ann Booth BOLTON and died June 24, 1909 in Provo. She married October 19, 1905 in Provo Willie

James **TAYLOR** who was born January 1, 1878 in Springville, Utah son of Hyrum J. **TAYLOR** and Angeline **EDWARDS** and died November 22, 1958 in Provo.

697- **SMITH** Hyrum (*Hyrum, James, Joseph, Daniel, Jasper, John, Jasper, John*) was born October 29, 1872 in Provo, Utah son of Hyrum **SMITH** and Julia **HUNTSMAN** and died February 27, 1923 in Provo. He married October 10, 1897 in Provo Olive **STAGG** who was born May 15, 1877 in Provo daughter of George **STAGG** and Olive **WHITE** and died May 11, 1950 in Provo.
Children born in Provo, Utah:

|       |                                                                          |
|-------|--------------------------------------------------------------------------|
|       | i- **SMITH** Glen born February 26, 1899 and died in Colton               |
|       | ii- **SMITH** Hyrum born December 9, 1899 and died April 14, 1900         |
| 849-  | iii- **SMITH** Jessie born May 20, 1901                                   |
| 850-  | iv- **SMITH** Ruth born October 19, 1902                                  |
| 851-  | v- **SMITH** Lola Lavon born April 9, 1904                                |
| 852-  | vi- **SMITH** Alice born November 27, 1906                                |
| 853-  | vii- **SMITH** Darroll born September 21, 1907                            |
| 854-  | viii- **SMITH** Olive S. born June 23, 1910                               |
|       | ix- **SMITH** George born September 16, 1911 and died April 14, 1909 in Provo |
| 855-  | x- **SMITH** Georgia born May 14, 1913 and died April 14, 1914 in Provo   |
| 856-  | xi- **SMITH** Elmer Alvin born September 3, 1915                          |
| 857-  | xii- **SMITH** Kenneth born March 4, 1919                                 |
| 858-  | xiii- **SMITH** Eugene Richard born September 23, 1920                    |

698- **SMITH** Albert Harry (*John, James, Joseph, Daniel, Jasper, John, Jasper, John*) was born August 17, 1888 in Provo, Utah son of John **SMITH** and Julia Ett **BOWEN** and died June 22, 1971 in Payson, Utah. He married December 14, 1910 in Provo Beatrice **RODEBACK** born October 21, 1892 in Hoytsville, Utah and died October 8, 1972.

699- **SMITH** James Hastings (*John, James, Joseph, Daniel, Jasper, John, Jasper, John*) was born June 24, 1891 in Provo, Utah son of John **SMITH** and Julia Ett **BOWEN** and died January 9, 1975. He married in Price, Utah Gladys **WALTON** daughter of John **WALTON** and Martha **GASKELL** and died July 10, 1989.

700- **CLARK** Enoch Alpheus (*Sarah Ann, James, Joseph, Daniel, Jasper, John, Jasper, John*) was born October 22, 1864 in Provo, Utah son of Enoch Alpheus **CLARK** and Sarah Ann **SMITH** and died November 22, 1938 in Salt Lake City. He married June 1, 1889 in Provo, Utah Josephine Marie **KLESS** born April 16, 1873 in Wuerttemberg, Germany daughter of Maximillian **KLESS** and Josephine **BRATH**. Unknown children

701- **CLARK** James Henry (*Sarah Ann, James, Joseph, Daniel, Jasper, John, Jasper, John*) was born November 8, 1865 in Provo, Utah son of Enoch Alpheus **CLARK** and Sarah Ann **SMITH** and died February 10, 1949 in Provo. He married in Provo November 13, 1893 Mary Aleapha **BARNETT** who was born June 18, 1876 in Harrison, Iowa and died March 8, 1940 in Springville, Utah.

702- SMITH Joseph William (*Joseph, James, Joseph, Daniel, Jasper, John, Jasper, John*) was born November 27, 1884 in Provo, Utah son of Joseph SMITH and Isabelle Lucinda PACE and died June 28, 1922 in Provo. He married (1) November 15, 1920 (spouse unknown) and married (2) October 26, 1921 in Los Angeles, Cal. Alma Carlotta KARIOTH born January 29, 1884 in Sachsen, Germany daughter of Heinrich and Bertha KARIOTH. She died August 22, 1959 in Provo and he married (3) June 9, 1960 Martha Joella LOTT born December 13, 1889 in Provo daughter of Isaiah B. LOTT and Lavonia ANDREWS.

703- SMITH Martha Ella (*Henry, James, Joseph, Daniel, Jasper, John, Jasper, John*) was born October 8, 1884 in Provo, Utah daughter of Henry SMITH and Alveretta H. CONOVER and died July 23, 1931. She married January 15, 1903 in Provo George Melvin CLINGER who was born May 29, 1882 in Provo son of George Francis CLINGER and Anna Marie JOHNSON and died March 28, 1957.

704- RUMSEY Donald Howard (*Frances L. Lanning, William Lanning, Jasper Lanning, Elizabeth, John, Jasper, John*) was born July 16, 1911 in Newfield, NY son of Elmer Clarence RUMSEY and Frances L. LANNING and died 1982 in Ithaca, NY. He married (1) Doris Leonard Button WILSON who was born July 24, 1911 and died March 17, 1997 in Cortland, NY. He married (2) July 21, 1934 Vivian Doris FISH born September 13, 1917 in Ithaca, NY daughter of Frank FISH and Bessie C. WILKINSON and died February 5, 1993 in Watertown, NY, buried Adams cemetery.
Children:
        i- RUMSEY Yvonne Marie born January 8, 1936 in Ithaca and died June 4, 1987 in Adams, NY. She married August 24, 1952 in Ithaca Gerald Lester SNYDER born January 21, 1936 in Dryden, NY and died December 29, 1959 in Willow Glen, NY. They had 3 children. She married (2) June 4, 1967 Frederick Elmer SHOEMAKER who was born April 14, 1930 son of Elmer Martin SHOEMAKER and Elsie Marie WEAVER. They had 1 son.

705- LAWTON Carolyn Louise (*Caroline, Peter, Benjamin, Israel, Israel, Jasper, Jasper, John*) was born January 28, 1902 in Wilmington, Delaware daughter of Charles Clark LAWTON and Caroline Louise SMITH and died December 26, 1987 in Van Nuys, Cal. She married April 7, 1920 in Los Angeles Vern Ira BIDWELL who was born January 31, 1901 in Severy, Ks. son of Marshall Ira BIDWELL and died August 17, 1963 in Hermiston, Ore., buried Carmichael cemetery
Children:
        i- BIDWELL Helen Louise born April 15, 1924 in Holywood, Ca. She married (1) unknown spouse in Pasadena, Cal. February 3, 1945 and married (2) November 4, 1961 in Los Angeles Frederick Alexander PECHECEK who was born February 27, 1897 in Yankton, Co. son of Frank Joseph PECHECEK and Rose STRANSKY and died July 25, 1977 in Glendale, Cal., both buried in Forest Lawn Memorial Park

706- ALBERTSON Emily Frances (*Sarah Clarissa White, John White, Mercy Tindall,*

Joseph Tindall, Abigail, Thomas, Jasper, John) was born February 17, 1857 in Great
Meadow, NJ daughter of Coursen ALBERTSON and Sarah Clarissa WHITE and died 1931.
She married November 27, 1879 John BLACKWELL born ca 1850.
Children:
    i- BLACKWELL Clara Jean born May 26, 1885 and married Duncan Albert
DOBIE born 1880
    ii- BLACKWELL Jessalyn Edith born September 18, 1888 and married Llewellyn
JAMES born ca 1880

707-   ALBERTSON John White (*Sarah Clarissa White, John White, Mercy Tindall,
Joseph Tindall, Abigail, Thomas, Jasper, John*) was born December 20, 1858 in Great
Meadows, NJ son of Coursen Henry ALBERTSON and Sarah Clarissa WHITE and died
1943. He married April 28, 1892 Annie Jane GRAY who was born 1867 and died 1944.
Children:
    i- ALBERTSON Mary Clarissa born July 13, 1893 and died 1918
    ii- ALBERTSON Mabel Gray born December 22, 1894 and died 1962
    iii- ALBERTSON Edith Lutie born February 27, 1896 and died 1982. She married
Randolph HUGG born 1889 and died 1969
    iv- ALBERTSON Coursen Henry born January 24, 1898 and died 1977
    v- ALBERTSON Margaret Rice born July 14, 1899 and died September 24, 1909
    vi- ALBERTSON Bertha Delia born July 11, 1901 and died 1997. She married
Walter A. TINDALL born 1897 and died 1990
    vii- ALBERTSON Annie Amelia born February 7, 1903 and died 1973
    viii- ALBERTSON John W. born August 6, 1905 and died August 8, 1905
    ix- ALBERTSON Milton Hoagland born June 11, 1907 and died September 26,
1909
    x- ALBERTSON Frances Bethany born February 10, 1910 and died 1971. She
married Frederick Robert SPINK

708-   ALBERTSON Kerr Freeman (*Sarah Clarissa White, John White, Mercy Tindall,
Joseph Tindall, Abigail, Thomas, Jasper, John*) was born February 12, 1860 son of Coursen
Henry ALBERTSON and Sarah Clarissa WHITE and died 1939. He married (1) June 10,
1891 Mary C. HUNTSBERGER born 1869 and (2) Helen BOULTER born 1860.

709-   ALBERTSON Anna Bird (*Sarah Clarissa White, John White, Mercy Tindall, Joseph
Tindall, Abigail, Thomas Jasper, John*) was born March 15, 1853 daughter of Henry
Coursen ALBERTSON and Sarah Clarissa WHITE and died 1958. She married December
25, 1884 in Oxford, NJ Levi W. HOAGLAND who was born 1857 son of Theodore
HOAGLAND and Rebecca K. MACKEY and died 1943.
Children:
    i- HOAGLAND Grace Lane born December 15, 1885
    ii- HOAGLAND Watson Levi born June 19, 1888
    iii- HOAGLAND Amos Coursen born August 21, 1890
    iv- HOAGLAND Ethel May born April 27, 1894

182

710- **ALBERTSON** William Coursen (*Sarah Clarissa White, John White, Mercy Tindall, Joseph Tindall, Abigail, Thomas, Jasper, John*) was born March 27, 1865 son of Henry Coursen **ALBERTSON** and Sarah Clarissa **WHITE** and died 1946. He married October 30, 1888 Mary Louise **SHIPMAN** born 1870.
Children:
    i- **ALBERTSON** Anna Morris born July 9, 1891
    ii- **ALBERTSON** William Coursen Jr. born December 18, 1898
    iii- **ALBERTSON** Morris Shipman born April 5, 1901
    iv- **ALBERTSON** son

711- **ALBERTSON** Milton Hoagland (*Sarah Clarissa White, John White, Mercy Tindall, Joseph Tindall, Abigail, Thomas, Jasper, John*) was born March 10, 1869 in NJ son of Henry Coursen **ALBERTSON** and Sarah Clarissa **WHITE** and died 1953. He married December 19, 1911 Edith **LEONARD** born 1873 in Flushing, LI.

712- **ALBERTSON** Jennie Clarissa (*Sarah Clarissa White, John White, Mercy Tindall, Joseph Tindall, Abigail, Thomas, Jasper, John*) was born October 18, 1871 in NJ daughter of Henry Coursen **ALBERTSON** and Sarah Clarissa **WHITE** and died 1952. She married November 17, 1898 David Newton **HENRY** born 1866.

713- **STAGGS** Mildred May (*George B. Staggs, Mary Berry, Susannah, Thomas H., Elijah, Thomas, Jasper, John*) was born May 28, 1884 in Opello, Ar. daughter of George B. **STAGGS** and Anna Josephine **THOMPSON** and died March 16, 1969 in Pope Co. Ar. She married February 3, 1901 in Pope Co. John William **HOTTINGER** who was born June 18, 1878 in Ohio and died March 10, 1958 in Little Rock, Ar.
Children born in Dover, Pope Co. Ar.:
    i- **HOTTINGER** Bertie Maude born November 28, 1901, married November 1928 Julius **WHITE** and had 1 daughter
    ii- **HOTTINGER** William Doke born December 21, 1903, married Jessie **LEWIS**
    iii- **HOTTINGER** Bertha Mae born November 6, 1905, married 1928 Earl **SHINN**
    iv- **HOTTINGER** Kirby Anderson born January 4, 1908 and died August 8, 1956 in Lee's Summit, Mo., married May 6, 1933 Margaretha Magdeline **BRINKMAN**, 2 sons
    v- **HOTTINGER** Maggie Gladys married ____ **BERRY**
    vi- **HOTTINGER** Charles Raymond born October 25, 1911 and died October 25, 1911 in Russellville, Ar.
    vii- **HOTTINGER** John Robert born February 2, 1914 and died March 27, 1935 in Dover, Ar.
    viii- **HOTTINGER** son
    ix- **HOTTINGER** daughter

714- **STAGGS** George Lewis (*George B. Staggs, Mary Berry, Susannah, Thomas H., Elijah, Thomas, Jasper, John*) was born July 8, 1886 son of George B. **STAGGS** and Anna Josephine **THOMPSON** and died August 5, 1947 in Little Rock, Ar. He married Lizzie **GIBSON**.

Chidren:

    i- STAGGS Everett

    ii- STAGGS Charles Milton born September 25, 1907 in Russellville, Ar. and died April 26, 1978 in Benton, Ar. He married ___ PASSMORE and had 2 children

    iii- STAGGS Jessie married 1928 Earl SHINN

    iv- STAGGS Jasper born August 10, 1913 and died September 19, 1985 in Pope Co. Ar.

715- STAGGS Walter Columbus (*George B. Staggs, Mary Berry, Susannah, Thomas H., Elijah, Thomas, Jasper, John*) was born April 1, 1892 in Woodruff Co. Ar. son of George B. STAGGS and Anna Josephine THOMPSON and died December 26, 1952 in Pope Co. Ar. He married June 28, 1913 Lucille Ann STEWART who was born February 16, 1893 in Ar. and died September 9, 1978 in Portland, Ore.

Children born in Dover, Ar.:

    i- STAGGS Myrick Earl born May 4, 1912 and died May 8, 1986 in Idabel, Ok. He married September 6, 1924 Grace DAVIS born March 20, 1912 in Burneyville, Ok. and died August 3, 1980. They had 2 daughters and 2 sons

    ii- STAGGS Douglas born June 17, 1913 and died January 25, in Portland, Ore. He married ___ MC KIBBEN

    iii- STAGGS daughter

    iv- STAGGS daughter

    v- STAGGS son

716- STAGGS William Robert (*George B. Staggs, Mary Berry, Susannah, Thomas H., Elijah, Thomas, Jasper, John*) was born August 3, 1894 in Woodruff Co. Ar. son of George B. STAGGS and Anna Josephine THOMPSON and died February 6, 1945. He married February 9, 1919 Eva BARTON who was born July 25, 1895 in Pope Co. Ar. and died July 23, 1932 in Pope Co.

Children born Pope Co. Ar.:

    i- STAGGS James Robert born June 28, 1920 and died February 2, 2000 at Ft. Smith, Ar. He married ___ MC FARREN and had 2 sons, James Gary born November 16, 1942 at Ft. Smith Ar. and died February 1988 and another son.

    ii- STAGGS Charles Thurman August 17, 1921 and died March 17, 1987 in Fayetteviile, Ar. He married ___ SIMPSON

    iii- STAGGS Edwin Duane born August 23, 1926 and died April 19, 1992 in Prairie Grove, Ar. He married ___ HEGI

717- STAGGS Charles H. (*George B. Staggs, Mary Berry, Susannah, Thomas H., Elijah, Thomas, Jasper, John*) was born August 23, 1896 in Opello, Ar. son of George B. STAGGS and Anna Josephine THOMPSON and died June 22, 1969. He married October 29, 1916 in New Hope, Ar. Nora L. EUBANKS born November 10, 1895 in New Hope, Ar. and died September 15, 1977, buried New Hope cemetery.

Children:

    i- STAGGS son born January 4, 1918 and died same day

184

    ii- **STAGGS** son
    iii- **STAGGS** daughter
    iv- **STAGGS** Charles Rue born December 16, 1924 in New Hope, Ar. and died
February 18, 1977 in Pope Co., buried new Hope cemetery. He married ____ **STEWART**
and had 3 children
    v- **STAGGS** Robert Ernest born October 3, 1927 in New Hope, Ar. and died
April 6, 1987. He married (1) Barbara **COVERT** and (2) ____ **DUNCAN** and had 2
children
    vi- **STAGGS** daughter

718-    **BATES** Beaulah Beatrice (*Florence Staggs, Nancy J. Berry, Susannah, Thomas H.,
Elijah, Thomas, Jasper, John*) was born June 1, 1907 in Eldorado, Ok. daughter of William
Webster **BATES** and Florence Arminda **STAGGS** and died November 30, 1996 in Lufkin,
Tx. She married December 21, 1925 in Quanah, Tx. Irving **CHENAULT** who was born
January 12, 1902 in Brazos Co. Tx. and died April 10, 1963, buried in Peach Tree
cemetery.
Children:
    i- **CHENAULT** daughter
    ii- **CHENAULT** Billy Lloyd born January 16, 1932 in Mullican, Tx. and died
October 12, 1990 in Delta Co. Col. He married ____ **FORSTHOFF** and had 3 children
    iii- **CHENAULT** daughter

719-    **MELTON** Mary Helen (*Minnie P. Knox, John B. Knox, Elijah Knox, Cynthia,
Elijah, Thomas, Jasper, John*) was born November 15, 1913 in Tx. daughter of John Gordon
**MELTON** and Minnie Pearl **KNOX** and died September 21, 2001 in Los Angeles, Cal. She
married December 9, 1934 in Harbor City, Cal. James Robert
**BLOOMER** who was born September 4, 1913 in Wabash, Ind. son of John Wellman
**BLOOMER** and Floy Edith **HUBBARD** and died September 27, 1971 in Harbor City, Cal.
Children:
    i- **BLOOMER** Linda Lea born February 2, 1939 in Los Angeles and died April 2,
2001
    ii- **BLOOMER** Robert

720-    **SCOTT** Sidney Ann (*Adnie Malott, Francis Malott, Ann, Absolom, John, Samuel,
Jasper, John*) was born Jun 1866 in Clermont Co. Ohio daughter of Isaac H. **SCOTT** and
Adnie **MALOTT** and died November 20, 1931 in Iroquois Co. Ill. She married July 1,
1882 in Iroquois Co. Ill. George Warvel **BALSER** who was born March 3, 1861 in
Williamsburg, Ohio son of Peter **BALSER** and Sarah **WATT** and died December 17, 1926
in Iroquois Co. Ill. They are buried in Amity cemetery.
Children in Iroquois Co. Ill.:
859-    i- **BALSER** Ella Elvida born May 1884
860-    ii- **BALSER** Sarah Addie born January 23, 1886 in Ash Grove
    iii- **BALSER** Bessie born January 17, 1890, married July 3, 1908 Benjamin Hamer
**COOK**

185

iv- **BALSER** John H. born January 22, 1892 in Milford, Ill. and died October 16, 1946 in Chicago, Ill, buried Amity cemetery
861-    v- **BALSER** Charlotta A. born June 13, 1894 in Milford
vi- **BALSER** Ettie Maude Mae born December 19, 1900
vii- **BALSER** Eddie

721-    **SCOTT** Lillian D. (*Adnie Malott, Francis L. Malott, Ann, Absolom, John, Samuel, Jasper, John*) was born October 3, 1868 in Brown Co. Ohio daughter of Isaac H. **SCOTT** and Adnie **MALOTT** and died February 21, 1944, buried Maple Grove cemetery. She married December 31, 1888 in Glenwood, Ill. William **HAWTHORNE**.
Children born Highland Co. Ohio:
i- **HAWTHORNE** Cordie Lee born February 28, 1892
ii- **HAWTHORNE** Everette Ray

722-    **SCOTT** John (*Adnie Malott, Francis L. Malott, Ann, Absolom, John, Samuel, Jasper, John*) was born September 6, 1872 in Brown Co. Ohio son of Isaac H. **SCOTT** and Adnie **MALOTT** and died June 5, 1947 in Winona, Ill. He married Lillian **BURGETT** who was born April 14, 1878 in Milford, Ill and died March 13, 1947 in Kankakee, Ill. They are buried in Maple Grove cemetery.
Children:
i- **SCOTT** Helen born July 21, 1912 in Milford and died September 5, 1983 in Danville, Ill. She married September 21, 1933 Jesse **SHOUFLER**
ii- **SCOTT** Lloyd died February 1961 in Robinsdale, Mn., buried Snelling National cemetery. Served WWI

723-    **SCOTT** Margaret L. (*Adnie Malott, Francis L. Malott, Ann, Absolom, John, Samuel, Jasper, John*) was born September 15, 1875 in St. Martin, Ohio daughter of Isaac H. **SCOTT** and Adnie **MALOTT** and died November 3, 1957 in Sheldon, Ill. She married George **BREEDING** who was born March 28, 1865 in Cincinnati, Oh. and died August 18, 1945 in Milford, Ill. They are buried in Maple Grove cemetery.
Children:
i- **BREEDING** Clarence born January 25, 1892 in Ash Grove Twp. and died June 10, 1967 in Watseka, Ill., buried Maple Grove cemetery. He married July 2, 1915 Catherine K. **SHAFER** who was born November 21, 1893 in Chippewa Falls, Wis.
ii- **BREEDING** Walter L. born September 15, 1895 in Milford, Ill and died July 23, 1972 in Hoopeston, Ill., buried Maple Grove
iii- **BREEDING** Ada married ____ **SIMS** and lived in Cal.

724-    **HOWELL** Albert Summers (*Marquis de Lafayette Howell, Anna Corwin, Elizabeth Biles, George Biles, Christian, Joshua, Jasper, John*) was born April 17, 1879 in W. Branch, Mi. son of Marquis de Lafayette **HOWELL** and Helen Leach **SUMMERS**. He married June 14, 1906 Effie Viola **BROWN** daughter of Vesbusuis **BROWN**.
Children born in Chicago, Ill.:
i- **HOWELL** Vernon Albert born June 30, 1906

ii- **HOWELL** Kenneth Summers born June 6, 1910
iii- **HOWELL** Glen Orvil born October 12, 1914

725- **HOWELL** Mabelle (*William B. Howell, Anna Corwin, Elizabeth Biles, George Biles, Christian, Joshua, Jasper, John*) was born November 18, 1881 in Avon Twp. Mi. daughter of William Biles **HOWELL** and Alice Beckwith **NEWBERRY** and died July 26, 1970 in Rochester, Mi. She married September 19, 1900 in Avon Twp. Bert **FRANK** who was born August 30. 1869 in Avon Twp. and died November 1, 1969 in Rochester, Mi., buried Mt. Avon cemetery.
Children born Lake Linden, Mi.:
862-     i- **FRANK** Bruce Kent born April 10, 1903 and died August 16, 1992
863-     ii- **FRANK** Bernice Mildred born April 4, 1905
864-     iii- **FRANK** Robert Howell born May 24, 1909
         iv- **FRANK** Marion Alice born March 21, 1913 and died March 21, 1917 in Lake Linden, Mi.
865-     v- **FRANK** Phillip Lucius born 1918
         vi- **FRANK** Margaret Anna born April 4, 1918, died same day
866-     vii- **FRANK** Maida Mary born February 22, 1917 (adopted) and died December 2004
867-     viii- **FRANK** Nancy Louise born 1923 in Rochester, Mi.

726- **HOWELL** Chester Arthur (*William B. Howell, Anna Corwin, Elizabeth Biles, George Biles, Christian, Joshua, Jasper, John*) was born April 4, 1883 in Rochester, Mi. son of William Biles **HOWELL** and Alice Beckwith **NEWBERRY** and died June 5, 1968 in Haney, British Columbia, Canada. He married (1) June 11, 1911 Daisy **LOVELL** who was born 1890 and died June 1920 in Rochester, Mi. He married (2) October 4, 1930 Martha Sarah (**WILLEY**) **WHITE** who was born February 2, 1888 in Swan River, Manatoba, Canada and died August 1857 in Haney, British Columbia, Canada.
Children by first marriage:
868-     i- **HOWELL** Harry born October 17, 1912
869-     ii- **HOWELL** Gladys born October 30, 1914 in Minitonas, Can. and died June 18, 1998 in Rochester, Mi.
Child by second mariage:
         iii- **HOWELL** William B. born 1933 in Haney, B. C. and married Lorraine Norma **LITTERMAN**

727- **HOWELL** Anna Alice (*William B. Howell, Anna Corwin, Elizabeth Biles, George Biles, Christian, Joshua, Jasper, John*) was born October 16, 1887 in Rochester, Mi. daughter of William B. **HOWELL** and Alice Beckwith **NEWBERRY** and died May 29, 1960 in Pontiac, Mi. She married August 22, 1922 in Toledo, Ohio Howard Knickerbocker **MC COTTER** who was born January 2, 1879 in Vermontville, Mi. and died July 10, 1942 in Pontiac, Mi., buried Mt. Avon cemetery.
Child born Rochester Twp. Mi.:
870-     i- **MC COTTER** Lee Newberry born March 16, 1925

728- **HOWELL** John Stinson II (*William B. Howell, Anna Corwin, Elizabeth Biles, George Biles, Christian, Joshua, Jasper, John*) was born April 20, 1891 in Rochester, Twp. Mi. son of William Biles **HOWELL** and Alice Beckwith **NEWBERRY**. He married (1) February 22, 1910 in Rochester, Mi. Arvilla **BAUCKE** who was born December 18, 1884 in Arizona and died March 3, 1959 in Rochester, Mi. He married (2) March 1, 1930 Martha Gerrard **LACY**.
Children by first marriage:
    i- **HOWELL** Ronald (twin) born December 10. 1910 and died December 14, 1910
    ii- **HOWELL** William Donald (twin) born December 10, 1910 in Cal. and died
January 4, 1918 in Rochester, Mi., buried Mt. Avon
871-   iii- **HOWELL** Robert V. born January 9, 1913
872-   iv- **HOWELL** Neil V. born January 22, 1914
873-   v- **HOWELL** Edith Marie born March 18, 1918
874-   vi- **HOWELL** John Stinson III born December 24, 1919
Children by second marriage:
875-   vii- **HOWELL** Milo Lacy born 1932
876-   viii- **HOWELL** Claire E. born 1932

729- **HOWELL** Milo Max (*William B. Howell, Anna Corwin, Elizabeth Biles, George Biles, Christian, Joshua, Jasper, John*) was born July 18, 1897 in Rochester, Mi. twin son of William B. **HOWELL** and Alice Beckwith **NEWBERRY** and died June 26, 1959 in Rochester, Mi. He married June 5, 1919 Harriet F. **OWEN** who was born 1895 in Collier, Ohio and died December 20, 1979 in Rochester, Mi., buried Mt. Avon cemetery.
Children born Rochester, Mi.:
877-   i- **HOWELL** Alis Lee born September 14, 1920
    ii- **HOWELL** Harold born June 15, 1922 an died June 15 1922
878-   iii- **HOWELL** Bruce Owen born 1923

730- **HOWELL** Leah Ruth (*William B. Howell, Anna Corwin, Elizabeth Biles, George Biles, Christian, Joshua, Jasper, John*) was born April 20, 1901 in Rochester, Mi. daughter of William B. **HOWELL** and Alice Beckwith **NEWBERRY** and died July 16, 1998 in Rochester Hills, Mi. She married May 19, 1921 Mason **CASE** who was born 1900 in Avon Twp. Mi. and died February 7, 1963, buried Mt. Avon.
Children born Avon Twp. Mi.
879-   i- **CASE** Betty Jean born April 4, 1922
880-   ii- **CASE** Mary Lou born February 7, 1924

731- **RAUB** Charles J. (*Sarah Ann Lundy, Margaret Vliet, Ann Biles, George Biles, Christian, Joshua, Jasper, John*) was born June 2, 1882 in Warren Co. NJ son of Albert Sylvester **RAUB** and Sarah Ann **LUNDY** and died February 1977. He married Grace Emma **WEST** who was born 1884 daughter of Jacob E. **WEST** and Mary M. **HOWELL** and died July 4, 1954.
One known child:
    i- **RAUB** Mary Sarah born September 5, 1912 and died January 13, 1973

188

732-    **VAN KEUREN** Ila (*Alice Russell, Hulda Nicholson, Sally, William, Joshua, Joshua, Jasper, John*) was born February 7, 1900 in Fremont, NY daughter of James **VAN KEUREN** and Alice **RUSSELL** and died September 1987 in Leicester, NY. She married James M. **ALEXANDER** born April 25, 1896 and died October 1976 in Rochester
Children:
881-      i- **ALEXANDER** William James
          ii- **ALEXANDER** John
          iii- **ALEXANDER** Albert
          iv- **ALEXANDER** Virginia married Richard **KIRKPATRICK**
          v- **ALEXANDER** Mary

733-    **BURDETT** Donald Sawyer (*Anna Russell, Hulda Nicholson, Sally, William, Joshua, Joshua, Jasper, John*) was born September 22, 1893 son of Francis **BURDETT** and Anna D. **RUSSELL** and died June 14, 1984 in Almond, NY, buried Almond Rural cemetery. He married (1) September 22, 1914 Blanche **WOOD** who was born January 22, 1898 daughter of William **WOOD** and Sarah **WILLIAMS** and died September 25, 1981. He married (2) in Hornell, NY September 1, 1934 Bernice **RANGER** who was born June 5, 1902 in Hornell, NY daughter of Curt D. **RANGER** and Maria Antoinette **NICHOLSON** (see #543)
Children:
882-      i- **BURDETT** Robert Donald born May 12, 1916
883-      ii- **BURDETT** Anna Ruth born June 30, 1920
          iii- **BURDETT** Betsy Ann born January 27, 1937
884-      iv- **BURDETT** Donna Sue born September 30, 1940
          v- **BURDETT** Janice Marie

734-    **BURDETT** Joel Dean (*Anna Russell, Hulda Nicholson, Sally, William, Joshua, Joshua, Jasper, John*) was born August 12, 1896 son of Francis **BURDETT** and Anna D. **RUSSELL** and died April 6, 1974. He married February 22, 1922 in Hornellsville, NY Mary (Polly) **ALLEN** who was born February 1, 1899 in Almond, NY and died 2004, buried Hornellsville, NY.
Children born in Hornell, NY:
          i- **BURDETT** infant born December 13, 1922 in Hornell, NY and died December 14, 1922
885-      ii- **BURDETT** Hobart Murray born October 30, 1923
886-      iii- **BURDETT** Marianna Virginia born January 29, 19__
887-      iv- **BURDETT** Margaret Viola born September 14, 19__
888-      v- **BURDETT** Paul Shelby May 24, 19__
889-      vi- **BURDETT** Joel Dean Jr. born December 23, 19__
          vii- **BURDETT** Donald Sidney born September 3, 19__
890-      viii- **BURDETT** James Milton born August 22, 19__
          ix- **BURDETT** Douglas Malcom born May 9, 1942 and died April 25, 1944 in Hornellsville, NY

735-    **BURDETT** Pauline Hulda (*Anna Russell, Hulda Nicholson, Sally, William, Joshua,*

*Joshua, Jasper, John*) was born in Hornellsville, NY May 25, 1898 daughter of Francis **BURDETT** and Anna D. **RUSSELL** and died September 23, 1980. She married July 15, 1922 in Fremont, NY James Howard **CROSSETT** who was born February 11, 1898 in S. Dansville, NY son of Orra **CROSSETT** and Mary **DEITER** and died in Dansville, NY in 1985. They are buried Woodlawn cemetery in Almond, NY
Children:
891-    i- **CROSSETT** Francis Paul born October 4, 1923 in Fremont
892-    ii- **CROSSETT** Paulina Mary April 25, 1926 in Hornell, NY
893-    iii- **CROSSETT** James Howard Jr. born Hornell, NY

736-    **BURDETT** Murray Roscoe (*Anna Russell, Hulda Nicholson, Sally, William, Joshua, Joshua, Jasper, John*) was born May 24, 1902 son of Francis **BURDETT** and Anna D. **RUSSELL** and died in Hornell, NY December 2, 1987. He married March 30, 1925 Florence **REIGELSPERBER** who was born in Wayland, NY October 23, 1900 daughter of George **REIGELSPERBER** and Flora **TUCKER** and died November 29, 1987. They are buried in Mt. Pleasant cemetery in Howard, NY

737-    **BURDETT** Beatrice Kathleen (*Anna Russell, Hulda Nicholson, Sally, William, Joshua, Joshua, Jasper, John*) was born in Fremont, NY July 6, 1904 daughter of Francis **BURDETT** and Anna D. **RUSSELL** and died August 4, 2000. She married July 15, 1922 Herman Winfield **SMITH** son of James **SMITH** and Elizabeth **DEITER**.
Children:
        i- **SMITH** Dorothy May
        ii- **SMITH** Marion Elizabeth
        iii- **SMITH** Clair Burdett born August 1, 1928 in Painted Post, NY
894-    iv- **SMITH** Anna Nancy

738-    **BURDETT** Roy Francis (*Anna D. Russell, Hulda Nicholson, Sally, William, Joshua, Joshua, Jasper, John*) was born August 16, 1906 in Fremont, NY son of Francis **BURDETT** and Anna D. **RUSSELL** and died July 3, 1991. He married Dorothy L. **MEENS** who was born 1905 and died July 1, 2001.
Children:
        i- **BURDETT** Lawrence Roy married Ann **SHUMAN** daughter of Albert Cornwell **SHUMAN** and Eleanor **CROMBIE**. Their son Steven Roy married Barbara (unknown maiden name) and had 2 children Lisa Ann and Eric Paul
        ii- **BURDETT** Rodney Earl married Jane **VALENTINE**. Their daughter Christine Rene married Eric Dean **PLATT** and had 2 children Samuel Russell and Leah Catherine

739-    **BURDETT** Abby Lena (*Anna D. Russell, Hulda Nicholson, Sally, William, Joshua, Joshua, Jasper, John*) was born in Fremont, NY December 6, 1907 daughter of Francis **BURDETT** and Anna D. **RUSSELL** and died November 25, 1992. She married (1) February 19, 1929 Harold **WAY** who was born in Churchville, NY May 5, 1906 son of Harvey and Ethel **WAY**. She married (2) in Churchville, NY June 28, 1962 Richard **LEARN** who died 1973

190

Children:
895-     i- WAY Betty Jane
        ii- WAY Harriet Ethel married John BARTLETT
896-    iii- WAY Carol Ann
        iv- WAY Kathryn T. married William FERGUSON born Rochester, NY son of
Kenneth FERGUSON and Edith DEWEY and had 2 children, Heather Catherine and Scott
Kenneth
        v- WAY Pamela Sue married Fred KISSELL son of Ralph D. and Edith M.
KISSELL and had 2 children Aaron John and Abbie Marcelle

740-    BURDETT James Wilson (*Anna Russell, Hulda Nicholson, Sally, William, Joshua,
Joshua, Jasper, John*) was born December 29, 1912 son of Francis BURDETT and Anna D.
RUSSELL and died November 28, 1999 in Dansville, NY. He married in Fremont, NY
January 20, 1934 Dorothy Grace BEECHER who was born in Atlanta, NY September 27,
1914 daughter of Dana C. BEECHER and Annie AKINS and died July 19, 1995 in N.
Dansville, NY, buried in Clearview cemetery in Cohocton, NY.
Children:
897-     i- BURDETT Joanne Louise
898-    ii- BURDETT James Wilson II

741-    BURDETT Elmer Paul (*Mary E. Russell, Hulda Nicholson, Sally, William, Joshua,
Joshua, Jasper, John*) was born May 19, 1891 in Howard, NY son of Murray C.
BURDETT and Mary Elsie RUSSELL and died July 1978. He married Cora Louise
STEVENS who was born May 10, 1900 in Coudersport, Pa. daughter of William A.
STEVENS and Marcia THOMPSON and died August 18, 1978 in Hornell, NY.
Children:
899-     i- BURDETT Steven Murray
        ii- BURDETT Mathew Steven

742-    BURDETT Shirley Russell (*Mary E. Russell, Hulda Nicholson, Sally, William,
Joshua, Joshua, Jasper, John*) was born February 19, 1893 in Steuben Co. NY son of
Murray C. BURDETT and Mary Elsie RUSSELL and died November 14, 1968 in Fremont,
NY. He married Marion Jeannette STEVENS who was born May 3, 1903 and died
December 1976.
One child:
        i- BURDETT Betty Lou married ____ CONSTANTINO, had one child Kelly Lee

743-    BURDETT Mildred (Mary) Wadsworth (*Mary E. Russell, Hulda Nicholson, Sally,
William, Joshua, Joshua, Jasper, John*) was born September 30, 1894 in Steuben Co. NY
daughter of Murray C. BURDETT and Mary Elsie RUSSELL and died January 1981. She
married Lewis Fay DAVIS who was born May 25, 1896 son of Fay E. DAVIS and Minnie
SCHAUMBERG and died February 3, 1967 in Hornell, NY. He married (2) Laura M.
FARTHING
Children:

900-    i- DAVIS Charles Fay
901-    ii- DAVIS Herman M.
902-    iii- DAVIS Dorothy June

744-    BURDETT Ethel Vance (*Mary E. Russell, Hulda Nicholson, Sally, William, Joshua, Joshua, Jasper, John*) was born September 7, 1900 in Steuben Co. NY daughter of Murray C. BURDETT and Mary E. RUSSELL and died June 4, 1993 in St. James, Suffolk Co. NY. She married Duncan Ross MUNRO who was born April 5, 1904 in NY.
Children:
903-    i- MUNRO William Duncan born October 28, 1927 in Old Westbury, NY
904-    ii- MUNRO Alan Ross
        iii- MUNRO David Angus married Martha Leigh MC DONALD and had 2 children Leigh Anne and David Ross

745-    BURDETT Charles K. (*Mary E. Russell, Hulda Nicholson, Sally, William, Joshua, Joshua, Jasper, John*) was born April 25, 1904 in Fremont, NY son of Murray C. BURDETT and Mary E. RUSSELL and died in Fremont May 1996 He married March 2, 1924 Margaret E. HALL born December 7, 1908 daughter of William HALL and Bertha HEATH and died August 26, 1995. He married (2) December 10, 1939 in Genessee, Pa. Elizabeth Neree HODSON born February 20, 1913 in Moravia, NY daughter of Kenneth R. DAZELL and Henrietta THOMAS and died March 1, 2004.
Child by first marriage:
905-    i- BURDETT Robert Duncan born September 5, 1928
Children by second marriage:
906-    ii- BURDETT Susan Jo born August 6, 1940
        iii- BURDETT Barbara Jane born March 3, 1942 married Jacob Richard METZLER and had 2 children, Gretchen and Erica
        iv- BURDETT Charles Kenneth Jr. married Susan MUSIAL and had 3 children, Jeffrey, Christopher and Sarah
        v- BURDETT Mary Elsie

746-    RUSSELL Harold H. (*Joel Dean Russell, Hulda Nicholson, Sally, William, Joshua, Joshua, Jasper, John*) was born in Steuben Co. NY son of Joel Dean RUSSELL and Nellie MOORE. He married Kathlyn HARRIS.
Children:
        i- RUSSELL Jack W. born September 12, 1934 and died Janduary 23 1999
        ii- RUSSELL Richard Dean born 1925 in Howard, NY and died 1931
        iii- RUSSELL Robert
        iv- RUSSELL Joel
        v- RUSSELL Thomas
        vi- RUSSELL Shirley

747-    RUSSELL Harrison (*Joel D. Russell, Hulda Nicholson, Sally, William, Joshua, Joshua, Jasper, John*) was born August 20, 1906 in Framont, NY son of Joel Dean Russell and Nellie **MOORE** and died July 15, 1940 in Hornellsville, NY. He married Auretta E. **VAN ZILE** born April 4, 1914 in Canisteo, NY and died February 5, 1998 in Leesburg, Ala., buried Howard, NY

Chldren:

     i- **RUSSELL** Betty married Mr. **BARBER**
     ii- **RUSSELL** James
     iii- **RUSSELL** Theodore

748-    **CONDERMAN** Gordon S. (*Addie, Alonzo, Abram, William, Joshua, Joshua, Jasper, John*) was born December 10, 1891 son of Martin **CONDERMAN** and Addie **SMITH** and died October 30, 1970.. He married Ethel **JAYNES** born February 22, 1893 daughter of Walter **JAYNES**. They are buried in Mt. Pleasant cemetery in Howard, NY. No death date for Ethel.

Children:

907-     i- **CONDERMAN** Betty Jayne born December 2, 1918
908-     ii= **CONDERMAN** Doris Erva born February 14, 1920

749-    **CONDERMAN** Ethel (*Addie, Alonzo, Abram, William, Joshua, Joshua, Jasper, John*) was born in Howard, NY daughter of Martin **CONDERMAN** and Addie **SMITH**. She married Ernest **CARWITH**. nfi

Children:

     i- **CARWITH** Mildred
     ii- **CARWITH** Jack

750-    **ROBERTS** Mernie (*Nellie, Alonzo, Abram, William, Joshua, Joshua, Jasper, John*) was born September 22, 1891 in Hornellsville, NY daughter of Herbert Vern **ROBERTS** and Nellie **SMITH** and died 1980. She married (1) Edward **TOURNER** who died 194_ and she married (2) Paul **VALLERY** who was born January 21, 1872 and died 1963. They are buried Rural cemetery in Hornell. One child adopted by first marriage:

     i- **TOURNER** Eugene married Betty **GOOD** and had children, Nancy, Larry, Rhea, Tommy and others

751-    **ROBERTS** Florence Janet (*Nellie, Alonzo, Abram, William, Joshua, Joshua, Jasper, John*) was born July 22, 1893 in Hornellsville, NY daughter of Herbert Vern **ROBERTS** and Nellie **SMITH** and died October 24, 1917. She married February 14, 1910 Frank E. **DODGE** born 1890 son of Frank W. **DODGE** and Sadie **USLER**.

One child:

     i- **DODGE** Gaylord born 1910

752-    **ROBERTS** Hazel (*Nellie, Alonzo, Abram, William, Joshua, Joshua, Jasper, John*) was born July 25, 1895 in Hornellsville, NY daughter of Herbert Vern **ROBERTS** and Nellie **SMITH** and died July 10, 1958. She married September 7, 1925 in Hornell, NY Charles S. **OSTRANDER** who was born 1882 son of William H. **OSTRANDER** and Hattie **PARSONS** and died May 17, 1948. They are buried in Clearview cemetery in Cohocton,

NY. No issue but Charles had 4 children by first marriage.

753- **ROBERTS** Gertrude Mae (*Nellie, Alonzo, Abram, William, Joshua, Joshua, Jasper, John*) was born October 26, 1903 in Hornellsville, NY daughter of Herbert Vern **ROBERTS** and Nellie **SMITH** and died September 9, 1981 in Hornellsville. She married September 4, 1921 in Hornell, NY Clayton Joseph **ROE** who was born September 20, 1900 in Canisteo, NY son of Joseph **ROE** and Lillian **HALLETT** and died December 5, 1990, buried Hillside cemetery.
Children:
909-    i- **ROE** Leroy Edwin born February 5, 1927
910-    ii- **ROE** Keith Leon born May 15, 1927
911-    iii- **ROE** Audrey Lillian born February 8, 1931
912-    iv- **ROE** Alma Jeannette born September 6, 1932
913-    v- **ROE** Carol Anita born February 27, 1946

754- **SMITH** Clifford (*Alonzo Jr., Alonzo, Abram, William, Joshua, Joshua, Jasper, John*) was born January 25, 1905 in Hornellsville, NY son of Alonzo **SMITH** Jr. and Pearl **JOHNSON** and died February 4, 1961. He married April 21, 1926 Julia Emma **LAIN** who was born March 23, 1905 daughter of William **LAIN** and died April 8, 1984 in Hornellsville. They are buried in Hope cemetery in Hornell.
Children:
914-    i- **SMITH** Lawrence Edwin born October 3, 1927
915-    ii- **SMITH** Carolyn Jean born March 31, 1930
916-    iii- **SMITH** Elaine Gwendolyn born January 23, 1938
917-    iv- **SMITH** Joan Coralee born August 4, 1944

755- **SMITH** Mildred (*Alonzo Jr. Alonzo, Abram, William, Joshua, Joshua, Jasper, John*) was born 1914 in Hornellsville, NY daughter of Alonzo **SMITH** Jr. and Pearl **JOHNSON**. She married Gilbert **BUTLER** who was born 1902 and died 1967. She married (2) Mr. **ZIMMERMAN**
Children:
        i- **BUTLER** James
        ii- **BUTLER** Sarah
        iii- **BUTLER** Nancy married George **GAMER** and had son Thomas

756- **GRIFFIN** Arthur Wendell (*Bertha, Alonzo, Abram, William, Joshua, Joshua, Jasper, John*) was born November 29, 1908 in Hornellsville, NY son of David **GRIFFIN** and Bertha **SMITH** and died January 16, 1979. He married May 20, 1972 Frances Rosetta **CHAPMAN** born August 6, 1936.
One Step daughter:
918-    i- **CHAPMAN** Louisa Maria born February 12, 1970

757- **GRIFFIN** Lyle David (*Bertha, Alonzo, Abram, William, Joshua, Joshua, Jasper, John*) was born March 22, 1910 in Hornellsville, NY son of David **GRIFFIN** and Bertha

SMITH. He married December 24, 1935 Marie Florence **NORTHRUP** born April 16, 1912 daughter of Guy **NORTHRUP** and Inez **WHEELER** and died October 26, 2003. They are buried in Rural cemetery.

Children adopted:

919-    i- **GRIFFIN** Linda Marie born May 25, 1950

920-    ii- **GRIFFIN** Barbara Sue

758-    **GRIFFIN** Anna Elizabeth (*Bertha, Alonzo, Abram, William, Joshua, Joshua, Jasper, John*) was born June 13, 1914 in Hornellsville, NY daughter of David **GRIFFIN** and Bertha **SMITH** and died June 26, 2004, buried Lakeview cemetery in Brockport, NY. She married June 14, 1933 Basil **FREEBORN**. They were divorced and she married (2) Harold **RICHARDSON** who died 1976.

Children by first marriage:

     i- **FREEBORN** Harold Franklin born September 1, 1934 and died 1989

     ii- **FREEBORN** Nellie Grace born January 30, 1936 married Jack **LAMPHIER** of Addison, NY

     iii- **FREEBORN** Harry Grant born February 24, 1940, married Sharon (unknown maiden name) and resided Harrison Valley, Pa.

Children by second marriage:

     iv- **RICHARDSON** Robert David born December 14, 1949, married Laurie (unknown maiden name) resided Rochester, NY

     v- **RICHARDSON** Richard J. resided Hornell, NY

759-    **GRIFFIN** Bernice Loretta (*Bertha, Alonzo, Abram, William, Joshua, Joshua, Jasper, John*) was born May 19, 1924 in Hornellsville, NY daughter of David **GRIFFIN** and Bertha **SMITH**. She married October 1, 1942 James Charles **COOK** born March 19, 1918.

Children:

921-    i- **COOK** Sandra Lee born March 16, 1943

922-    ii- **COOK** Duane Charles born November 20, 1945

923-    iii- **COOK** Brenda Sue born July 16, 1947

924-    iv- **COOK** Darlene Marie born January 29, 1950

925-    v- **COOK** Sheila Dawn born April 4, 1954

760- **GRIFFIN** Luella Arline (*Bertha, Alonzo, Abram, William, Joshua, Joshua, Jasper, John*) was born March 15, 1927 in Hornellsville, NY daughter of David **GRIFFIN** and Bertha **SMITH**. She married January 16, 1945 Alva William **CRAMER** born March 14, 1918.

Children:

926-    i- **CRAMER** Wendy Lou born September 6, 1946

927-    ii- **CRAMER** David Lee born July 20, 1951

761-    **FISHER** Norman F. (*Clinton D. Fisher, Flora, Abram. William, Joshua, Joshua, Jasper, John*) was born in Canisteo, NY in March/April 25, 1896 son of Clinton D. **FISHER** and Laura Lannah **HAMMER** and died 1978. Unknown if married or children

762- **FISHER** Donald L. (*Clinton D. Fisher, Flora, Abram, William, Joshua, Joshua, Jasper, John*) was born December 22, 1902 in Canisteo, NY son of Clinton D. **FISHER** and Laura Lannah **HAMMER** and died at his daughter's in Alfred, NY October 5, 2004. He married in 1926 Katherine **SMITH** who was born 1902 and died 1970. They are buried in Hilside cemetery in Canisteo.
Children:
      i- **FISHER** June E. married (1) March 23, 1952 James F. **ROYSTON** and married
(2) \_\_\_ **HITCHCOCK**
      ii- **FISHER** Donald married June 27, 1954 in Canisteo, NY Jeanne S. **CORNELL** daughter of Lewis R. **CORNELL** and Jeannett **STREETER**
      iii- **FISHER** Marilyn born 1930 and died 2003. She married Charles E. **GILLETTE** son of William **GILLETTE** and Marie **HARTWICK**


763- **BEATTIE** Leo Milton (*Alta Fisher, Flora, Abram, William, Joshua, Joshua, Jasper, John*) was born September 17, 1895 in Hornellsville, NY (or Elmira, NY) son of Sherman **BEATTIE** and Alta **FISHER** and died December 20, 1954 in Canisteo, NY. He married June 20, 1917 in Canisteo Catherine Mae **CORNISH** who was born February 1, 1897 in Jasper, NY daughter of Charles Wesley **CORNISH** and Rhoda **VAN SKIVER** and died November 1976 in N. Hornell, NY. They are buried in Hillside cemetery in Canisteo, NY
Children born in Canisteo, NY:
929-     i- **BEATTIE** Virginia Eileen born July 23, 1918
930-     ii- **BEATTIE** Donald Sherman born May 20, 1921
931-     iii- **BEATTIE** Lois born July 27, 1923


764- **BEATTIE** Isabel G. (*Alta Fisher, Flora, Abram, William, Joshua, Joshua, Jasper, John*) was born September 1, 1897 in Hornellsville, NY daughter of Sherman Grant **BEATTIE** and Alta **FISHER** and died December 9, 2003 in Hornell, NY. She married November 23/27, 1918 in Hartsville, NY Howard Judson **POST** who was born August 16, 1895 in Chester, NY son of David E. **POST** and Kate **TERWILLIGER** and died February 1978 in Allegany Co. NY.
Children born in Hartsville, NY:
      i- **POST** Howard Milton born December 3, 1919 and died in Andover, NY
      ii- **POST** Beatrice M. born 1921
      iii- **POST** Gertrude L. born 1922 married John **STICKLE**
      iv- **POST** Miriam born 1927 and died Long Island, married James **SCOVAZZO**
      v- **POST** Vida B. born 1927 and died Concord, Cal. She married Eugene **GRAU**
932-     vi- **POST** Marjorie born after 1930


765- **BEATTIE** Ina Gladys (*Alta Fisher, Flora, Abram, William, Joshua, Joshua, Jasper, John*) was born April 9, 1901 in Hornellsville, NY daughter of Sherman Grant **BEATTIE** and Alta **FISHER** and died April 30, 1929 in Nunda, NY. She committed suicide by drinking rat poison when she found out that her husband was cheating on her, buried Hope cemetery in Hornell, NY. She married March 26, 1924 Howard E. **COFFIN** who was born November 12, 1901 in Perry, NY son of George **COFFIN** and Edith **DE VINNEY** and died

April 1970 in Nunda, NY.
Children:
      i- COFFIN James B. born 1926
      ii- COFFIN William E. born 1928

766-    GATES Pauline Alveretta (*Lena, Hobart, Abram, William, Joshua, Joshua, Jasper, John*) born October 13, 1916 the adopted daughter of Merton GATES and Lena Mary SMITH and died October 22, 2002 at Bethany Manor in Horseheads, NY. She married in Hornell, NY February 27, 1943 Thomas Scott CLANCY who was born June 6, 1910 son of Edward V. CLANCY and Theresa Mary VEILIE and died February 1, 1971, buried St. Mary's Catholic cemetery in Corning.
Children born in Hornell, NY:
933-      i- CLANCY Barbara Ann born August 11, 1943
934-      ii- CLANCY Dianne Kathleen February 24, 1946
935-      iii- CLANCY Elizabeth Jane May 25, 1950
         iv- CLANCY Delores Jean born May 29, 1953

767-    BUTLER Milton (*Edith, Hobart, Abram, William, Joshua, Joshua, Jasper, John*) was born August 31, 1912 in Knoxville, Pa. son of Delevan R. BUTLER and Edith Almira SMITH and died January 22, 1990. He married December 19, 1931 Eva HARRINGTON who still lives in Knoxville, Pa.
Children:
      i- BUTLER Larry Dean born June 18, 1932 and died July 4, 1932, buried Butler Hill cemetery
936-     ii- BUTLER Koeth Erwin born November 15, 1934
        iii- BUTLER Esther Dawn born January 13, 1937 and died September 1938
937-     iv- BUTLER Daryl Merlin born March 23, 1941
938-     v- BUTLER Kean Allen born June 12, 1943
939-     vi- BUTLER Wyona Jean born April 15, 1944
940-     vii- BUTLER Kermit David born February 14, 1946

768-    BUTLER Esther Belle (*Edith, Hobart, Abram, William, Joshua, Joshua, Jasper, John*) was born February 3, 1919 in Knoxville, Pa. daughter of Delevan R. BUTLER and Edith Almira SMITH. She married Lawrence LADD born 1900 and died 1971. They resided in Elmira Heights, NY. They had 1 child who was stillborn.

769-    SMITH Ernest Glen (*Frank, Hobart, Abram, William, Joshua, Joshua, Jasper, John*) was born September 13, 1920 in Hornellsville, NY son of Frank H. SMITH and Charlotte (Lottie) BOSSARD. He married August 23, 1958 Mrs. Fern (BUCHINGER) HANKINS born August 15, 1924 in Dalton, NY daughter of John BUCHINGER and Ida Eliza FLINT. She died August 11, 1996 in Hornell, NY and is buried in Dalton, NY. Ernest died January 27, 1998 and is buried in Rural cemetery in Hornellsville, NY.
Children:
941-     i- SMITH Sandra Janine born February 9, 1961

942-    ii- SMITH Steven Franklin born January 24, 1965
Fern had two children by her first marriage:
        i- HANKINS Samuel John born March 27, 1948
        ii- HANKINS Shirley born November 2, 1951

770-    SMITH Mary Louise (*Frank, Hobart, Abram, William, Joshua, Joshua, Jasper, John*) was born May 30, 1928 in N. Hornell, NY daughter of Frank H. SMITH and Charlotte (Lottie) BOSSARD. She married June 2, 1951 in Rochester, NY Eugene George JACKSON who was born September 6, 1923 in Rochester, NY son of Wilbert JACKSON and Gertrude E. TINDAL. Eugene served in Co. E. 320th Infantry during World War II and was injured during the Battle of the Bulge for which he received the purple heart. He worked for the Defense Department in Rochester until he retired in 1977. He died June 3, 1989 in Canandaigua, NY and is buried in the Friends cemetery in Farmington, NY.
Children:
943-    i- JACKSON Edward Frank born January 25, 1948 and adopted by Eugene.
944-    ii- JACKSON Allen Eugene born May 25, 1953
945-    iii- JACKSON Richard Jay born November 21, 1954
946-    iv- JACKSON Cheryl Ann (twin) born February 11, 1956
947-    v- JACKSON Gary Lee (twin) born February 11, 1956
948-    vi- JACKSON Brian Ernest born February 13, 1959
949-    vii- JACKSON Susan Elizabeth born March 26, 1960
950-    viii- JACKSON Kevin Scott born April 5, 1961

771-    LEIBY Frances (*Arthur Leiby, Frances D., Philetus, Joshua Jr., Joshua, Joshua, Jasper, John*) was born in Tioga Co. Pa. daughter of Arthur LEIBY an died 1980. She married Ernest Robert NOWLAN who was born August 7, 1907 son of Truman NOWLAN and Ella TAYLOR and died December 26, 2000 in Gillette, Pa., buried Forest Lawn Memorial Park in Elmira, NY. He married (2) Gertrude Purcell WINSLOW.
One child:
        i- LEIBY Wayne married Rita (unknown maiden name) lived Horseheads, NY and had 3 sons, Robert, Brian and Barry

772-    CHAMBERLAIN Harold B. (*Neva Bartlett, Jennie, Philetus, Joshua Jr., Joshua, Joshua, Jasper, John*) was born in Tioga Co. Pa. son of Albert Ulysses CHAMBERLAIN and Neva BARTLETT. He married June 2, 1933 Eloise SMITH.
Children:
        i- CHAMBERLAIN Richard November 19, 1934 in Sullivan Twp. Pa. and died February 28, 1991 in Sayre, Pa. He married in 1956 Phyllis KENNEDY daughter of Donald and Gertrude KENNEDY and had 4 children, Michael R. of Denver, Col., Donald H. of Mansfield, Pa. and Judy Lynn who married _____ BECKWITH of Waukesha, Wis. Also, an infant daughter who died April 7, 1957.

773-    BASTIAN Robert Jr. (*Cora Benson, Ellen (Ella) Watkins, Diantha, Joshua Jr., Joshua, Joshua, Jasper, John*) was born February 28, 1902 in Ralston, Pa. son of Robert

BASTIAN and Cora BENSON and died October 31, 1968 at Blossburg State Hospital. He married ____ WOODWARD who died before 1968.
Step children named in obit both of Ralston, Pa.:

     i- BASTIAN Eugene
     ii- BASTIAN Juanita who married ____ ANDERSON

774- BASTIAN Ella (*Cora Benson, Ellen (Ella) Watkins, Diantha, Joshua Jr., Joshua, Joshua, Jasper, John*) was born in Tioga Co. Pa. daughter of Nathan BASTIAN and Cora BENSON. She married Roy J. BURLEIGH who was born 1901 and died September 10, 1973, buried in Besley cemetery.
Children:

     i- BURLEIGH Edith
     ii- BURLEIGH Nathan born 1928 and died March 9, 1998. He married Dolores E. BAILEY
     iii- BURLEIGH Leroy married Francine ?

775- MC CLURE Lee W. (*Edith Benson, Ellen (Ella) Watkins, Diantha, Joshua Jr., Joshua, Joshua, Jasper, John*) was born 1911 in Tioga Co. Pa. son of Mark J. MC CLURE and Edith BENSON and died April 7, 1986. He married Maria EHLERS who was born 1898 and died September 13, 1990. They are buried in Watson cemetery.
Children:

     i- MC CLURE Lavere W. of Bloomsburg
     ii- MC CLURE Richard M. of State College
     iii- MC CLURE Wendell L. of Mansfield, Pa.
     iv- MC CLURE Marshall L. of Roseville, Pa.
     v- MC CLURE Mary Lee who married ____ TROWBRIDGE of Wellsboro, Pa.

776- CHAMBERLAIN Maurice (*Edith Rumsey, Charles Rumsey, Mary, Joshua Jr., Joshua, Joshua, Jasper, John*) was born October 21, 1917 in Tioga Co. Pa. son of Frank C. CHAMBERLAIN and Edith RUMSEY and died May 31, 1988 in Towanda, Pa., buried Watson cemetery. He married Marion WHITTEKER.
Children:

     i- CHAMBERLAIN Gerald of Tully, NY
     ii- CHAMBERLAIN Cleo married ____ BALDWIN of Standing Stone
     iii- CHAMBERLAIN Maureen married ____ MORGAN
     iv- CHAMBERLAIN Gail married ____ DULL
     v- CHAMBERLAIN Sue married ____ BECK of Towanda, Pa.

777- SHERMAN Lyle B. (*Nettie Richmond, Oscar Richmond, Annanias Richmond, Anna, Joshua, Joshua, Jasper, John*) was born January 14, 1897 in Tioga Co. Pa. son of John Wesley SHERMAN and Nettie RICHMOND and died February 4, 1972 in Wellsboro, Pa. He married Iva Matilda SMITH who was born July 9, 1903 daughter of Emerson SMITH and Addie MAKLEY.
Children:

i- SHERMAN Delphine married Bradley COPP of Cherry Flats

ii- SHERMAN Lynn Tracy married January 16, 1964 in Mainesburg, Pa. Sylvia Jane WEBSTER daughter of Donald WEBSTER

951-    iii- SHERMAN Arthur L. born September 12, 1932

iv- SHERMAN Donald of Orlando, Fl. and Ks.

v- SHERMAN Walter married in Elk Run, Pa. February 26, 1956 Priscilla CARSON daughter of Stuart CARSON

vi- SHERMAN Milton married Karen _____

vii- SHERMAN Joseph married Velma Ann JONES

viii- SHERMAN Dorothy May born October 30, 1936, married Robert SMITH

ix- SHERMAN Mabel Marie married James L. BRADLEY

778-    SHERMAN Oscar Richmond (*Nettie Richmond, Oscar Richmond, Annanias Richmond, Anna, Joshua, Joshua, Jasper, John*) was born November 11, 1900 in Sullivan Twp. Pa. son of John Wesley SHERMAN and Nettie RICHMOND and died July 29, 1990 in Sullivan Twp. He married (1) December 26, 1998 Mary Rosella ISCHLER who was born January 2, 1904 in Potters Bank, Pa. and died March 22, 1942 in Homer City, Pa. He married (2) June 9, 1945 Mildred WINEMAN who was born April 17, 1903 in Homer City, Pa. daughter of Elmer WINEMAN and Rosa HUTCHINSON and died November 16, 1993. They are buried in Tioga Memorial Gardens in Wellsboro, Pa.

Children by first marriage:

i- SHERMAN Constance Louise who married August 23, 1952 Raymond Lewis SIREN son of Urho SIREN and Lillian WALTERS, removed to Pittsburgh, Pa.

ii- SHERMAN John Wesley who married Mary Evelyn (unknown maiden name), removed to Lusby, Md.

779-    SHERMAN Florence (*Nettie Richmand, Oscar Richmond, Annanias Richmond, Anna, Joshua, Joshua, Jasper, John*) was born January 21, 1906 in Richmond Twp. Pa. daughter of John Wesley SHERMAN and Nettie RICHMOND and died January 24, 1997 in Broad Acres Nursing Home in Wellsboro, Pa. She married Earl Dean TICE who was born 1900 and died September 1950, buried Gray Valley cemetery.

Children:

i- TICE Esther married Charles SMITH of New Holland, Pa.

ii- TICE Lucille married Leo PACKARD of Mansfield, Pa.

iii- TICE Mary married Lee HARVEY of Mansfield, Pa.

iv- TICE Marjorie married James CRANDLE of Troy, Pa.

v- TICE Richard married Joanne (unknown maiden name)

vi- TICE Frank married Nancy (unknown maiden name)

vii- TICE Harold married Shirley WILSON

viii- TICE James married Dora CHILSON

780-    SMITH Morris (*Edith Ann Richmond, Dayton Richmond, Albert Richmond, Anna, Joshua, Joshua, Jasper, John*) was born ca 1895 in Tioga Co. Pa. son of Hobart M. SMITH and Edith Ann RICHMOND. He married June 3, 1922 Fanny Louise BIXBY who was

born December 24, 1904 and moved to Watkins Glen, NY.
Children:

      i- SMITH Wayne born May 13, 1925
      ii- SMITH Leland born April 2, 1927

781- **CARD** Rachel (*Edith Ann Richmond, Dayton Richmond, Albert Richmond, Anna, Joshua, Joshua, Jasper, John*) was born in Pa. daughter of Leon Elmo **CARD** and Edith Ann **RICHMOND** and died 1988 in Horseheads, NY. She married James Manley **DARROW** who was born 1912 in Pa. and died August 20, 1991 in Horseheads, NY. They are buried in Maple Grove cemetery.
Children:

      i- **DARROW** Richard, married Lillian ____, lived Elmira
      ii- **DARROW** Robert married Hazel ____, lived Gillett, Pa.
      iii- **DARROW** Marlene married Richard **WHITSON** of Wellsburg
      iv- **DARROW** Merub married ____ **FILES**, lived Horseheads, NY
      v- **DARROW** Judy married Duane **WETZEL** of Troy, Pa.

782- **CONGDON** Edgar Fayette (*Henry Earl Congdon, Ella Ruggles, Melissa Richmond, Anna, Joshua, Joshua, Jasper, John*) was born October 8, 1906 in South Creek, Pa. son of Henry Earl **CONGDON** and Mayme DeEtta **SAWDY** and died February 20, 1990 in Troy, Pa. He married 1927 Leone **PELLOR** who was born April 20, 1906 daughter of ____ Delos **PELLOR** and Edna **PATTERSON** and died February 4, 1993. They are buried in Gilette cemetery.
Children:

      i- **CONGDON** Robert Earl born October 24, 1927 and died 1973. He married Betty **WALKER**
      ii- **CONGDON** Leslie married Darlene, lived Millerton, Pa.
      iii- **CONGDON** Karl married Shirley, lived Mansfield, Pa.
      iv- **CONGDON** Donna married Stanley **MOKRZYNSKI**

783- **POTTER** Ralph Frederick (*Susan Vorhees, Ida Swick, Susan, Daniel, Joshua, Joshua, Jasper, John*) was born August 13, 1910 in Hector, NY son of Fred **POTTER** and Susan **VORHEES** and died November 16, 1889 in Wellsville, NY, buried Wellsville. He married in Wellsville June 23, 1934 Marguerite Beulah **STRONG** who was born July 6, 1910 in Elmira, NY daughter of Elmer D. **STRONG** and Mae S. **DUTTON**.
Child:

      i- **POTTER** a daughter who married Blaine Eugene **AUSTIN** born November 10, 1934 in Wellsville son of William Wellington **AUSTIN** and Mary Adeline **WILLIAMS** and died September 12, 1994 in Wellsville. He is buried in Woodlawn cemetery in Wellsville.

784- **POTTER** Leon Arthur (*Susan Vorhees, Ida Swick, Susan, Daniel, Joshua, Joshua, Jasper, John*) was born August 5, 1912 in Hector, NY son of Fred **POTTER** and Susan **VORHEES** and died December 11, 1978. He married Josephine **VOSSLER** and had 2 sons.

785- **WHEELER** Jay (*Susan Vorhees, Ida Swick, Susan, Daniel, Joshua, Joshua, Jasper, John*) was born in Hector, NY son of Frank **WHEELER** and Susan **VORHEES**. He married (spouse unknown) and had 3 children.

786- **VORHEES** Lyle Robert (*William Vorhees, Ida Swick, Susan, Daniel, Joshua, Joshua, Jasper, John*) was born March 28, 1918 in Hector, NY son of William **VORHEES** and Theresa Stillwell **SWICK**. He married April 9, 1949 in Big Flats, NY Myrtle Electa **USHER** born February 20, 1921 in Hector, NY daughter of Orrin Kniffin **USHER** and Winifred **SMITH**. They had 8 children.

787- **LESSITER** Ruby Minnie (*Edith Viola, Horace, Elijah, Joshua, Platt, Joshua, Jasper, John*) was born in Grattan, Mi. July 23, 1919 daughter of William James **LESSITER** and Edith Viola **SMITH**. She married in Colorado Springs, Col. February 2, 1943 Richard John **LONGSTREET**. Unknown children

788- **LESSITER** Wayne Jay (*Edith Viola, Horace, Elijah, Joshua, Platt, Joshua, Jasper, John*) was born February 9, 1924 in Grattan, Mi. son of William James **LESSITER** and Edith Viola **SMITH** and died June 16, 1980 in Alma, Mi. He married (1) February 21, 1953 Barbara **CRAIG** and married (2) November 26, 1979 Mrs. Beverly **CUNNINGHAM**. Unknown children

789- **LESSITER** Priscilla Beth (*Edith Viola, Horace, Elijah, Joshua, Platt, Joshua, Jasper, John*) was born December 16, 1930 in Grattan, Mi. daughter of William James **LESSITER** and Edith Viola **SMITH**. She married December 16, 1950 in Belding, Mi. Jack Chaney **HAMMEL** born September 14, 1928 in Detroit, Mi. son of John Christopher **HAMMEL** and Tracie Mabel **CHANEY**.
One child adopted:
    i- **HAMMEL** Tracy Ann born July 28, 1960 in Atlanta, Ga.

790- **SMITH** Harvey W. (*Horace W., Horace F. George W., Joshua, Platt, Joshua, Jasper, John*) was born November 7, 1925 in Tompkins co. NY son of Horace Walker **SMITH** and Ruth **HARVEY**. He married July 21, 1950 Joan **WESTBROOK** born July 7, 1932 daughter of Frederick Hamilton **WESTBROOK** and Clara Mae **LETTS**.
Child:
952-    i- **SMITH** Melissa May born October 7, 1966

791- **COLE** Walter W. (*Grant Cole, Elizabeth Deremer, Hannah, Joshua, Platt, Joshua, Jasper, John*) was born December 1892 in Tompkins Co. NY son of Grant and Margaret W. **COLE** and died by 1933. He married Helen (unknown maiden name) who married (2) ____ **SIMONDS** and moved to Patterson, NJ.
One child:
    i- **COLE** Valerie Vivian born 1915

792- **YOUNG** Ezra Lawrence Jr. (*Grace Fulmer, Martha Deremer. Hannah, Joshua,

*Platt, Joshua, Jasper, John*) was born January 1891 in Tompkins Co. NY son of Ezra YOUNG and Grace FULMER and died September 5, 1930. He married Elizabeth KELLOGG who was born 1893 and died 1981. They are buried in Grove cemetery.
Children:
> i- YOUNG Lawrence Phillip born August 23, 1915
> ii- YOUNG daughter born August 23, 1917
> iii- YOUNG Joan K. born 1928 and died 1946, buried Grove cemetery

793-   DIMMICK Eva M. (*Frank Dimmick, Melissa Richards, Platt Richards, Johannah, Platt, Joshua, Jasper, John*) was born 1883 in Trumansburg, NY daughter of Frank DIMMICK and Cora DAGGETT and died May 14, 1969 in Binghamton, NY. She married Ernest B. ALLEN who was born 1888 and died 1966.
One known child:
> i- ALLEN Gladys born 1908, married Sebastian ALIG and had 5 children, Norman, Ronald, William and two others

794-   DIMMICK Mabel (*Frank Dimmick, Melissa Rochards, Platt Richards, Johannah, Platt, Joshua, Jasper, John*) was born in Trumansburg, NY July 22, 1888 daughter of Frank DIMMICK and Cora DAGGETT and died March 23, 1912. She married John BULLIVANT who died December 16, 1941 in hospital in Seneca Falls, NY. He married (2) her sister Frances (see #796)
One child:
> i- BULLIVANT Frederick C.

795-   DIMMICK Clark (*Frank Dimmick, Melissa Richards, Platt Richards, Johannah, Platt, Joshua, Jasper, John*) was born August 1890 in Trumansburg, NY son of Frank DIMMICK and Cora DAGGETT and died 1956. He married Bessie May (unknown maiden name) born 1892 and died 1977.
Children:
> i- DIMMICK Harold Buster born 1912 and died 1927
953-   ii- DIMMICK Carlton Lewis born 1915
954-   iii- DIMMICK Thelma born 1917
955-   iv- DIMMICK Sylvia born 1919
> v- DIMMICK Edward Kenneth born 1923

796-   DIMMICK Frances (*Frank Dimmick, Melissa Richards, Platt Richards, Johannah, Platt, Joshua, Jasper, John*) was born 1895 in Trumansburg, NY daughter of Frank DIMMICK and Cora DAGGETT. She married John BULLIVANT as his second wife. (see #794)
Children:
> i- BULLIVANT Walter J.
960-   ii- BULLIVANT Robert born 1916
> iii- BULLIVANT Katherine married ____ BLUE
> iv- BULLIVANT James E. born 1922 and died 1972 (spouse unknown) and had 3

203

children John, James and Jeffrey
    v- **BULLIVANT** Donald
    vi- **BULLIVANT** John Jr.
    vii- **BULLIVANT** Marion

797- **DIMMICK** Dorothy Cora (*Frank Dimmick, Melissa Richards, Platt Richards, Johannah, Platt, Joshua, Jasper, John*) was born March 2, 1897 in Tompkins Co. NY daughter of Frank **DIMMICK** and Cora **DAGGETT** and died August 31, 1954. She married Herbert **AUSTIC** who was born February 17, 1894 son of Herbert **AUSTIC** and Emily **TURNER** of England and died July 1993. They are buried in Grove cemetery.
Children born Tompkins Co. NY:
956-    i- **AUSTIC** Clinton H. born March 15, 1918
957-    ii- **AUSTIC** Albert William born January 24, 1920
958-    iii- **AUSTIC** Evelyn May born June 10, 1923
959-    iv- **AUSTIC** Edward Frank born May 14, 1927
Note: other possible children were Scott E. and Harold C. born 1912 and died 1927, buried Grove cemetery

798- **FRAZIER** George Daniel (*Samuel Frazier, Emeline Richards, Platt Richards, Johannah, Platt, Joshua, Jasper, John*) was born 1893 in Tompkins Co. NY son of Samuel **FRAZIER** and Dessie Demund **CURRY** and died May 13, 1969. He married (1) Leora Maude **CALKINS** who was born June 2, 1890 in Ithaca, NY and died February 14, 1893. They were divorced and he married (2) Goldy T. (unknown maiden name). They were divorced November 14, 1941 in Ithaca and he married (3) Marion **MC MILLAN** who was born January 20, 1914 in Messhoppen, Pa. daughter of Ulysses **MC MILLAN** and Helen **ROOT** and died July 13, 1974 in Strong Memorial Hospital in Rochester, NY. They are buried in Grove cemetery.
Children by first marriage:
961-    i- **FRAZIER** Harry Joseph born January 26, 1912 in Hector
962-    ii- **FRAZIER** Mary Dessie born January 18, 1920 in Ithaca
    iii- **FRAZIER** Harold born November 14, 1920 in Ithaca and died May 30, 1956

799- **FRAZIER** Fred P. (*Charles Frazier, Emeline Richards, Platt Richards, Johannah, Platt, Joshua, Jasper, John*) was born in Ulysses, NY son of Charles **FRAZIER** and Mary L. **SHINDLEDECKER** and died July 6, 1973. He married Gertrude **LOVELL** who was born July 29, 1903 in Lodi, NY daughter of Dr. James E. **LOVELL** and Delia **BEARDSLEE** and died July 17, 1979 in Jacksonville, NY. They are buried in Grove cemetery.
Children:
963-    i- **FRAZIER** Ervin L. born June 5, 1930
964-    ii- **FRAZIER** Charles R. born April 6, 1934
965-    iii- **FRAZIER** Margaret born 1938

800- **CHURCH** Margaret Hattie (*Carrie L. Richards, Emeline Richards, Platt Richards,*

*Johannah, Platt, Joshua, Jasper, John)* was born 1909 in Tompkins Co. NY daughter of
Everal **CHURCH** and Carrie L. **RICHARDS** and died September 20, 1989, buried Grove
cemetery. She married William **POYER**.
Children:
      i- **POYER** Carolyn Louise married Paul **WHITE**
      ii- **POYER** William Henry married Helen **WAY**
      iii- **POYER** Merton Everel married Betty **EVANS**
      iv- **POYER** Raymond Edward married June **TEETER**
      v- **POYER** Robert married Betty Ann **ANDERSON**
      vi- **POYER** Ronald Anson married Elizabeth **SHOEMAKER**
Note: Also buried on same plot #1421 in Grove cemetery are Albert P. who died June 15,
1962 age 2 yrs and Joyce who died August 1997 age 56 yrs.

801-   **RATHBUN** Ruth Edna (*Edna Sarah Poppino, Harry Poppino, Alice Amelia,
Lafayette, Jasper, Joshua, Jasper, John)* was born October 27, 1939 in Tompkins Co. NY
daughter of Seymour **RATHBUN** and Edna Sarah **POPPINO**. She married January 23,
1957 Roger Moesel **GOYETTE** son of Harvey **GOYETTE** and Bessie **MOESEL**.
Children:
      i- **GOYETTE** Roger Moesel Jr. born September 26, 1959, married February 2,
1986 Kelly **KUHMA** and divorced
      ii- **GOYETTE** Karen Ruth born November 23, 1960
966-   iii- **GOYETTE** Teresa born May 10, 1962

802-   **RATHBUN** Keith Morris (*Edna Sarah Poppino, Harry Poppino, Alice Amelia,
Lafayette, Jasper, Joshua, Jasper, John)* was born June 12, 1941 in Tompkins Co. NY son
of Seymour **RATHBUN** and Edna Sarah **POPPINO** and died April 23, 1967, buried Grove
cemetery. He married (1) Beverly **COVERT** and married (2) Vera Marie **HATHAWAY**
daughter of George and Vera **HATHAWAY**.
Child by first marriage:
967-   i- **RATHBUN** Bradley Lewis born April 15, 1963

803-   **RATHBUN** Glenn Harry (*Edna Sarah Poppino, Harry Poppino, Alice Amelia,
Lafayette, Jasper, Joshua, Jasper, John)* was born September 1, 1942 in Tompkins Co. NY
son of Seymour **RATHBUN** and Edna Sarah **POPPINO**. He married (1) June 6, 1970
Loretta **HODGE** daughter of Merriette **HODGE** and Cynthia **SIMPSON**. He married (2)
July 1, 1982 her sister Lois **HODGE**. He married (3) August 7, 1985 Ann **WOOD** daughter
of Marshall James **WOOD** and Mary Jane **SWICK**.
Children by first marriage:
      i- **RATHBUN** Glenn Seymour born July 7, 1964
968-   ii- **RATHBUN** Leon Merritt born August 19, 1966
Child by third marriage:
      iii- **RATHBUN** Edna Marie born February 23, 1990 (adopted)

804-   **RATHBUN** Paul Eugene (*Edna Sarah Poppino, Harry Poppino, Alice Amelia,*

*Lafayette, Jasper, Joshua, Jasper, John*) was born February 16, 1947 in Tompkins Co. NY son of Seymour **RATHBUN** and Edna Sarah **POPPINO**. He married (1) December 10, 1977 Donna **FISH**, married (2) February 1972 Barbara **SEARS** and (3) July 2, 1976 Linda **HODGE** daughter of Merriette **HODGE** and Cynthia **SIMPSON**
Child by first marriage:
    i- **RATHBUN** Tina Marie born September 7, 1967
Child by second marriage:
    ii- **RATHBUN** Timothy Michael born January 18, 1970

805-   **RATHBUN** Carol Lynn (*Edna Sarah Poppino, Harry Poppino, Alice Amelia, Lafayette, Jasper, Joshua, Joshua, John*) was born September 18, 1957 in Tompkins Co. NY daughter of Seymour **RATHBUN** and Edna Sarah **POPPINO**. She married May 30, 1952 David **LAWRENCE** son of William Wallace **LAWRENCE** and Marjorie Rapold **NEWTON**
One child:
    i- **LAWRENCE** Michelle Renee born December 17, 1982

806-   **MILLER** Edwin C. (*Bert Miller, William H. Miller, Elizabeth, Obadiah, Obadiah, Joshua, Jasper, John*) was born 1912 son of Bert and Bess **MILLER** and died 1986 in Trumansburg, NY. He married Dorothy **JORDAN** who was born 1916 and died 1984. They are buried in Grove cemetery.
Children:
    i- **MILLER** Carol married July 6, 1963 Richard **LAVOIE** son of Arthur **LAVOIE**
    ii- **MILLER** Edwin J. born 1946 and died June 23, 1964, buried Grove cemetery
    iii- **MILLER** James

807-   **MC LALLEN** Levi Herbert (*Flora E. Mason, Adeline Ganoung, Berentha, Obadiah, Obadiah, Joshua, Jasper, John*) was born May 6, 1906 in Tompkins Co. NY son of Herbert Leslie **MC LALLEN** and Flora Elizabeth **MASON** and died August 25, 1972. He married Belle **MC MAHON** who was born 1906 and died June 23, 1994 in Trumansburg, NY. They are buried in Grove cemetery.
Child:
    i- **MC LALLEN** George F. born September 23, 1928/29 and died June 2, 1945 of gunshot wound, buried Grove cemetery

808-   **MC LALLEN** Raymond Mason (*Flora E. Mason, Adeline Ganoung, Berentha, Obadiah, Obadiah, Joshua, Jasper, John*) was born November 12, 1912 son of Herbert Leslie **MC LALLEN** and Flora Elizabeth **MASON** and died August 4, 1989. He married (1) August 11, 1934 Pauline **GORDON** who was born 1905 and died March 28, 1967 and married (2) August 24, 1968 Josephine **BOWER** who was born 1909 and died November 4, 1981.
Children by first marriage:
    i- **MC LALLEN** Dennis born April 24, 1937, married January 13, 1968 in Endicott, NY Gloria J. **MILLER** born February 25, 1928 daughter of Frank **MILLER** and

Althea **GUNSET**. No issue
969-    ii- **MC LALLEN** Ronald born September 6, 1941

809-    **MASON** Mary Evelyn (*Herman J. Mason, Adeline Ganoung, Berentha, Obadiah, Obadiah, Joshua, Jasper, John*) was born June 21, 1907 daughter of Herman J. **MASON** and Georgianna **BOND** and died July 14, 1988. She married July 11, 1930 Charles Eliphalet **DEMPSEY** who was born March 25, 1896 and died July 10, 1971. They are buried in Grove cemetery. He married (1) Irma **LA LONDE** who died in childbirth. They had 2 children Elizabeth Jane born June 5, 1923 and Monica Veronica born September 22, 1925.
Children:
970-    i- **DEMPSEY** Robert Charles born August 2, 1931
971-    ii- **DEMPSEY** Norma Jean born July 11, 1932
972-    iii- **DEMPSEY** John Mason born September 14, 1941

810-    **SMITH** Esther Ellen (*Olin, John B., Francis, Annanias, Obadiah, Joshua, Jasper, John*) was born September 20, 1916 in Genoa, NY daughter of Olin J. **SMITH** and Edna Esther **BROKAW** and died 1997, buried Rural cemetery. She married June 30, 1943 Michael Curtis **PERRY** who was born August 10, 1916 in Detroit, Mi. son of Samuel **PERRY** and Helen **ADINHOFFER** and died July 16, 2005 at son's in Clarksville, Ga., buried Alfred Rural cemetery. He served in US Army Air Force during World War II
Children:
973-    i- **PERRY** David Michael born September 5, 1946, married Tommie ?
   ii- **PERRY** Duane James born April 11, 1948, married August 3, 1980 Paulette **JULIUS** born 1950, lived San Francisco, Ca.
974-    iii- **PERRY** Marcia Ellen born July 20, 1951, married Richard **DRUMM** of Fabius, NY

811-    **SMITH** Rodney Olin (*Olin, John B., Francis, Annanias, Obadiah, Joshua, Jasper, John*) was born in Hornell, NY February 19, 1922 son of Olin J. **SMITH** and Edna Esther **BROKAW** and died February 8, 1996 in Chrystal City, Fl. He married in Canisteo, NY August 20, 1946 Delores **O'DELL** daughter of Frank M. **O'DELL** and Della W. **JACKSON**. He is buried in Woodlawn cemetery in Canisteo
Children:
   i- **SMITH** Kathy married Thomas **OSTRANDER** of Horseheads, NY
   ii- **SMITH** James of Bath, NY, married Jackie ?
   iii- **SMITH** Robert of Bath, NY married Edna ?

812-    **STORM** Jane J. (*Gertrude K., John B., Francis, Annanias, Obadiah, Joshua, Jasper, John*) was born November 6, 1926 in Detroit, Mi. daughter of Fred **STORM** and Gertrude Katherine **SMITH**. She married July 8, 1950 James **CONSTABLE** born 1922. Children born in Detroit, Mi.:
   i- **CONSTABLE** Mark born 1951
   ii- **CONSTABLE** Diana born 1953
   iii- **CONSTABLE** Marta born 1955

813-   **STORM** John S. (*Gertrude K., John B., Francis, Annanias, Obadiah, Joshua, Jasper, John*) was born November 18, 1928 in Detroit, Mi. son of Fred **STORM** and Gertrude Katherine **SMITH**. He married July 24, 1954 Rosemary **KANE** born 1933 in Detroit, Mi.
Children born in Detroit, Mi.:
    i- **STORM** Mathew born 1955
    ii- **STORM** Susan born 1957

814-   **STORM** Joan E. (*Gertrude K., John B., Francis, Annanias, Obadiah, Joshua, Jasper, John*) was born December 13, 1930 in Detroit, Mi. son of Fred **STORM** and Gertrude Katherine **SMITH**. She married May 30, 1955 Robert W. **MC LAUGHLIN** born September 1, 1926 in Rawlatt, Pa.
Children born in Penn Yan, NY:
    i- **MC LAUGHLIN** Karen S. born March 9, 1956
    ii- **MC LAUGHLIN** Bruce S. born July 9, 1958
    iii- **MC LAUGHLIN** Scott S. born May 2, 1960
    iv- **MC LAUGHLIN** Marc S. born March 21, 1963
    v- **MC LAUGHLIN** Greg S. born May 22, 1965

815-   **SMITH** Raymond F. Jr. (*Raymond, John B., Francis, Annanias, Obadiah, Joshua, Jasper, John*) was born December 23, 1926 son of Raymond F. **SMITH** Sr. and Bernice Louisa **HAVENS**. He married August 1947 Sarah **KOUP**. They were living in Tacoma, Wa. in 1981.
Children born in NJ:
    i- **SMITH** Raymond F. III born July 2, 1950
    ii- **SMITH** Ricky Thomas born February 10, 1952
    iii- **SMITH** Rhonda Jean born September 9, 1953
    iv- **SMITH** Robert David born June 28, 1958

816-   **SMITH** Phyllis Jean (*Raymond, John B., Francis, Annanias, Obadiah, Joshua, Jasper, John*) was born April 7, 1928 daughter of Raymond F. **SMITH** and Bernice Louisa **HAVENS**. She married October 18, 1946 Robert Ernest **OLIVER**.
Children:
975-     i- **OLIVER** Sally Jean born October 12, 1947 in Ithaca, NY
    ii- **OLIVER** William Charles born August 7, 1957 in Syracuse
    iii- **OLIVER** Nancy Ann born November 14, 1961 in Syracuse

817-   **SMITH** Eldora (*Ralph, John B., Francis, Annanias, Obadiah, Joshua, Jasper, John*) was born April 8, 1925 in N. Hornell, NY daughter of Ralph **SMITH** and Esther **ROE**. She married in Cal. July 25, 1943 Minor Henry **PATTERSON** born January 8, 1921 in Ithaca, NY son of Henry Thomas **PATTERSON** and Bessie Elizabeth **ROLFE**.
Children born in Ithaca NY:
976-     i- **PATTERSON** James Michael born August 10, 1944
977-     ii- **PATTERSON** Joyce Linda born May 3, 1947

208

978-    iii- **PATTERSON** Jane Eldora born January 14, 1951
979-    iv- **PATTERSON** Joanne born August 7, 1955

818-    **PARSONS** John Walter (*Ethel Hunt, Eleanor E., Francis, Annanias, Obadiah, Joshua, Jasper, John*) was born July 30, 1932 son of Walter D. **HUNT** and Claud V. **PARSONS** and Ethel Katherine **HUNT**. He married December 1959 (spouse unknown)
Children:
        i- **PARSONS** Claude Douglas born October 17, 1960
        ii- **PARSONS** Leo Edwin born July 10, 1963
        iii- **PARSONS** Steven born October 1, 1965

819-    **BROWN** Howard Frederick (*Frederick T. Brown, Manley C. Brown, Melissa, Robert T., Obadiah, Joshua, Jasper, John*) was born April 10, 1938 in Cortland, NY son of Frederick Tichenor **BROWN** and Edith Iona **REYNOLDS**. He married April 9, 1960 in Ithaca, NY Marilyn Elizabeth **REHBEIN** born August 19, 1937 in Mc Graw, NY.
Children:
        i- **BROWN** Susan Iona born November 7, 1942 in Cortland, NY, married August 27, 1964 Lawrence Robert **MATSON** born February 9, 1940.
        ii- **BROWN** Linda Jean born February 14, 1947 in Ithaca, NY, married September 4, 1965 in Cortland, NY Thomas William **ARDIS** born June 16, 1941 in Cortland, NY

820-    **TAGGART** Cecil (*Laura M., Clement D., William, Clement, Obadiah, Joshua, Jasper, John*) was born 1898 in Tompkins Co. NY son of William **TAGGART** (born in Ireland) and Laura Mae **SMITH** and died October 28, 1947, buried in Woodlawn cemetery in Newfield, NY. He married (1) Martha **DASSANCE** and (2) Mildred **RAE**.
Children:
        i- **TAGGART** Curtis D. born 1927 and died 1927
        ii- **TAGGART** son (nfi)

821-    **TAGGART** Mabel (*Laura M., Clement D., William, Clement, Obadiah, Joshua, Jasper, John*) was born 1904 in Tompkins Co. NY daughter of William **TAGGART** and Laura Mae **SMITH**. She married Roy F. **MC INTYRE** who was born 1895 and died age 56 yrs.
Children:
980-    i- **MC INTYRE** Ray B. born November 11, 1924
981-    ii- **MC INTYRE** Hazel Mae born February 12, 1926

822-    **TAGGART** Robert (*Laura M., Clement D., William, Clement, Obadiah, Joshua, Jasper, John*) was born 1909 in Tompkins Co. NY son of William **TAGGART** and Laura Mae **SMITH** and died 1962, buried Woodlawn cemetery in Newfield, NY. He married Mary **BROWN**
Children:
        i- **TAGGART** John A. born 1934 and died 1973, buried Woodlawn cemetery in Newfield, NY

ii- **TAGGART** Paul

823-    **VANN** Mark Newman (*Carl W. Vann, Fred Vann, Julia M., Clement, Obadiah, Joshua, Jasper, John*) was born February 4, 1952 son of Carl Wilbert **VANN** and Bertha Elizabeth **NEWMAN**. He married May 22, 1976 Sanja Jean **HALL** born December 27, 1954.
Children:
    i- **VANN** Mathew Bruce born April 19, 1979
    ii- **VANN** Justin Mark born May 12, 1981

824-    **VANN** Bruce Carl (*Carl W. Vann, Fred Vann, Julia M., Clement, Obadiah, Joshua, Jasper, John*) was born February 14, 1953 son of Carl Wilbert **VANN** and Bertha Elizabeth **NEWMAN**. He married Karen Alice **MARTIN** born April 6, 1966.
Children:
    i- **VANN** Sally Bea born August 3, 1989
    ii- **VANN** Eliza Alice born September 1, 1991

825-    **VANN** Linda (*Alvin Gilbert Vann, Fred Vann, Julia M., Clement, Obadiah, Joshua, Jasper, John*) was born September 9, 1951 daughter of Alvin Gilbert **VANN** and Olive **ADAMS**. She married Robert **MIX** born September 15, 1954.
Children:
982-    i- **MIX** Monica born December 31, 1972
    ii- **MIX** Michael born December 6, 1974
    iii- **MIX** Mathew born September 25, 1980

826-    **VANN** Kathy (*Alvin Gilbert Vann, Fred Vann, Julia M., Clement, Obadiah, Joshua, Jasper, John*) was born August 26, 1958 daughter of Alvin Gilbert **VANN** and Olive **ADAMS**. Spouse unknown. had 2 children, Laura born October 21, 1981 and Erin born June 2, 1985

827-    **SMITH** James G. (*Gilbert C., Cornelius, Gilbert C., John T., Obadiah, Joshua, Jasper, John*) was born November 7, 1932 son of Gilbert Cole and Louise **SMITH**. He married (1) Ivy (unknown maiden name) and married (2) Chom (unknown maiden name) born August 8, 1946.
Children by first marriage:
    i- **SMITH** Gilbert Cornelius born August 6, 1965
    ii- **SMITH** Ina born August 8, 1970, married ____ **BALL**

828-    **SMITH** Frances (*Gilbert C., Cornelius, Gilbert C., John T., Obadiah, Joshua, Jasper, John*) was born June 16, 1946 daughter of Gilbert Cole and Marjorie Helen **SMITH**. She married Charles **WEHNER** born October 26, 1943.
Children:
983-    i- **WEHNER** Heidi born April 7, 1969
    ii- **WEHNER** Holly born May 19, 1971

829-    **PETER** Edward C. II (*Anita, Gilbert C., Gilbert C., John T., Obadiah, Joshua, Jasper, John*) was born May 8, 1929 son of Edward **PETER** and Anita **SMITH**. He married May 9, 1953 Jean Audrey **FORESTEIRE** who was born April 24, 1929 daughter of Anthony F. **FORESTEIRE** and Angeline Mary **WHITE**.
Children:
984-        i- **PETER** Jean Audrey born January 25, 1954
            ii- **PETER** Edward Compston III born May 20, 1955
985-        iii- **PETER** Mary Ann born April 6, 1957
            iv- **PETER** Anita Smith born July 28, 1964

830-    **FRUDD** Eugene (*Margaret Griswold, Emma Cole, Emeline, John T., Obadiah, Joshua, Jasper, John*) was born August 9, 1924 son of Charles **FRUDD** and Margaret **GRISWOLD**. He married December 14, 1951 Odial **KIMBLE** born May 13, 1929.
Children:
            i- **FRUDD** Vernon born February 9, 1953
            ii- **FRUDD** Wayne born June 29, 1954
            iii- **FRUDD** Warren born August 3, 1955, married May 14, 1981 Jennifer Joan **DEAN** born February 8, 1956 and had 3 daughters
            iv- **FRUDD** Virginia Marie born January 18, 1957
            v- **FRUDD** Clarice born March 6, 1961, died March 29, 1963
            vi- **FRUDD** Sharon Kaye born December 26, 1962 died same day

831-    **ARDEN** Carol (*Dorothy, Frank T., Herman T., John T., Obadiah, Joshua, Jasper, John*) was born September 16, 1964 daughter of Richard **ARDEN** and Dorothy **SMITH**. She married (1) Scott **VESLEY** born May 12, 1959 son of Edwin **VESLEY** and Ellen **NESS**. They were divorced and she married (2) Mark **SMITH**.
Children by first marriage:
            i- **VESLEY** Heather born July 3, 1983
            ii- **VESLEY** Sean Edwin born September 17, 1985
            iii- **VESLEY** Tracey Ellen born October 22, 1988
Children by second marriage:
            iv- **ARDEN** Paul Vincent born October 22, 1991
            v- **SMITH** June Devonna born September 1993

832-    **ARDEN** Robert (*Dorothy, Frank T., Herman T., John T., Obadiah, Joshua, Jasper, John*) was born January 3, 1968 son of Richard **ARDEN** and Dorothy **SMITH**. He married Melissa **BENNETT** born May 14, 1969 daughter of Elmer and Sharon **BENNETT**.
Children:
            i- **ARDEN** Nicholas Bennett born January 8, 1991
            ii- **ARDEN** Tyler Robert born July 11, 1993

833-    **WHITAKER** Nellie Grace (*Fidelia Lyon, Lorenzo Lyon, Priscilla, Joshua, Annanias, Joshua, Jasper, John*) was born August 17, 1887 in Waterloo, Mi. daughter of Charles Benjamin **WHITAKER** and Fidelia **LYON** and died March 16, 1971 in Mesa, Az. She

married Pyrl John **HARPHAM** born May 5, 1887 in Pleasant Lake, Ind. son of John **HARPHAM** and Loatta **DELLER** and died July 1965. They are buried in Mr. Zion cemetery in Pleasant Lake.
One known child born in Huntington, Ind.:
986-      i- **HARPHAM** Virginia Ruth born December 10, 1917

834-    **DAVID** Lora Agnes (*Miles R. David, Sarah K. Georgia, Lovina, Joshua, Annanias, Joshua, Jasper, John*) was born July 1, 1886 in Bengal, Mi. daughter of Miles R. **DAVID** and Alice Adelia **GILLETT** and died January 29, 1967 in Corry, Pa. She married Robert E. **RETHERFORD** who was born May 31, 1882 in Marion, Ind. son of Miner **RETHERFORD** and Mary Elizabeth **MARKS** and died January 3, 1939 in Corry, Pa. They are buried in Pine Grove cemetery.
Children:
          i- **RETHERFORD** Richard Robert born November 27, 1910 in Dayton, Ohio and drowned in Chenango River, Binghamton, NY December 19, 1923
987-      ii- **RETHERFORD** Phyllis Joan born March 14, 1915 in Rochester, NY
988-    iii- **RETHERFORD** Roberta Flora born November 16, 1918 in Rochester, NY
989-     iv- **RETHERFORD** Mary Alice May 18, 1920

835-    **DAVID** Floyd (*Frank E. David, Sarah Georgia, Lovina, Joshua, Annanias, Joshua, Jasper, John*) was born in Gratiot Co. Mi. son of Frank E. **DAVID** and Maud **HIPKONS**. He married Marguerite Elmira **OSTRAND** born June 27, 1893 in Gladwin, Mi. daughter of Silas Wright **OSTRAND** and Margaret Elmira **KING** and died October 31, 1984 in Lansing, Mi.
Children:
          i- **DAVID** Donald born 1912
         ii- **DAVID** Chester born 1915
        iii- **DAVID** Royal born 1919
         iv- **DAVID** Erma born 1920
          v- **DAVID** Sylvia born 1923

836-    **DAVID** Archie (*Frank E. David, Sarah Georgia, Lovina, Joshua, Annanias, Joshua, Jasper, John*) was born 1893 in Gratiot Co. Mi. son of Frank E. **DAVID** and Maud **HIPKONS** and died 1957. He married Anna **HUMMEL** born 1890 in Isabella Co. Mi. daughter of William Adolph **HUMMEL** and Catherine **SMITH**.
Children:
          i- **DAVID** Ola K. born 1913
         ii- **DAVID** Ralph W. born 1915
990-    iii- **DAVID** Vivian Irene born 1916

837-    **GEORGIA** Hazel (*Fred Georgia, Schuyler Georgia, Lovina, Joshua, Annanias, Joshua, Jasper, John*) was born in Mi. daughter of Fred Dudley **GEORGIA** and Caddie **BROWN**. She married Verne **EAGLE**
One child:

991-     i- **EAGLE** Georgia born June 17, 1921

838-     **FISH** Helen Elma (*Myrtle E. Freese, Margaret Anna, Lewis H., Joshua, Annanias, Joshua, Jasper, John*) was born June 9, 1892 daughter of Charles E. **FISH** and Myrtle E. **FREESE** and died August 8, 1981. She married Ralph F. **TILTON** who was born May 20, 1893 and died July 20, 1981. (see #474) Unknown children

839-     **FISH** Wesley Elwood (*Myrtle E. Freese, Margaret Anna, Lewis H., Joshua, Annanias, Joshua, Jasper, John*) was born August 15, 1896 son of Charles E. **FISH** and Myrtle E. **FREESE** and died August 4, 1969. He married Ella Eleanor **RICHARDSON** who died November 9, 1969.
One child:
       i- **FISH** Phyllis married Donald **HUGHES** and had 3 children, Donald, David and Laurel

840-     **FREESE** Mary Edith (*Willard Freese, Margaret Anna, Lewis H. Joshua, Annanias, Joshua, Jasper, John*) was born November 28, 1913 daughter of Willard **FREESE** and Helen M. **GRAY**. She married April 24, 1943 George Henry **WARD** who was born June 19, 1915 son of George Lester **WARD** and Mary Elosia **SCHROFFT** and died September 16, 1988.
Children:
       i- **WARD** John Willard born June 13, 1947, married June 6, 1970 Marjorie Ann **HOCKER**
       ii- **WARD** Kathleen Ann born July 6, 1952
       iii- **WARD** Jean Louise born December 4, 1958, married Charles **SCHWARTZ** and were divorced

841-     **FREESE** Myrtle May (*Lewis O. Freese, Margaret Anna, Lewis H., Joshua, Annanias, Joshua, Jasper, John*) was born May 10, 1903 in Enfield, NY daughter of Lewis Orville **FREESE** and Elizabeth Josephine **DUNSTER**, last know residence was White House, Tn. She married (1) September 25, 1923 Thomas Theodore **CORNELL** who was born May 6, 1901 and died January 5, 1965. She married (2) March 26, 1935 Clifford **VAN MARTER** who was born July 1, 1903 and died April 27, 1972.
Child by first marriage:
992-     i- **CORNELL** Barbara May born September 20, 1924
Child by second marriage:
       ii- **VAN MARTER** Sadie Elizabeth born July 17, 1938

842-     **FREESE** Cora Luella (*Lewis O. Freese, Margaret Anna, Lewis H., Joshua, Annanias, Joshua, Jasper, John*) was born May 30, 1907 in Enfield, NY daughter of Lewis Orville **FREESE** and Elizabeth Josephine **DUNSTER** and died December 6, 1994. She married June 29, 1927 Cleo **FREESE** who was born September 1, 1900 in Newfield, NY son of Charles Delmar **FREESE** and Melinda **KRESGE** and died 1984 in Ithaca, NY. Children born in Ithaca, NY:

993-    i- **FREESE** Marion Louise born December 20, 1927
994-    ii- **FREESE** Betty Marie born June 30, 1929
995-    iii- **FREESE** Jane Elizabeth born December 19, 1932
996-    iv- **FREESE** Robert Cleo born September 29, 1936
        v- **FREESE** Richard Lewis born November 20, 1940 and died in Interlaken, NY
June 2, 1943, buried Hayt's cemetery
997-    vi- **FREESE** Charles Roger born August 1, 1944
998-    vii- **FREESE** Ronald Edward born March 19, 1946
999-    viii- **FREESE** Marcia Jean born May 23, 1947
        ix- **FREESE** Janice Lorraine born July 5, 1949 and died in Interlaken, NY July 9,
1950, buried Hayt's cemetery

843-    **TEETER** Ann Margaret (*Mary E. Freese, Margaret Anna, Lewis H., Joshua,
Annanias, Joshua, Jasper, John*) was born March 20, 1902 in Newfield, NY daughter of
Luther **TEETER** and Mary Edith **FREESE** and died February 21, 1980 in Lakeland, Fl.
She married October 8, 1920 Leon M. **LAUGHLIN** who was born November 14, 1892 in
Van Etten, NY son of William Hiram **LAUGHLIN** and Ida Arvilla **MC DANIELS** and died
November 27, 1965 in Ithaca, NY.
Children:
        i- **LAUGHLIN** Barbara born December 23, 1921 (see #980)    1000-    ii-
**LAUGHLIN** James Laverne born June 24, 1935

844-    **ACKLEY** Homer Howell (*Walter F. Ackley, Olive Rose Summerton, Thomas
Summerton, Sally, Annanias, Joshua, Jasper, John*) was born September 25, 1908 in NY
State son of Walter F. **ACKLEY** and Clara May **HOWELL** and died August 15, 2003 in
Malabar, Fl., buried Evergreen cemetery in Spencer, NY  He married Elma **DUNHAM**.
Children:
        i- **ACKLEY** Donald Glen born August 29, 1949, married (1) July 1983 Sheryl
Lynn **SINK** and married (2) Cherie Ann **JARRY** born February 18, 1962, lived Palm Bay
Fl. in 2003
        ii- **ACKLEY** Lester married twice, 2 children, moved to Cleveland, Ohio
1001-    iii- **ACKLEY** William Howell and wife Eileen lived Mewark, Valley, NY in 2003

845-    **ACKLEY** Charles William (*Alvah Charles Ackley, Olive Rose Summerton, Thomas
Summerton, Sally, Annanias, Joshua, Jasper, John*) was born March 31, 1915 in Lockwood,
NY son of Alvah Charles **ACKLEY** and Clara May **HOWELL** and died February 7, 2004
in Springville, NY, buried Prospect Park in Sidney, Delaware Co. NY.  He married March
3, 1937 Frances Evelyn **TRIPP** born May 16, 1915 daughter of Glen Scott **TRIPP** and Ruth
Frances **SEELEY**.
Children:
1002-    i- **ACKLEY** Joyce Ruth born June 4, 1944
        ii- **ACKLEY** John Charles born September 5, 1946, married September 9, 1978
Diane Barbara **SEIFERT**, lived W. Hempstead, NY

## Tenth Generation

846-   **SMITH** Eugenia Abigail (*Halma B., Halma, James, Joseph, Daniel, Jasper, John, Jasper, John*) was born November 19, 1888 in Springville, Utah daughter of Halma Bolton **SMITH** and Florena **CLARK**.  She married May 9, 1907 in Salt Lake City, Utah John Emmett **BIRD** who was born December 25, 1887 in Springville, Utah son of James Oliver **BIRD** and Lydia Sylvania **HERRINGTON**
Children:
         i- **BIRD** Rena Setella born July 12 1908 and married Albion W. **CAINE**.  Their daughter married Larry **BUSHMAN**
         ii- **BIRD** Ina born July 3, 1916, married December 26, 1931 in Melad, Idaho David **REYNOLDS** born February 28, 1918 in Pocatello, Idaho son of George **REYNOLDS**.
They had 3 daughters
         iii- **BIRD** Gene Emmett born July 31, 1918 in Springville, Utah and died November 29, 1943, married May 7, 1943 Illa **CLYDE**

847-   **SMITH** Claude Halma (*Halma B., Halma, James, Joseph, Daniel, Jasper, John, Jasper, John*) was born November 30, 1890 in Springville, Utah son of Halma Bolton **SMITH** and Florena **CLARK** and died October 29, 1950 in Anaheim, Cal.  He married April 11, 1925 Feral Yoder **ASHBY** who was born December 21, 1904 in Elwood, Nebraska daughter of Fred Spencer **ASHBY** and Myrtle **ALBERTINE**.  Her first husband was William **SCHIFFER**.
One child:
         i- **SMITH** Bonnie Mae born February 26, 1926 in Buena Park, Cal.  She married October 27, 1944 Bergen Marshall **DAVIS** born November 4, 1924 in Artesia, Cal. son of Harold Milton **DAVIS** and Anna Bertha **HARVEY**.  They had 3 sons and 2 daughters

848-   **SMITH** Georgianna (*Halma B., Halma, James, Joseph, Daniel, Jasper, John, Jasper, John*) was born September 23, 1895 in Springville, Utah daughter of Halma Bolton **SMITH** and Florena **CLARK**.  She married September 18, 1919 in Anaheim, Cal. James Marius **PEDERSON** born January 16, 1894 in American Fork, Utah son of Antone James and Petra **PEDERSON**.
One child:
         i- **PEDERSON** Marjorie born July 9, 1921 in Santa Ana, Cal. and married April 21, 1946 William Marshall **TODD** born October 26, 1921 son of Carl William **TODD** and Frances Willard **LEONARD**

849-   **SMITH** Jessie (*Hyrum, Hyrum, James, Joseph, Daniel, Jasper, John, Jasper, John*) was born May 20, 1901 in Provo, Utah daughter of Hyrum **SMITH** and Olive **STAGG** and died October 10, 1966 in Heber City, Utah.  She married August 16, 1920 in Provo Elmer Benson **LONG** who was born September 11, 1901 in Diamond, Utah.

Children:

    i- **LONG** Max born July 24, 1921 in Ogden, Utah and died April 26, 1989 in Provo, Utah

    ii- **LONG** Permelia Marie born January 4, 1922 and married October 6, 1938 in Provo Alvin B. **LEWIS** born December 17, 1919 and died July 16, 1992 in Provo

    iii- **LONG** Elmer Benson born April 13, 1924 and died 1984 in Pleasant Grove, Utah

    iv- **LONG** William Dwayne born September 8, 1927 and died December 11, 1993

850-    **SMITH** Ruth (*Hyrum, Hyrum, James, Joseph, Daniel, Jasper, John, Jasper, John*) was born October 19, 1902 in Provo, Utah daughter of Hyrum **SMITH** and Olive **STAGG** and died October 1, 1936 in Huntington Park, Cal. She married January 3, 1922 in Provo Albert Walter **HARPER** born June 3, 1902 in Payson, Utah and died in Inglewood, Cal.
Children:

    i- **HARPER** Betty Lou born August 13, 1923 in Watttis, Ut.

    ii- **HARPER** Gloria Ruth born September 23, 1926 in Wattis

    iii- **HARPER** Velda Mae born May 31, 1929 Spanish Forks, Ut.

    iv- **HARPER** son

851-    **SMITH** Lola Lavon (*Hyrum, Hyrum, James, Joseph, Daniel, Jasper, John, Jasper, John*) was born April 9, 1904 in Provo, Utah daughter of Hyrum **SMITH** and Olive **STAGG** and died April 14, 1943 in Utah. She married July 25, 1924 in Salt Lake City Robert Milton **MAXFIELD** son of Robert Burns **MAXFIELD** and Cynthia Jane **WILSON** who died February 17, 1903 in Lakeview, Utah. She married (2) Thomas Loren **KEEL** born May 21, ____ son of John H. **KEEL** and Artemicia **OWEN**.

852-    **SMITH** Alice (*Hyrum, Hyrum, James, Joseph, Daniel, Jasper, John, Jasper, John*) was born November 27, 1906 in Provo, Utah daughter of Hyrum **SMITH** and Olive **STAGG** and died July 25, 1958 in Springville, Utah. She married January 17, 1929 in Nephi, Utah Moses Leon **SHEPHERD** who was born January 25, 1906 in Springville, Utah and died April 30, 1989 in Provo. They had 5 children.

853-    **SMITH** Darroll (*Hyrum, Hyrum, James, Joseph, Daniel, Jasper, John , Jasper, John*) was born September 21, 1907 in Provo, Utah son of Hyrum **SMITH** and Olive **STAGG** and died December 13, 1969 in Provo. He married December 3, 1930 in Provo Ethel Juanita **BRUNDAGE** born December 3, 1917 in Duchesne, Utah.

854-    **SMITH** Olive S. (*Hyrum, Hyrum, James, Joseph, Daniel, Jasper, John, Jasper, John*) was born June 23, 1910 in Provo, Utah daughter of Hyrum **SMITH** and Olive **STAGG** and died October 7, 1955 in Los Angeles, Cal. She married May 19, 1928 in Provo Phillip Leo **ROPER** who was born August 12, 1909 in Albion, Idaho son of Charles Henry **ROPER** and Hope Wayne **DACK** and died March 6, 1966 in Compton, Cal., buried Orem, Utah. They had 2 children.

216

855-	**SMITH** Georgia (*Hyrum, Hyrum, James, Joseph, Daniel, Jasper, John, Jasper, John*) was born May 14, 1913 in Provo, Utah daughter of Hyrum **SMITH** and Olive **STAGG** and died November 5, 1992 in Orem, Utah. She married June 26, 1937 in Los Angeles, Cal. Francis **ROPER** born October 5, 1912 in Albion, Idaho and died March 21, 1986 in Phoenix, Ar., buried Orem, Utah. They had 2 children. She married (2) Roy **WEST**

856-	**SMITH** Elmer Alvin (*Hyrum, Hyrum, James, Joseph, Daniel Jasper, John, Jasper, John*) was born September 3, 1915 in Provo, Utah son of Hyrum **SMITH** and Olive **STAGG** and died November 6, 1983 in Orem, Utah. He married in 1945 Melba Marie **PETERS** born February 14, 1922. They were divorced, unknown children.

857-	**SMITH** Kenneth (*Hyrum, Hyrum, James, Joseph, Daniel, Jasper, John, Jasper, John*) was born March 4, 1919 in Provo, Utah son of Hyrum **SMITH** and Olive **STAGG**. He married Margie Doreen Holly **MC DONALD** and they were divorced, unknown children.

858-	**SMITH** Eugene Richard (*Hyrum, Hyrum, James, Joseph, Daniel Jasper, John, Jasper, John*) was born September 23, 1923 in Provo, Utah son of Hyrum **SMITH** and Olive **STAGG**. He married March 3, 1929 in Ely, Nev. Glenda Joyce **PIERCE** born June 19, 1929 in Sigurd, Utah daughter of Wilford **PIERCE** and Alice **AVEY**. They had 2 children.

859-	**BALSER** Ella Elvida (*Sidney Ann Scott, Adnie Malott, Francis L. Malott, Ann, Absolom, John, Samuel, Jasper, John*) was born May 1884 in Iroquois Co. Ill. daughter of George Warvel **BALSER** and Sidney Ann **SCOTT** and died 1923 in Wis. She married in Iroquois Co. March 3, 1909 Charles William **HARNESS** who was born February 20, 1887 in Milford, Ill. son of Asa John **HARNESS** and Rebecca **REEVES** and died August 27, 1958 in Milford. They are buried in Maple Grove cemetery.
Children:
	i- **HARNESS** John Alonzo born November 11, 1911 in Iroquois Co. and died September 17, 1987 in Hoopeston, Vermillion Co. Ill., buried Floral Hill cemetery. He married (1) unknown, married (2) October 10, 1946 in Kennton, Ind. Belle **FARRAR** born April 26, 1894 in Woodland, Ill. and died November 20, 1979 in Watseka, Ill., buried Body cemetery. He married (3) November 7, 1981 (unknown). He had 1 daughter by first marriage Karen Sue born February 17, 1938 and died May 4, 1939
	ii- **HARNESS** Anna R. born September 15, 1915 in St. James, Mn. and died October 13, 1995. She married June 11, 1947 Elmer D. **WILLIAMS** who was born March 12, 1922 in Cissna Pk. Ill. and died October 20, 1995 in Watseka, Ill.
	iii- **HARNESS** Genevieve Louise born August 4, 1920 in La Salle, Mn. and died October 5, 1955 in Watseka. She married October 23, 1945 Harold **PARRO** who was born June 10, 1923 in Milford, Ill. and died May 26, 1982. They are buried in Maple Grove cemetery.

860- **BALSER** Sarah Addie (*Sidney Ann Scott, Adnie Malott, Francis L. Malott, Ann, Absolom, John, Samuel, Jasper, John*) was born January 23, 1886 in Ash Grove, Ill. daughter of George Warvel **BALSER** and Sidney Ann **SCOTT** and died September 8, 1962 in Watseka, Ill. She married in Watseka December 13, 1905 John Milton **HOLT** who was born February 22, 1877 in Otway, Ohio son of James **HOLT** and Martha **STEVENS** and died April 17, 1964. They are buried in Sugar Creek Chapel cemetery.
Children born in Iroquois Co. Ill.:

    i- **HOLT** Blanche Mae born March 20, 1906 and died March 3, 1942 in Danville, Ill. She married August 29, 1924 Clarence A. **GOSSETT** who was born April 29, 1902 in Cropsey, Ill.

    ii- **HOLT** Herbert Lee born August 27, 1907, married January 21, 1928 Maude Pearl **LONGFELLOW**

    iii- **HOLT** Dorothy Marie born July 16, 1909, married Hubert **GOSSETT** and had son Donald Eugene **GOSSETT** born September 12, 1928 in Milford, Ill. and died January 2, 1996, buried GAR cemetery.

    iv- **HOLT** Harold Raymond born May 12, 1911 and died August 6, 1911 in Stoddard Twp. Ill., buried Maple Grove cemetery

1003-    v- **HOLT** Donald George born September 25, 1912

    vi- **HOLT** Russell Leon born April 8, 1916 and died May 16, 1982 in Urbana, Ill., buried Floral Hill cemetery

    vii- **HOLT** Mary Frances born April 20, 1922 and died January 7, 1989 in Milford, Ill

    viii- **HOLT** Ruth Louise born December 8, 1930 and died January 7, 1931, buried Amity cemetery

861- **BALSER** Charlotta (*Sidney Ann Scott, Adnie Malott, Francis L. Malott, Ann, Absolom, John, Samuel, Jasper, John*) was born June 13, 1894 in Milford, Ill. daughter of George Warvel **BALSER** and Sidney Ann **SCOTT** and died November 27, 1982 in West Bend, Wis. She married July 20, 1910 Charles Marion **COOK** who was born November 21, 1880 in Kingston, Tn. and died 1965 in West Bend. They are buried in Washington Co. Memorial Park.
Children:

    i- **COOK** Charles died in action World War II August 24, 1944

    ii- **COOK** Richard L. died before 1982

862- **FRANK** Bruce Kent (*Mabelle Howell, William B. Howell, Anna Corwin, Elizabeth Biles, George Biles, Christian, Joshua, Jasper, John*) was born April 10, 1903 in Lake Linden, Mi. son of Bert **FRANK** and Maybelle **HOWELL** and died August 16, 1992. He married September 21, 1928 Chrystal **SPROULE** born November 22, 1907.
Child:

1004-    i- **FRANK** Victoria Amanda born 1943

863- **FRANK** Bernice Mildred (*Mabelle Howell, William B. Howell, Anna Corwin, Elizabeth Biles, George Biles, Christian, Joshua, Jasper, John*) was born April 4, 1905 in

Lake Linden, Mi. daughter of Bert FRANK and Mabelle HOWELL and died August 16, 1992 in Avon Twp. Mi. She married June 28, 1930 Lewis Bertram ARSCOTT who was born November 7, 1903 and died September 20, 1985 in Avon Twp., buried Mt. Avon cemetery.
Children born in Avon Twp. Mi.:
1005-     i- ARSCOTT Patricia A. born 1934
1006-     ii- ARSCOTT Lewis David born 1937
1007-     iii- ARSCOTT James Bertram born December 17, 1942 and died June 11, 1966 in Avon Twp. Mi.

864-     FRANK Robert Howell (*Mabelle Howell, William B. Howell, Anna Corwin, Elizabeth Biles, George Biles, Christian, Joshua, Jasper, John*) was born May 24, 1909 in Lake Linden, Mi. son of Bert FRANK and Mabelle HOWELL and died October 2003 in Imley City, Mi. He married October 1, 1932 Zela Beth WINGER who was born March 23, 1911 and died April 17, 1984 in Avon Twp. Mi. They are buried in Mt. Avon cemetery.
Children:
1008-     i- FRANK Robert Howell II born 1942
1009-     ii- FRANK Betty Marion born 1946

865-     FRANK Phillip Lucius (*Mabelle Howell, William B. Howell, Anna Corwin, Elizabeth Biles, George Biles, Christian, Joshua, Jasper, John*) was born 1918 in Avon Twp, Mi. twin son of Bert FRANK and Mabelle HOWELL. He married Apri 5, 1947 Edna Rice NORMAN who born 1912 and died September 19, 2000 Framingham, Ma.
Children:
1010-     i- FRANK Wendy born 1948
          ii- FRANK Phillip Lucius II born 1952 (unknown spouse). He had 1 child Phillip Vincent

866-     FRANK Maida Mary (*Mabelle Howell, William B. Howell, Anna Corwin, Elizabeth Biles, George Biles, Christian, Joshua, Jasper, John*) was born February 22, 1917 in Avon Twp: Mi. adopted daughter of Bert FRANK and Mabelle HOWELL and died December 2004. She married May 7, 1948 Chester NORMAN who died May 25, 1966. She married (2) October 17, 1970 Clarence HAWKINS.
Child by first marriage:
          i- NORMAN Diane Louise born 1951, married Charles VOGT

867-     FRANK Nancy Louise (*Mabelle Howell, William B. Howell, Anna Corwin, Elizabeth Biles, George Biles, Christian, Joshua, Jasper, John*) was born 1923 in Avon Twp. Mi. daughter of Bert FRANK and Mabelle HOWELL. She married March 16, 1946 Ozelle WHITE who was born September 23, 1918 in Cave Creek, Tn. and died June 2000 in Riverdale, Md.
Children born in Ann Arbor, Mi.
          i- WHITE William Scott born 1948
1011-     ii- WHITE Lawrence born June 2, 1950 and died August 10, 1999 in Brunswick,

Md.

iii- WHITE Kathleen Louise born 1951
1012-    iv- WHITE Alicia born 1953

868-    HOWELL Harry (*Chester A. Howell, William B. Howell, Anna Corwin, Elizabeth Biles, George Biles, Christian, Joshua, Jasper, John*) was born October 17, 1912 son of Chester Arthur HOWELL and Daisy LOVELL and died 1980.  He married May 13, 1939 in Tisdale, Sasketchewan, Canada Irene Annie FURGER who was born October 7, 1915.
Children:
1013-    i- HOWELL Frances Marie born 1939 in Tisdale
         ii- HOWELL Margaret Ann born 1943 in Ft. Williams, Ont.

869-    HOWELL Gladys (*Chester A. Howell, William B. Howell, Anna Corwin, Elizabeth Biles, George Biles, Christian, Joshua, Jasper, John*) was born October 30, 1914 in Minitonas, Canada daughter of Chester Arthur HOWELL and Daisy LOVELL and died June 18, 1998 in Rochester Hills, Mi.  She married June 24, 1939 Frederick LAATZ who was born September 26, 1914 and died October 18, 1976 in Detroit, Mi.  They are buried in Mt. Avon cemetery.
Child born in Detroit, Mi.:
1014-    i- LAATZ William Frederick born 1950

870-    MC COTTER Lee Newberry (*Anna A. Howell, William B. Howell, Anna Corwin, Elizabeth Biles, George biles, Christian, Joshua, Jasper, John*) was born March 16, 1925 in Rochester, Mi. son of Howard Knickerbocker MC COTTER and Anna Alice HOWELL and died November 3, 1990 in Rochester Hills, Mi., buried in Mt. Avon cmetery.  He married July 24, 1943 in Romeo, Macomb Co. Mi. Eleanor Irene PALMER who was born 1925 in Avon Twp. Mi. daughter of Irl PALMER and Eleanor DUNLOP.
Children born in Rochester, Mi.:
1015-    i- MC COTTER Catherine Ann born 1944
1016-    ii- MC COTTER Carol Lynn born 1945
1017-    iii- MC COTTER Constance Lee born 1946
1018-    iv- MC COTTER Richard Lee born 1947

871-    HOWELL Robert V. (*John S. Howell, William B. Howell, Anna Corwin, Elizabeth Biles, George Biles, Christian, Joshua, Jasper, John*) was born January 9, 1913 son of John Stinson HOWELL and Arvella BAUCKE.  He married (1) in 1937 Margie GUSTAFON and (2) December 7, 1939 Vivian Eugenia HERMANN who was born February 21, 1917.  He married (3) August 17, 1956 Alan Mae SHIP who was born August 9, 1919.
Children:
         i- HOWELL Johnny born September 15, 1940, died same day
         ii- HOWELL Robert Mason born 1941
         iii- HOWELL Daniel Herman born 1943
         iv- HOWELL Donald Gran born 1945

872- **HOWELL** Neil V. (*John S. Howell, William B. Howell, Anna Corwin, Elizabeth Biles, George Biles, Christian, Joshua, Jasper, John*) was born January 22, 1914 son of John Stinson **HOWELL** and Arvella **BAUCKE**. He married June 20, 1936 Alice V. **CORNER** who was born May 14, 1917.
Children:
1019-     i- **HOWELL** Valerie Virginia born 1937
          ii- **HOWELL** Neil V. II born 1943
          iii- **HOWELL** Karen born 1945


873- **HOWELL** Edith Marie (*John S. Howell, William B. Howell, Anna Corwin, Elizabeth Biles, George Biles, Christian, Joshua, Jasper, John*) was born 1918 daughter of John Stinson **HOWELL** and Arvella **BAUCKE**. She married January 26, 1955 Thomas Dewey **BENNETT**.
Children:
          i- **BENNETT** Thomas Dewey II born 1956
          ii- **BENNETT** John Murray born 1957


874- **HOWELL** John Stinson III (*John S. Howell, William B. Howell, Anna Corwin, Elizabeth Biles, George Biles, Christian, Joshua, Jasper, John*) was born 1919 son of John Stinson **HOWELL** and Arvella **BAUCKE**. He married 1911 Barbara Ann **BRADBURY** born 1924.
Children:
          i- **HOWELL** Marion Nannette born 1945, married 1965 Nathan H. **THOMAS** Jr.
          ii- **HOWELL** Susan Carol born 1948, married 1970 David John **IRVIN**
          iii- **HOWELL** John Stinson IV born 1953
          iv- **HOWELL** William Ronald born 1954


875- **HOWELL** Milo Lacy (*John S. Howell, William B. Howell, Anna Corwin, Elizabeth Biles, George Biles, Christian, Joshua, Jasper, John*) was born 1922 son of John Stinson **HOWELL** and Arvilla **BAUCKE**. He married 1952 Maxine **WALDRON** born 1931.
Children:
          i- **HOWELL** Patricia Ann born 1951
          ii- **HOWELL** Debra Lea born 1954
          iii- **HOWELL** Michael Kelly born 1957


876- **HOWELL** Clarie E. (*John S. Howell, William B. Howell, Anna Corwin, Elizabeth Biles, George Biles, Christian, Joshua, Jasper, John*) was born 1932 daughter of John Stinson **HOWELL** and Arvilla **BAUCKE**. She married in 1950 John William **MITCHELL**.
Children:
          i- **MITCHELL** John Patrick lived 24 hours
          ii- **MITCHELL** Kathleen Elizabeth Howell born 1953
          iii- **MITCHELL** Martha Jane born 1955
          iv- **MITCHELL** Karen Kay Howell born 1959

877- **HOWELL** Alis Lee (*Milo Max Howell, William B. Howell, Anna Corwin, Elizabeth Biles, George Biles, Christian, Joshua, Jasper, John*) was born September 14, 1920 daughter of Milo Max **HOWELL** and Harriet F. **OWEN** and died January 29, 1994 in Rochester, Mi. She married August 29. 1940 William G. **BRIDGE** who was born April 25, 1917 and died January 28, 1984 in Pontiac, Mi. They are buried in Mt. Avon cemetery.
Children:
>  i- **BRIDGE** Gary George born June 24, 1942 and died in auto accident April 2, 1958 in Avon Twp. Mi.

1020-  ii- **BRIDGE** Susan Lee born 1943
1021-  iii- **BRIDGE** Sallie Jo born 1948
1022-  iv- **BRIDGE** Polly Ann born 1955
>  v- **BRIDGE** Michael George born September 3, 1958 and died March 29, 1984 in Avon Twp. Mi.

878- **HOWELL** Bruce Owen (*Milo M. Howell, William B. Howell, Anna Corwin, Elizabeth Biles, George Biles, Christian, Joshua, Jasper, John*) was born 1923 in Rochester Twp. Mi. son of Milo Max **HOWELL** and Harriet F. **OWEN**. He met Elsie M. **MESSLER** and married (2) June 14, 1957 Nancy Jo Ann **MORIARETY** who was born 1938 and died August 11, 1986 in Rochester Twp. Mi., buried Mt. Avon cemetery.
Children by first marriage:
>  i- **HOWELL** Danny Bruce born 1948
>  ii- **HOWELL** Dwight Raymond born 1951

Children by second marriage:
>  iii- **HOWELL** Sherrie Lynn born 1960
>  iv- **HOWELL** Andy Lynn born 1962

879- **CASE** Betty Jean (*Leah R. Howell, William B. Howell, Anna Corwin, Elizabeth Biles, George Biles, Christian, Joshua, Jasper John*) was born April 4, 1922 in Rochester Twp. Mi. daughter of Mason **CASE** and Leah Ruth **HOWELL** and died September 11, 1971 in Rochester Twp. She married December 16, 1961 Lee **SLAZINSKI**.
Child:
1023-  i- **SLAZINSKI** David Anton

880- **CASE** Mary Lou (*Leah R. Howell, William B. Howell, Anna Corwin, Elizabeth Biles, George Biles, Christian, Joshua, Jasper, John*) was born February 7, 1924 in Rochester Twp. Mi. daughter of Mason **CASE** and Leah Ruth **HOWELL** and died April 15, 1993 in Houston, Tx. She married October 2, 1948 Dale Elwood **CYPHER** who was born 1918 and died August 20. 1986. They are buried in Mt. Avon cemetery.
Children:
1024-  i- **CYPHER** Steven D. born 1950
1025-  ii- **CYPHER** John Mason born 1952

881- **ALEXANDER** William James (*Ila Van Keuren, Alice Russell, Hulda Nicholson, Sally, William, Joshua, Joshua, Jasper, John*) was born January 29, 1924 son of James M.

ALEXANDER and Ila VAN KEUREN and died June 21, 1992 in Rochester, NY. He married Dorothy (unknown maiden name)
Children:
  i- ALEXANDER Kathleen married ____ CROLLI lived Pa.
  ii- ALEXANDER Keith resided Pa.
  iii- ALEXANDER Sharon married ____ WALBURN
  iv- ALEXANDER Timothy resided Alexandria, Va.

882- BURDETT Robert Donald (*Donald S. Burdett, Anna D. Russell, Hulda Nicholson, Sally, William Joshua, Joshua, Jasper, John*) was born May 12, 1916 in Hornell, NY son of Donald Sawyer BURDETT and Blanche WOOD and died September 16, 1998. He married Doris Evelyn MAYNARD.
One child:
  i- BURDETT Carol Linda

883- BURDETT Anna Ruth (*Donald S. Burdett, Anna D. Russell, Hulda Nicholson, Sally, William, Joshua, Joshua, Jasper, John*) was born January 30, 1920 in Hornell, NY daughter of Donald Sawyer BURDETT and Blanche C. WOOD. She married Harold K. SEAMAN born August 2, 1914.
Child:
  i- SEAMAN Sandra Lee married David K. BURDETT and had 2 children Diana and Stephen C.

884- BURDETT Donna Sue (*Donald S. Burdett, Anna D. Russell, Hulda Nicholson, Sally, William, Joshua, Joshua, Jasper, John*) was born September 30, 1940 daughter of Donald S. BURDETT and Blanche WOOD. She married Lee RYAN.
Children:
  i- RYAN Eric Lee born January 19, 1980 and died next day
  ii- RYAN Jeffrey Donald
  iii- RYAN Jennifer Louise
  iv- RYAN Heidi Marie

885- BURDETT Hobart Marion (*Joel D. Burdett, Anna Russell, Hulda Nicholson, Sally, William, Joshua, Joshua, Jasper, John*) was born in Howard, NY October 21, 1923 son of Joel D. BURDETT and Polly ALLEN and died April 4, 1965 in Hartsville, NY, buried Rural cemetery. He married November 13, 1954 in Roulette, Pa. Joyce MEHLENBACKER who was born September 23, 1932 in Canisteo, NY daughter of Harvey MEHLENBACKER and Madeline F. PHILLIPSON. He served in US Army Airforce in World War II.
Children:
  i- BURDETT David Murray died April 23, 1955 in Willetts, Cal., buried Arkport, NY
1026- ii- BURDETT Mark Dwight
  iii- BURDETT Wayne Francis married Dana M. PRITCHARD and had 3 children

Katie Marie, Daniella Rene and Samuel David

      iv- **BURDETT** Wendy Sue married Bruce **JORDAN** and had 2 children Christian David and Stephen Michael

      v- **BURDETT** Tracy Raymond married Karen Louise **ANDREWS** and had 3 children Joshua Raymond, Nicholas Joel and Caleb

886-    **BURDETT** Marianna Virginia (*Joel D. Burdett, Anna Russell, Hulda Nicholson, Sally, William, Joshua, Joshua, Jasper, John*) was born January 29, 19__ in Hornell, NY daughter of Joel D. **BURDETT** and Polly **ALLEN**. She married July 1954 Peter **MATLEGA**. They were divorced. Last known residence in Dundee, NY.

887-    **BURDETT** Margaret Viola (*Joel D. Burdett, Anna Russell, Hulda Nicholson, Sally, William, Joshua, Joshua, Jasper, John*) was born September 14, 19__ in Hornell, NY daughter of Joel D. **BURDETT** and Polly **ALLEN**. She married in Hornellsville, NY May 1, 1947 William O. **DRAKE** who was born in Hornell, NY March 10, 19__ son of William Henry **DRAKE** and Mary **PERRY**, served World War II.
Children:
      i- **DRAKE** William James
      ii- **DRAKE** Daniel Wayne
      iii- **DRAKE** Douglas Malcolm

888-    **BURDETT** Paul Shelby (*Joel D. Burdett, Anna Russell, Hulda Nicholson, Sally, William, Joshua, Joshua, Jasper, John*) was born in Hornell, NY May 24, 19__ son of Joel D. **BURDETT** and Polly **ALLEN**. He married in Bowie, Tx. Betty Jean **FRANKLIN** who was born June 26, 19__ in Bowie, Tx. daughter of Jesse James **FRANKLIN** and Minnie Estelle **GEORGE**.
One child:
      i- **BURDETT** Paul Shelby Jr.

889-    **BURDETT** Joel Dean (*Joel D. Burdett, Anna Russell, Hulda Nicholson, Sally, William, Joshua, Joshua, Jasper, John*) was born in Hornell, NY December 23, 19__ son of Joel Dean **BURDETT** and Polly **ALLEN**. He married 1953 in Painted Post, NY Geraldine K. **HICKEY** who was born November 1, 1927 in Painted Post daughter of John **HICKEY** and Stella **SMITH** and died January 4, 1994 in Hornell. Children:
      i- **BURDETT** Robin Ann
      ii- **BURDETT** Rocky Allen married Linda **DAVISON** and had one child Polly Tanner **BURDETT**

890-    **BURDETT** James Milton (*Joel D. Burdett, Anna Russell, Hulda Nicholson, Sally, William, Joshua, Joshua, Jasper, John*) son of Joel D. **BURDETT** and Polly **ALLEN**. He married February 9, 1962 in Bath, NY Joyce A. **DOWNEY** daughter of Kenneth **DOWNEY** and Ann **BOBOWNIK**. They were divorced and he married (2) September 17, 1966 in Arkport, NY Anna Rae **HAYNES** who was born July 9, 19__ in N. Hornell, NY daughter of Edward Christian **HAYNES** and Fannie Eliza **BRIGGS**.

Children:
 i- **BURDETT** Andrew Allen married Danielle ST. LAURENT and had one child Drew Thomas **BURDETT**
 ii- **BURDETT** James Edward married Pamela Jean **CLARK** and had 3 children, Ashley Ann, James Christian and Abigail Lynn
 iii- **BURDETT** Paula Deanna married Gabriel Catalin RUSU
 iv- **BURDETT** Rebecca Ann married Kenneth Paul DELANO

891- **CROSSETT** Francis Paul (*Pauline H. Burdett, Anna D. Russell, Hulda Nicholson, Sally, William, Joshua, Joshua, Jasper, John*) was born October 4, 1923 in Fremont, NY son of James Howard **CROSSETT** and Pauline Hulda **BURDETT** and died February 28, 2004 in Elmira, NY. He married January 28, 1946 in Canisteo, NY Maxine **HOWE** born May 26, 1925 in Canisteo, NY and died March 21, 2000 in Bath, NY.
Children:
 i- **CROSSETT** Lawrence Paul married Carolyn **HEDDRON** and had 3 children Tracy Lynn, Kelly Nichole and Michael Lawrence
 ii- **CROSSETT** David born January 18, 1948 and died March 3, 1952
 iii- **CROSSETT** Thomas married Martha **BONACOLE** and had 3 children Jennifer L., Janice Patricia and Thomas David

892- **CROSSETT** Paulina Hulda (*Pauline H. Burdett, Anna D Russell, Hulda Nicholson, Sally, William, Joshua, Joshua, Jasper, John*) was born April 25, 1926 in Hornell, NY daughter of James Howard **CROSSETT** and Pauline Hulda **BURDETT** and died December 29, 2004 in Almond, NY. She married Lewis Halsey **WHEELER** who was born July 15, 1925 and died November 2, 2004.
Children:
 i- **WHEELER** Carol Lynn married Jeffrey Brian **CHAPIN** and had 2 children Adell Kimberly and Daniel Wade
 ii- **WHEELER** Michael Scot married Mary E. **BEIHL** and had 3 children Carrie Lynn, Michelle and Stephanie Diane
 iii- **WHEELER** Stephen David married Barbara Jean **O'MALLEY** and had 2 children Emily Rachel and Jessica Halsey

893- **CROSSETT** James Howard Jr. (*Pauline H. Burdett, Anna D. Russell, Hulda Nicholson, Sally, William, Joshua, Joshua, Jasper, John*) was born in Hornell, NY son of James Howard **CROSSETT** and Pauline Hulda **BURDETT**. He married Katherine M. **JOHONN**
Children:
 i- **CROSSETT** Mark James married Barbara **POWERS** and had 2 children Jason William and Katie Elizabeth
 ii- **CROSSETT** John Ray married Patti **JAY** and had 3 children Andrew Jay, Daniel James and Breanne Louise
 iii- **CROSSETT** Mary Kay married Alan D. **GOULD** and had 3 children David Alan, Benjamin James and April Marie

iv- CROSSETT Linda Ann married James Grafton WALLACE and had 2 children James Crossett and Peter Gratton

894- SMITH Anna Nancy (*Beatrice Burdett, Anna D. Russell, Hulda Nicholson, Sally, William, Joshua, Joshua, Jasper, John*) was born in Steuben Co. NY daughter of Herman SMITH and Beatrice Kathleen BURDETT. She married July 15, 1961 in Corning, NY John H. MILLER son of John B. MILLER and Anna MC KEOWN.
Children:
 i- MILLER Keith Burdett
 ii- MILLER Kevin Thomas

895- WAY Betty Jane (*Abby Burdett, Anna D. Russell, Hulda Nicholson, Sally, William, Joshua, Joshua, Jasper, John*) was born in NY State daughter of Harold WAY and Abby Lena BURDETT. She married Gerald BARTON son of Walter BARTON and Mary DE RUYSCHER.
Children:
 i- BARTON Joyce Ann married Mathew WAGNER and had 2 children Paul Mathew who married Debbie TUCHIRELLO. She married (2) Lewis TIEKE and had son Jeffrey Gerald
 ii- BARTON Steven Gerald married Nancy FETTER and had 3 children, Michael Steven, Randall Walter and Adam Douglas

896- WAY Carol Ann (*Abby Burdett, Anna D. Russell, Hulda Nicholson, Sally, William, Joshua, Joshua, Jasper, John*) was born in NY State daughter of Harold WAY and Abby Lena BURDETT. She married James JACKSON son of Willett C. JACKSON and Nellie BOWEN.
Children:
 i- JACKSON Diane Carol married Ronald PERRY and had 2 children Eric and Ryan Way
 ii- JACKSON James Harold married Laurie Ann MAHER and had 3 children Christopher James, Joseph Charles and William Arlis
 iii- JACKSON Jean Lynnette married Thomas J. KUTER and had 3 children, Andrew James, Karol Ann and Lauren Jean
 iv- JACKSON Joan Denise married Dickson HAWTHORNE son of James HAWTHORNE Judith Ann FLOOD and had 3 children Jordan Denise, James Colby and Janelle Rae

897- BURDETT Joanne Louise (*James W. Burdett, Anna D. Russell, Hulda Nicholson, Sally, William, Joshua, Joshua, Jasper, John*) was born in NY State daughter of James Wilson BURDETT and Dorothy Grace BEECHER. She married (1) Chester Grant BERGER son of Dana Grant BERGER and Ruth Charlotte KIEFER. She married (2) Lowell CONRAD son of George CONRAD and Gladys MACHAN.
Children by first marriage:
 i- BERGER Diana Jo married Jeffrey COTTOM and had daughter Alysia Ray

226

ii- **BERGER** Michelle Louise
Child by second marriage:
   iii- **CONRAD** Elizabeth Julianna

898-   **BURDETT** James Wilson II (*James W. Burdett, Anna D. Russell, Hulda Nicholson, Sally, William Joshua, Joshua, Jasper, John*) was born in Steuben Co. NY son of James Wilson **BURDETT** and Dorothy Grace **BEECHER**. He married (1) Jeannette **ASHBY** daughter of Chester **ASHBY** and Alma **JOHNSON** and married (2) Lucille **PARAVATO** daughter of Frank **PARAVATO** and Josephine **DI SALVA**.
Children by first marriage:
   i- **BURDETT** James W. III married (1) Mary **MORSE** daughter of John **MORSE** and Audrey **HENDERSON** and married (2) Veronica **FOCHT** and had daughter Alexandria Dorothy
   ii- **BURDETT** Lisa Dorothy married Thomas Victor **MIKOLAJCZYK** son of Frank **MIKOLAJCZYK** and Barbara **GROWER** and had 2 children Allyssa Nicole and Morgan Brittany
   iii- **BURDETT** Barbara Alma married Jack Erwin **RYAN** son of Raymond **RYAN** and Mary **MAC MASTERS**
   iv- **BURDETT** Julia Ann Burns

899-   **BURDETT** Steven Murray (*Elmer P. Burdett, Mary Elsie Russell, Hulda Nicholson, Sally, William, Joshua, Joshua, Jasper, John*) was born August 24, 1938 in Hornell, NY son of Elmer Paul **BURDETT** and Cora Louise **STEVENS**. He married Carol Jane **MEEKS** born December 25, 1940 daughter of Francis **MEEKS** and Phyllis **WEAVER**.
Children:
   i- **BURDETT** Kathleen Marie married Timothy R. **KEOHANE** son of James and Helen **KEOHANE** and had 3 children Eva Grace, Joel Timothy and Cora Hope
   ii- **BURDETT** Mathew Steven married Laurel Ann **BIENIAS** and had 2 children, Broderick Mathew and Colin Judd

900-   **DAVIS** Charles Fay (*Mildred W. Burdett, Mary E. Russell, Hulda Nicholson, Sally, William, Joshua, Joshua, Jasper, John*) was born in Steuben Co. NY son of Lewis Fay **DAVIS** and Mildred Wadsworth **BURDETT**. He married Grace G. **GOODWIN**.
Children:
   i- **DAVIS** Kevin C.
   ii- **DAVIS** Leslie G. married Kim **KENDRICK** and had 2 children, Angela Hope and Andrew. She married (2) Greg **PORTER**

901-   **DAVIS** Herman (*Mildred W. Burdett, Mary E. Russell, Hulda Nicholson, Sally, William, Joshua, Joshua, Jasper, John*) was born in Steuben Co. NY son of Lewis Fay **DAVIS** and Mildred Wadsworth **BURDETT**. He married Erla Jean **MC GREGOR**.
Children:
   i- **DAVIS** Laurie Ann married Michael **WHITEMAN** and had a son Joshua
   ii- **DAVIS** Jeffrey Scott

902- DAVIS Dorothy June (*Mildred W. Burdett, Mary E. Russell, Hulda Nicholson, Sally, William, Joshua, Joshua, Jasper, John*) was born in Steuben Co. NY daughter of Lewis Fay DAVIS and Mildred Wadsworth BURDETT. She married Stanley Kyle SMITH son of Ernest C. SMITH and Mary M. OATLEY.
Children:
1027-    i- SMITH Carol Evelyn
1028-    ii- SMITH Lowell Charles
1029-    iii- SMITH Marcia Faye
1030-    iv- SMITH Joanne Kyle
1031-    v- SMITH Dale Stanley
         vi- SMITH Allyn Oatley born April 10, 1954 and died November 11, 1973

903-    MUNRO William Duncan (*Ethel Vance Burdett, Mary E. Russell, Hulda Nicholson, Sally, William, Joshua, Joshua, Jasper, John*) was born October 28, 1829 in Old Westbury, NY son of Duncan Ross MUNRO and Ethel Vance BURDETT and died January 1972. He married June G. (unknown maiden name)
Children:
         i- MUNRO Cameron Douglas married Joy MILHAVEN and had 2 children William Duncan and Allison Joy
         ii- MUNRO Elizabeth Vance married (1) Arthur VON KELLER and married (2) Mr. CONRAD, one child by second marriage Sarah Elizabeth CONRAD
         iii- MUNRO Janet Ellen married Christopher Brent COLEMAN and had 2 children Jordan Elyse and Rachel Ann

904-    MUNRO Alan Ross (*Ethel Vance Burdett, Mary E. Russell, Hulda Nicholson, Sally, William, Joshua, Joshua, Jasper, John*) was born in NY State son of Duncan Ross MUNRO and Ethel Vance BURDETT . He married Connie (unknown maiden name).
Children:
         i- MUNRO Duncan
         ii- MUNRO Peter
         iii- MUNRO Donald
         iv- MUNRO Carol
         v- MUNRO Jean
         vi- MUNRO Meg
         vii- MUNRO Christopher

905-    BURDETT Robert Duncan (*Charles K. Burdett, Mary E. Russell, Hulda Nicholson, Sally, William, Joshua, Joshua, Jasper, John*) was born September 5, 1928 in Hornell, NY son of Charles Kenneth BURDETT and Margaret HALL and died September 16, 2001 in Sayre, Pa. He married Caroline GAFFNEY daughter of Francis F. GAFFNEY and Ann Marie BATES.
One child:
         i- BURDETT Karen married William BUSH and had son Bryan

228

906- **BURDETT** Susan Jo (*Charles K. Burdett, Mary E. Russell, Hulda Nicholson, Sally, William, Joshua, Joshua, Jasper, John*) was born in Steuben Co. NY daughter of Charles Kenneth **BURDETT** and Elizabeth Neree **HODSON**. She married David **WILLIS**.
Children:
    i- **WILLIS** Michael Ryan
    ii- **WILLIS** Andrea Linnie married Christopher **COOKE**
    iii- **WILLIS** Barbara Lehigh married Jeffrey L. **ROBINSON** and had 2 children
Allison Kaye and Kelly

907- **CONDERMAN** Betty Jayne (*Gordon Conderman, Addie, Alonzo, Abram, William, Joshua, Joshua, Jasper, John*) was born December 2, 1918 daughter of Gordon **CONDERMAN** and Ethel **JAYNES**. She married December 12, 1941 Ervin **LYKE** born September 9, 1919.
Children:
    i- **LYKE** Walter Ervin born May 6, 1948 and died same day
    ii- **LYKE** Andrea Diane born November 19, 1949

908- **CONDERMAN** Doris Erva (*Gordon Conderman, Addie, Alonzo, Abram, William, Joshua, Joshua, Jasper, John*) was born February 14, 1920 daughter of Gordon **CONDERMAN** and Ethel **JAYNES**. She married October 12, 1938 Wilbur **MEAD** who was born April 23, 19__.
Children:
    i- **MEAD** Larry Ray born April 30, 1941
    ii- **MEAD** Roger Gordon born December 21, 1943

909- **ROE** Leroy Edwin (*Gertrude Roberts, Nellie, Alonzo, Abram, William, Joshua, Joshua, Jasper, John*) was born February 5, 1927 son of Clayton Joseph **ROE** and Gertrude Mae **ROBERTS** and died December 1978. He married December 17, 1949 Dorothy Lee **STEWART** who was born September 8, 1931/2.
Adopted children:
    i- **ROE** Jon Stewart born June 2, 1953. He married May 18, 1988 Gretchen (unknown maiden name)
    ii- **ROE** Terry Michael born March 1, 1958 He married (1) Robin (unknown maiden name) and had 2 children. They were divorced and he had a child with Tammy Freeman Boyle (White), Brandi Lee born September 2, 1995. In June 2004 he married Patti

910- **ROE** Keith Leon (*Gertrude Roberts, Nellie, Alonzo, Abram, William, Joshua, Joshua, Jasper, John*) was born May 15, 1929 in Hornell, NY son of Clayton Joseph **ROE** and Gertrude **ROBERTS** and died June 4, 2004. He married October 8, 1955 Janet Elizabeth **SLATER** born April 4, 1931/2.
Children:
    i- **ROE** Mark Dean born September 23, 1956 in N. Hornell. He married July 1977 Stephanie (unknown maiden name) and had 2 children Kristen and Stephen
    ii- **ROE** Kyle Allen born December 31, 1957 in N. Hornell. He married in

Denver, Col. Doreen **PETERSON**, 1 son Sean born 1998
    iii- **ROE** Todd Jay born March 2, 1964, no children

911-     **ROE** Audrey Lillian (*Gertrude Roberts, Nellie, Alonzo, Abram, William, Joshua, Joshua, Jasper, John*) was born February 8, 1931 in Hornell, NY daughter of Clayton Joseph **ROE** and Gertrude Mae **ROBERTS**. She married (1) October 10, 1958 Ernest Roger **MORRIS** born September 27, 1934. They were divorced in 1972 and she married (2) Dwight Francis **MILES**. They were divorced.
Children by first marriage:
    i- **MORRIS** Joseph Ernest born May 12, 1960
    ii- **MORRIS** James Andrew born June 5, 1964
    iii- **MORRIS** Kathleen Elizabeth born March 17, 1970

912-     **ROE** Alma Jeannette (*Gertrude Roberts, Nellie, Alonzo, Abram, William, Joshua, Joshua, Jasper, John*) was born September 6, 1932 in Hornell, NY daughter of Clayton Joseph **ROE** and Gertrude **ROBERTS**. She married April 12, 1953 Edwin Richard **DUNHAM** born August 22, 1931/2 and died December 11, 1990. He was cremated and his ashes are buried in Maine or New Brunswick, Canada.
Children:
1032-     i- **DUNHAM** Christine Kay born February 17, 1953
    ii- **DUNHAM** Cynthia Sue born January 16, 1955, married Michael **MAJESKY**.
They were divorced, no children
1033-     iii- **DUNHAM** Rebecca Lynn born August 15, 1957
    iv- **DUNHAM** David Richard born February 2, 1960, married Beth **BELDEN** born March 16, 1961 and had 1 child David Richard Jr. born February 13, 1986 in Syracuse, NY

913-     **ROE** Carol Anita (*Gertrude Roberts, Nellie, Alonzo, Abram, William, Joshua, Joshua, Jasper, John*) was born February 27, 1946 in Hornell, NY daughter of Clayton Joseph **ROE** and Gertrude **ROBERTS**. She married May 27, 1967 Robert Royce **DICKEY** who was born November 4, 1945.
Children:
1034-     i- **DICKEY** Karen Elizabeth born February 5, 1969
1035-     ii- **DICKEY** Heather Michele born October 14, 1971

914-     **SMITH** Lawrence Edwin (*Clifford, Alonzo Jr., Alonzo, Abram, William, Joshua, Joshua, Jasper, John*) was born October 3, 1927 in Hornell, NY son of Clifford **SMITH** and Julia Emma **LAIN**. He married June 24, 1951 in Almond, NY Loretta Jeanette **FRENCH** born June 1, 1933. No issue.

915-     **SMITH** Carolyn Jean (*Clifford, Alonzo Jr., Alonzo, Abram, William, Joshua, Joshua, Jasper, John*) was born March 31, 1930 in Hornell, NY daughter of Clifford **SMITH** and Julia Emma **LAIN** and died July 2, 2002. She married George Edward **DOLL** born December 5, 1930. They were divorced and she married (2) August 5, 1953 Ebenezer **MASON** in Bath, NY who died August 2004.

Children by first marriage born in Hornell, NY:
> i- **DOLL** Carol Ann born November 15, 1950
> ii- **DOLL** Stephen Edward born January 18, 1952
> iii- **DOLL** Daniel John born December 10, 1953

Children by second marriage born in Hornell, NY:
> i- **MASON** Heather Julia born April 21, 1976

916- **SMITH** Elaine Gwendolyn (*Clifford, Alonzo Jr., Alonzo, Abram, William, Joshua, Joshua, Jasper, John*) was born January 23, 1938 in Hornell, NY daughter of Clifford **SMITH** and Julia Emma **LAIN**. She married May 30, 1957 in Howard, NY Francis William **O'DELL** who was born October 30, 1935 in Woodhull, NY and died February 28, 1991, buried in the O'Dell family cemetery in Howard.
Children:
> i- **O'DELL** Francis William Jr. born December 25, 1958 in Philadelphia, Pa. He has 1 daughter Melissa Anne who married July 10, 1999 Steven Robert **CODDINGTON**.
> ii- **O'DELL** Timothy Wayne born February 5, 1960 in N. Hornell, NY
> iii- **O'DELL** Jonathan Warren born December 18, 1961 in N. Hornell, NY
> iv- **O'DELL** Geoffrey Wade born April 12, 1963 in Hornell, NY. He married July 10, 1999 Cheryl Lynn **GREEN** who had a daughter Rachel Ann born September 4, 1996. They have 1 son Lucas Isaiah born October 20, 2004.
> v- **O'DELL** Darlene Kaye born June 9, 1964 in Hornell, NY

917- **SMITH** Joan Coralee (*Clifford, Alonzo Jr., Alonzo, Abram, William, Joshua, Joshua, Jasper, John*) was born August 4, 1944 in Hornell, NY daughter of Clifford **SMITH** and Julia Emma **LAIN**. She married January 26, 1962 in Howard, NY Wayne Douglas **MASON** born September 17, 1939.
Children born in Hornell, NY:
> i- **MASON** Donna Marie born July 17, 1962 and died December 17, 1991
> ii- **MASON** Julie Ann born July 10, 1963 married Clarence **GRANGER**. They have 2 children Jill Marie born March 5, 1981 who married July 26, 2004 David **JACKSON** and have 2 children, Dawson Hunter born May 10 2002 and Derek Jacob born August 4, 2005. David has a son Devon Jon born July 31, 1992. Also, a daughter Lida who married ____ **SEAMAN** who have 2 children Toree Leanne born August 27, 2001 and William Michael **DELANEY** born September 2, 2004.
> iii- **MASON** Wayne Douglas Jr. born October 20, 1966, married October 2, 1993 Rae Ann **WIDMER**. They have 2 children Dustin Robert born August 17, 1995 and Francesca Marie born May 10, 1997

918- **CHAPMAN** Louisa Maria (*Arthur Griffin, Bertha, Alonzo, Abram, William, Joshua, Joshua, Jasper, John*) was born February 12, 1970 daughter of Frances Rosetta **CHAPMAN** and step-daughter of Arthur Wendell **GRIFFIN**. She married July 9, 1888 Frank **HEBERER**
Children:
> i- **HEBERER** James Lee born December 8, 1986

ii- **HEBERER** Sara Jean born December 30, 1988
iii- **HEBERER** Tricia Ann born September 22, 1992

919-    **GRIFFIN** Linda Marie (*Lyle Griffin, Bertha, Alonzo, Abram, William Joshua, Joshua, Jasper, John*) was born May 25, 1950 and adopted by Lyle **GRIFFIN** and Marie Florence **NORTHRUP**. She married Tom **BERRY**. They were divorced and she married (2) George **DOOLEY**
One child:
        i- **DOOLEY** George David

920-    **GRIFFIN** Barbara Sue (*Lyle Griffin, Bertha, Alonzo, Abram, William, Joshua, Joshua, Jasper, John*) was born in Steuben Co. NY and adopted by Lyle **GRIFFIN** and Marie Florence **NORTHRUP**. She married Steve **COVELL**. They were divorced and she married (2) Steven **BOSSARD** who was born October 21, 1956 son of James **BOSSARD** and Bonnie **CARLIN** and died 2002 in Hornell, NY. They were divorced and she married (3) Arlie **HARWOOD**
Child by first marriage:
        i- **COVELL** Kelly
Child by second marriage:
        ii- **BOSSARD** Tammy born March 10, 1981 in Hornell, NY

921-    **COOK** Sandra Lee (*Bernice Griffin, Bertha, Alonzo, Abram, William, Joshua, Joshua, Jasper, John*) was born March 16, 1943 daughter of James Charles **COOK** and Bernice **GRIFFIN**. She married January 14, 1961 John C. **JACKSON** born March 26, 1941.
Children:
        i- **JACKSON** James Milton born May 24, 1961
        ii- **JACKSON** Lori Louise born August 11, 1963
        iii- **JACKSON** John C. Jr. born July 8, 1964

922-    **COOK** Duane Charles (*Bernice Griffin, Bertha, Alonzo, Abram, William, Joshua, Joshua, Jasper, John*) was born November 20, 1945 son of James Charles **COOK** and Bernice **GRIFFIN**. He married July 26, 1968 Donna Lynn **BROWN** born July 10, 1948.
Children:
        i- **COOK** Heather Therese born November 16, 1970
        ii- **COOK** Christopher Garland born July 23, ____
        iii- **COOK** Heidi Lynn born July 16, ____

923-    **COOK** Brenda Sue (*Bernice Griffin, Bertha, Alonzo, Abram, William, Joshua, Joshua, Jasper, John*) was born July 16, 1947 dau of James Charles **COOK** and Bernice **GRIFFIN**. She married July 24, ____ Warren Ross **CLINE** born November 30, ____.
Children:
        i- **CLINE** Kimberly Sue born March 28, 1967
        ii- **CLINE** David Jeffery born April 29, 1968

iii- **CLINE** Lisa Ann born September 4, 1970
iv- **CLINE** Jason Ross born May 11, 1973

924-     **COOK** Darlene Marie (*Bernice Griffin, Bertha, Alonzo, Abram, William, Joshua, Joshua, Jasper, John*) was born January 29, 1950 dau of James Charles **COOK** and Bernice **GRIFFIN**. She married November 4, 1967 Randie Norman **BREWER** born November 13, 1945.
Children:
      i- **BREWER** Beth Ann born March 2, 1968
      ii- **BREWER** Michelle Rene born March 12, 1971

925-     **COOK** Sheila Dawn (*Bernice Griffin, Bertha, Alonzo, Abram, William, Joshua, Joshua, Jasper, John*) was born April 4, 1954 daughter of James Charles **COOK** and Bernice **GRIFFIN**. She married July 7, ____ Robert Eugene **BROWN** born January 19, ____.
Children:
      i- **BROWN** Rene Eileen born December 10, 1974
      ii- **BROWN** Robin Ellane born November 4, 1976
      iii- **BROWN** Ryan Eric born May 23, 1978
      iv- **BROWN** Rustin Edmond born May 13, 1980

926-     **CRAMER** Wendy Lou (*Luella Griffin, Bertha, Alonzo, Abram, William, Joshua, Joshua, Jasper, John*) was born September 6, 1946 dau of Alva William **CRAMER** and Luella **GRIFFIN**. She married May 8, 1965 Raymond Arnold **WHEATON** who was born May 5, 1940 and died August 8, 1993.
Children:
      i- **WHEATON** Julie Lynn born July 19, 1967
      ii- **WHEATON** Christina Lee born June 22, 1971
      iii- **WHEATON** William Arnold born November 11, 1972

927-     **CRAMER** David Lee (*Louella Griffin, Bertha, Alonzo, Abram, William, Joshua, Joshua, Jasper, John*) was born July 20, 1951 son of Alva William **CRAMER** and Louella **GRIFFIN**. He married Elizabeth **JONES** born April 4, ____. They were divorced and he married (2) Maty **WAE** born November 13, ____. They were divorced and he married (3) Kathy **WALTON**.
Children by first marriage:
      i- **CRAMER** Amy Lee born September 26, 1969
      ii- **CRAMER** Elizabeth (step daughter) born June 21, ----
Children by second mariage:
      iii- **CRAMER** Walter (adopted) born September 24, 1980
      iv- **CRAMER** Corina born April 29, 1983
Children by third marriage:
      v- **CRAMER** Ashley born February 12, ____
      vi- **CRAMER** David Arthur born March 3, 1991

928- **CRAMER** Stephen Louis (*Luella Griffin, Bertha, Alonzo, Abram, William, Joshua, Joshua, Jasper, John*) was born June 15, 1960 son of Alva William **CRAMER** and Luella **GRIFFIN**. He married Melody _____ born December 1, ___. They were divorced and he married (2) Karen **WILKINS** born May 15, ___.
Children by first marriage:
      i- **CRAMER** Stephen Jr. born February 1, 1981
      ii- **CRAMER** Jason born October 7, 1983
Children by second marriage:
      iii- **WILKINS** Julie Ann (step daughter) born _____
      iv- **CRAMER** Garrett born _____

929- **BEATTIE** Virginia Eileen (*Leo Beattie, Alta Fisher, Flora, Abram, William, Joshua, Joshua, Jasper, John*) was born July 23, 1918 in Hornell, NY daughter of Leo **BEATTIE** and Catherine **CORNISH** and died December 9, 2003 in Hornell, NY. She married December 17, 1936 in Letchworth, NY Ernest Demeral **WISE** who was born June 9, 1913 in Avoca, NY son of William **WISE** and Emma **SHILOH** and died April 14, 1975 in Hornell, NY. They are buried in Hillside cemetery in Canisteo, NY
Children born in Hornell, NY:
1036-    i- **WISE** Douglas Milton born October 11, 1937
      ii- **WISE** Gary Ernest born June 1940 (stillborn), buried Mt. Pleasant cemetery in Howard, NY
      iii- **WISE** Carolyn Eileen born June 1941, died November 26, 1941, buried Mt. Pleasant cemetery in Howard, NY
1037-    iv- **WISE** Patricia Ann born July 12, 1944

930- **BEATTIE** Donald Sherman (*Leo Beattie, Alta Fisher, Flora, Abram, William, Joshua, Joshua, Jasper, John*) was born May 20, 1921 in Hornell, NY son of Leo **BEATTIE** and Catherine **CORNISH** and died March 6, 2000 in Alexandria, Va. He married in Thelma, Mass. Virginia **MAQUIRE** who was born September 4, 1923 in Pittsburgh, Pa. and died March 6, 2000 in Alexandria, Va. They are buried in Hillside cemetery in Canisteo, NY
Children:
      i- **BEATTIE** James born October 5, 1955 in Cleveland, Oh.
      ii- **BEATTIE** Thomas born May 26, 1958 in Cleveland, Oh.
      iii- **BEATTIE** Donald born May 21, 1964 in Alexandria, Va.

931- **BEATTIE** Lois (*Leo Beattie, Alta Fisher, Flora, Abram, William, Joshua, Joshua, Jasper, John*) was born July 27, 1923 in Canisteo, NY daughter of Leo **BEATTIE** and Catherine **CORNISH** and died in Mc Auley Manor in N. Hornell, NY November 5, 2002. She married August 6, 1945 in Canisteo, NY Donald H. **MC KEE** who was born June 14, 1922 in Grover, Pa. son of Charles **MC KEE** and Florence **BALTZER** and died January 13, 2004 in Bath, NY. They are buried in Bath National cemetery.
Children:
      i- **MC KEE** Daniel H. married July 25, 1981 Brenda Jean **FELTON**

ii- **MC KEE** Donald James married May 12, 1972 in Resquehoning, Pa. Mary Theresa **BALES**
iii- **MC KEE** David
iv- **MC KEE** Michael married Melissa **POMEROY**
v- **MC KEE** Barry Lee
vi- **MC KEE** Alan J. married May 29, 1982 in Canisteo, NY Rene Marie **FORSHAY**

932- **POST** Marjorie (*Isabel G. Beattie, Alta Fisher, Flora, Abram, William, Joshua, Joshua, Jasper, John*) was born after 1930 and died in Penn Yan, NY. She married Milton **UPDYKE**.
Child:
i- **UPDYKE** Milton

933- **CLANCY** Barbara Ann (*Pauline Gates, Lena, Hobart, Abram, William, Joshua, Joshua, Jasper, John*) was born August 11, 1943 in Hornell, NY daughter of Thomas Scott **CLANCY** and Pauline Alveretta **GATES**. She married (1) January 13, 1962 Reginald E. **NELSON** who was born December 31, 1939 son of Earl **NELSON** and Lillian **RIFFLE**. She married (2) August 24, 1974 George F. **CLARKE**.
Children:
i- **NELSON** Richard Thomas born July 12, 1962. He married April 27, 1996 Inge and had one daughter Hanna Josephine
ii- **NELSON** Jeffrey Earl born September 15, 1963
iii- **NELSON** Chandra Elaine born July 7, 1969. She married March 9, 1991 Charles Mark **STULL** son of David **STULL** and Maria **RUOCCO**. They have one son Tyler Bryon born February 24, 1994 and 1 daughter Giavonna Natalie born August 9, 2005
iv- **CLARKE** Steven David born February 24, 1977

934- **CLANCY** Dianne Kathleen (*Pauline Gates, Lena, Hobart, Abram, William, Joshua, Joshua, Jasper, John*) was born February 24, 1946 in Hornell, NY daughter of Thomas Scott **CLANCY** and Pauline Alveretta **GATES**. She married July 10, 1964 J. Thomas **RECOTTA** who was born June 16, 1942 and died April 13, 2002.
Children:
i- **RECOTTA** Robert Thomas born January 21, 1965. He married September 9, 1991 Carrie **STAINBROOK** daughter of Keith and Linda **STAINBROOK** and had 1 daughter Emily Rose. He married (2) Ann (Beecher) **WILSON** daughter of Terry and Pat **BEECHER**. She had 3 children Joshua, Ellen and Jacob.
ii- **RECOTTA** James Paul born February 16, 1968

935- **CLANCY** Elizabeth Jane (*Pauline Gates, Lena, Hobart, Abram, William, Joshua, Joshua, Jasper, John*) was born May 25, 1950 in Hornell, NY daughter of Thomas Scott **CLANCY** and Pauline Alveretta **GATES**. She married October 24, 1970 Lucian **ABRUZZO** son of Benjamin and Julia **ABRUZZO** who died November 20, 1986.
Children:

i- ABRUZZO Benjamin Scott born January 9, 1972
ii- ABRUZZO Natalie Shannon born May 9, 1974

936- **BUTLER** Koeth Erwin (*Milton Butler, Edith, Hobart, Abram, William, Joshua, Joshua, Jasper, John*) was born November 15, 1934 in Knoxville, Pa. son of Milton **BUTLER** and Eva **HARRINGTON**. He married August 15, 1953 Marjorie **PROTZMAN** born December 28, 1933 in Troupsburg, New York.
Children:
1038-     i- **BUTLER** Lorry Dean born September 10, 1957
1039-    ii- **BUTLER** Larena Jean born June 12, 1959

937- **BUTLER** Daryl Merlin (*Milton Butler, Edith, Hobart, Abram, William, Joshua, Joshua, Jasper, John*) was born March 23, 1941 in Knoxville, Pa. son of Milton **BUTLER** and Eva **HARRINGTON**. He married January 16, 1963 Portia Clair **ROTH**.
Children:
1040-     i- **BUTLER** Bryan Mark born June 13, 1964
1041-    ii- **BUTLER** Cheryl Suzanne born January 18, 1966
1042-   iii- **BUTLER** Andrea Kay born August 11, 1967
         iv- **BUTLER** James Daryl born August 12, 1970, married May 29, 1995 Melissa **BRIGGS**

938- **BUTLER** Kean Allen (*Milton Butler, Edith, Hobart, Abram, William, Joshua, Joshua, Jasper, John*) was born June 12, 1943 in Knoxville, Pa. son of Milton **BUTLER** and Eva **HARRINGTON**. He married January 23, 1965 June **EGGLESTON** who died October 16, 1999. He married (2) February 8, 2003 Connie **OSBORN**.
Children:
1043-     i- **BUTLER** DeAnn born September 10, 1965
1044-    ii- **BUTLER** Thomas Alan born March 15, 1969
         iii- **BUTLER** David born August 2, 1973

939- **BUTLER** Wyona Jean (*Milton Butler, Edith, Hobart, Abram, William, Joshua, Joshua, Jasper, John*) was born April 15, 1944 in Knoxville, Pa. daughter of Milton **BUTLER** and Eva **HARRINGTON**. She married September 9, 1961 Claude **MARSH** who died January 20, 1993.
Children:
1045-     i- **MARSH** Kelly Dawn born April 27, 1962
1046-    ii- **MARSH** Darla born February 21, 1964
         iii- **MARSH** Steven Bruce born September 6, 1966 and died same day

940- **BUTLER** Kermit David (*Milton Butler, Edith, Hobart, Abram, William, Joshua, Joshua, Jasper, John*) was born Feruary 14, 1946 in Knoxville, Pa. son of Milton **BUTLER** and Eva **HARRINGTON**. He married November 20, 1971 Rebecca **KLING**.
Children:
         i- **BUTLER** Bobby Jo born September 1977

ii- **BUTLER** Joshua born March 21, 1981

941- **SMITH** Sandra Janine (*Ernest, Frank, Hobart, Abram, William, Joshua, Joshua, Jasper, John*) was born February 9, 1961 in Hornell, NY daughter of Ernest G. **SMITH** and Fern Buchinger **HANKINS**. She is presently living in Wellsville, NY.
Children:
    i- **HURD** Scot Lee born June 11, 1985
    ii- **HURD** Shannon Marie born January 15, 1988

942- **SMITH** Steven Franklin (*Ernest, Frank, Hobart, Abram, William, Joshua, Joshua, Jasper, John*) was born January 24, 1965 in Hornell, NY son of Ernest G. **SMITH** and Fern (**BUCHINGER**) **HANKINS**. He married October 18, 1986 Denise **LARNARD** born July 16, 1969 in Ft. Dix, New Jersey daughter of Mark **LARNARD** and Donna **BURNS**. They are presently living in Hornell, NY
Children:
    i- **SMITH** Amanda Marie born January 30, 1987
    ii- **SMITH** Brandy Nicole born July 28, 1988
    iii- **SMITH** Steven Mark born May 25, 1990
    iv- **SMITH** Michael Glen born February 2, 1992
    v- **SMITH** Mathew Logan born January 30, 2000
    vi- **SMITH** Timothy Joseph born January 14, 2002

943- **JACKSON** Edward Frank (*Mary, Frank, Hobart, Abram, William, Joshua, Joshua, Jasper, John*) was born January 25, 1948 in Rochester, New York son of Mary Louise **SMITH**. He was adopted by her husband Eugene G. **JACKSON**. He married (1) July 10, 1969 Kathleen **WILSON** born December 7; 1951 daughter of Donald and Leola **WILSON**. They were divorced and he married (2) Fay Aundry **MERRILL** daughter of Albert **MERRILL** and Mildred **DUVALL**. They were divorced and he is presently living in Macedon, New York,
Children by first marriage:
    i- **JACKSON** Daniel Lee born January 13, 1970 in Newark, NY
    ii- **JACKSON** Michael Scot born June 21 1973 in Clifton Springs, NY
Child by second marriage:
1047-     iii- **JACKSON** Carrie Lynn born July 10, 1977 in Clifton Springs, NY

944- **JACKSON** Allen Eugene (*Mary, Frank, Hobart, Abram, William, Joshua, Joshua, Jasper, John*) was born May 25, 1953 in Rochester, NY son of Eugene G. **JACKSON** and Mary L. **SMITH**. He married (1) April 29, 1972 in Palmyra, NY Debria **SIMMONS** born March 25, 1954 daughter of William and Delerea **SIMMONS**. They were divorced and he married (2) June 23, 1983 Gail (**DURKEE**) **LENT** who was born June 11, 1954 daughter of Ira **DURKEE** and Ardith **COOK** and died September 10, 1999. He married (3) November 1, 2003 Betsey **LOREN** who was born January 3, 1960. She has 3 daughters Melissa, Crystal and Sandy **GANO** and 3 foster daughters Raychel, Amanda and Sadiemae.
Children by first marriage:

1048- i- JACKSON Caprice born September 29, 1972 in Clifton Springs, NY
1049- ii- JACKSON Joshua Allen born August 5, 1975 in Frankfurt, Germany
Children by second marriage:
  iii- JACKSON Jeromy Eugene born March 7, 1980 son of Gail and adopted by
Allen, married and has 3 children
  iv- JACKSON Kyle Paul born August 2, 1982 and died September 5, 1982. He is
buried in the Palmyra cemetery
  v- JACKSON Mary Beth born December 10, 1988 in Rochester, NY and died
September 21, 2005 in Ontario, NY. She is buried in Chateaugay, NY with her Mother.
  vi- WATERS Jeremy born August 22, 1980, is married and lives in Mi. He has a
daughter

945-    JACKSON Richard Jay (*Mary, Frank, Hobart, Abram, William, Joshua, Joshua,
Jasper, John*) was born November 21, 1954 in Rochester, NY son of Eugene G. JACKSON
and Mary L. SMITH. He married (1) November 15, 1972 in Rochester, NY Cathy
SCHEERENS born February 15, 1955. They were divorced and he married (2) October 22,
1977 Ethel WALTON They were divorced and he married (3) March 15, 1985 Deborah
BAKER BEUG. They were divorced and he married (4) December 7, 1991 Debbie (BEAL)
WHITE born May 16, 1957 in Lyons, NY daughter of Arthur BEAL and Shirley DRATT.
They are presently living in Farmington, NY.
Children by first marriage:
1050-    i- JACKSON Richard Jay II born June 11, 1973 in Rochester, NY
1051-    ii- JACKSON John Paul born June 14, 1974 in Germany
Child by second marriage:
  iii- JACKSON Amy Lynn born March 31, 1979 in Clifton Springs, NY
Children by fourth marriage:
  iv- JACKSON Amber Lynn born November 28, 1989 Newark, NY
  v- JACKSON Seth Richard born December 30, 1991 Newark, NY

946-    JACKSON Cheryl Ann (*Mary, Frank, Hobart, Abram, William, Joshua, Joshua,
Jasper, John*) was born February 11, 1956 in Rochester, NY twin daughter of Eugene G.
JACKSON and Mary L. SMITH. She married December 18, 1973 Roderick W. E. BRAY
born October 26, 1953 son of George BRAY and Ethel WEICHBRODT. They were
divorced and Cheryl is presently living in Farmington, NY
Children born in Rochester, NY:
1052-    i- BRAY Jeremy Allen born December 31, 1974
1053-    ii- BRAY Jason Eugene born September 28, 1978

947- JACKSON Gary Lee (*Mary, Frank, Hobart, Abram, William, Joshua, Joshua,
Jasper, John* ) was born February 11, 1956 in Rochester, NY twin son of Eugene, G.
JACKSON and Mary L. SMITH. He married August 11, 1979 in Newark, NY Bonnie Lee
NARY born July 30, 1957 daughter of Eric NARY and Sharon WALDORF. They were
divorced and he married (2) November 6, 2004 Tina (MAYNARD) BOADWAY born July
16, 1967 in Bronx, NY daughter of Carl MAYNARD and Elizabeth CAPOZZI. She had 2

238

children by first marriage, Cody Lloyd born August 18, 1995 and Ryan Steven born May 12, 1997. They are presently living in Farmington, NY.
One child by first marriage, adopted:
    i- JACKSON Christopher Lee born August 7, 1989

948- JACKSON Brian Ernest (*Mary, Frank, Hobart, Abram, William, Joshua, Joshua, Jasper, John*) was born February 13, 1959 in Rochester, NY son of Eugene G. JACKSON and Mary L. SMITH. He married (1) July 16, 1980 Jodie WAGER born November 13, 1960. They were divorced and he married (2) Elizabeth (NOTO) HUNTLEY born June 7, 1961 daughter of Louis NOTO and Jean KEENAN. Brian was killed in a car-train accident November 12, 1994 in Macedon, NY, buried in Lakeview cemetery in Pultneyville, NY.
Child by first marriage:
    i- JACKSON Gregory Brian born September 16, 1981
Children by second marriage:
    ii- JACKSON Ian Eugene born July 29, 1989
    iii- JACKSON Taylor Lynn born November 10, 1992

949- JACKSON Susan Elizabeth (*Mary, Frank, Hobart, Abram, William, Joshua, Joshua, Jasper, John*) was born March 26, 1960 in Rochester, NY daughter of Eugene G. JACKSON and Mary L. SMITH. She married June 23, 1979 Lonnie Allison EVERETT born October 5, 1947 in Canandaigua, NY son of Floyd EVERETT and Iona SPEARS. They were divorced and Susan is presently living in Farmington, NY. Lonnie died in a house fire at my home December 25, 1998 and is buried in Friend's cemetery in Farmington, NY.
Children:
1054-    i- EVERETT Jeffrey Aaron born November 11, 1979
    ii- EVERETT Joseph Clark born December 26, 1983
    iii- EVERETT James Lee (twin) born November 1, 1986
    iv- EVERETT Jennifer Ann (twin) born November 1, 1986

950- JACKSON Kevin Scot (*Mary, Frank, Hobart, Abram, William, Joshua, Joshua, Jasper, John*) was born April 5, 1961 in Rochester, NY son of Eugene G. JACKSON and Mary L. SMITH. He married (1) September 9, 1989 Kandi Lynn JACKSON born August 23, 1964 daughter of David JACKSON and Roberta RUSH. They were divorced and he married (2) April 23, 1995 Barbara Joan SHEA born December 15, 1960 daughter of Robert SHEA and Florence WEAVER. They are presently living in Fairport, NY.
Children by second marriage:
    i- JACKSON Robert Brian born July 31, 1995
    ii- JACKSON Kelly Shea born June 11, 1997

951- SHERMAN Arthur L. (*Lyle Sherman, Nettie Richmond, Oscar Richmond, Annanias Richmond, Anna, Joshua, Joshua, Jasper, John*) was born September 12, 1932 in Mansfield, Pa. son of Lyle B. SHERMAN and Iva SMITH and died January 26, 2004 at the Care Home in Mainesburg, Pa., buried Tioga Memorial Gardens. He married (1) September 27,

1959 Mary **YOUMANS** daughter of Ralph **YOUMANS** and married (2) Helen **SHANNON**.
Children:
  i- **SHERMAN** Curtis A.
  ii- **SHERMAN** Kimberly married Steven **AUMICK**
Also had 2 stepsons and a step daughter

952-  **SMITH** Melissa May (*Harvey, Horace W., Horace F., George W., Joshua, Platt, Joshua, Jasper, John*) was born October 7, 1966 daughter of Harvey **SMITH** and Joan **WESTBROOK**. She married Steve **PORTER**.
Children (twins):
  i- **PORTER** Krystal Mae born November 15, 1990 and died March 14, 1991, buried Lakeview cemetery in Interlaken, NY
  ii- **PORTER** Cody Austin born November 15, 1990

953-  **DIMMICK** Carlton Lewis (*Clark Dimmick, Frank Dimmick, Melissa Richards, Platt Richards, Johannah, Platt, Joshua, Jasper, John*) was born in Tompkins Co. NY son of Clark and Bessie May **DIMMICK** and died 1987. He married (1) Lorraine **PRIANO** born 1921, married (2) Kay (unknown maiden name) and (3) Theresa **CAPOZZI**.
One child:
1055-    i- **DIMMICK** Patricia born 1953

954-  **DIMMICK** Thelma (*Clark Dimmick, Frank Dimmick, Melissa Richards, Platt Richards, Johannah, Platt, Joshua, Jasper, John*) was born 1917 in Tompkins Co. NY daughter of Clark and Bessie May **DIMMICK**. She married Willard **NEISS**.
Children:
  i- **NEISS** Delos married Mae Ellen **MORTON**
1056-   ii- **NEISS** Carl

955-  **DIMMICK** Sylvia (*Clark Dimmick, Frank Dimmick, Melissa Richards, Platt Richards, Johannah, Platt, Joshua, Jasper, John*) was born 1919 in Tompkins Co. NY daughter of Clark and Bessie May **DIMMICK**. Name of spouse unknown.
Children:
1057-    i- **DIMMICK** Ronald born 1938
         ii- **DIMMICK** Melvin born 1941
1058-   iii- **DIMMICK** David A. born 1944
         iv- **CARR** Donna born 1948

956-  **AUSTIC** Clinton H. (*Dorothy Dimmick, Frank Dimmick, Melissa Richards, Platt Richards, Johannah, Platt, Joshua, Jasper, John*) was born March 15, 1918 in Tompkins Co. NY son of Herbert **AUSTIC** and Dorothy **DIMMICK** and died March 3, 2002 in Trumansburg, NY. He married April 12, 1940 Frances **WAGER**. He married (2) September 15, 1952 Mary "Fern" **HAYES** born September 8, 1932.
Child by first marriage:
1059-    i- **AUSTIC** Charles Clinton born July 28, 1940

Children by second marriage:
1060-    ii- AUSTIC Victor Eugene born February 5, 1952
1061-    iii- AUSTIC Barbara Ann born September 16, 1954
1062-    iv- AUSTIC Linda Sue born November 3, 1956
        v- AUSTIC Terry Lee born November 29, 1965
        vi- AUSTIC Cynthia Marie born April 22, 1968

957-    AUSTIC Albert William (*Dorothy Dimmick, Frank Dimmick, Melissa Richards, Platt Richards, Johannah, Platt, Joshua, Jasper, John*) was born January 20, 1920 in Trumansburg, NY son of Herbert AUSTIC and Dorothy DIMMICK and died February 8, 1996 in Trumansburg. He married April 21, 1940 Helen Elizabeth PAYNE who was born March 19, 1922 daughter of Leon R. PAYNE and Elsie FRAREY and died July 10, 1993. They are buried in Grove cemetery
Children:
1063-    i- AUSTIC Richard Edward born April 10, 1941
1064-    ii- AUSTIC William Albert born January 9, 1943
1065-    iii- AUSTIC Douglas John born April 12, 1935
1066-    iv- AUSTIC Bruce James born December 30, 1952
1067-    v- AUSTIC Herbert Leon born March 15, 1957

958-    AUSTIC Evelyn May (*Dorothy Dimmick, Frank Dimmick, Melissa Richards, Platt Richards, Johannah, Platt, Joshua Jasper, John*) was born June 10, 1923 in Tompkins Co. NY daughter of Herbert AUSTIC and Dorothy DIMMICK and died January 14, 1993. She married September 7, 1941 Earl RICHAR who was born July 3, 1922 son of Lawrence R. and Stella C. RICHAR and died July 1993. They are buried in Grove cemetery.
Children:
1068-    i- RICHAR Joyce Ann born June 14, 1940
1069-    ii- RICHAR Alfred Earl born September 18, 1943
1070-    iii- RICHAR James Edward born December 18, 1946
        iv- RICHAR Gary John born June 27, 1948 and died August 13, 1967. He served in World War II.

959-    AUSTIC Edward Frank (*Dorothy Dimmick, Frank Dimmick, Melissa Richards, Platt Richards, Johannah, Platt, Joshua, Jasper, John*) was born May 14, 1927 in Tompkins Co. NY son of Herbert AUSTIC and Dorothy DIMMICK. He married January 4, 1947 Hildreth HURLBUT born October 4, 1923.
Children:
1071-    i- AUSTIC Duwayne Edward born August 26, 1948
        ii- AUSTIC Dorothy Jean born March 18, 1952, married October 28, 1978 Timothy Carson CRANE, divorced November 29, 1983
1072-    iii- AUSTIC Janet Lee born December 9, 1955
        iv- AUSTIC Garrett born April 2, 1958

960-    BULLIVANT Robert F. (*Frances Dimmick, Frank Dimmick, Melissa Richards, Platt*

*Richards, Johannah, Platt, Joshua, Jasper, John*) was born 1916 son of John **BULLIVANT** and Frances **DIMMICK** and died 1982. He married Barbara **ARMSTRONG** born 1920. They are buried in Grove cemetery.

Children:

    i- **BULLIVANT** Ronald
    ii- **BULLIVANT** Thomas
    iii- **BULLIVANT** Douglas
    iv- **BULLIVANT** Robert

961-    **FRAZIER** Harry Joseph (*George D. Frazier, Samuel Frazier, Emeline Richards, Platt Richards, Johannah, Platt, Joshua, Jasper, John*) was born January 25, 1912 in Tompkins Co. NY son of George Daniel **FRAZIER** and Leora Maud **CALKINS** and died 1983 in Ithaca, NY. He married Helen **HAMILTON** who was born August 4, 1906 and died 1981. They are buried in Grove cemetery.

Child:
1073-    i- **FRAZIER** Harry Joseph Jr. born June 16, 1940

962-    **FRAZIER** Mary Dessie (*George D. Frazier, Samuel Frazier, Emeline Richards, Platt Richards, Johannah, Platt, Joshua, Jasper, John*) was born January 18, 1913 in Ithaca, NY daughter of George Daniel **FRAZIER** and Leora Maud **CALKINS** and died March 13, 1978 in Johnson City, NY. She married November 12, 1929 in Danby, NY Herbert Edward **UNDERWOOD** who was born January 14, 1908 son of George Fred **UNDERWOOD** and Lillian **TAYLOR** and died October 26, 1979 in Johnson City, NY. They are buried in Lisle Center cemetery.

Children:

    i- **UNDERWOOD** Lillian Bell born April 27, 1930
1074-    ii- **UNDERWOOD** George Herbert Jr. born July 7, 1931
1075-    iii- **UNDERWOOD** Charles Samuel born October 15, 1932
1076-    iv- **UNDERWOOD** Mary Leora born December 21, 1933
1077-    v- **UNDERWOOD** Barbara Jean born March 24, 1935
1078-    vi- **UNDERWOOD** Betty Lee born April 3, 1936
1079-    vii- **UNDERWOOD** Dorothy born March 20, 1937
1080-    viii- **UNDERWOOD** Frederick Curtis March 29, 1938
1081-    ix- **UNDERWOOD** Harry Sanford born February 23, 1940
    x- **UNDERWOOD** Douglas R. born April 5, 1944 married Myra Sue **WOODWARD** born July 4, 1946 and had daughter Sherrill Ann born March 14, 1965
    xi- **UNDERWOOD** Gary Lee born December 12, 1950

963-    **FRAZIER** Erwin L. (*Fred P. Frazier, Charles Frazier, Emeline Richards, Platt Richards, Johannah, Platt, Joshua, Jasper, John*) was born June 5, 1930 in Ulysses, NY son of Fred P. **FRAZIER** and Gertrude **LOVELL**. He married November 22, 1950 Carol **ADAMS** daughter of Robert E. **ADAMS**

Children:

    i- **FRAZIER** Roxanne Elizabeth born July 1957

ii- **FRAZIER** Regina born July 1957 (adopted)

964- **FRAZIER** Charles (*Fred P. Frazier, Charles Frazier, Emeline Richards, Platt Richards, Johannah, Platt, Joshua, Jasper, John*) was born April 6, 1934 in Tompkins Co. NY son of Fred P. **FRAZIER** and Gertrude **LOVELL**. He married (1) Joyce **BACON** and married (2) Elsie **LONGSTREET**.
Child by first marriage:
  i- **FRAZIER** Marty born May 5, 1957 and died November 1993
Child by second marriage:
  ii- **FRAZIER** Kristine Irene born November 26, 1968/9

965- **FRAZIER** Margaret (*Fred P. Frazier, Charles Frazier, Emeline Richards, Platt Richards, Johannah, Platt, Joshua, Jasper, John*) was born 1938 in Tompkins Co. NY daughter of Fred P. **FRAZIER** and Gertrude **LOVELL**. She married (1) Roger **HAZARD** and married (2) Alvin **BICKAL** son of George **BICKAL** of Ludlowville, NY.
Children by first marriage:
  i- **HAZARD** Terry Lynn born April 9, 1957
  ii- **HAZARD** Douglas Eugene born May 17, 1959
Child by second marriage:
  iii- **BICKAL** Karen Leilani born October 2, 1965

966- **GOYETTE** Teresa (*Ruth Edna Rathbun, Harry Poppino, Alice Amelia, Lafayette, Jasper, Joshua, Jasper, John*) was born May 10, 1962 daughter of Roger Moesel **GOYETTE** and Ruth Edna **RATHBUN**. She married (1) December 16, 1078 Ross **TERWILLIGER** and married (2) December 24, 1990 Scott **BEVERLY**.
Child by first marriage:
  i- **TERWILLIGER** Barbara Jo born April 16, 1979, married April 25, 1997 Buzzy Sherman **WEBER** born October 8, 1977 son of Walter S. **WEBER** and Ann Marie **WOOD**
Children by second marriage:
  i- **BEVERLY** Joshua Scott born March 1, 1985
  ii- **BEVERLY** Matthew born March 11, 1987

967- **RATHBUN** Bradley Lewis (*Keith Morris Rathbun, Harry Poppino, Alice Amelia, Lafayette, Jasper, Joshua, Jasper, John*) was born April 15, 1963 son of Keith Morris **RATHBUN** and Beverly **COVERT**. He married July 5, 1987 Marjorie **CHAMPION**.
One child:
  i- **RATHBUN** Bradley Lewis Jr. born April 24, 1991

968- **RATHBUN** Leon Merritt (*Glenn H. Rathbun, Harry Poppino, Alice Amelia, Lafayette, Jasper, Joshua, Jasper, John*) was born August 19, 1966 son of Glenn Harry **RATHBUN** and Loretta **HODGE**. He married Stephanie Annette Christina **CLINE**.
One child:
  i- **RATHBUN** Sarah Lee Rose born July 12, 1995

969-    MC LALLEN Ronald Alan (*Raymond M. Mc Lallen, Flora E. Mason, Adeline Ganoung, Berentha, Obadiah, Obadiah, Joshua, Jasper, John*) was born September 6, 1941 son of Raymond M. MC LALLEN and Pauline GORDON. He married Pam (unknown maiden name) born August 26, 1944.
Children:
    i- MC LALLEN Andrew born January 8, 1970
    ii- MC LALLEN Frank born July 1964 (adopted by Ronald)

970-    DEMPSEY Robert Charles (*Mary E. Mason, Herman J. Mason, Adeline Ganoung, Berentha, Obadiah, Obadiah, Joshua, Jasper, John*) was born August 2, 1931 son of Charles Eliphalet DEMPSEY and Mary Evelyn MASON. He married April 12, 1958 Margaret Jean RANDALL who was born July 14, 1930 in Cortland, NY daughter of Floyd J. RANDALL and Ruby A. PFORTER.
Children:
    i- DEMPSEY Susan Joan born January 5, 1959
    ii- DEMPSEY Christopher Charles born September 10, 1960, married Diane DEVLON and had one child
    iii- DEMPSEY Nanette Lee born July 7, 1962, married Jeffrey Woodrow STELL born September 27, 1961 son of Douglas Seward STELL and Harriet CHELL
    iv- DEMPSEY Colleen Mary born January 23, 1966, married Joseph Peter CUNNINGHAM born October 15, 1965 son of Joseph CUNNINGHAM and Elizabeth KNOPFLER. No issue

971-    DEMPSEY Norma Jean (*Mary E. Mason, Herman J. Mason, Adeline Ganoung, Berentha, Obadiah, Obadiah, Joshua, Jasper, John*) was born July 11, 1932 daughter of Charles Eliphalet DEMPSEY and Mary Evelyn MASON. She married August 22, 1954 Palmer Dexter TRUE born March 6, 1933 in Orange, NJ son of Howard Dexter TRUE and Ruth Calender MC MURTRIE. They were divorced in 1979.
Children:
1082-    i- TRUE Ellen Elizabeth born April 22, 1959 Corning, NY
1083-    ii- TRUE Bruce Dexter born January 27, 1961 Corning, NY
1084-    iii- TRUE Brian born April 27, 1966 in Elmira, NY

972-    DEMPSEY John Mason (*Mary E. Mason, Herman J. Mason, Adeline Ganoung, Berentha, Obadiah, Obadiah, Joshua, Jasper, John*) was born September 14, 1941 son of Charles Eliphalet DEMPSEY and Mary Evelyn MASON. He married April 11, 1970 in Lackawanna, NY Helen Marie KANEY born May 22, 1943 in Lackawanna, NY daughter of Terrence T. KANEY and Helen MERRICK.
Children born in Buffalo, NY:
    i- DEMPSEY John Kaney born September 11, 1974
    ii- DEMPSEY Catherine Bridget born July 25, 1979

973-    PERRY David Michael (*Esther, Olin, John B., Francis, Annanias, Obadiah, Joshua, Jasper, John*) was born September 5, 1946 in Hornell, NY son of Michael Curtis

PERRY and Esther Ellen SMITH. He married October 3, 1969 Carol SIKES.
One child:
      i- PERRY Dawn born October 4, 1972

974-    PERRY Marcia Ellen (*Esther, Olin, John B., Francis, Annanias, Obadiah, Joshua, Jasper, John*) was born July 20, 1951 in Hornell, NY daughterh of Michael Curtis PERRY and Esther Ellen SMITH. She married August 19, 1972 Richard C. DRUMM born August 19, 1972.
Children:
      i- DRUMM Geoffrey born March 3, 1976
     ii- DRUMM Timothy born July 28, 1979

975-    OLIVER Sally Jean (*Phyllis, Raymond F., Raymond F., John B., Annanias, Obadiah, Joshua, Jasper, John*) was born October 12, 1947 in Ithaca, NY daughter of Phyllis Jean SMITH and Robert Ernest OLIVER. She married September 9, 1967 Robert L. RICE.
Children:
      i- RICE Susan Jean born March 16, 1971
     ii- RICE Robert Burton born June 1, 1972

976-    PATTERSON James Michael (*Eldora J., Ralph, John B., Francis, Annanias, Obadiah, Joshua, Jasper, John*) was born August 10, 1944 in Ithaca, NY son of Miner Henry PATTERSON and Eldora Jane SMITH. He married July 22, 1967 Judy Linda DRAPPO born October 23, 1948 in Syracuse, NY
Children:
      i- PATTERSON Kristina Marie born June 20, 1971 in Annaheim, Cal.
     ii- PATTERSON Ryan Michael born September 17, 1973 in Bellflower, Cal.

977-    PATTERSON Joyce Linda (*Eldora J., Ralph, John B., Francis, Annanias, Obadiah, Joshua, Jasper, John*) was born May 3, 1947 in Ithaca, NY daughter of Miner Henry PATTERSON and Eldora Jane SMITH. She married April 2, 1966 Larry Herman KROHN born June 18, 1944 in Duluth, Mn.
Children born in Westminster, Cal.:
      i- KROHN Katrina Lynn born February 14, 1969
     ii- KROHN Keith Allen born January 18, 1971

978-    PATTERSON Jane Eldora (*Eldora J., Ralph, John B., Francis, Annanias, Obadiah, Joshua, Jasper, John*) was born January 14, 1951 in Ithaca, NY daughter of Miner Henry PATTERSON and Eldora Jane SMITH. She married October 16, 1976 Grant George ASHBY born November 23, 1937 in Salt Lake City, Ut.
One child born in Salt Lake City:
      i- ASHBY Michelle Aldora born April 19, 1984

979-    PATTERSON Joanne (*Eldora J., Ralph, John B., Francis, Annanias, Obadiah,

*Joshua, Jasper, John*) was born August 7, 1955 in Ithaca, NY daughter of Miner Henry PATTERSON and Eldora Jane SMITH. She married in Oceanside, Cal. April 20, 1979 John Wyatt SIMON born January 29, 1945 in Oakland, Cal. They were divorced.
Children born in Murray, Utah:
      i- SIMON Nathan Wyatt (twin) born September 24, 1980
      ii- SIMON Stephanie Jane (twin) born September 24, 1980

980-    MC INTYRE Ray B. (*Mabel Taggart, Laura M., Clement D., William, Clement, Obadiah, Joshua, Jasper, John*) was born November 11, 1924 in Tompkins Co. NY son of Roy F. MC INTYRE and Mabel TAGGART and died August 13, 1987. He married Barbara LAUGHLIN (see #843).
Children:
1085-    i- MC INTYRE Wayne Arthur born April 29, 1953
1086-    ii- MC INTYRE Elaine Margaret born March 21, 1955

981-    MC INTYRE Hazel Mae (*Mabel Taggart, Laura M., Clement D., William, Clement, Obadiah, Joshua, Jasper, John*) was born February 12, 1926 daughterr of Roy F. MC INTYRE and Mabel TAGGART. She married (1) Lawrence PEET and married (2) Elmer VAN OSTRAND.
Child by first marriage:
      i- PEET Beverly Joan married Douglas MC CRAE
Children by second marriage:
      ii- VAN OSTRAND Mickie Lynne
      iii- VAN OSTRAND James

982-    MIX Monica (*Linda Vann, Alvin G. Vann, Fred Vann, Julia M., Clement, Obadiah, Joshua, Jasper, John*) was born December 31, 1972 daughter of Robert MIX and Linda VANN. She married William BOYLAN born December 18, 1969.
Child:
      i- BOYLAN Joseph born July 4, 1990

983-    WEHNER Heidi (*Frances, Gilbert C., Cornelius, Gilbert C., John T., Obadiah, Joshua, Jasper, John*) was born April 7, 1969 daughter of Charles WEHNER and Frances SMITH. She married October 28, 1989 Steve PANZICA born September 26, 1964.
Child:
      i- PANZICA Emmy Lila born July 2, 1994

984-    PETER Jean Audrey (*Edward C. Peter, Anita, Gilbert C., Gilbert C., John T., Obadiah, Joshua, Jasper, John*) was born January 25, 1954 daughter of Edward C. PETER II and Jean Audrey FORESTEIRE. She married 1975 Ronald Wesley LARSEN who was born April 10, 1948 son of Wesley LARSEN and Florence STROM.
Children:
      i- LARSEN Audrey Jean born November 30, 1976
      ii- LARSEN Peter Anthony born March 5, 1979

iii- **LARSEN** Veronica Ann born February 5, 1984
iv- **LARSEN** John Edward born July 24, 1988

985- **PETER** Mary Ann (*Edward C. Peter, Anita, Gilbert C., Gilbert C., John T., Obadiah, Joshua, Jasper, John*) was born April 6, 1957 daughter of Edward Compston **PETER** and Jean Audrey **FORESTEIRE**. She married May 2, 1987 Keith Alan **KIRBY** who was born April 18, 1956.
Children:
      i- **KIRBY** Ryan Anthony born April 23, 1988
      ii- **KIRBY** Robert Edward born September 15, 1994

986- **HARPHAM** Virginia Ruth (*Nellie G. Whitaker, Fidelia Lyon, Lorenzo Lyon, Priscilla, Joshua, Annanias, Joshua, Jasper, John*) was born December 10, 1917 in Huntington, Ind. daughter of Pyrl John **HARPHAM** and Nellie Grace **WHITAKER**. She married December 25, 1938 in Auburn, Ind. Dale Lamar **HARPHAM** who was born July 6, 1917 in Montcalm Co. Mi. son of Arthur John **HARPHAM** and Maude **SWAGER** and died December 4, 1943 in Martinsville, Ind. They had 1 son and 1 daughter.

987- **RETHERFORD** Phyllis Joan (*Lora A. David, Miles R. David, Sarah K. Georgia, Lovina, Joshua, Annanias, Joshua, Jasper, John*) was born March 14, 1916 in Rochester, NY daughter of Robert **RETHERFORD** and Lora Agnes **DAVID** and died September 22, 2001 in Phoenix, Az. She married (1) George **MOSS** and married (2) August 30, 1940 Arthur Joseph **WEIS** born April 22, 1913 in Brighton, NY son of Francis Sebastian **WEISS** and Margaret J. **KEYES**. They had 3 children.

988- **RETHERFORD** Roberta Flora (*Lora A. David, Miles R. David, Sarah K. Georgia, Lovina, Joshua, Annanias, Joshua, Jasper, John*) was born November 16, 1918 in Rochester, NY daughter of Robert **RETHERFORD** and Lora Agnes **DAVID**. She married March 28, 1938 Herbert A. **SMITH** born December 29, 1906 in Lima, NY son of Herbert **SMITH** and Elizabeth **GREEN** and died July 23, 1980 in Homestead, Pa. They had 7 children,

989- **RETHERFORD** Mary Alice (*Lora A. David, Miles R. David, Sarah K. Georgia, Lovina, Joshua, Annanias, Joshua, Jasper, John*) was born May 18, 1920 in Rochester, NY daughter of Robert **RETHERFORD** and Lora Agnes **DAVID**. She married March 28, 1938 in Clymer, NY Wilbur G. **BALDWIN** born November 14, 1914 in Erie, Pa. son of Ralph **BALDWIN** and Oleta Marguerite **JOHNSON**. They had 6 children. She married (2) ____ **WESTON**

990- **DAVID** Vivian Irene (*Archie David, Frank E. David, Sarah Georgia, Lovina, Joshua, Annanias, Joshua, Jasper, John*) was born 1916 in Gratiot Co. Mi. daughter of Archie and Anna **DAVID**. She married Clare Ernest **BETZ** born 1915 in Saginaw, Mi.
Child:
1087-   i- **BETZ** Margie born February 28, 1944

991- **EAGLE** Georgia (*Hazel Georgia, Fred D. Georgia, Schuyler Georgia, Lovina, Joshua, Annanias, Joshua, Jasper, John*) was born June 17, 1921 in Mi. daughter of Verne **EAGLE** and Hazel **GEORGIA** and died November 25, 1994. She married Charles T. **HUTSON**.
One child:
    i- **HUTSON** John

992- **CORNELL** Barbara Ann (*Myrtle E. Freese, Lewis O. Freese, Margaret Anna, Lewis H. Joshua, Annanias, Joshua, Jasper, John*) was born September 20, 1924. She married in Denver, Col. February 20, 1946 Charles Richard **HEDSTROM** born July 12, 1913 in Flagstaff, Az. and she married (2) Asa Dalton **BONHAM** born 1919.
Children by first marriage:
    i- **HEDSTROM** David Edwin born Denver, Col.
    ii- **HEDSTROM** Joseph Kenneth born Denver Col.
    iii- **HEDSTROM** Louise Elaine born Seattle, Wa., has 2 children Chrysta Lynne born June 17, 1983 and Mykll Emanuell born November 28, 1987

993- **FREESE** Marion Louise (*Cora L. Freese, Lewis O. Freese, Margaret Anna, Lewis H., Joshua, Annanias, Joshua, Jasper, John*) was born December 20, 1927 in Ithaca, NY daughter of Cleo **FREESE** and Cora Luella **FREESE**. She married February 17, 1945 Gordon Harvey **KLINE** son of Harvey Romaine **KLINE** and Hazel June **TERBUSH**. They were divorced and he died August 6, 1989 in Cortland, NY, buried Willow Grove cemetery in Dryden, NY.
Children born in Ithaca, NY:
1088-    i- **KLINE** Linda Jean born August 7, 1945
1089-    ii- **KLINE** Nancy Lee born October 30, 1946
    iii- **KLINE** David Gordon born April 17, 1947, married in Perry City, NY Catherine Elizabeth **SIRRINE**. They were divorced
1090-    iv- **KLINE** Robert Bradford born December 12, 1958
    v- **KLINE** Lisa Jayne born March 1, 1962

994- **FREESE** Betty Marie (*Cora L. Freese, Lewis O. Freese, Margaret Anna, Lewis H., Joshua, Annanias, Joshua, Jasper, John*) was born in Ithaca, Ny daughter of Cleo **FREESE** and Cora Luella **FREESE** and died in Interlaken, NY February 23, 1952. She married May 12, 1944 Carl Norton **TRACY** who was born November 12, 1927 in Sidney, NY son of Earl Frederick **TRACY** and Heloise **NORTON**.
Children:
1091-    i- **TRACY** Richard Carl born August 22, 1944
1092-    ii- **TRACY** Shirley Ann born December 20, 1945
    iii- **TRACY** Bruce Burnham born December 1948 and died in Perry City, NY 1968, buried Grove cemetery
    iv- **TRACY** Joan Elaine born November 1, 1950

995- **FREESE** Jane Elizabeth (*Cora L. Freese, Lewis O. Freese, Margaret Anna, Lewis H., Joshua, Annanias, Joshua, Jasper, John*) was born December 19, 1932 in Ithaca, NY

daughter of Cleo **FREESE** and Cora Luella **FREESE**.  She married January 22, 1955 Robert William **THOMPSON** who was born March 23, 1933 in Seneca Falls, NY son of Robert Henry **THOMPSON** and Edith May **BURNHAM** and died July 5, 1982 in Interlaken, NY.
Children born in Waterloo, NY:
1093-    i- **THOMPSON** Robert Michael born September 28, 1959
1094-    ii- **THOMPSON** Lorrie Jayne born July 17, 1962
1095-    iii- **THOMPSON** Vicki Lu born August 16, 1967

996-    **FREESE** Robert Cleo (*Cora L. Freese, Lewis O. Freese, Margaret Anna, Lewis H., Joshua, Annanias, Joshua, Jasper, John*) was born September 29, 1936 in Enfield, NY son of Cleo **FREESE** and Cora Luella **FREESE**.  He married June 25, 1960 in Brooklyn, NY Mary Ellen **DONALDSON** who was born December 5, 1939 in Brooklyn, NY daughter of Robert **DONALDSON** and Helen **GORNOCK**.
Children born in Ithaca, NY:
        i- **FREESE** Mark Joseph born May 5, 1971 in Waterloo, NY, married April 18, 1992 in Montreat, NC Patricia Elaine **OWENS**
        ii- **FREESE** Kelly Marie born June 28, 1963 in Waterloo, NY, married Jay **COX** and had daughter Malissa Ann born June 16, 1985
        iii- **FREESE** Heather Joan born October 22, 1969 in Winston Salem, NC

997-    **FREESE** Charles Roger (*Cora L. Freese, Lewis O. Freese, Margaret Anna, Lewis H., Joshua, Annanias, Joshua, Jasper, John*) was born August 1, 1944 in Ithaca, NY son of Cleo **FREESE** and Cora Luella **FREESE**  He married (1) October 4, 1967 in the USN chapel of Mayport, Fl. Betty Jean **ANDERSON**.  He married (2) Colleen Rose **CHAMBERLAIN** who was born April 28, 1952 daughter of Raymond Earl **CHAMBERLAIN** and Donna Carol **MAC CAINE**.
Children by first marriage:
1096-    i- **FREESE** Connie Marie born June 2, 1970 in Waterloo, NY
        ii- **FREESE** Cindy Ann born January 16, 1975 in Waterloo, NY
Children by second marriage:
        iii- **FREESE** Nichole Lynn born April 2, 1977 in Ithaca, NY

998-    **FREESE** Ronald Edward (*Cora L. Freese, Lewis O. Freese, Margaret Anna, Lewis H., Joshua, Annanias, Joshua, Jasper, John*) was born in Ithaca, NY March 19, 1946 son of Cleo **FREESE** and Cora Luella **FREESE**.  He married May 5, 1978 in Ovid, NY Janet **BRUST** who was born October 5, 1951 in Ithaca, NY daughter of Earl **BRUST** and Emily **ROBINSON**.
Children born in Ithaca, NY:
        i- **FREESE** Carrie Jay born July 7, 1982
        ii= **FREESE** Scott Christopher born September 16, 1986

999-    **FREESE** Marcia Jean (*Cora L. Freese, Lewis O. Freese, Margaret Anna, Lewis H., Joshua, Annanias, Joshua, Jasper, John*) was born May 23, 1947 in Ithaca, NY daughter of

Cleo FREESE and Cora Luella FREESE. She married August 6, 1965 in Ovid, NY
Charles STEPHENS son of Dumont STEPHENS and Irene PORTER who died May 28,
1981 in Interlaken, NY, buried Sheldrake cemetery.
Children:
1097-    i- STEPHENS Donald Eugene born April 29, 1966
1098-    ii- STEPHENS Jeffrey Scott born December 5, 1969
1099-    iii- STEPHENS Randall Joseph born November 1970

1000- LAUGHLIN James Laverne (*Ann Margaret Teeter, Mary Edith Freese, Margaret
Anna, Lewis H., Joshua, Annanias, Joshua, Jasper, John*) was born January 24, 1925 in
Ithaca, NY son of Leon M. LAUGHLIN and Ann Margaret TEETER. He married
Marjorie OLSON who was born May 8, 1937 daughter of Edwin OLSON and Jane
DRAKE.
Children:
         i- LAUGHLIN Randall James born August 9, 1959 and died April 15, 1996
         ii- LAUGHLIN Gregory Leon born October 16, 1960, married Christine LAINE
and had son Mitchell
         iii- LAUGHLIN Deborah Ann born June 7, 1967
         iv- LAUGHLIN Diane Elizabeth born December 30, 1969 and died January 1970,
lived 59 hours

1001- ACKLEY William Howell (*Homer H. Ackley, Walter F. Ackley, Olive Rose
Summerton, Thomas Summerton, Sally, Annanias, Joshua, Jasper, John*) was born in Tioga
Co. NY son of Homer Howell ACKLEY and Elma DUNHAM, He married Eileen
HARROWER daughter of Tom L. and Sylvia HARROWER.
Children:
         i- ACKLEY Brian
         ii- ACKLEY David

1002- ACKLEY Joyce Ruth (*Charles W. Ackley, Alvah C. Ackley, Olive Rose Summerton,
Thomas Summerton, Sally, Annanias, Joshua, Jasper, John*) was born June 4, 1944 in Tioga
Co. NY daughter of Charles William ACKLEY and Frances Evelyn TRIPP. She married
June 21, 1964 Barton Conrad BUSH son of B. Keith BUSH,
Children:
         i- BUSH Richard Keith born November 29, 1967
         ii- BUSH Charles Mitchell born June 14, 1970
         iii- BUSH Jeremy Conrad born October 29, 1972

### Eleventh Generation

1003- HOLT Donald George (*Sarah Addie Balser, Sidney Ann Scott, Adnie Malott, Francis*

*L. Malott, Ann, Absolom, John, Samuel Jasper, John*) was born September 25, 1912 in Milford Twp. Ill. son of John Milton **HOLT** and Sarah Addie **BALSER** and died February 26, 1967 in Watseka, Ill. He married in Hoopston, Ill. April 10, 1936 Marjory Irene **WHEELER** who was born July 28, 1917 in Milford, Ill daughter of Thomas Ulysses Grant **WHEELER** and Maude **HARNESS** and died June 25, 1998 in Indianapolis, Ind.
Children:

    i- **HOLT** Marilyn Ruth born August 15, 1939 in Prairie Green Twp. Ill and died January 20, 1999 in Carbondale, Ill., buried Masonic and Oddfellows cemetery. She was married Twice.

    ii- **HOLT** Larry James born August 17, 1945 in Danville, Ill and died December 28, 1945

**1004- FRANK** Victoria Amanda (*Bruce K. Frank, Mabelle Howell, William B. Howell, Anna Corwin, Elizabeth Biles, George Biles, Christian, Joshua, Jasper, John*) was born 1943 in Mi. daughter of Bruce Kent **FRANK** and Chrystal **SPROULE**. She married in 1966 Leroy Earl **KEIFER** born 1938.
Children:

    i- **KEIFER** Jacob Joseph Howell born 1968

    ii- **KEIFER** Nathaniel Kent born born 1971

**1005- ARSCOTT** Patricia A. (*Bernice M. Frank, Mabelle Howell, William B. Howell, Anna Corwin, Elizabeth Biles, George Biles, Christian, Joshua, Jasper, John*) was born 1934 daughter of Lewis Bertram **ARSCOTT** and Bernice Mildred **FRANK**. She married in 1956 in Rochester, Mi. Robert **JOHNSON** born 1943.
Children:

    i- **JOHNSON** Kathleen born 1959. She married Mark **MEDINA** in 1983 and had 2 children Ruthann J. born 1986 and Rachel Arscott born 1990

    ii- **JOHNSON** Timothy born 1962. He married in 1984 Kathy **PETRIE** and had son Joshua

    iii- **JOHNSON** Thomas born 1964

**1006- ARSCOTT** Lewis David (*Bernice M. Frank, Mabelle Howell, William B. Howell, Anna Corwin, Elizabeth Biles, George Biles, Christian, Joshua, Jasper, John*) was born 1937 son of Lewis Bertram **ARSCOTT** and Bernice Mildred **FRANK**. He married in 1966 Allison **WEEBER** who was born 1943.
Children:

    i- **ARSCOTT** Sara Andrea born 1967

    ii- **ARSCOTT** David Bertram born 1971

**1007- ARSCOTT** James Bertram (*Bernice M. Frank, Mabelle Howell, William B. Howell, Anna Corwin, Elizabeth Biles, George Biles, Christian, Joshua, Jasper, John*) was born December 17, 1942 in Mi. son of Lewis Bertram **ARSCOTT** and Bernice Mildred **FRANK** and died June 11, 1966 in Rochester, Mi., buried Mt. Avon cemetery. He married April 7, 1959 Christine **BLUM** who was born 1940.

Children:
    i- **ARSCOTT** Patricia Louise born 1960. She married in 1987 Paul **BERLITZ** and had 2 children Nadine Louise born 1985 and Kirara Lynn born 1989.
    ii- **ARSCOTT** William Lewis born 1961
    iii- **ARSCOTT** James Mathew born 1964

1008- **FRANK** Robert Howell II (*Robert H. Frank, Mabelle Howell, William B. Howell, Anna Corwin, Elizabeth Biles, George Biles, Christian, Joshua, Jasper, John*) was born 1942 in Mi. son of Robert Howell **FRANK** and Zela Beth **WINGER**. He married in 1964 Constance J. **FLEEMAN**.
Children:
    i- **FRANK** Robert Howell III born 1970
    ii- **FRANK** William born 1975

1009- **FRANK** Betty Marion (*Robert H. Frank, Mabelle Howell, William B. Howell, Anna Corwin, Elizabeth Biles, George Biles, Christian, Joshua, Jasper, John*) was born 1946 daughter of Robert Howell **FRANK** and Zela Beth **WINGER**. She married 1966 Michael **REDDISH**.
Children:
    i- **REDDISH** Theodore born 1969
    ii- **REDDISH** Molly born 1971

1010- **FRANK** Wendy (*Phillip L. Frank, Mabelle Howell, William B. Howell, Anna Corwin, Elizabeth Biles, George Biles, Christian, Joshua, Jasper, John*) was born 1948 daughter of Phillip Lucius **FRANK** and Edna Rice **NORMAN**. She married 1986 Kenneth **TIPPETT**.
Children:
    i- **TIPPETT** Noah Memphis born 1983
    ii- **TIPPETT** Montana 'Anna' born 1987

1011- **WHITE** Lawrence (*Nancy L. Frank, Mabelle Howell, William B. Howell, Anna Corwin, Elizabeth Biles, George Biles, Christian, Joshua, Jasper, John*) was born June 2, 1950 in Ann Arbor, Mi. son of Ozell **WHITE** and Nancy Louise **FRANK** and died August 10, 1999 in Brunswick, Md. He married in 1972 in Eagle, Pa. Shirley **SORENSON** who was born 1950.
Children:
    i- **WHITE** Christopher Lawrence born 1982 in Salem, Mass.
    ii- **WHITE** Andrew Dane born 1984 in Salem, Mass.
    iii- **WHITE** Eric Thomas born 1987 in Brunswick, Md.

1012- **WHITE** Alicia (*Nancy L. Frank, Mabelle Howell, William B. Howell, Anna Corwin, Elizabeth Biles, George Biles, Christian, Joshua, Jasper, John*) was born 1953 in Ann Arbor, Mi. daughter of Ozell **WHITE** and Nancy Louise **FRANK**. She married 1979 in Md. Michael **BUSH** born 1950 in Md.
Children:

  i- **BUSH** Nathaniel Patrin born 1983 in Washington, DC
  ii- **BUSH** Courtney Ann born 1990 in Silver Springs, Md.

1013- **HOWELL** Frances Marie (*Harry Howell, Chester A. Howell, William B. Howell, Anna Corwin, Elizabeth Biles, George Biles, Christian, Joshua, Jasper, John*) was born 1939 in Tisdale, Sasketchewan, Canada daughter of Harry **HOWELL** and Irene Annie **FURGER**. She married 1959 Ronald J. **SYNCOX** born 1937.
Children:
  i- **SYNCOX** Frances Joy born 1960
  ii- **SYNCOX** Ronald Joseph born 1961

1014- **LAATZ** William Frederick (*Gladys Howell, Chester A. Howe,, William B. Howell, Anna Corwin, Elizabeth Biles, George Biles, Christian, Joshua, Jasper, John*) was born 1950 in Detroit, Mi. son of Frederick **LAATZ** and Gladys **HOWELL**. He married in 1972 in Rochester, Mi. Dawn Marie **HURLEY**.
Children:
  i- **LAATZ** Richard Frederick born 1978
  ii- **LAATZ** Robert Charles born 1979 in Rochester Hills, Mi. He married in 2002 in Greensburg, Ind. Shannon Marie **RICH** and had daughter Madison Elise born 2004 in Indianapolis, Ind.

1015- **MC COTTER** Catherine Ann (*Lee N. Mc Cotter, Anna A. Howell, William B. Howell, Anna Corwin, Elizabeth Biles, George Biles, Christian, Joshua, Jasper, John*) was born 1944 in Rochester, Avon Twp. Mi. daughter of Lee Newberry **MC COTTER** and Eleanor Irene **PALMER**. She married in 1967 James Anthony **POULS** who was born 1943 in Detroit, Mi. son of Mathew **POULS** and Johannah **HAJEK**.
Children born in Rochester Hills, Mi.:
  i- **POULS** Brad Allen born 1977
  ii- **POULS** Scott Ryan born 1979. He married in 2004 in Pontiac, Mi. Cristel Holly **KENT** who was born 1980 in Jackson, Mi. and had daughter Holly Ann born 2004.

1016- **MC COTTER** Carol Lynn (*Lee N. Mc Cotter, Anna A. Howell, William B. Howell, Anna Corwin, Elizabeth Biles, George Biles, Christian, Joshua, Jasper, John*) was born 1945 in Rochester, Avon Twp. Mi. daughter of Lee Newberry **MC COTTER** and Eleanor Irene **PALMER**. She married in 1970 in Rochester, Mi Gordon **REBRESH** who was born 1944 in Detroit, Mi.
Children born in Ann Arbor, Mi.:
  i- **REBRESH** Kristi Lee born 1977
  ii- **REBRESH** Kerri Lynn born 1979

1017- **MC COTTER** Constance Lee (*Lee N. Mc Cotter, Anna A. Howell, William B. Howell, Anna Corwin, Elizabeth Biles, George Biles, Christian, Joshua, Jasper, John*) was born 1946 in Rochester, Avon Twp. Mi. daughter of Lee Newberry **MC COTTER** and Eleanor Irene **PALMER**. She married 1968 in Warren, Mi. Charles William **PARZYCH**

who was born 1941 in New Britain, Ct.
Children:
>    i- **PARZYCH** Marcianna born 1971 in Detroit, Mi.
>    ii- **PARZYCH** Charles William III born 1973 in Detroit, Mi.
>    iii- **PARZYCH** Joseph Michael born 1979 in Rochester Hills

1018- **MC COTTER** Richard Lee (*Lee N. Mc Cotter, Anna A. Howell, William B. Howell, Anna Corwin, Elizabeth Biles, George Biles, Christian, Joshua, Jasper, John*) was born 1947 in Rochester, Avon Twp. Mi. son of Lee Newberry **MC COTTER** and Eleanor Irene **PALMER**. He married (1) in 1967 in Pontiac, Mi. Catherine Grace **CHIERA** who was born 1947 and he married (2) in 1983 in Oxford, Mi. Krystal Kay **HOOVER** who was born 1958 in Pontiac, Mi.
Children by first marriage:
>    i- **MC COTTER** Kevin Michael born 1968 in Avon Twp. Mi. He met Kim **HYDE** and had sons Andrew born 1989 and Zachory born 1993
>    ii- **MC COTTER** Kelly Lynn born 1972 in Rochester Hills. Mi.
Child by second marriage:
>    iii- **MC COTTER** Keith Daniel born 1976 in Pontiac, Mi.

1019- **HOWELL** Valerie Virginia (*Neil V. Howell, John S. Howell, William B. Howell, Anna Corwin Elizabeth Biles, George Biles, Christian, Joshua, Jasper, John*) was born 1937 daughter of Neil V. **HOWELL** and Alice **CORNER**. She married Jerry L. **EAVES** in 1959
Children:
>    i- **EAVES** Virginia Lynn born 1960
>    ii- **EAVES** Elizabeth Ann born 1961

1020- **BRIDGE** Susan Lee (*Alis L. Howell, Milo M. Howell, William B. Howell, Anna Corwin, Elizabeth Biles, George Biles, Christian, Joshua, Jasper, John*) was born 1943 daughter of William G. **BRIDGE** and Alis Lee **HOWELL**. She married 1959 Dennis Max **HOHF** born 1941.
Children:
>    i- **HOHF** Gary Dennis born 1960. He married in 1982 Janet **MC CLASIN**, had 2 children Chelsea born 1984 and Carly born 1987
>    ii- **HOHF** Steven Dennis born 1963. He married Julie M. **MONTROSS** and had son Michael Earl born 1991
>    iii- **HOHF** Elizabeth Susan born 1964 married David **LITTLESON**

1021- **BRIDGE** Sallie Jo (*Alis L. Howell, Milo M. Howell, William B. Howell, Anna Corwin, Elizabeth Biles, George Biles, Christian, Joshua, Jasper, John*) was born 1948 daughter of William G.     **BRIDGE** and Alis Lee **HOWELL**. She married John **TOEPEL** in 1969.
Children:
>    i- **TOEPEL** Jennifer Susan born 1970
>    ii- **TOEPEL** Rebecca Marie born 1978

1022- **BRIDGE** Polly Ann (*Alis L. Howell, Milo M. Howell, William B. Howell, Anna Corwin, Elizabeth Biles, George Biles, Christian, Joshua, Jasper, John*) was born 1955 daughter of William G. **BRIDGE** and Alis Lee **HOWELL**. She married (1) 1976 in Rochrester, Mi. David **ALSPAUGH** and (2) in 1981 Terrance **OSPHAL**.
Child by first marriage:
 i- **ALSPAUGH** Jessica born 1977
Child by second marriage:
 ii- **OSPHAL** Melissa Lynn born 1984

1023- **SLAZINSKI** David Anton (*Betty J. Case, Leah R. Howell, William B. Howell, Anna Corwin, Elizabeth Biles, George Biles, Christian, Joshua, Jasper, John*) was born 1962 son of Lee **SLAZINSKI** and Betty Jean **CASE**. He married Susan **WELCH** in 1991
Children:
 i- **SLAZINSKI** Stephanie born 1989
 ii- **SLAZINSKI** Mason

1024- **CYPHER** Steven D. (*Mary Lou Case, Leah R. Howell, William B. Howell, Anna Corwin, Elizabeth Biles, George Biles, Christian, Joshua, Jasper, John*) was born 1950 son of Dale Elwood **CYPHER** and Mary Lou **CASE**. He married in 1985 Catherine **MELVILLE**.
Children:
 i- **CYPHER** Alexander born 1986
 ii- **CYPHER** Emily born 1989
 iii- **CYPHER** Sarah born 1990

1025- **CYPHER** John Mason (*Mary Lou Case, Leah R. Howell, William B. Howell, Anna Corwin, Elizabeth Biles, George Biles, Christian, Joshua, Jasper, John*) was born 1952 son of Dale Elwood **CYPHER** and Mary Lou **CASE**. He married (2) in 1979 Sharon Laurie **SIVY**.
Children:
 i- **CYPHER** Jacob Michael born 1989
 ii- **CYPHER** Elizabeth Mary born 1991

1026- **BURDETT** Mark Dwight (*Hobart Burdett, Joel D. Burdett, Anna Russell, Hulda Nicholson, Sally, William, Joshua, Joshua, Jasper, John*) was born in Steuben Co. NY son of Hobart Murray **BURDETT** and Joyce **MEHLENBACKER**. He married Bonnie Louise **BECKWITH**.
Children:
 i- **BURDETT** Stevie Brianna married Michael **PICKETT**, 1 child Trinity Joyce
 ii- **BURDETT** Michael David

1027- **SMITH** Carol Evelyn (*Dorothy J. Davis, Mildred W. Burdett, Anna D. Russell, Hulda Nicholson, Sally, William, Joshua, Joshua, Jasper, John*) was born in Steuben Co. NY daughter of Stanley K. **SMITH** and Doroty June **DAVIS**. She married David Vincent

BURNS son of Vincent Kenneth BURNS and Emma Lucille MEAD.
Children:
 i- BURNS Alana Carol married Charles A. O'TOOLE Jr. and had 2 children
Katie Alana and Brian Patrick
 ii- BURNS Pamela June married Joseph WOODS and had 2 children Colleen
Keating and Mariah June

1028- SMITH Lowell Charles (*Dorothy J. Davis, Mildred W. Burdett, Anna D. Russell,
Hulda Nicholson, Sally, William, Joshua, Joshua, Jasper, John*) was born in Steuben Co.
NY son of Stanley K. SMITH and Dorothy June DAVIS. He married Bonnie
SCHWINGEL.
Children:
 i- SMITH Alisa A.
 ii- SMITH Heather J. married Christopher PASSERO
 iii- SMITH Aaron L.
 iv- SMITH Lindsay F.

1029- SMITH Marcia Faye (*Dorothy J. Davis, Mildred W. Burdett, Anna D. Russell, Hulda
Nicholsdon, Sally, William, Joshua, Joshua, Jasper, John*) was born in Steuben Co. NY
daughter of Stanley K. SMITH and Dorothy June DAVIS. She married Albert Charles
BURNS son of Durwood BURNS and Edna Aldine STUART.
Children:
 i- BURNS Christine Faye married Earl William HARP Jr. and had 3 children
Heather Faye, Sarah Elizabeth and Kyle Ross
 ii- BURNS Eric Charles married Tiffany Shay CHRISTOPHER daughter of James
CHRISTOPHER and had son Cody Mathew
 iii- BURNS Ryan Guy married Toni Jo PIAZZA
 iv- BURNS Casey Albert
 v- BURNS Allyn Joseph
 vi- BURNS Michelle Suzanne

1030- SMITH Joanne Kyle (*Dorothy J. Davis, Mildred W. Burdett, Anna D. Russell, Hulda
Nicholson, Sally, William, Joshua, Joshua, Jasper, John*) was born in Steuben Co. NY
daughter of Stanley K. SMITH and Dorothy June DAVIS. She married Roger
WILLIAMSON son of George WILLIAMSON and Genevieve TURNER.
Children:
 i- WILLIAMSON Brett married Lynelle AHEARN and had 2 children Luke
Minor and Jacob Stanley
 ii- WILLIAMSON Curt
 iii- WILLIAMSON Tara married Todd WELTY
 iv- WILLIAMSON Tammy Jo
 v- WILLIAMSON Ted Mathew

1031- SMITH Dale Stanley (*Dorothy J. Davis, Mildred W. Burdett, Anna D. Russell, Hulda

256

Nicholson, Sally, William, Joshua, Joshua, Jasper, John) was born in Steuben Co. NY son of Stanley Kyle SMITH and Dorothy June DAVIS. He married Lucy Ann FOX daughter of George C. FOX and Sandra BALL.
Children:
   i- SMITH Elizabeth married Ronald Ray CLARK and had 2 children Mathew Dale and Daniel George
   ii- SMITH Jason Allyn
   iii- SMITH Andrew Lewis
   iv- SMITH Rachel Louise
   v- SMITH Dale Adam

1032- DUNHAM Christine Kay (Alma J. Roe, Gertrude, Nellie, Alonzo, Abram, William, Joshua, Joshua, Jasper, John) was born February 17, 1953 in N. Hornell, NY daughter of Edwin Richard DUNHAM and Alma Jeannette ROE. She married (1) Charles FLANDERS and (2) John Joseph PETRILLI born December 5, 1945.
Children by second marriage born in Hornell, NY:
   i- PETRILLI Jamie Marie born October 29, 1988
   ii- PETRILLI Danielle Elizabeth born February 8, 1993

1033- DUNHAM Rebecca Lynn (Alma J. Roe, Gertrude Roberts, Nellie, Alonzo, Abram, William, Joshua, Joshua, Jasper, John) was born August 15, 1957 in N. Hornell, NY daughter of Edwin Richard DUNHAM and Alma Jeannette ROE. She married December 6, 1974 Robert Allen KILBURY born March 20, 1955.
Children born in Hornell, NY:
   i- KILBURY Mathew Robert born January 26, 1975, married Stephanie FLAMINI and had 4 children Korin born 1997, Kyle born 2001, Kaleb born 2005 and Koby born 2005
   ii- KILBURY Jennifer Ann born January 16, 1978, married Daniel MOORE and had 1 child Chelby born 2004
   iii- KILBURY Bradley born June 17, 1983

1034- DICKEY Karen Elizabeth (Carol Roe, Gertrude Roberts, Nellie, Alonzo, Abram, William, Joshua, Joshua, Jasper, John) was born February 5, 1969 in Hornell, NY daughter of Robert Royce DICKEY and Carol Anita ROE. She married in Aquana, Guam December 11, 1989 Christopher Shane LYONS born May 9, 1969 in Miss.
Children:
   i- LYONS Joshua Shane born July 20, 1991 at Travis AFB
   ii- LYONS Alexis Michelle born June 9, 1998 Anchorage, AK

1035- DICKEY Heather Michelle (Carol Roe, Gertrude Roberts, Nellie, Alonzo, Abram, William Joshua, Joshua, Jasper, John) was born October 14, 1971 in Hornell, NY daughter of Robert Royce DICKEY and Carol Anita ROE. She married August 13, 1994 Eric Michael BISCHOF born March 16, 1971 in Marquette, Mi.
One child:
   i- BISCHOF Trae Dickey born September 1, 1999 in Gaylord, Mi.

1036- **WISE** Douglas Milton (*Virginia E. Beattie, Leo Beattie, Alta Fisher, Flora, Abram, William, Joshua, Joshua, Jasper, John*) was born October 11, 1937 in Hornell, NY son of Ernest **WISE** and Virginia Eileen **BEATTIE** and died January 29, 1981 in Canandaigua, NY. He married (1) Delores **COOMBS** (2) June 7, 1958 in Hornell, NY Sandra Louise **AMIDON** daughter of Walter **AMIDON** and Tressa **BROWN** and married (3) July 19, 1974 Darlene Spencer **MATHIAS** who was born September 12, 1936.
Children by second marriage:
 i- **WISE** Catherine Mary born March 2, 1959 married Dennis **MULLIKIN** son of Roy and Lou **MULLIKIN** born June 20, 1956 in Hornell, NY. They have 2 children born in Hornell, NY Jessica born November 12, 1980 and Johnathon born February 2, 1987. Jessica has 1 child James Dennis **HENSHAW** born September 28, 2000 in Hornell, NY
 ii- **WISE** Stephanie Elaine born April 2, 1961 in Canisteo, NY married (1) June 1981 in Hornell, NY Michael **HANRAHAN** and had 1 child Nikki Lynn born October 2, 1980 in Canandaigua, NY who married February 18, 2000 in Ok. Curtis Eugene **BISHOP** II who was born March 6, 1980 and they have 1 child Curtis Eugene III born August 3, 2000. Stephanie married (2) July 2, 1989 in Miami, Fl. James Edward **NAYLOR** born December 15, 1988 in Ark. son of Melvin **NAYLOR** and Shirley **ERLICH** and they have a daughter Rachel born March 16, 1996 in Sweden.
 iii- **WISE** Monica Lee born April, 30, 1963 in N. Hornell, NY. She married Michael Francis **METACALE** born April 25, 1960 in Hornell, NY son of Francis **METACALE** and Margaret **REYNOLDS**. They have 2 children Christopher born February 16, 1985 in Kingston, NY and Ryan born February 26, 1989 in Sayre, Pa.
 iv- **WISE** Mathew John born August 14, 1964. He married (1) Terri **COOK** and had 2 children Nicholas born August 30, 1986 and Mathew John born November 23, 1987. He has another child with Courtney **BAKER**, Brandon Michael born August 3, 2003
Child by third marriage:
 iii- **WISE** Andrea born April 20, 1975 in Canandaigua, NY, married May 20, 2000 in Canandaigua Jonathan Lee **EARNST**

1037- **WISE** Patricia Ann (*Virginia Beattie, Leo Beattie, Alta Fisher, Flora, Abram, William, Joshua, Joshua, Jasper, John*) was born July 12, 1944 in Hornell, NY daughter of Ernest **WISE** and Virginia E. **BEATTIE**. She married in Hornell, NY Gary **DAVIS** son of Edwin **DAVIS**.
Children:
 i- **DAVIS** William M. born August 23, 1964
 ii- **DAVIS** Christoher Todd born February 25, 1965, married June 13, 1992 Julie Ann **ELLINGTON**
 iii- **DAVIS** Melinda Sue born January 4, 1971, married July 15, 2000 in Hornell, NY William **BISHOP**

1038- **BUTLER** Lorry Dean (*Koeth Butler, Milton Butler, Edith, Hobart, Abram, William, Joshua, Joshua, Jasper, John*) was born September 10, 1957 son of Koeth Erwin **BUTLER** and Marjorie **PROTZMAN**. He married in 1978 May **STAFFORD**.
One child:

i- **BUTLER** Erin Marie born May 29, 1979 and has 1 child Brayden born July 29, 2001

1039- **BUTLER** Larena Jean (*Koeth Butler, Milton Butler, Edith, Hobart, Abram, William, Joshua, Joshua, Jasper, John*) was born June 12, 1959 in Tioga Co. Pa. daughter of Koeth Erwin **BUTLER** and Marjorie **PROTZMAN**. She married August 27, 1977 Craig **OWLETT**.
Children:
    i- **OWLETT** Wade Michael born August 31, 1980
    ii- **OWLETT** Clinton Dennis born August 23, 1982

1040- **BUTLER** Bryan Mark (*Daryl Butler, Milton Butler, Edith, Hobart, Abram, William, Joshua, Joshua, Jasper, John*) was born June 13, 1964 in Tioga Co. Pa. son of Daryl Merlin **BUTLER** and Portia Clair **ROTH**. He married January 9, 1985 Kimberly Rae **SCOTT**
Children:
    i- **BUTLER** Jeffrey Milton born June 10, 1991
    ii- **BUTLER** Kelsey Grace born September 30, 1993

1041- **BUTLER** Cheryl Suzanne (*Daryl Butler, Milton Butler, Edith, Hobart, Abram, William, Joshua, Joshua, Jasper, John*) was born January 18, 1966 in Tioga Co. Pa. daughter of Daryl Merlin **BUTLER** and Portia Clair **ROTH**. She married July 12, 1985 Scott **BUNTING**
Children:
    i- **BUNTING** Jennifer Lynn born September 9, 1987
    ii- **BUNTING** Kasey Elizabeth born January 3, 1991
    iii- **BUNTING** Lindsay Rae born May 2, 1996

1042- **BUTLER** Andrea Kay (*Daryl Butler, Milton Butler, Edith, Hobart, Abram, William, Joshua, Joshua, Jasper, John*) was born August 11, 1967 in Tioga Co. Pa. daughter of Daryl Merlin **BUTLER** and Portia Clair **ROTH**. She married September 23, 1994 Clay **ALLISON**.
Children:
    i- **ALLISON** Justin Clay born May 14, 1996
    ii- **ALLISON** Kelly Hope born October 23, 2002

1043- **BUTLER** DeAnn (*Kean Butler, Milton Butler, Edith, Hobart, Abram, William, Joshua, Joshua, Jasper, John*) was born September 10, 1965 daughter of Kean Allen **BUTLER** and June **EGGLESTON**. She married April 1991 Brian **CARRIGAN**.
Children:
    i- **CARRIGAN** Katherine born March 21, 1995
    ii- **CARRIGAN** Connor born June 28, 2000

1044- **BUTLER** Thomas Alan (*Kean Butler, Milton Butler, Edith, Hobart, Abram, William, Joshua, Joshua, Jasper, John*) was born March 15, 1969 in Tioga Co. Pa. son of Kean Allen

BUTLER and June EGGLESTON. He married August 4, 1999 Kimberly FORSYTHE.
Children:
    i- BUTLER Emma June born October 23, 2000
    ii- BUTLER Anna Marie born June 23, 2002
    iii- BUTLER Richard Alan born April 18, 2004

1045- MARSH Kelly Dawn (*Wyona Butler, Milton Butler, Edith, Hobart, Abram, William, Joshua, Joshua, Jasper, John*) was born April 27, 1962 daughter of Wyona Jean BUTLER and Claude MARSH. She married (1) March 10, 1979 Joe LEON and (2) David DANIELS.
Child by first marriage:
    i- LEON Breanne born July 10, 1979
Children by second marriage:
    ii- DANIELS Brooke born March 3, 1985
    iii- DANIELS Timothy born May 10, 1991

1046- MARSH Darla (*Wyona Butler, Milton Butler, Edith, Hobart, Abram, William, Joshua, Joshua, Jasper, John*) was born February 21, 1964 daughter of Wyona Jean BUTLER and Claude MARSH. She married (1) September 18, 1982 Emery CHILDRESS and married (2) October 17, 1999 Bill BALANCE.
Children by first marriage:
    i- CHILDRESS Emery J. born March 3, 1985
    ii- CHILDRESS Chad born September 18, 1989
Child by second marriage:
    iii- BALANCE Julia Claudette born March 16, 2000

1047- JACKSON Carrie Lynn (*Edward Jackson, Mary, Frank, Hobart, Abram, William, Joshua, Joshua, Jasper, John*) was born July 10, 1977 in Clifton Springs, NY daughter of Edward Frank JACKSON and Fay Aundry MERRILL. She married 2004 Kevin STEVENS.
Children:
    i- JACKSON Megan Elizabeth born July 26, 1997
Children of Jonathan LAWRENCE and Carrie JACKSON
    ii- LAWRENCE Shaylee Nicole born May 24, 1999
    iii- LAWRENCE Kasey Koral born March 12, 2002

1048- JACKSON Caprice (*Allen Jackson, Mary, Frank, Hobart, Abram, William, Joshua, Joshua, Jasper, John*) was born September 29, 1972 in Clifton Springs, NY daughter of Allen JACKSON and Debria SIMMONS. She married (1) Neil DE BUYSER. They were divorced and she married (2) Andrew CAHILL in Newark, NY
Children born in Newark, NY:
    i- DE BUYSER Abbie Lynn born May 16, 1997
    ii- CAHILL Mc Kenzie Virginia Mary Rae born May 23, 2000

260

1049- JACKSON Joshua Allen (*Allen Jackson, Mary, Frank, Hobart, Abram, William Joshua, Joshua, Jasper, John*) was born August 5, 1975 in Frankfurt, Germany son of Allen JACKSON and Debria SIMMONS. He married in 1997 in Newark, NY Jessica VELTE. They were divorced.
Children:
    i- JACKSON Blake Allen born April 22, 1998
    ii- JACKSON Brynne Angela born January 22, 2002

1050- JACKSON Richard Jay II (*Richard Jackson, Mary, Frank, Hobart, Abram, William, Joshua, Joshua, Jasper, John*) was born June 11, 1973 in Rochester, NY son of Richard JACKSON and Cathy SCHEERENS. He married Brandy KNEPP born September 25, 1973 daughter of Richard Eugene KNEPP and Linda Frances WILLIAMS.
Children:
    i- JACKSON Kacey born January 11, 1994
    ii- JACKSON Eric Jay born June 4, 1995
    iii- JACKSON Tessa Ann born August 8, 1997

1051- JACKSON John Paul (*Richard Jackson, Mary, Frank, Hobart, Abram, William, Joshua, Joshua, Jasper, John*) was born June 14, 1974 in Heilbron, Germany son of Richard JACKSON and Cathy SCHEERENS. He married (1) December 31, 1998 Carrie BOUSMAN. They were divorced and he married (2) June 7, 2003 Lisa BAUCMAN born November 2, 1972 in Rochester, NY.
One child:
    i- JACKSON Zander Christopher born September 19, 2004

1052- BRAY Jeremy Allen (*Cheryl Jackson, Mary, Frank, Hobart, Abram, William, Joshua, Joshua, Jasper, John*) was born December 31, 1974 in Rochester, NY son of Roderick Eugene BRAY and Cheryl Ann JACKSON. He married February 11, 2005 Jamie MC CALL who was born February 8, 1980.
One child:
    i- BRAY Brian Ashton born September 13, 1996

1053- BRAY Jason Eugene (*Cheryl Jackson, Mary, Frank, Hobart, Abram, William, Joshua, Joshua, Jasper, John*) was born September 29, 1978 in Rochester, NY son of Roderick Eugene BRAY and Cheryl Ann JACKSON. He married December 10, 2004 April DOMBROSKI.
Children:
    i- DOMBROSKI Randi Marie born June 24, 1999
    ii- DOMBROSKI Alexandra Carolyn born March 13, 2003
    iii- BRAY Dillon Michael born October 27, 2005
    iv- KEELEY Grace Jane born June 11, 2001

1054- EVERETT Jeffrey Aaron (*Susan Jackson, Mary, Frank, Hobart, Abram, William, Joshua, Joshua, Jasper, John*) was born November 11, 1979 in Newark, NY son of Lonnie

Allison EVERETT and Susan Elizabeth JACKSON. He married September 14, 2002 Christie CONHEADY.
Children:

   i- EVERETT-GRESTY Jacob born November 11, 1997
   ii- EVERETT Allison Louise born May 24, 2003

1055- DIMMICK Patricia (*Carlton Dimmick, Clark Dimmick, Frank Dimmick, Melissa Richards, Platt Richards, Johannah, Platt, Joshua, Jasper, John*) was born 1953 in Tompkins Co. NY daughter of Carlton Lewis DIMMICK and Theresa CAPOZZI. She married Daniel Ernest WALP born 1951
Children:

   i- WALP Daniel Carlton born 1972, married Tracy Lynn CORSON and had son Jordan Michael WALP born 1991
   ii- WALP Jackalynne Machelle born 1977
   iii- WALP Joseph Daniel born 1979

1056- NEISS Carl (*Thelma Dimmick, Clark Dimmick, Frank Dimmick, Melissa Richards, Platt Richards, Johannah, Platt, Joshua, Jasper, John*) was born in Tompkins Co. NY son of Willard NEISS and Thelma DIMMICK. He married Mary Frances BERKLEY.
Children:

   i- NEISS Carl Dean born 1960
   ii- NEISS Kevin Francis born 1966

1057- DIMMICK Ronald (*Sylvia Dimmick, Clark Dimmick, Frank Dimmick, Melissa Richards, Platt Richards, Johannah, Platt, Joshua, Jasper, John*) was born 1938 in Tompkins Co. NY son of Sylvia DIMMICK and (?). He married Rita GRAF.
Children:

   i- DIMMICK Thomas married Sheryl (?).
   ii- DIMMICK Suraya married Brian JANIS and had 2 children, Nicolas born 1990 and Marjon Holly born 1992
   iii- DIMMICK Jasmine married Bobby WILSON and had 2 children Beau Justin born 1984 and Kyle Austin born 1987

1058- DIMMICK David A. (*Sylvia Dimmick, Clark Dimmick, Frank Dimmick, Melissa Richards, Platt Richards, Johannah, Platt, Joshua, Jasper, John*) was born 1944 in Tompkins Co. NY son of Sylvia and (?) DIMMICK. He married Joyce GROVER.
Children:

   i- DIMMICK Frank D. who married Teresa BUTLER born 1967 and had son Brandon Michael born 1990
   ii- DIMMICK Ronald Lee born 1968
   iii- DIMMICK Michael Edward born 1973

1059- AUSTIC Charles Clinton (*Clinton H. Austic, Dorothy Dimmick, Frank Dimmick, Melissa Richards, Platt Richards, Johannah, Platt, Joshua, Jasper, John*) was born July 29.

1940 in Tompkins Co. NY son of Clinton Herbert AUSTIC and Frances WAGER. He married Sharon HESS born July 16, 1941.
Children:
  i- AUSTIC Dedra Cheryl born July 11, 1963
  ii- AUSTIC David Charles born August 15, 1965, married Mary Jo WILSON born July 20, 1969
  iii- AUSTIC Candace Lynn born November 22, 1972

1060- AUSTIC Victor Eugene (*Clinton H. Austic, Dorothy Dimmick, Frank Dimmick, Melissa Richards, Platt Richards, Johannah, Platt, Joshua, Jasper, John*) was born February 5, 1952 in Tompkins Co. NY son of Clinton Herbert AUSTIC and Mary HAYES. He married Cindy Lou (unknown maiden name).
Children:
  i- AUSTIC Rebecca Sue born November 2, 1974
  ii- AUSTIC Dustin Eugene born January 30, 1976

1061- AUSTIC Barbara Ann (*Clinton H. Austic, Dorothy Dimmick, Frank Dimmick, Melissa Richards, Platt Richards, Johannah, Platt, Joshua, Jasper, John*) was born September 17, 1954 in Tompkins Co. NY daughter of Clinton Herbert AUSTIC and Mary HAYES. She married ____ CORNELL.
Children:
  i- CORNELL Tracy Lynn born September 24, 1973
  ii- CORNELL Jennifer Lou born August 30, 1975
  iii- CORNELL Melissa Jo born April 13, 1977

1062- AUSTIC Linda Sue (*Clinton H. Austic, Dorothy Dimmick, Frank Dimmick, Melissa Richards, Platt Richards, Johannah, Platt, Joshua, Jasper, John*) was born November 3, 1956 in Tompkins Co. NY daughter of Clinton H. AUSTIC and Mary HAYES. She married (1) ____ COMBS and ____ COLLINS
Children by first marriage:
  i- COMBS Chrystal Marie born April 3, 1975
  ii- COMBS Frederick Paul born November 14, 1976
Children by second marriage:
  i- COLLINS Tonya Lynn born January 4, 1980
  ii- COLLINS Cetesha Sharon born August 19, 1982

1063- AUSTIC Richard Edward (*Albert W. Austic, Dorothy Dimmick, Frank Dimmick, Melissa Richards, Platt Richards, Johannah, Platt, Joshua, Jasper, John*) was born April 10, 1941 in Tompkins Co. NY son of Albert William AUSTIC and Helen Elizabeth PAYNE. He married Patricia Ann THOMPSON born September 23, 1941.
Children:
  i- AUSTIC Karen Lynn born April 2, 1967
  ii- AUSTIC Susan Elaine born June 5, 1967/9?
  iii- AUSTIC Nancy Elizabeth born February 23, 1975

1064- AUSTIC William Albert (*Albert W. Austic, Dorothy Dimmick, Frank Dimmick, Melissa Richards, Platt Richards, Johannah, Platt, Joshua, Jasper, John*) was born January 9, 1943 in Tompkins Co. NY son of Albert William AUSTIC and Helen Elizabeth PAYNE. He married January 16, 1965 Janice Louise RUSSELL born July 24, 1944
Children:
  i- AUSTIC Kelly Lynn born August 17, 1967
  ii- AUSTIC Dianne Louise born August 30, 1971
  iii- AUSTIC Shannon Lynn born August 14, 1977

1065- AUSTIC Douglas John (*Albert W. Austic, Dorothy Dimmick, Frank Dimmick, Melissa Richards, Platt Richards, Johannah, Platt, Joshua, Jasper, John*) was born April 2, 1946 in Tompkins Co. NY son of Albert William AUSTIC and Helen Elizabeth PAYNE. He married September 4, 1966 Paula Kay INGRAHAM born July 1, 1946.
Children:
  i- AUSTIC Debra Sue born October 5, 1967
  ii- AUSTIC Amy Elizabeth born December 9, 1968
  iii- AUSTIC Beth Marie born May 27, 1970

1066- AUSTIC Bruce James (*Albert W. Austic, Dorothy, Dimmick, Frank Dimmick, Melissa Richards, Platt Richards, Johannah, Platt, Joshua, Jasper, John*) was born December 30, 1952 in Tompkins Co. NY son of Albert William AUSTIC and Helen Elizabeth PAYNE. He married October 21, 1972 Judith Josephine SCHRAFICK born March 7, 1954.
Children:
  i- AUSTIC Benjamin Albert born April 8, 1977
  ii- AUSTIC Erin Elizabeth born June 25, 1979
  iii- AUSTIC Gregory Bruce born November 6, 1980

1067- AUSTIC Herbert Leon (*Albert W. Austic, Dorothy Dimmick, Frank Dimmick, Melissa Richards, Platt Richards, Johannah, Platt, Joshua, Jasper, John*) was born March 15, 1957 in Tompkins Co. NY son of Albert William AUSTIC and Helen Elizabeth PAYNE. He married June 7, 1980 Sharon Ann SWIFT.
Children:
  i- AUSTIC Shawn Ann born May 24, 1985
  ii- AUSTIC Herbert Daniel born February 8, 1988

1068- RICHAR Joyce Ann (*Evelyn May Austic, Dorothy Dimmick, Frank Dimmick, Melissa Richards, Platt Richards, Johannah, Platt, Joshua, Jasper, John*) was born June 14, 1940 in Tompkins Co. NY daughter of Earl RICHAR and Evelyn May AUSTIC. She married John Cycil CHAMPION born November 17, 1947.
Children:
  i- CHAMPION Carol Ann born June 19, 1968
  ii- CHAMPION John Gary born January 27, 1970
  iii- CHAMPION Chris Marie born August 14, 1972

1069- **RICHAR** Alfred Earl (*Evelyn M. Austic, Dorothy Dimmick, Frank Dimmick, Melissa Richards, Platt Richards, Johannah, Platt, Joshua, Jasper, John*) was born September 18, 1943 in Tompkins Co. NY son of Earl **RICHAR** and Evelyn May **AUSTIC**. He married January 4, 1964 Mary Ann **THOMPSON** born January 7, 1944.
Children:
      i- **RICHAR** Patrick Allen born February 1, 1969 (adopted)
     ii- **RICHAR** James Alfred born January 24, 1981 (adopted)

1070- **RICHAR** James Edward (*Evelyn May Austic, Dorothy Dimmick, Frank Dimmick, Melissa Richards, Platt Richards, Johannah, Platt, Joshua, Jasper, John*) was born December 18, 1946 in Tompkins Co. NY son of Earl **RICHAR** and Evelyn May **AUSTIC**. He married (1) Linda **HANKINSON** born October 5, 1948. They were divorced and he married (2) Jean Sylvia (?) **FRENCH**. She had son Michael **FRENCH** born February 2, 1966.
Children:
      i- **RICHAR** Terri Lynn born November 28, 1970
     ii- **RICHAR** Kim Marie born November 8, 1973

1071- **AUSTIC** Duwayne Edward (*Edward F. Austic, Dorothy Dimmick, Frank Dimmick, Melissa Richards, Platt Richards, Johannah, Platt, Joshua, Jasper, John*) was born August 26, 1948 son of Edward Frank **AUSTIC** and Hildreth **HURLBUT**. He married Donna **HOUSEWORTH**. They were divorced and he married (2) Jo Ann **BAKER**
Children:
      i- **AUSTIC** Angela Sue born April 25, 1967
     ii- **AUSTIC** Lisa Ann born January 2, 1970
    iii- **AUSTIC** Christopher Edward born February 16, 1972
    iv- **AUSTIC** Zachary Edward born August 28, 1988
Note: also has step daughter Valerie **BAKER**

1072- **AUSTIC** Janet (*Edward F. Austic, Dorothy Dimmick, Frank Dimmick, Melissa Richards, Platt Richards, Johannah, Platt, Joshua, Jasper, John*) was born December 9, 1955 daughter of Edward Frank **AUSTIC** and Hildreth **HURLBUT**. She married February 11, 1978 Robert Harrison **CASTERLINE**.
One child:
      i- **CASTERLINE** Michele Lynn born March 19, 1973

1073- **FRAZIER** Harry Joseph Jr. (*Harry J. Frazier, George D. Frazier, Samuel Frazier, Emeline Richards, Platt Richards, Johannah, Platt, Joshua, Jasper, John*) was born June 6, 1940 son of Harry Joseph **FRAZIER** and Leora Maude **CALKINS**. He married Jeannette Doris **ADAMS** born August 27, 1940.
Children:
      i- **FRAZIER** Luanne Doris born September 24, 1961
     ii- **FRAZIER** Laurie Jean born June 2, 1964

1074- **UNDERWOOD** George Herbert (*Mary Dessie Frazier, George D. Frazier, Samuel Frazier, Emeline Richards, Platt Richards, Johannah, Platt, Joshua, Jasper, John*) was born July 7, 1931 in Broome Co. son of Herbert Edward **UNDERWOOD** and Mary Dessie **FRAZIER**. He married (1) Joyce **COLE** and (2) Rose **DIANGELO**.
Child by first marriage:
    i- **UNDERWOOD** Susan Lynn born November 29, 1954
Children by second marriage:
    ii- **UNDERWOOD** Lori Ann born May 6, 1958
    iii- **UNDERWOOD** George Herbert Jr. born June 13, 1961

1075- **UNDERWOOD** Charles Samuel (*Mary Dessie Frazier, George D. Frazier, Samuel Frazier, Emeline Richards, Platt Richards, Johannah, Platt, Joshua, Jasper, John*) was born October 15, 1932 in Broome Co. NY son of Herbert Edward **UNDERWOOD** and Mary Dessie **FRAZIER**. He married Jean **FAUX** born January 26, 1935.
Children:
    i- **UNDERWOOD** Terri Lee born December 13, 1954
    ii- **UNDERWOOD** James Robert born June 7, 1959
    iii- **UNDERWOOD** Lisa Jean born August 9, 1963
    iv- **UNDERWOOD** John Charles born May 1, 1965

1076- **UNDERWOOD** Mary Leora (*Mary Dessie Frazier, George D. Frazier, Samuel Frazier, Emeline Richards, Platt Richards, Johannah, Platt, Joshua, Jasper, John*) was born December 21, 1933 in Broome Co. NY daughter of Herbert Edward **UNDERWOOD** and Mary Dessie **FRAZIER**. She married Leonard J. **COLE** born May 23, 1931.
Children:
    i- **COLE** Connie born June 24, 1957
    ii- **COLE** Randall James born July 7, 1958
    iii- **COLE** Gregory born August 28, 1959
    iv- **COLE** Sherrie Ellen born March 21, 1965
    v- **COLE** unknown

1077- **UNDERWOOD** Barbara Jean (*Mary Dessie Frazier, George D. Frazier, Samuel Frazier, Emeline Richards, Platt Richards, Johannah, Platt, Joshua, Jasper, John*) was born March 24, 1935 in Broome Co. NY daughter of Herbert Edward **UNDERWOOD** and Mary Dessie **FRAZIER**. She married Joseph Francis **HAMILTON** born December 25, 1927 in Broome Co. NY
Children:
    i- **HAMILTON** Michael Joseph born January 9, 1963
    ii- **HAMILTON** Carol Ann born July 7, 1965

1078- **UNDERWOOD** Betty Lee Margaret (*Mary Dessie Frazier, George D. Frazier, Samuel Frazier, Emeline Richards, Platt Richards, Johannah, Platt, Joshua, Jasper, John*) was born April 3, 1936 in Broome Co. NY daughter of Herbert Edward **UNDERWOOD** and Mary Dessie **FRAZIER**. She married Willis **JUDD** born April 16, 1931.

266

Children:
    i- JUDD Debra Lynn born December 19, 1955
    ii- JUDD Donna Marie born November 22, 1956
    iii- JUDD Stephen Michael born February 16, 1962

1079- **UNDERWOOD** Dorothy (*Mary Dessie Frazier, George D. Frazier, Samuel Frazier, Emeline Richards, Platt Richards, Johannah, Platt, Joshua, Jasper, John*) was born March 20, 1937 in Broome Co. NY daughter Herbert Edward **UNDERWOOD** and Mary Dessie **FRAZIER**. She married George Caesar **ALTAVILLA** born February 6, 1936.
Children:
    i- **ALTAVILLA** Joseph Anthony born May 1, 1954
    ii- **ALTAVILLA** Ann Marie born January 18, 1966

1080- **UNDERWOOD** Frederick Curtis (*Mary Dessie Frazier, George D. Frazier, Samuel Frazier, Emeline Richards, Platt Richards, Johannah, Platt, Joshua, Jasper, John*) was born March 29, 1938 in Broome Co. NY son of Herbert Edward **UNDERWOOD** and Mary Dessie **FRAZIER**. He married Laura Jean **RUPERT** born January 7, 1941.
Children:
    i- **UNDERWOOD** Linda Lee born March 25, 1960
    ii- **UNDERWOOD** Frederick Curtis Jr. born March 28, 1961
    iii- **UNDERWOOD** Sharon Kim born May 14, 1962
    iv- **UNDERWOOD** Kenneth Wayne born June 18, 1963
    v- **UNDERWOOD** Jodie Marie born April 10, 1965

1081- **UNDERWOOD** Harry Sanford (*Mary Dessie Frazier, George D. Frazier, Samuel Frazier, Emeline Richards, Platt Richards, Johannah, Platt, Joshua, Jasper, John*) was born February 23, 1940 in Broome Co. NY son of Herbert Edward **UNDERWOOD** and Mary Dessie **FRAZIER**. He married Thelma **LINCOLN** born May 21, 1942.
Children:
    i- **UNDERWOOD** Darlene Marie born October 9, 1959
    ii- **UNDERWOOD** Cynthia Lou born October 31, 1960
    iii- **UNDERWOOD** Lisa Marchelle born January 21, 1964
    iv- **UNDERWOOD** Herbert Edward born November 29, 1965

1082- **TRUE** Ellen Elizabeth (*Norma J. Dempsey, Mary E. Mason, Herman J. Mason, Adeline Ganoung, Berentha, Obadiah, Obadiah, Joshua, Jasper, John*) was born April 22, 1959 in Corning, NY daughter of Palmer Dexter **TRUE** and Norma Jean **DEMPSEY**. She married August 8, 1987 in Sudbury, Mass. Louis John **DI CERBO** born May 20, 1956 in Schenectady, NY son of Alphonso **DI CERBO** and Margery **BLACKFORD**.
One child:
    i- **DI CERBO** John Louis born October 3, 1989

1083- **TRUE** Bruce Dexter (*Norma J. Dempsey, Mary E. Mason, Herman J. Mason, Adeline Ganoung, Berentha, Obadiah, Obadiah, Joshua, Jasper, John*) was born January 27, 1961 in

Corning, NY son of Palmer Dexter TRUE and Norma Jean DEMPSEY. He married July 23, 1988 in Jericho, NY Wendy Louise MILLIGAN born November 8, 1965 in Portsmouth, Va. daughter of James Michael MILLIGAN and Dorothea Mary BURNS.
One child:
    i- TRUE Sarah Elizabeth born April 19, 1993

1084- TRUE Brian (*Norma J. Dempsey, Mary E. Mason, Herman J. Mason, Adeline Ganoung, Berentha, Obadiah, Obadiah, Joshua, Jasper, John*) was born April 27, 1966 in Elmira, NY son of Palmer Dexter TRUE and Norma Jean DEMPSEY. He married Renae Ann THOMAS born September 14, 1964 daughter of Arthur Dale THOMAS and Caroline Ann RUST.
One child:
    i- TRUE Eugenia Ann born January 26, 1992 in Elk Grove Village, Ill.

1085- MC INTYRE Wayne Arthur (*Barbara Laughlin, Ann Margaret Teeter, Mary Edith Freese, Margaret Anna, Lewis H., Joshua, Annanias, Joshua, Jasper, John*) was born April 29, 1953 in Tompkins Co. NY son of Ray B. MC INTYRE and Barbara LAUGHLIN. He married Nancy BILL who was born November 5, 1952 daughter of Donald BILL and Phyllis WIXON.
Children:
    i- MC INTYRE Lynne Odelia born January 5, 1981
    ii- MC INTYRE Lee Edward born January 11, 1986

1086- MC INTYRE Elaine Margaret (*Barbara Laughlin, Ann Margaret Teeter, Mary Edith Freese, Margaret Anna, Lewis H. Joshua, Annanias, Joshua, Jasper, John*) was born March 21, 1955 daughter of Ray B. MC INTYRE and Barbara LAUGHLIN. She married (1) Brian O'CONNOR born November 15, 1955 son of James O'CONNOR and Jane CLEARY. She married (2) Bernard PERRY born January 12, 1961 son of Niclolas and Mary PERRY.
Children by first marriage:
    i- O'CONNOR Carolyn Ericka born June 16, 1976
    ii- O'CONNOR Mathew John born November 13, 1979
    iii- O'CONNOR Patrick Michael born March 14, 1982
Children by second marriage:
    iv- PERRY Curtis Daniel born September 24, 1986
    v- PERRY Miles David

1087- BETZ Margie (*Vivian David, Archie David, Frank David, Sarah Georgia, Lovina, Joshua, Annanias, Joshua, Jasper, John*) was born February 28, 1944 in Mi. daughter of Clare Ernest BETZ and Vivian Irene DAVID. She married (1) Hubert ROSE born January 10, 1940 in Ashley, Mi. son of Milan ROSE and Pearl WALKER and died July 15, 2000 in Lansing, Mi. and married (2) Kenneth James CLAYTON.
Children by first marriage:
    i- ROSE Paula Jean born September 23, 1963

    ii- **ROSE** Patricia Ann born March 6, 1966
    iii- **BETZ** Lisa Marie born July 17, 1972
Children by second marriage:
    iv- **CLAYTON** Joel Scott born June 1976
    v- **CLAYTON** Shannon Marie born June 1980


1088- **KLINE** Linda Jean (*Marion L. Freese, Cora L. Freese, Lewis O. Freese, Margaret Anna, Lewis H., Joshua, Annanias, Joshua, Jasper, John*) was born August 7, 1945 in Ithaca, NY daughter of Gordon Harvey **KLINE** and Marion L. **FREESE**. She married (1) August 24, 1963 Clayton **HARRIS** and married (2) in 1975 John G. **CLARK**.
Children by first marriage:
    i- **HARRIS** Stacey L. born 1964, married James Howard **SMITH** and had 2 children, Kayla Ann born 1987 and Jennifer K. born 1990
    ii- **HARRIS** Michael D. born 1969
Child by second marriage:
    iii- **CLARK** Jerald G. born September 26, 1976 in Ithaca, NY


1089- **KLINE** Robert Bradford (*Marion L. Freese, Cora L. Freese, Lewis O. Freese, Margaret Anna, Lewis H., Joshua, Annanias, Joshua, Jasper, John*) was born December 12, 1958 in Ithaca, NY son of Gordon Harvey **KLINE** and Marion Louise **FREESE**. He married February 14, 1986 in Deltona, Fl. Felice Diane **ALTMAN**.
One child:
    i- **KLINE** Ashley born January 13, 1989


1090- **KLINE** Nancy Lee (*Marion L. Freese, Cora L. Freese, Lewis O. Freese, Margaret Anna, Lewis H., Joshua, Annanias, Joshua, Jasper, John*) was born October 30, 1946 in Ithaca, NY daughter of Gordon Harvey **KLINE** and Marion Louise **FREESE**. She married August 21, 1965 in Perry City, NY Ronald Earl **BOWER** who was born February 28, 1946 in Elmira, NY
Children born in Ithaca, NY:
    i- **BOWER** Ronda Lee born November 9, 1967
    ii- **BOWER** Deanna Michelle born September 10, 1072
    iii- **BOWER** Joshua Ryan born November 13, 1982


1091- **TRACY** Richard Carl (*Betty Marie Freese, Cora L. Freese, Lewis O. Freese, Margaret Anna, Lewis H., Joshua, Annanias, Joshua, Jasper, John*) was born August 22, 1944 in Ithaca, NY son of Carl Norton **TRACY** and Betty Marie **FREESE**. He married (1) June 5, 1965 in Kissimmee, Fl. Marsha Ann **MOORE**. They were divorced and he married (2) Clela (JoAnn) Louise **MELLOTT** born September 19, 1950.
Children by first marriage born in Florida:
    i- **TRACY** Richard Carl Jr. born April 28, 1966, married June 30, 1990 Jimer Lynn **JOHNSON**
    ii- **TRACY** David Bruce born August 1, 1967
    iii- **TRACY** Steven Carl born December 1, 1969

iv- **TRACY** Robert Anthony born October 7, 1970, married December 2, 1990 Libby **PARISH** with daughter Holly **PARISH**. They had son Robert Anthony **TRACY** born July 26, 1990.
Child by second marriage:
vi- **TRACY** Linda married ____ **HOLLINGSWORTH** and had one son David Lee born March 9, 1992

1092- **TRACY** Shirley Ann (*Betty Marie Freese, Cora L. Freese, Lewis O. Freese, Margaret Anna, Lewis H., Joshua, Annanias, Joshua, Jasper, John*) was born December 26, 1956 in Tompkins Co. daughter of Carl Norton **TRACY** and Betty Marie **FREESE**. She married July 20, 1963 in Ovid, NY William Lewis **HANCY** born November 3, 1942.
Children:
i- **HANCY** Richard William born August 27, 1966, married May 19, 1990 Judith M. **FRIEDA**
ii- **HANCY** Wayne Carl born June 18, 1969

1093- **THOMPSON** Robert Michael (*Jane E. Freese, Cora L. Freese, Lewis O. Freese, Margaret Anna, Lewis H., Joshua, Annanias, Joshua, Jasper, John*) was born September 28, 1959 in Waterloo, NY son of Robert William **THOMPSON** and Jane Elizabeth **FREESE**. He married April 2, 1983 in Orlando, Fl. Wendy Lee **REID** who was born June 21, 1964 at Wurtsmouth AFB, Mi. daughter of Robert **REID** and Elaine **WEIDMAN**.
Children:
i- **THOMPSON** Robert Allen born April 12, 1986 Ithaca, NY

1094- **THOMPSON** Lorrie Jane (*Jane E. Freese, Cora L. Freese, Lewis O. Freese, Margaret Anna, Lewis H., Joshua, Annanias, Joshua, Jasper, John*) was born July 17, 1962 in Waterloo, NY daughter of Robert William **THOMPSON** and Jane Elizabeth **FREESE**. She married in Auburn, NY Thomas Charles **WAZNICA** born November 20, 1962 in Syracuse, NY son of Frederick Martin **WAZNICA** and Mary Agnes **DAVIS**
Children born in Syracuse, NY:
i- **WAZNICA** Katherine Jayne born March 28, 1992
Quintuplets born in Syracuse
ii- **WAZNICA** Sara Jayne born September 22, 1993. one month before the other quintuplets and died same day, buried Interlaken
iii- **WAZNICA** Thomas Charles born October 20, 1993
iv- **WAZNICA** Daniel Robert born October 20, 1993
v- **WAZNICA** Jonathan Frederick born October 20, 1993
vi- **WAZNICA** Rebekah Jayne born October 20, 1993
vii- **WAZNICA** David Nathaniel born May 18, 1995

1095- **THOMPSON** Vicki Lou (*Jane Freese, Cora L. Freese, Lewis O. Freese, Margaret Anna, Lewis H., Joshua, Annanias, Joshua, Jasper, John*) was born August 16, 1911 in Tompkins Co. NY daughter of Robert William **THOMPSON** and Jane Elizabeth **FREESE**. She married June 16, 1990 Vasit **LEIDY** son of William and Sriprapa

1096- **FREESE** Connie Marie (*Charles Freese, Cora L. Freese, Lewis O. Freese, Margaret Anna, Lewis H., Joshua, Annanias, Joshua, Jasper, John*) was born June 2, 1970 daughter of Charles R. **FREESE** and Betty Jean **ANDERSON**. She married at Seneca Army Depot in Romulus, NY March 3, 1990 Brad **SAMPLE**.
One child:
> i- **SAMPLE** Kyle born January 11, 1991

1097- **STEPHENS** Donald Eugene (*Marcia J. Freese, Cora L. Freese, Lewis O. Freese, Margaret Anna, Lewis H., Joshua, Annanias, Joshua, Jasper, John*) was born April 29, 1966 son of Charles **STEPHENS** and Marcia Jean **FREESE**. He married Roseanne (unknown maiden name)
Children:
> i- **STEPHENS** Christopher Donald born February 2, 1991
> ii- **STEPHENS** Kelly Margaret born October 14, 1992
> iii- Christine Brock
> iv- Timothy Brock

1098- **STEPHENS** Jeffrey Scott (*Marcia J. Freese, Cora L. Freese, Lewis O. Freese, Margaret Anna, Lewis H., Joshua, Annanias, Joshua, Jasper, John*) was born December 5, 1969 son of Charles **STEPHENS** and Marcia Jean **FREESE**. He married August 11, 1990 in Marengo, Ohio Christa Rana **BOWLING**.
One child:
> i- **STEPHENS** Samantha Ann born February 25, 1992

1099- **STEPHENS** Randall Joseph (*Marcia J. Freese, Cora L. Freese, Lewis O. Freese, Margaret Anna, Lewis H., Joshua, Annanias, Joshua, Jasper, John*) was born November 1970 son of Charles **STEPHENS** and Marcia Jean **FREESE**. He married March 1991 Julie **DE GIACONE**.
One child:
> i- **STEPHENS** Zachary born June 7, 1991

# Index

BEAM
   Avis 173
BEARD
   John 83
BEARDSLEY
   Asa 108
   Brank 108
   Elmer 108
   Frank 158
   Hattie 108
   Herbert 159
   Maggie 108
   Martha 108
   Olive 159
   Robert 159
BEATTIE
   Donald 195, 233
   Ina 146, 195
   Isabel 146, 195
   James 233
   Leo 146, 195
   Lois 195, 233
   Sherman 146
   Thomas 233
   Virginia 195,
      233
BEATTY
   Electa 89
   John 89
   Mary 89
   Sarah 81
   William 88, 89
BECK
   ___ 198
BECKWITH
   ___ 197
   Bonnie 254
BEEBE
   Benjamin 50
   Della 50
   Edgar 50
BEECHER
   Dorothy 190
BEEKMAN
   J. Russell 34
BEIHL
   Mary 224
BELDEN
   Beth 229
BELK
   Minnie 82
BELL
   William 142
BELLOWS
   Geraldine 154
BENEDICT
   Fred 147
BENHAM
   Elizabeth 41
BENNETT
   Carrie 79
   John 220

   Melissa 210
   Naira 159
   Thomas 220
BENSON
   Bertha 96, 150
   Colie 96
   Cora 96, 150
   Edith 96, 150
   Ella 96
   Nathan 96
   Pearl 96
BERGEN
   Lammetje 5
BERGER
   Chester 225
   Diana 225
   Michelle 226
BERGLAND
   John 169
BERKLEY
   Mary 261
BERLITZ
   Kirara 251
   Nadine 251
   Paul 251
BERRY
   ___ 182
   Ada 83
   Alfred 40, 83
   Alice 84
   Alton 136
   Annie 137
   Bonnie 134
   Burton 40, 82,
      83,
      136
   Clayton 83
   Columbus 40
   Della 84
   Elizabeth 83
   Elmore 83
   Eva 83
   Georgia 83
   Hugh 137
   James 40, 82,
      84,
      137
   Jarret 40, 82
   Jessie 134
   John 83, 136
   Joseph 82, 134
   Julius 84
   Laura 134
   Lehman 136
   Lehmon 136
   Martha 82, 135
   Mary 40, 82,
      83,
      136
   Mary Elizabeth
      134
   Minnie 84

   Myrtle 83
   Nancy 40, 83,
      134
   Nannie 83, 135
   Otis 137
   Resin 40, 82
   Roy 136
   Samuel 83
   Serena 40, 83
   Susan 82
   Syble 137
   Thomas 40, 83,
      134
   Tom 231
   Walter 83
   Willard 136
   William 84, 134,
      137
   Willie 82, 135
BETZ
   Clare 246
   Lisa 268
   Margie 246, 267
BEUG
   Deborah 237
BEVERLY
   Joshua 242
   Matthew 242
   Scott 242
BICKAL
   Alvin 242
   Karen 242
BIDWELL
   Clara 164
   Helen 180
   Vern 180
BIENIAS
   Laurel 226
BILES
   Abraham 7
   Anna 17, 43, 88
   Annanias 17, 43
   Caroline 88
   Cora 88
   Electa 17, 43,
      89
   Elizabeth 17, 42,
      88
   George 7, 17,
      42, 88
   James 88
   Jane 17, 42, 43
   John 7
   Mary 17, 88
   Mary Elizabeth
      43
   Paul 88
   Polly 42
   Rachel 17, 43
   Samuel 7
   Sara 7
   Sarah 88

292

Theodore 177
MELLOTT
    Clela 268
MELTON
    J. B. 139
    John 139
    Mary 139, 184
MELVILLE
    Catherine 254
MERCELL
    Lillian 145
MERRILL
    Charles 114
    Fay 236
    Wallace 114
MERRITT
    Mildred 101
MERSHON
    Caleb 30
    Frances 30, 74
    Jasper 30
    Joseph 30
    Louisa 30, 75
    Mary 30
    Samuel 11, 30
    William 11, 30
MESICK
    Edna 145
MESSENGER
    Effie 88
MESSLER
    Benjamin 133
    Elizabeth 23
    Elsie 221
    James 133
    Mary 133
    Robert 133
METACALE
    Christopher 257
    Michael 257
    Ryan 257
METZLER
    Erica 191
    Gretchen 191
    Jacob 191
MEYERS
    Elizabeth 130
MIDDLETON
    Mary 80
MIKOLAJCYK
    Morgan 226
MIKOLAJCZYK
    Allyssa 226
    Thomas 226
MILES
    Dwight 229
MILHAVEN
    Joy 227
MILLER
    Adelaide 116, 166
    Bert 116, 166

Bessie 116
Carol 205
Carrie 64, 116
Charles 64
Edith 166
Edward 132
Edwin 166, 205
Elizabeth 23
Frank 64
Fred 116
Gloria 205
Howard 118
Hugh 116
J. Edwin 116
James 135, 136, 205
John 78, 166, 225
Judson 64, 116
Julia 166
Keith 225
Kevin 225
Lillian 132
Margaret 116, 166
Nettie 116
Olin 64, 116
Onia 136
Paul 132
Richard 166
Ruth 116
Thomas 92
Versie 135
Ward 64
William 64, 116
MILLIGAN
    Wendy 267
MILLNITS
    ___ 148
MINER
    Theodore 152
MINTZ
    ___ 156
MISNER
    Julia 110
MITCHELL
    Elizabeth 38
    Jenny 176
    John 220
    Karen 220
    Kathleen 220
    Lida 178
    Martha 220
    Meda 142
    Theodore 142
MIX
    Mathew 209
    Michael 209
    Monica 209, 245
    Robert 209
MOKRZYNSKI
    Stanley 200

MONTROSS
    Julie 253
MOORE
    Albert 59
    Catherine 59
    Charles 141
    Chelby 256
    Daniel 256
    Edith 102
    Elizabeth 26
    Elmer 141
    Emma 59
    George 102
    Grace 109
    Harold 131
    Henrietta 37
    Hulda 102
    Irene 109
    Iva May 100
    John 58, 141, 144
    Louisa 173
    Luella 109
    Marsha 268
    Mary 59
    Mary A. 22
    Nellie 144
    Oliver 59, 109
    Owen 102
    Rolland 109
MOREY
    Eugene 117
    Harry 117
    Paul 117
MORGAN
    ___ 198
MORIARETY
    Nancy 221
MORRIS
    ___ 59
    Ernest 229
    James 229
    Joseph 229
    Kathleen 229
    Minnie 138
    Willie 138
MORRISON
    Annetta 142
    Charles 141
    Francis 141
    Harry 142
    William 141
MORROW
    Hazel 177
MORSE
    Biancy 123
    Mary 226
MORTIMER
    Susan 36
MORTON
    Mae 239
MOSHER

307

WHEATON
    Christina 232
    Julie 232
    Raymond 232
    William 232
WHEELER
    Carol 224
    Carrie 224
    Emily 224
    Frank 154
    Jay 154, 201
    Jessica 224
    Lewis 224
    Marjory 250
    Michael 224
    Michelle 224
    Stephanie 224
    Stephen 224
WHIPPLE
    Ida 105
WHITAKER
    Charles 172
    Nellie 172, 210
    Ruhamah 149
WHITCOMB
    Adell 111
    Benjamin 112,
        164
    Carroll 164
    Ethel 164
    Forman 112,
        164
    Francis 164
    Gurdon 112, 164
    Harold 164
    Hattie 111, 160
    Herman 112
    Hermon 164
    Howard 164
    John 112
    Judd 165
    Leon 164
    Lester 165
    Losey 164
    Lucy 111
    Marguerite 164
    Mary 164
    Nathaniel 112
    Percy 164
    Robert 111
    Warren 112, 164
WHITE
    Alice 156
    Alicia 219, 251
    Andrew 251
    Calarissa 81
    Caroline 38
    Charlie 81
    Charlotta 16
    Christopher 251
    Debbie 237
    Deborah 38

Edson 81
Elida 81
Elizabeth 72,
    134
Eric 251
Fanny 81
Fritz 96
George 81
Hiram 81, 134
Huldah 38
James 38
John 38, 81
Joseph 38
Julius 182
Kathleen 219
Lawrence 218,
    251
Lucille 96
Margaret 38, 81
Mary 142
Mercy 38, 81
Nada 156
Ozelle 218
Oziel 38, 81
Paul 204
Penninah 38
Persis 81
Robert 156
Sarah 38, 81,
    133
William 38, 81,
    134,
    218
WHITEMAN
    Joshua 226
    Michael 226
WHITING
    Vern 129
WHITNEY
    Almina 65
WHITSON
    Richard 200
WHITTAKER
    ____ 151
WHITWORTH
    Pegram 121
WICKLIFFE
    C. E. 82
WIGHTMAN
    Anna 23
WILKINS
    Julie 233
    Karen 233
WILLEY
    Martha Sarah
    186
WILLIAMS
    Cora 126
    Elmer 216
    Ermel 151
    Gladys 175
    Howard 175

Lawrence 175
Lewis 126
Lynn 98, 151
Matilda 54
Nellie 151
Orson 98
Perry 175
Richard 176
Winton 126
WILLIAMSON
    Brett 255
    Curt 255
    Jacob 255
    Luke 255
    Mary E. 121
    Roger 255
    Rosemary 169
    Tammy 255
    Tara 255
    Ted 255
WILLIS
    Andrea 228
    Barbara 228
    David 228
    Michael 228
WILSON
    Amelia 20
    Ann 234
    Annette 121
    Beau 261
    Bobby 261
    Donald 131
    Doris 180
    Ellen 234
    Grant 132
    Henry 64
    Jacob 234
    Joshua 234
    Julia 46
    Kathleen 236
    Kyle 261
    Mary Jo 262
    Shirley 199
WIND
    Jerusha 8
WINEMAN
    Mildred 199
WINGER
    Zela 218
WINSLOW
    Gertrude 197
WISE
    Andrea 257
    Annie 136
    Brandon 257
    Carolyn 233
    Catherine 257
    Douglas 233,
    257
    Ernest 233
    Eugene 136
    Gary 233

308

www.ingramcontent.com/pod-product-compliance
Lightning Source LLC
Chambersburg PA
CBHW061716270326
41928CB00011B/1998